ABOUT THE Q'EQCHI' LINGUISTIC COMMUNITY

(Chi rix li xmolamil aatinob'aal Q'eqchi')

The Q'eqchi' are the predominant Maya group in the central highlands and northern lowlands of Guatemala. Geographically, Q'eqchi' is the largest Maya language community in Guatemala. Q'eqchi' is widely spoken in the departments of Quiche' (northern), in Alta and Baja Verapaz, Isabal, Petén and to a lesser extent southern Belize and parts of Mexico and El Salvador (see Figure 1).

The Q'eqchi' language is nart of the greater Quiche'an language family (see Figure 2  ⁿⁱᵗᵒʳʸ of the Q'eqchi' runs from Coban ar the west along the Sierra Yal˙ stward to Lanquin / Cahabon n the east. Historically, the Q'e arginalized by more powerful g alas whose ancient territory was a step ... ne point in the post-conquest period it is estimated that the ωtal Q'eqchi'-speaking population was reduced to only 5,000 individuals. In the last hundred years the Q'eqchi' have increased numerically and geographically. They immigrated (or were forced) to the lowlands of Izabal and Belize and then to the lowlands of northern Alta Verapaz and the Peten. These migrations have made the Q'eqchi' language the widest spoken Mayan language of Guatemala as understood by geographic area.

The Q'eqchi' Maya consider themselves heirs of the rich culture and history of the ancient Maya. The Q'eqchi' homeland encompasses the only Maya territory never conquered militarily by the Spanish (Tezulutlan). The Q'eqchi' language is derived from Proto-Mayan and there are many examples of shared vocabulary between Proto-Mayan and Q'eqchi'. Although Q'eqchi' is a member of the Quiche'an language family, its geographic proximity through history to the Cholean languages of their closest neighbors also left its mark on the vocabulary and grammar.

In the classic period (ca. 200bc to 800ad) and into the post-classic period, urban centers flourished in Chichen (between Chamelco and Santa Cruz), Chamelco, Coban, Ulpan, Chijolom and Lanquin. Today, some of these are only ruins, such as Chichen, Ulpan and Chijolom. Others continue as urban centers, for example: Chamelco, Coban and Lanquin.

Q'eqchi's nearest relative is Uspantec, a small language group west of the Rio Negro. Nothing much else is closely related to Q'eqchi'. Other Quiche'an languages seem to share more in common (the preceding passages are based largely on Cahill, 2014).

In sharp contrast to other Mayan linguistic communities where the indigenous language is on a path to extinction, Q'eqchi' is a thriving language (see Figure 3). Q'eqchi' is without a doubt the most rapidly expanding indigenous language in the Americas (Romero, 2012). Consider, for example:

- There are now more than 1 million speakers; this places Q'eqchi' 2nd among all 30 living Mayan languages (CODISRA, 2010).

- The number of native speakers has more than doubled in the last 25 years.

- The current geographic footprint of the Q'eqchi' linguistic community (QLC) covers as much area as all other Guatemala Maya groups combined.

- The area encompassed by the QLC is expanding within Guatemala, and includes a significant number of speakers in southern Belize and Mexico and El Salvador as well.

Q'EQCHI' MAYAN DICTIONARY - FIRST EDITION

Molob'aal Aatin Q'eqchi' ~ Inkles - Xb'een Xpuktasinkil

Q'EQCHI' MAYAN DICTIONARY

Molob'aal Aatin Q'eqchi' ~ Inkles

FIRST EDITION / Xb'een Xpuktasinkil

Q'EQCHI' MAYAN DICTIONARY - FIRST EDITION

Molobb'aal Aatin Q'eqchi' ~ Inkles - Xb'een Xpuktasinkil

A Mayaglot book.

Online resources associated with this work are located at mayaglot.com.

Email communication can be sent to *info@mayaglot.com*.

Cover art credit: MINEDUC (Recursos Educativos del Portal Educativo, Ministerio de Educación Guatemalteca).

ISBN-13: 978-0692602096 (Mayaglot)

ISBN-10: 0692602097

BISAC: Foreign Language Study / Native American Languages

TABLE OF CONTENTS

XTUSULAL

AUTHOR'S NOTE

(Li naxch'olob' laj tz'iib'ahom re)

This book is intended to fill a gap not yet well covered by other published Q'eqchi' language materials. While in recent years professional linguists have produced a number of excellent Q'eqchi' grammars, vocabularies and bilingual lexicons, they almost always pair Q'eqchi' exclusively with Spanish. This means that native speakers of English or Q'eqchi' who don't speak Spanish must first acquire Spanish before undertaking serious study in either language. It is my hope that this book might be a useful resource, for example, for the non-Spanish speaking medical or religious volunteer working in Q'eqchi' communities as well as for Q'eqchi' speakers seeking to work or study in English-speaking countries.

This goal of facilitating language learning has informed my choices on how to structure and develop this reference tool. For example, I have included some conveniences like illustrations, variant word forms, and occasional comments on how particular features of the language are used by modern speakers in an effort to make the book as user-friendly as possible. In essence, I have created the dictionary I wish I had had over 25 years ago when I first started studying Q'eqchi'. In addition, this version contains a comprehensive overview of Q'eqchi' grammar for English-speaking Q'eqchi' language students.

I have also included many additional items where possible such as neologisms developed by Q'eqchi' linguists from Q'eqchi' word stock to describe the modern world, alongside the many Spanish and even English loanwords that have also become embedded in the language. Some of the neologisms seem a bit strained or awkward, but many are quite elegant—in many cases they will be understood intuitively by native speakers even if they have not used the term before.

Q'eqchi' is still evolving as a written language and as such there is not universal agreement on spelling and punctuation conventions, let alone adoption of newly developed terms. Where possible I have included variant forms in terms of pronunciation, spelling and usage as they exist in the dialectal variations of Q'eqchi'. This effort is not exhaustive and I refer any interested readers to the bibliography at the back of this book for sources on additional work on dialectal variation in Q'eqchi'. Fortunately, due to the historical evolution of the language there is a high degree of mutual intelligibility (despite ongoing processes of divergence) and Q'eqchi' speakers from the lowlands and the highlands usually understand each other.

Users will note that the English used in this dictionary is largely of the Standard American variety, though there are some Britishisms too. (Q'eqchi' speakers in Belize might remind you that Belize only achieved its independence from Great Britain in 1981!)

This dictionary is not an attempt to document a dying language. Q'eqchi' is alive and currently undergoing a dynamic expansion in its vocabulary, educational standards, and literary arts. With growing interest and activity on the part of native speakers to explore and develop their language as a primary manifestation of their culture and heritage, it will be fascinating to see how the spoken and written language continues to progress in the coming years. I chronicle some of these happenings on a weblog at *mayaglot.com*, where I'm also happy to receive feedback and suggestions on how to improve this work.

Jeffrey B Frazier
December 11, 2015

ACKNOWLEDGMENTS

Special thanks and warm regards to those who provided technical insight and/or financial support for this project: Michael Horlick, Liz Saint Rain, Kelly Nuttall, and others too shy to be mentioned here.

XB'ANTIOXINKIL

Nawaj xb'antioxinkil chijunileb' lin looy aj Q'eqchi'. Wankeb' k'ila poyanam xine'xtenq'a xtzolb'al li aatinob'aal Q'eqchi' chiru k'ila chihab' ut chekuy taxaq inmaak wi xsach sa' inch'ool wiib' oxib' eek'ab'a'.

Ninb'antioxi re aj Domingo Bol ut re aj Benjamin Rax (Senahú), jo' ajwi' re aj Alberto Coy (Seamay) ut laj Juan Can (Sacsuha). Ninb'antioxi re li xBlanca Azucena Noack Cajbon (intzolonel sa' li ch'ina tzoleb'aal Muqb'il B'e) jo' ajwi' laj Josué Oswaldo Xol Botzoc (Cobán), ut laj Ramón Chocooj (El Estor).

Aajel ru ajwi' xb'antioxinkil chiru laj Carlos Tiul ut chixjunil lix junkab'al sa' li xteepal Chupón chi re li palaw Izabal. Ninb'antioxi re li rixaqil Margarita de Tiul ut chijunileb' li ralal xk'ajoleb': Lucrecia Petrona, Ingris Mayaliy, Carlos Enrique, Kinberly Gabriela, ut Brayan Orlando. Ninb'antioxi eere ink'ulb'al sa' eerochoch ut lee ch'ina iklees wiib' oxib' kutan.

Sa' xchoyb'al, ninb'antioxi chiru li xNiik re...lix saasal ru lix nawom. Naq laa'in xwil li xk'anjel xink'e reetal li rusilal. Xb'aan naq a'an x'ala sa' inch'ool xb'aanunkil li molob'aal aatin a'in ut xk'eb'al jun ilb'al li usilal. At insaq'e, sa' junaq kutan tatink'ut chaawu laa k'ab'a' mayab'.

- Q'eqchi' has the highest proportion of monolingual speakers in all Guatemalan Mayan linguistic communities.

- Q'eqchi' has the highest rate of literacy among all Guatemalan Mayan linguistic communities. Reported at 10.3% in 2010, but still three times greater than K'iche', the next closest Mayan language (CODISRA, 2010).

- Q'eqchi' is culturally and linguistically assimilative, with a word stock reflecting absorption of words and concepts from other Mayan languages—both living and extinct. Q'eqchi' has a long history of assimilating other groups (indigenous and European) into its linguistic community.

- Since 1996, a number of native Q'eqchi' speakers have trained as professional linguists and published a growing body of professional descriptive and didactic linguistic resources.

- The language is in vigorous use, with standardization and literature being sustained through a widespread system of institutionally supported education (Lewis, 2014).

Figure 1 – Geography of Q'eqchi' Linguistic Community

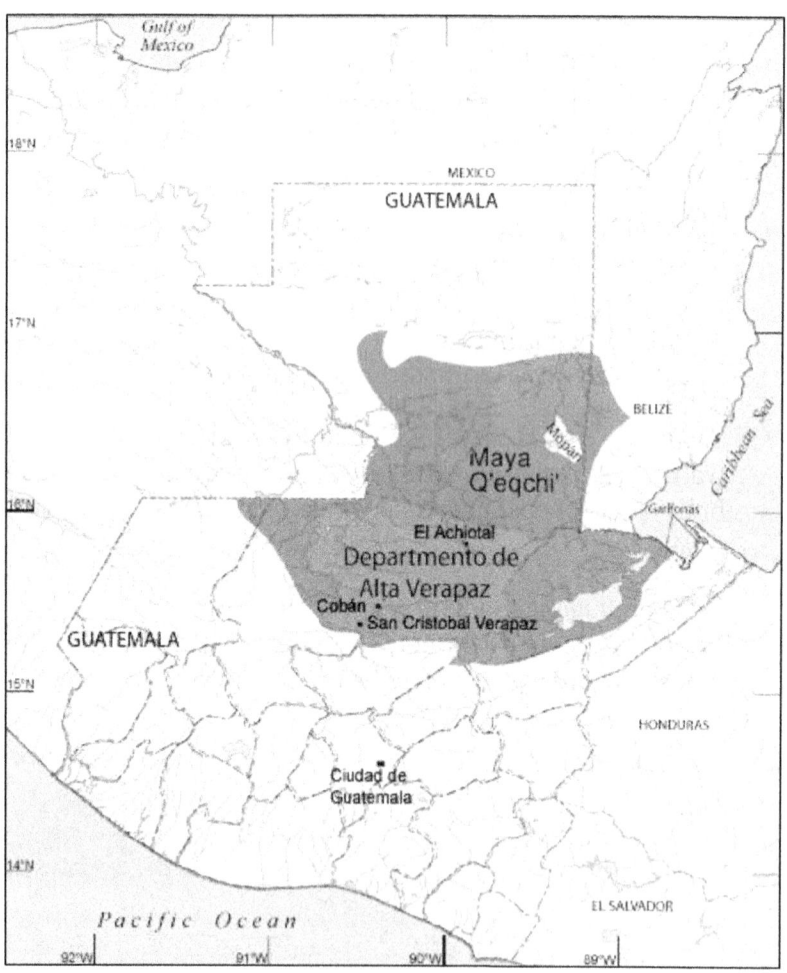

Graphic credit: Dan Cole; Indigenous Geography Project, Smithsonian's National Museum of the American Indian.

Figure 2 – Mayan Language Tree

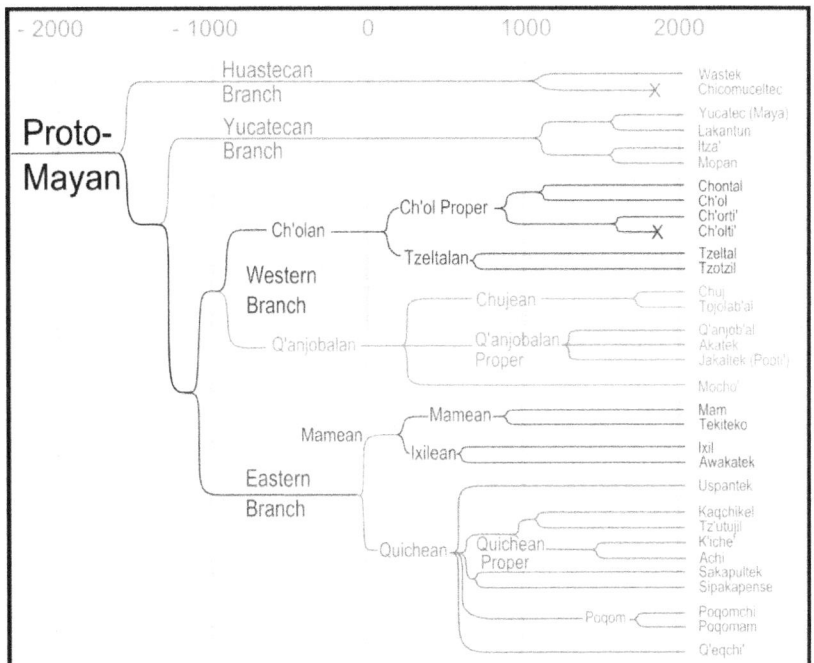

Source: A genealogy tree for the Mayan languages, based on an earlier tree by Maunus. From Wikimedia Commons, the free media repository. Permission is granted to copy, distribute and/or modify this document under the terms of the GNU Free Documentation License, Version 1.2 or any later version published by the Free Software Foundation.

Figure 3 – Place of Q'eqchi' Amongst World Languages

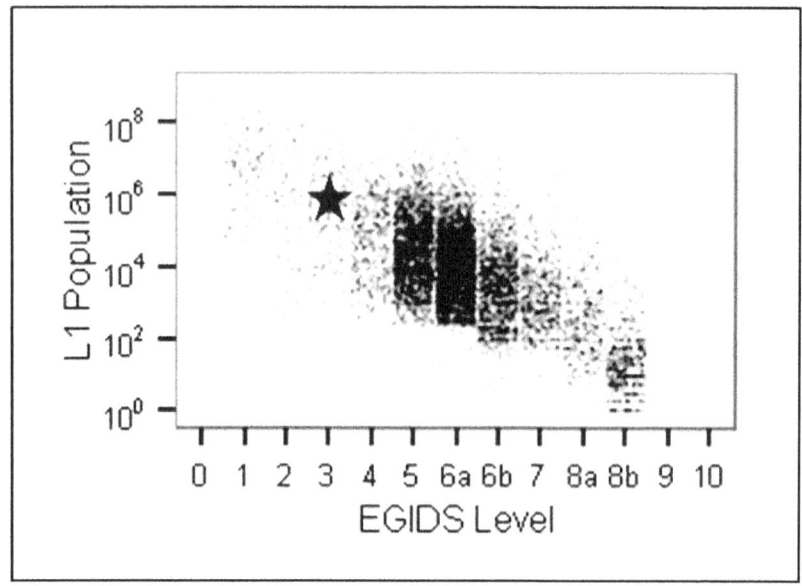

This graph shows the place of Q'eqchi' within the cloud of all living languages. Each language in the world is represented by a small dot that is placed on the grid in relation to its population (in the vertical axis) and its level of development or endangerment (in the horizontal axis), with the largest and strongest languages in the upper left and the smallest and weakest languages (down to extinction) in the lower right. The population value is the estimated number of first language (L1) speakers; it is plotted on a logarithmic scale (where $10^0 = 1$; $10^2 = 100$; $10^4 = 10,000$; $10^6 = 1,000,000$; $10^8 = 100,000,000$). The value for the development versus endangerment dimension is the estimated level on the EGIDS scale (Expanded Graded Intergenerational Disruption). The EGIDS level for Q'eqchi' in its primary country is 4 (Educational), meaning that the language is in vigorous use, with standardization and literature being sustained through a widespread system of institutionally supported education (Lewis, 2014).

HOW TO USE THIS BOOK

(Chan ru roksinkil li tasal hu a'in)

This dictionary builds upon the *Q'eqchi' Mayan Thematic Dictionary* previously produced from this database and available in print on-demand through Amazon.com and an extended network of international publishers. In this version the arrangement of entries in the Q'eqchi'-to-English section is presented alphabetically rather than by theme. This approach offers advantages to native Q'eqchi' speakers learning English in that one can more easily locate the Q'eqchi' word in question and learn its English equivalent(s).

There are three principal sections in this version of the Q'eqchi' ~ English Dictionary:

- **Section I** contains a simple introduction to Q'eqchi' orthography and pronunciation for English speakers that are new to Q'eqchi', as well as a comprehensive overview of Q'eqchi' grammar that outlines the principal parts of speech and how they are formed into proper inflections, conjugations, and sentences. This grammar is new to this version of the dictionary and as far as I can tell it is the only Q'eqchi' grammar written in English available in print, so I have tried to make it as comprehensive as possible within the space constraints of this book.

- **Section II** is an alphabetical list of Q'eqchi' words followed by their parts of speech and English equivalent(s). Many of the entries are illustrated. This section also contains a number of new and updated entries not found in the first edition of the *Q'eqchi' Mayan Thematic Dictionary.*

- **Section III** is a reversal index that contains an alphabetical listing of the English words corresponding to all of the Q'eqchi' entries in Section II.

I have also included a few helpful notes on grammatical usage and evidence for borrowed words where possible, as explained elsewhere and referenced in the appendix. In addition, this version includes entries for many Q'eqchi' place names and their etymologies and English meanings. While not yet complete, these entries are not found in the first edition of the *Q'eqchi' Mayan Thematic Dictionary*.

As of the date of this publication, an experimental online version of this bilingual dictionary can be accessed on the Internet at *mayaglot.com*. In the future I hope to include many more features, both digitally and in expanded and revised versions of both dictionaries in print form.

I

INTRODUCTION TO
Q'EQCHI' MAYAN

Xch'olob'ankil Re Li
Aatinob'aal Q'eqchi' Mayab'

CONTENTS

(Xtusulal)

OVERVIEW OF Q'EQCHI' MAYAN

(Chi rix Q'eqchi' Mayab')

All the Mayan languages are descended from Proto-Mayan, which is thought to have arisen some 5,000 years ago in the Western highlands of Guatemala. The Mayan language family is a rather large one: there are 8 official Mayan languages in Mexico and 21 in Guatemala. In Guatemala, the four largest Mayan languages are Kaqchikel, K'ichee', Mam, and Q'eqchi', all with more than 500,000 speakers.

Although the Mayan languages are largely mutually unintelligible, they all share some common features that distinguish them from other language groups. An interesting feature of Mayan languages is that they are ergative. Ergative languages are characterized by complex verb systems that treat the subjects of intransitive verbs differently from the subjects of transitive verbs.

Q'eqchi' is a flourishing language that is experiencing growth and expansion both in the number of speakers and the geographic territory of its linguistic community. Q'eqchi' is also a well-studied and documented language with modern rules that have been elaborated in terms of writing, punctuation, and style. This brief guide provides an overview of the principal rules governing proper Q'eqchi' writing, pronunciation, and grammar along with examples of usage for each topic.

Q'EQCHI' ALPHABET

(Ch'oltz'iib' Q'eqchi')

Modern Mayan languages, especially in Guatemala, are now written using a Latin alphabet which was first standardized by the Guatemalan Academy of Mayan Languages in 1986. The standard modern Q'eqchi' alphabet uses the following letters and symbols:

Upper case letters: A AA B' CH CH' E EE H I II J K K' L M N O OO P Q Q' R S T T' TZ TZ' U UU W X Y '

Lower case letters: a aa b' ch ch' e ee h i ii j k k' l m n o oo p q q' r s t t' tz tz' u uu w x y '

Unused letters: Letters in the English and Spanish alphabets not typically used in Q'eqchi' orthography: C c, D d, F f, G g, LL ll, Ññ, RR rr, V v, Z z.

Note: The letter B' in Q'eqchi' is always accompanied by the glottalization symbol ('), and all vowels can also be glottalized.

The 33 letters in the Q'eqchi' alphabet can be divided as follows: 5 short vowels, 5 long vowels, and 23 consonants. Some of these letters share similar sound profiles with their English and Spanish version of the same letter, and some are used to represent sounds unique to Q'eqchi'.

LETTER GROUPINGS

(Xjachinkil Ru Li Ch'oltz'iib')

Short Vowels (Xna' tz'iib' seeb' xyaab')	Long Vowels (Xna' tz'iib' aal xyaab')	Consonants (Xyaab' tz'iib')
a, e, i, o, u	aa, ee, ii, oo, uu	b', ch, ch', h, j, k, k', l, m, n, p, q, q', r, s, t, t', tz, tz', w, x, y, '

Q'EQCHI' STYLE GUIDE

(Chaq'rab'il Tz'iib')

The following ten rules reflect modern conventions reagarding how to write well in Q'eqchi'[1].

1. In Q'eqchi', as in English, new sentences begin with a capital letter and end with a period.

2. In cases where an individual grapheme or letter is composed of more than one symbol (e.g., **ch, ch', tz, tz'**, and all long vowels), only the first symbol is capitalized. For example: ***Chaab'ilat.*** (You are good.); ***Aajel ru naq texchalq wik'in wuulaj.*** (You must come with me tomorrow.)

3. The apostrophe symbol (') is considered one of the 33 letters of the alphabet, and as such it is always written independently and not as an accent mark above any other letter. So, for example, it is written: ***k'anti', b'atz', tz'unun, b'a***, and not *bá, tzúnun*.

4. Exclamation marks (!) and question marks (?) are not used in written Q'eqchi', as intonation and meaning for exclamations and questions are usually evident from word choice and sentence structure.

5. All particles, articles, adverbs and pronouns are written as separate words. For example: ***chan, ab'aanan, chik, chi, sa' naq, re, ru, xb'aan, jo', ta, wi'***, and the like. Thus, it is always "chi rix" (behind, about) and not

---

[1] Much of the content in this section was adapted from: Oxom, Carlos. Li Tz'iib'ak ut Aatinak Chi Chaab'il Sa' Li Aatinob'aal Q'eqchi'. Coban, A.V. Guatemala, 2014.

"chirix"; likewise, it is always "chi ru" (in front of) and not "chiru".

6. Words that end in these consonant clusters: **nk, nq, mk, mq, lk, chk, rk,** are always preceded by a single vowel. So for example: *b'ichank, winq, kamk, awimq, chalk, sachk, wark,* and the like.

7. When writing conjugated verbs and possessive nouns the personal marker is always written with the verb or nouns as one word. So, for example: ***xinwa'ak*** (I ate); and, ***injolom*** (my head).

8. When conjugating intransitive verbs their endings are not dropped, as in these examples for *wa'ak* (to eat) and *uk'ak* (to drink): *xinwa'**ak**, xatwa'**ak**, xwa'**ak**, xoowa'**ak**, xexwa'**ak**, xe'wa'**ak**. Xin'uk'**ak**, xat-uk'**ak**, x'uk'**ak**, xoo'uk'**ak**, xex'uk'**ak**, xe'uk'**ak**.*

9. When conjugating transitive verbs their endings are dropped, as in these examples for *wa'ak* (to eat) and *wa'tesink* (to cause to eat) and *uk'ak* (to drink): *xinwa', xaawa', xwa', xqawa', xeewa', xe'xwa'. Xatinwa'tesi, xatxwa'tesi, xatqawa'tesi, xate'xwa'tesi. Xwuk', xaawuk', xruk', xquk', xeeruk', xe'ruk'.*

10. When conjugating intransitive verbs that begin with vowels, in order to not change the meaning of what is being written, an apostrophe (') is used after the personal marker. (In the second person singular a dash (-) is used instead so as not to confuse the letter (t) with the letter (t'). For example, the verb *ilok* (to see) conjugates in the present tense as: *nakin'ilok, nakat-ilok, na'ilok, nakoo'ilok, nekex'ilok, nake'ilok.*

Q'EQCHI' PHONETICS

(Xyaab'asinkil Aatinob'aal Q'eqchi')

Q'eqchi' pronunciation presents some challenges to most non-native speakers. Mayan languages have several glottalized or ejective consonants and they also make distinctions between short and long vowels; these sound features are often the most difficult thing for new learners of Q'eqchi' to pick up, but they are essential in that they distinguish meaning.

Examples of pronunciation

Q'eqchi' Vowels

Vowel	Pronunciation
a	Like the *a* in *father*.
aa	Like *a* only held longer.
e	Like the Spanish *e*, similar to the *a* in English *gate*.
ee	Like *e* only held longer.
i	Like the *i* in *police*.
ii	Like *i* only held longer.
o	Like the *o* in *note*.

oo	Like *o* only held longer.
u	Like the *u* in *flute*.
uu	Like *u* only held longer.

Q'eqchi' Diphthongs

Dipthong	Pronunciation
ay	Like English *eye*.
ey	Like *ey* in English *they*.
oy	Like *oy* in English *boy*.
uy	like the *uoy* in English *buoy*.

Q'eqchi' Consonants

Consonant	Pronunciation
b'	Like *b* in *boy*, only more plosive. To English speakers, it sounds as if Maya speakers are 'swallowing' the b sound, similar to the way *b* is pronounced in Vietnamese.
ch	Like *ch* in *chair*.

ch'	Like *ch*, only glottalized (pronounced with a slight pop or click.)
h	Like the *h* in *hay*.
j	Like the raspy *j* in Spanish *jalapeño*.
k	Like *k* in *key*.
k'	Like *k*, only glottalized (pronounced with a slight pop or click.)
l	Like *l* in *light*.
m	Like *m* in *moon*.
n	Like *n* in *night*.
p	Like the *p* in *pie*.
q	Like *k* only pronounced further back in the throat. This is similar to the *q* in Arabic.
q'	Like *q*, only glottalized (pronounced with a slight pop or click.)
r	Like Spanish *r*, somewhat like the *tt* in English *butter*.
s	Like the *s* in *sun*.

t	Like the *t* in *tell*.
t'	Like *t*, only glottalized (pronounced with a slight pop or click.)
tz	Like *ts* in *cats*.
tz'	Like *tz*, only glottalized (pronounced with a slight pop or click.)
w	Like *gw* in *Gwen*. Some speakers pronounce it like the *qu* in *quic*k (closer to the sound of the Q'eqchi' *k* followed by a *w*; alternatively, some pronounce it more like the *w* in the English *wheel* without an initial plosive.
x	Like *sh* in *shell*.
y	Like *y* in *yes*. Some speakers pronounce it more like the "ky" sound in *cute*.
'	A glottal plosive, like the one in the middle of the English exclamation "uh-oh". Represented in written Q'eqchi' using the apostrophe symbol.

Q'EQCHI' PARTS OF SPEECH

(Xk'ub'lal Aatinob'aal Q'eqchi'[2])

NOUNS

(K'ab'a'ej)

A noun is a word that can function grammatically as the main or only element of subjects of verbs, or of objects of verbs or prepositions. Nouns typically denote people, places and things.

PERSONAL MARKERS

(Xpoyanamil Li Eechanink K'ab'a'ej)

In Q'eqchi' personal markers combine with nouns to denote possession. If the noun begins with a vowel one set is used as prefixes; if a noun begins with a consonant another set is used.

Person (Xpoyanamil)	Pre-Vowel Marker (Xpoyanamil xna' tz'iib')	Pre-Consonant Marker (Xpoyanamil xyaab' tz'iib')
First person singular (1S)	w	in
Second person singular (2S)	aaw	aa
Third person singular (3S)	r	x
First person plural (1P)	q	qa
Second person plural (2P)	eer	ee
Third person plural (3P)	r-eb'	x-eb'

---

[2] Much of the content in this section was adapted from: Oxom, Carlos. Li Tz'iib'ak ut Aatinak Chi Chaab'il Sa' Li Aatinob'aal Q'eqchi'. Coban, A.V. Guatemala, 2014.

13

When a noun is possessed the personal marker is always written next to it to form a single word, as shown in the box below.

Person (Xpoyanamil)	Nouns Beginning with Vowels ochoch (house)	Nouns Beginning with Consonants punit (hat)
(1S) my	wochoch	inpunit
(2S) your	aawochoch	aapunit
(3S) his, her	rochoch	xpunit
(1P) our	qochoch	qapunit
(2P) your	eerochoch	eepunit
(3P) their	rochocheb'	xpuniteb'

TYPES OF NOUNS

(Xpaayil Ru K'ab'a'ej)

In Q'eqchi' there are many classes of nouns, each with its own name, standards for the written form, and manner of forming possession through use of personal markers, as described in the sections below.

COMMON NOUNS

(Komon K'ab'a'ej)

Common nouns are the names for people, places and things. For example: *ochoch, ixq, winq, kok'al, k'aleb'aal, tenamit, tzolom, nima', k'ayib'aal, tzoleb'aal, tz'i', kaxlan, aaq, awinq, ketomq, xul, b'anleb'aal, wa'leb'aal, che'* and the like. Note that in these examples we do not know who or where these things are

14

specifically (in which case they would be proper nouns); rather, as common nouns they refer to the generic form.

SUFFIX-DROPPING NOUNS

(K'ab'a'ej Natz'eqman Xtz'aqob')

In Q'eqchi' there is one class of nouns that drops its ending upon being possessed, as shown in the following tables. Note that the personal marker is shown here in boldface and is always written with the noun as one word.

Person (Xpoyanamil)	hi'b'ej (son-in-law)	iitz'inb'ej (younger sibling)	ixaqilb'ej (wife)
(1S) my	**in**hi'	**w**iitz'in	**w**ixaqil
(2S) your	**aa**hi'	**aaw**iitz'in	**aaw**ixaqil
(3S) his, her	**x**hi'	**r**iitz'in	**r**ixaqil
(1P) our	**qa**hi'	**q**iitz'in	**q**ixaqil
(2P) your	**ee**hi'	**ee**riitz'in	**ee**rixaqil
(3P) their	**x**hi'**eb'**	**r**iitz'in**eb'**	**r**ixaqil**eb'**

Person (Xpoyanamil)	xik'ej (ear)	oq'ej (foot, feet)	na'b'ej (mother)
(1S) my	**in**xik	**w**oq	**in**na'
(2S) your	**aa**xik	**aaw**oq	**aa**na'
(3S) his, her	**x**xik	**r**oq	**x**na'
(1P) our	**qa**xik	**q**oq	**qa**na'
(2P) your	**ee**xik	**ee**roq	**ee**na'
(3P) their	**x**xik**eb'**	**r**oq**eb'**	**x**na'**eb'**

SUFFIX-ADDING NOUNS

(K'ab'a'ej Nak'eeman Xtz'aqob')

This type of noun adds an ending or suffix when it is possessed, as shown below. Note that both the personal marker and the added suffix are shown here in boldface type, but that all elements combine to form one written word.

Person (Xpoyanamil)	b'aq (bone)	ich' (vein)	tib' (meat)	kik' (blood)
(1S) my	**in**b'aq**el**	**w**ich'**mul**	**in**tib'**el**	**in**kik'**el**
(2S) your	**aa**b'aq**el**	**aaw**ich'**mul**	**aa**tib'**el**	**aa**kik'**el**
(3S) his, her	**x**b'aq**el**	**r**ich'**mul**	**x**tib'**el**	**x**kik'**el**
(1P) our	**qa**b'aq**el**	**q**ich'**mul**	**qa**tib'**el**	**qa**kik'**el**
(2P) your	**ee**b'aq**el**	**eer**ich'**mul**	**ee**tib'**el**	**ee**kik'**el**
(3P) their	**x**b'aq**eleb'**	**r**ich'**muleb'**	**x**tib'**eleb'**	**x**kik'**eleb'**

DISCRETE NOUNS

(K'ab'a'ej Ink'a' Najala)

Upon being marked for possession these types of nouns do not change their base forms, meaning that they do not take or drop any affixes other than the personal marker, as shown below.

Person (Xpoyanamil)	ak'ach (turkey)	atz'am (salt)	xaab' (shoe)	k'aleb'aal (village)
(1S) my	**w**ak'ach	**w**atz'am	**in**xaab'	**in**k'aleb'aal
(2S) your	**aaw**ak'ach	**aaw**atz'am	**aa**xaab'	**aa**k'aleb'aal
(3S) his, her	**r**ak'ach	**r**atz'am	**x**xaab'	**x**k'aleb'aal
(1P) our	**qa**k'ach	**qa**tz'am	**qa**xaab'	**qa**k'aleb'aal
(2P) your	**eer**ak'ach	**eer**atz'am	**ee**xaab'	**ee**k'aleb'aal
(3P) their	**r**ak'ach**eb'**	**r**atz'am**eb'**	**x**xaab'**eb'**	**x**k'aleb'aal**eb'**

16

COMPOUND NOUNS

(Ch'utch'uukil K'ab'a'ej)

This class of noun is composed of two root words or stems that are combined together to form a new word with a single meaning, as in the following examples: *tz'alamche', saltul, chuche', ch'ohix, kaqkoj, k'iche'aaq, ak'waj, raxke'* and the like. As with other nouns, compound nouns can take personal markers for possession as illustrated in the following table.

Person (Xpoyanamil)	tz'alamche' (board)	k'iche'aaq (boar)	raxtul (graft)
(1S) my	intz'alamche'	ink'iche'aaq	inraxtul
(2S) your	aatz'alamche'	aak'iche'aaq	aaraxtul
(3S) his, her	xtz'alamche'	xk'iche'aaq	xraxtul
(1P) our	qatz'alamche'	qak'iche'aaq	qaraxtul
(2P) your	eetz'alamche'	eek'iche'aaq	eeraxtul
(3P) their	xtz'alamche'eb'	xk'iche'aaqeb'	xraxtuleb'

COMPLEX NOUNS

(Jachjookil K'ab'a'ej)

Like compound nouns, these nouns are composed of two words. However, with complex nouns each root maintains its own meaning and thus they are written as two words even though they function as a single noun when it comes to their possessive forms. For example: *kaxlan wa, kaxlan winq, kaxlan aatin, kok' aaq, xan tz'i', q'an is*, and the like. What is clear is that there are two distinct components of meaning in the noun. That is to say, for example, that with the word *kaxlan wa* (bread)

17

there are two components of meaning preserved in the complex noun: 1) *kaxlan*, which signifies something foreign; and, 2) *wa*, which means tortilla. Taken together they form "the tortillas of the foreigners", or in English simply "bread". These nouns take possessive markers as follows:

Person (Xpoyanamil)	kaxlan wa (bread)	kaxlan aatin (Spanish)
(1S) my	inkaxlan wa	inkaxlan aatin
(2S) your	aakaxlan wa	aakaxlan aatin
(3S) his, her	xkaxlan wa	xkaxlan aatin
(1P) our	qakaxlan wa	qakaxlan aatin
(2P) your	eekaxlan wa	eekaxlan aatin
(3P) their	xkaxlan waheb'	xkaxlan aatineb'

Person (Xpoyanamil)	kok' kaxlan (chicks)	q'an yaj (bloating)
(1S) my	inkok' kaxlan	inq'an yaj
(2S) your	aakok' kaxlan	aaq'an yaj
(3S) his, her	xkok' kaxlan	xq'an yaj
(1P) our	qakok' kaxlan	qaq'an yaj
(2P) your	eekok' kaxlan	eeq'an yaj
(3P) their	xkok' kaxlan eb'	xq'an yajeb'

When these nouns are possessed, only the first word takes the possessive. However, in the third person plural the marker encloses the entirety of the two words forming the noun, as shown. In cases where the noun ends with a vowel then the letter "**h**" is used between the ending vowel and the **eb'** suffix (e.g., *xkaxlan waheb'*). Other words that will take the "**h**" in these cases include: *u, o, hu, ch'ima, iswa* and the like.

18

POSSESSION-DERIVED NOUNS

(Eechaninb'il Xb'een K'ab'a'ej)

Like complex nouns, this class is formed using two discrete nouns but in this instance the first component is already possessed, as in the following examples: *xkux aq', re kab'l, rix u, xb'een aq, rix uq'm, ru'uj uq'm, rit oq, xxuk po'ot, rit telb',xxe' ch'ima.* Since the first noun in the grouping is already possessed, in these cases it is the second noun in the pair that takes further personal markers for possession, as shown below.

Person (Xpoyanamil)	xkux aq' (collar)	rix xul (hide)	xb'een aq (knee)
(1S) my	xkux waq'	rix inxul	xb'een waq
(2S) your	xkux aawaq'	rix aaxul	xb'een aawaq
(3S) his, her	xkux raq'	rix xxul	xb'een raq
(1P) our	xkux qaq'	rix qaxul	xb'een qaq
(2P) your	xkux eeraq'	rix eexul	xb'een eeraq
(3P) their	xkux raqeb'	rix xxuleb'	xb'een raqeb'

CONJOINED NOUNS

(Sumalil K'ab'a'ej)

In Q'eqchi' there are several examples of nouns that are formed through the pairing of two independent nouns with their own meanings that when joined together have become embedded in the language as a conjoined pair with respect to the meaning of the combination. In these cases the component nouns are written separately. For example: *xe' toon, alal k'ajolb'ej, oq uq', as iitz'in, na'b'ej yuwa'b'ej.* In these nouns each word in the pair is marked for possession by the appropriate personal marker.

Person (Xpoyanamil)	xe' toon (ancestors)	alal k'ajolb'ej (children)
(1S) my	inxe' intoon	walal ink'ajol
(2S) your	aaxe' aatoon	aawalal aak'ajol
(3S) his, her	xxe' xtoon	ralal xk'ajol
(1P) our	qaxe' qatoon	qalal qak'ajol
(2P) your	eexe' eetoon	eeralal eek'ajol
(3P) their	xxe' xtooneb'	ralal xk'ajoleb'

Person (Xpoyanamil)	oq uq' (extremities)	as iitz'in (brothers)
(1S) my	woq wuq'	was wiitz'in
(2S) your	aawoq aawuq'	aawas aawiitz'in
(3S) his, her	roq ruq'	ras riitz'in
(1P) our	qoq quq'	qas qiitz'in
(2P) your	eeroq eeruq'	eeras eeriitz'in
(3P) their	roq ruq'eb'	ras riitz'ineb'

ALWAYS-POSSESSED NOUNS

(K'ab'a'ej Junelik Eecchaninb'il)

This class of noun is permanently marked for possession and requires no further modification. For example: *ru, rix, xb'een, xxuk, re, rit, xtoon, xxe', ru'uj,* and the like. In their written forms these nouns stand alone and are not combined with other words, as in the following examples:

20

- *Pechpo chi **re** kab'l li tz'i'.* «The dog is curled up beside the house. »
- *Yookeb' chi b'atz'unk chi **rix** tzoleb'aal li kok'al.* "The children are playing behind the school."
- *Wank chaq sa' **xb'een** ochoch li mes.* « The cat was on the house. »
- *Yo chi q'ixink chi **ru** saq'e laj Sen.* « Sen is getting hot in the sun. »
- *Sa xtiwb'al **xxe'** li ch'ima.* « It's nice to chew those squash roots. »

In these sentences note that the always-possessed nouns (here in bold type) are written independently and never combined with another word.

NEVER-POSSESSED NOUNS

(K'ab'a'ej Maajunwa Eecchaninb'il)

Certain Q'eqchi' nouns never take a personal marker for possession, as in the Q'eqchi' worldview they cannot be owned by anyone. Examples include: *saq'e, hab', po, chaahim, choxa, choql, choxa ch'och', chu'ke, xokaq'ab'*, and the like.

SUPPLETIVE NOUNS

(K'ab'a'ej Kiib' Xyeeb'al)

Suppletion can be understood as the use of one word as the inflected form of another word when the two words are not cognate. For those learning Q'eqchi', suppletive forms will be seen as highly irregular, but they are only few in number. For example, in Q'eqchi' the word *kab'l* can mean both "house" and "town". It cannot, however, be possessed. In order to denote possession of a house, the term *ochoch* is used; and in order to denote possession of a town the term *tenamit* is used instead, as outlined in the following table:

Person (Xpoyanamil)	kab'l / ochoch (house)	kab'l / tenamit (town)
(1S) my	wochoch	intenamit
(2S) your	aawochoch	aatenamit
(3S) his, her	rochoch	xtenamit
(1P) our	qochoch	qatenamit
(2P) your	eerochoch	eetenamit
(3P) their	rochocheb'	xtenamiteb'

PROPER NOUNS

(Junesal K'ab'a'ej)

Proper nouns typically refer to people, places (including commerical establishments), and geographical features (such as rivers, mountains, etc.). As in English, proper nouns in Q'eqchi' are capitalized, as in the following examples:

tenamit (towns)	poyanam (people)	roqha' (rivers)	k'ayib'aal (stores)
Karcha	Tuk	Aj Uchte'	B'onb'il Pek
Raxruha'	Rux	Aj Q'aniha'	Xalab'e
Chisek	Pet	Aj Pemech	Oxib' Chaahim

DEMONYMS (OR GENTILICS)

(Aj Yeehol Na'ajej)

In order to denote personal place of origin in Q'eqchi' the particle « **Aj** » is used before the place name to form a noun. For example: *Aj Q'anpur, Aj Se'muy, Aj Chama', Aj Tolo'ox, Aj Karcha, Aj Kob'an, Aj Chisek, Aj Raxruha'* and the like.

- *Laa'in Aj Kob'an.* « I am from Coban. »
- *Ma laa'at Aj Karcha'.* « Are you from Carcha? »
- *Li winq aran, ma Aj Senahu a'an.* « Is that man from Senahu? »

PRONOUNS

(Ruuchil K'ab'a'ej)

Pronouns take the place of nouns in sentences and are used in place of the name of a specfic person or thing. In Q'eqchi' there are two types of personal pronouns, as outlined below:

Person (Xpoyanamil)	Independent Pronouns (Junesal ruuchil k'ab'a'ej)	Dependent Pronouns (Chapchookil ruuchil k'ab'a'ej)
First person singular (1S)	laa'in	in
Second person singular (2S)	laa'at	at
Third person singular (3S)	a'an	Ø
First person plural (1P)	laa'o	o
Second person plural (2P)	laa'ex	ex
Third person plural (3P)	a'aneb'	eb'

23

Independent pronouns are written as discrete words in a sentence, as shown here:

- *A'an xsak'ok re laj B'ex.* « **He/She** hit B'ex. »
- *Laa'o xootz'iib'ank re li hu.* « **We** wrote in the book. »
- *A'aneb' ke'kamsink re li kaxlan.* « **They** killed the chicken. »
- *Laa'in xintoqok re li tz'iib'leb'.* « **I** broke my pencil. »
- *Laa'ex texmesunq re li tzoleb'aal wulaj.* « **You all** will sweep the school tomorrow. »
- *Laa'at xattz'ajnink re linhu.* « **You** stained my book. »

Dependent prounouns are never written separately, but only in conjunction with the words they modify, as shown below.

Person (Xpoyanamil)	b'aq (bone)	oxib' (three)	yaj (sick)	wank (to be)	xul (naughty)
(1S) my	b'aqin	oxib'in	yajin	wankin	xulin
(2S) your	b'aqat	oxib'at	yajat	wankat	xulat
(3S) his, her	b'aq	oxib'	yaj	wank	xul
(1P) our	b'aqo	oxib'o	yajo	wanko	xulo
(2P) your	b'aqex	oxib'ex	yajex	wankex	xulex
(3P) their	b'aqeb'	oxib'eb'	yajeb'	wankeb'	xuleb'

Note from these examples that whenever dependent pronouns are used they are always written as a suffix to whatever noun they are modifying in the form of a single word. Also, in the third person singular the null sign "Ø" is not written out.

VERBS

(Xch'ool Aatin)

Verbs are used to indicate the action that is being carried out by someone or what is happening, happened, or will happen in any given sentence, as in the following examples (the verbs are shown in boldface):

- *Xt'ane' sa' sulul li ch'ina'al.* « The child **fell** in the mud. »
- *Xsak' laj Tuk lix Roos.* « Roos **hit** Tuk. »
- *Yo chi **b'atz'unk** sa' xmu kab'l li chi'ina'al.* « The child **is playing** in the hallway. »
- *Xtiw li ch'ina'al li tz'i'.* « The dog **bit** the child. »
- *Jwal **nawulak** chi ru **tz'iib'ak** laj Lu'.* « Lu' **likes to write**. »

TYPES OF VERBS

(Xpaayil Ru Xch'ool Aatin)

In Q'eqchi' there are two principal types of verbs: intransitive verbs and transitive verbs. Conjugating verbs from the base infinitive forms involves learning the inflections that correspond to the tense, person, and transitive/intransitive nature of each verb, as will be outlined in this section.

INFINITIVE VERB FORM

(Xch'ool Aatin Maak'a Xpoyanamil)

An infinitive is a verb that has not yet been conjugated to reflect person, tense, aspect, or any other feature of the action to which it refers. Examples of infinitive verbs in Q'eqchi' include: *xajok, uk'ak, tzolok, tz'iib'ak, se'ek, ilok, utz'uk, etz'unk, tz'aamank, rahok, ajok, hob'ok, ch'ajok, b'eek, iximak* and the like.

INTRANSITIVE VERBS

(Xch'ool Aatin Jun Xpoyanamil)

In the case of intransitive verbs there is only one agent involved in the action to which the verb refers. In other words, there is no direct object. In order to conjugate an intransitive verb you must first learn the affixes used to mark tense and person for the action.

TENSE MARKERS

(Xhoonalil Xch'ool Aatin)

In Q'eqchi', verb conjugations are inflected for both tense and person. There are five verb tenses and each one uses a prefix (or prefixes) according to the following table:

Verb Tenses & Prefixes (Xhoonalil Xch'ool Aatin)		Sample Verb (Xk'utb'al Xch'ool Aatin)
Remote past	**k**	wa'ak
Recent past	**x**	wa'ak
Present	**na**	wa'ak
Present	**nak**	wa'ak
Near Future	**t**	wa'a**q**
Potential Future	**ch**	wa'a**q**

In this table only the various tense marker prefixes are shown in bold—**"k"** for remote past (actions completed long ago), **"x"**

26

for recent past (actions completed recently), **"nak"** or **"na"** for present tense (currently ongoing actions), **"t"** for near future (that which is understood to take place soon), and **"ch"** for potential future actions that have not yet happened, and that may or may not happen in the future—often used as an expression of future imperative). Note that in the future tenses of intransitive verb conjugations that the final **"k"** becomes **"q"**.

PERSONAL MARKERS

(Xpoyanamil Xch'ool Aatin)

In order to conjugate intransitive verbs you must also use a personal marker in conjunction with the tense marker. The various personal markers are shown in the table below:

Person (Xpoyanamil)	Marker
First person singular (1S)	in
Second person singular (2S)	at
Third person singular (3S)	Ø
First person plural (1P)	oo
Second person plural (2P)	ex
Third person plural (3P)	e'

These markers are similar to the ones used as dependent personal pronouns and are placed after the tense marker but before the verb stem. (Note: In its written form the third person singular congugation does not write out the null symbol **"Ø"**.)

To illustrate, now consider two full verb conjugations—one beginning with a consonant and one beginning with a vowel.

Wa'ak

(to eat)

First the verb *wa'ak* (to eat), is conjugated in its various conjugations for tense and person. In this table only the various tense marker prefixes are shown in bold—**"k"** for remote past, **"x"** for recent past, **"nak"** or **"na"** for present tense, **"t"** for near future, and **"ch"** for potential future.

	Remote Past (Najteril hoonal)	**Recent Past** (Toje'il hoonal)	**Present** (Anaqwanil hoonal)	**Near Future** (Seeb'il hoonal)	**Potential Future** (Moqonil hoonal)
I	**k**inwa'ak	**x**inwa'ak	**na**kinwa'ak	**t**inwa'aq	**ch**inwa'aq
you	**k**atwa'ak	**x**atwa'ak	**na**katwa'ak	**t**atwa'aq	**ch**atwa'aq
s/he	**k**iwa'ak	**x**wa'ak	**na**wa'ak	**t**wa'aq	**ch**iwa'aq
we	**k**oowa'ak	**x**oowa'ak	**na**koowa'ak	**t**oowa'aq	**ch**oowa'aq
you	**k**exwa'ak	**x**exwa'ak	**na**kexwa'ak	**t**exwa'aq	**ch**exwa'aq
they	**k**e'wa'ak	**x**e'wa'ak	**na**ke'wa'ak	**t**e'wa'aq	**ch**e'wa'aq

Utz'uk

(to smell)

Next are full conjugations for the verb *utz'uk* (to smell), in its various conjugations for tense and person. In this table only the various personal marker affixes are shown in bold—**"in"** for first person singular, **"at"** for second person singlular, **"Ø"** for third person singular, **"oo"** for first person plural, **"ex"** for second person plural, and **"e'"** for third person plural.

Remote Past (Najteril hoonal)	Recent Past (Toje'il hoonal)	Present (Anaqwanil hoonal)	Near Future (Seeb'il hoonal)	Potential Future (Moqonil hoonal)
kin'utz'uk	xin'utz'uk	nakin'utz'uk	tin'utz'uq	chin'utz'uq
kat-utz'uk	xat-utz'uk	nakat-utz'uk	tat-utz'uq	chat-utz'uq
ki'utz'uk	x'utz'uk	na'utz'uk	t-utz'uq	chi'utz'uq
koo'utz'uk	xoo'utz'uk	nakoo'utz'uk	too'utz'uq	choo'utz'uq
kex'utz'uk	xex'utz'uk	nakex'utz'uk	tex'utz'uk	chex'utz'uq
ke'utz'uk	xe'utz'uk	nake'utz'uk	te'utz'uq	che'utz'uq

It is important to note the differing conventions for the written forms of conjugated verbs beginning with vowels. An apostrophe (') is used as a separator between the tense and person markers and the root verb, except that in the second person singular form and the thrid person singular form of the near future tense a dash symbol (-) is used following the "t", so as not to confuse it with the glottalized letter "t'". For example: *nakin'utz'uk, tat-utz'uq, nakoo'utz'uk, t-utz'uq.*

TRANSITIVE VERBS

(Xch'ool Aatin Kiib' Xpoyanamil)

Transitive verbs are different from intransitive verbs in that they can be marked for both the subjects and the objects of the action—that is, the doer of the action is not the same as the recipient of the action. This means that conjugated forms can have personal markers both for the subject and the object of the action being described. In some cases, only the personal marker for the doer of the action is used and it is understood that there is an object "it" based on the choice of verb conjugation.

29

In Q'eqchi' transitive verb conjugations use a set of personal markers based on whether the verb begins with a consonant or a vowel, as shown in the box below:

Person (Xpoyanamil)	Pre-Vowel Markers (Xpoyanamil xna' tz'iib')	Pre-Consonant Markers (Xpoyanamil xyaab' tz'iib')
First person singular (1S)	w	in
Second person singular (2S)	aaw	aa
Third person singular (3S)	r	x
First person plural (1P)	q	qa
Second person plural (2P)	eer	ee
Third person plural (3P)	e'r	e'x

FIRST TRANSITIVE CONJUGATION

(Xb'een Paay Xb'atz'unenkil Li Xch'ool Aatin Kiib' Xpoyanamil)

To conjugate the verb wa'ak (to eat) in its transitive form the personal markers: *in, aa, x, qa, ee, e'x* are used because this verb begins with a consonant. These are used in combination with the various tense markers for form a prefix that is then added to the verb stem formed by dropping the ending from the infinitive.

For example, with the verb *wa'ak* (to eat), the final **"ak"** is omitted leaving the root **"wa'"** to which the tense and personal markers are added. So for example, if one took the recent past first person singular marker "xin" and added it to the verb root **"wa'"** the resulting verb *xinwa'* would be translated in English as "I ate it." Likewise, the verb *xaawa'* would be translated as "You ate it." And so on. This is because transitive conjugations are understood to have both subjects and objects. Consider the variety of conjugations for the verb *wa'ak* (to eat) using this format, as shown in the following box:

Wa'ak

Remote Past (Najteril hoonal)	Recent Past (Toje'il hoonal)	Present (Anaqwanil hoonal)	Near Future (Seeb'il hoonal)	Potential Future (Moqonil hoonal)
kinwa'	xinwa'	nakinwa'	tinwa'	chinwa'
kaawa'	xaawa'	nakaawa'	taawa'	chaawa'
kixwa'	xxwa'	naxwa'	tixwa'	chixwa'
kiqawa'	xqawa'	naqawa'	tqawa'	chiqawa'
keewa'	xeewa'	nakeewa'	teewa'	cheewa'
ke'xwa'	xe'xwa'	nake'xwa'	te'xwa'	che'xwa'

Verbs beginning in a vowel combine with a different set of pre-vowel personal markers in their transitive conjugations, as with the verb *utz'uk* (to smell).

Utz'uk

Remote Past (Najteril hoonal)	Recent Past (Toje'il hoonal)	Present (Anaqwanil hoonal)	Near Future (Seeb'il hoonal)	Potential Future (Moqonil hoonal)
kiwutz'	xwutz'	nawutz'	tinwutz'	chiwutz'
kaawutz'	xaawutz'	nakaawutz'	taawutz'	chaawutz'
kirutz'	xrutz'	narutz'	trutz'	chirutz'
kiqutz'	xqutz'	naqutz'	tqutz'	chiqutz'
keerutz'	xeerutz'	nakeerutz'	teerutz'	cheerutz'
ke'rutz'	xe'rutz'	nake'rutz'	te'rutz'	che'rutz'

In the box above, the verb *utz'uk* (to smell) is conjugated in its transitive form using the personal markers for verbs beginning with vowels: ***w, aaw, r, q, eer, e'r***. As with the verb *wa'ak* (to eat), the formation *xwutz'* (with the first person singular recent past tense and personal markers added to the stem **"utz'"**) would be translated into English as "I smelled it." Similarly, *tinwutz'* would translate to "I will smell it" and so on. In these cases, even though the direct object of the action is not stated, it is understood.

SECOND TRANSITIVE CONJUGATION

(Xka' Paay Xb'atz'unenkil Li Xch'ool Aatin Kiib' Xpoyanamil)

For the second type of transitive conjugation both the subject and the object of the action are marked in the conjugation, using the following personal markers:

Personal Prefixes for Conjugating Transitive Verbs (Xpoyanamil b'atz'unenk xch'ool aatin kiib' xpoyanamil)			
Person	Intransitive & Transitive Markers	Pre-Consonant Markers (Xpoyanamil xyaab' tz'iib')	Pre-Vowel Markers (Xpoyanamil xna' tz'iib')
First person singular	in	in	w
Second person singular	at	aa	aaw
Third person singular	Ø	x	r
First person plural	oo	qa	q
Second person plural	ex	ee	eer
Third person plural	e'	e'x	e'r

In this conjugation of transitive verbs both personal markers (the one for the subject performing the action and the one for the object receiving the action) are used in conjunction with the verb and are written as one word. This is illustrated in the following tables, where the markers for the subject and the object are shown in boldface type for the verb *wa'ak* (to eat), which begins with a consonant, and also for the verb *utz'uk* (to smell), which begins with a vowel.

Wa'ak

Remote Past (Najteril hoonal)	Recent Past (Toje'il hoonal)	Present (Anaqwanil hoonal)	Near Future (Seeb'il hoonal)	Potential Future (Moqonil hoonal)
ki**nin**wa'	xa**tin**wa'	na**kin**wa'	too'**in**wa'	che**xin**wa'
ki**naa**wa'	xa**taa**wa'	na**kaa**wa'	too'**aa**wa'	che**xaa**wa'
ki**nx**wa'	xa**tx**wa'	na**x**wa'	too**x**wa'	che**xx**wa'
ki**nqa**wa'	xa**tqa**wa'	na**qa**wa'	too**qa**wa'	che**xqa**wa'
ki**nee**wa'	xa**tee**wa'	na**kee**wa'	too'**ee**wa'	che**xee**wa'
ki**ne'x**wa'	xa**te'x**wa'	xa**te'x**wa'	too'**e'x**wa'	che**xe'x**wa'

Utz'uk

Remote Past (Najteril hoonal)	Recent Past (Toje'il hoonal)	Present (Anaqwanil hoonal)	Near Future (Seeb'il hoonal)	Potential Future (Moqonil hoonal)
ki**nw**utz'	xa**tw**utz'	na**koow**utz'	te**xw**utz'	che'**w**utz'
ki**naaw**utz'	xa**taaw**utz'	na**koo'aaw**utz'	te**xaaw**utz'	che'**aaw**utz'
ki**nr**utz'	xa**tr**utz'	na**koor**utz'	te**xr**utz'	che'**r**utz'
ki**nq**utz'	xa**tq**utz'	na**kooq**utz'	te**xq**utz'	che'**q**utz'
ki**neer**utz'	xa**teer**utz'	na**koo'eer**utz'	te**xeer**utz'	che'**eer**utz'
ki**ne'r**utz'	xa**te'r**utz'	na**koo'e'r**utz'	te**xe'r**utz'	che'**e'r**utz'

The following articulation table illustrates how to combine the tense and personal markers for the verb *xuxb'ak* (to whistle) in a variety of conjugations and explains who is receiving the action.

Xuxb'ak

(to whistle)

Tense (Xhoonalil)		Person (Xpoyanamil)		Verb (Xch'ool Aatin)	Receiver (Aj k'ulul re)
k	Remote past	in	aa	kinaaxuxb'a'	"I" (laa'in) received the whistle
x	Recent past	at	in	xatinxuxb'a'	"You" (laa'at) received the whistle
nak	Present	Ø	e'x	nake'xxuxb'a	"He" (a'an) receives the whistle
nak	Present	oo	ee	nakooheexuxb'a	"We" (laa'o) receive the whistle
t	Near Future	ex	x	texxxuxb'a	"You" (laa'ex) will receive the whistle
ch	Potentia l Future	e'	qa	che'qaxuxb'a	"They" (a'aneb') will receive the whistle

INTRANSITIVE DERIVATIONS

(Xjalanil Xch'ool Aatin Jun Xpoyanamil)

In Q'eqchi', sometimes transitive verbs are formed from intransitive ones with the use of special suffixes. For example, the suffix **–siink** attaches to some intransitive verbs to create a transitive one, as in:

- *kaamk* (to die), becomes *kamsiink* (to kill).
- *ok* (to enter), becomes *oksiink* (to put inside).
- *wakliik* (to arise), becomes *waklisiink* (to raise up).

There are other variations as well. For example, the suffix -*tesiink* converts some intransitive verbs into transitive verbs with a causative function. For example:

- *wa'ak* (to eat), becomes *wa'tesiink* (to make eat).
- *kalaak* (to get drunk), becomes *kaltesiink* (to intoxicate).
- *xajok* (to dance), becomes *xajtesiink* (to make dance).

In these instances it is posible to conjugate these transitive verbs using the same tense and personal markers used in the first and second transitive conjugations previously described. This is illustrated in the following tables for the transitive version of the verb *xajok* (to dance). Note that in this conjugation, for example, the meaning of *xinxajtesi* becomes "I made it dance," where the direct object is understood. Likewise, in the second transitive conjugation the verb *xatinxajtesi* would translate as "I made you dance."

Xajtesiink

(to make dance)

Remote Past (Najteril hoonal)	Recent Past (Toje'il hoonal)	Present (Anaqwanil hoonal)	Near Future (Seeb'il hoonal)	Potential Future (Moqonil hoonal)
kinxajtesi	xinxajtesi	nakinxajtesi	tinxajtesi	chinxajtesi
kaaxajtesi	xaaxajtesi	nakaaxajtesi	taaxajtesi	chaaxajtesi
kixxajtesi	xxxajtesi	naxxajtesi	tixxajtesi	chixxajtesi
kiqaxajtesi	xqaxajtesi	naqaxajtesi	tqaxajtesi	chiqaxajtesi
keexajtesi	xeexajtesi	nakeexajtesi	teexajtesi	cheexajtesi
ke'xxajtesi	xe'xxajtesi	nake'xxajtesi	te'xxajtesi	che'xxajtesi

Xajtesiink

(to make dance)

Remote Past (Najteril hoonal)	Recent Past (Toje'il hoonal)	Present (Anaqwanil hoonal)	Near Future (Seeb'il hoonal)	Potential Future (Moqonil hoonal)
k**inin**xajtesi	x**atin**xajtesi	n**akin**xajtesi	too**'in**xajtesi	ch**exin**xajtesi
k**inaa**xajtesi	x**ataa**xajtesi	n**akaa**xajtesi	too**'aa**xajtesi	ch**exaa**xajtesi
k**inx**xajtesi	x**atx**xajtesi	n**ax**xajtesi	too**x**xajtesi	ch**exx**xajtesi
k**inqa**xajtesi	x**atqa**xajtesi	n**aqa**xajtesi	too**qa**xajtesi	ch**exqa**xajtesi
k**inee**xajtesi	x**atee**xajtesi	n**akee**xajtesi	too**'ee**xajtesi	ch**exee**xajtesi
k**ine'x**xajtesi	x**ate'x**xajtesi	x**ate'x**xajtesi	too**'e'x**xajtesi	ch**exe'x**xajtesi

In these examples note that the transitive conjugations have the personal markers following the tense marker and prior to the verb root. At times this will result in three consecutive consonants. For example, in the case of the verb *xajok* (to dance), which begins with **"x"**, and in the third person singular form of the potential future tense of its causative construction the addition of the second person plural marker **"ex"** along with the third person singular marker **"x"** results in *chexxxajtesi,* with the consonant combination "**xxx**". This happens in a number of other verb conjugations as well. These consonant combinations are always written together no matter how many consecutive consonants there are.

Note: In conjugating transitive verbs at times the apostrophe symbol **(')** or an **"h"** is used between personal markers to separate them because in Q'eqchi' consecutive vowels must be separated. For example, it is written: *too'eexajtesi (or*

*tooheexajtesi), nakoo'aawutz' (or nakoohaawutz'),
too'e'xxajtesi (or toohe'xxajtesi).*

PROGRESSIVE TENSES

(Xhoonalil Yo Xb'aanunkil Li Xch'ool Aatin)

Progressive verb tenses differ from the "perfect" tenses in that they express the ongoing nature of the action, whether it be in the past, present, or future. To form progressive tenses in Q'eqchi' an inflected form of the' verb *yook* (which indicates the ongoing nature of an action) combines with the personal markers for who is receiving the action and the transitive markers for verbs that begin with both consonants and vowels. These formations include markers or articles for tense and thus convey the aspects of past, present and future progression. First consider the various inflections of the verb *yook*:

Person (Xpoyanamil)		Past Progressive (Ak b'aanunb'il)	Present Progressive (Yo xb'aanunkil)	Future Progressive (Toj tb'aanumanq)
I	laa'in	yookin chaq	yookin	yooqin
you	laa'at	yookat chaq	yookat	yooqat
s/he	a'an	yoo chaq	yoo	yooq
we	laa'o	yooko chaq	yooko	yooqo
you	laa'ex	yookex chaq	yookex	yooqex
they	eb' a'an	yookeb' chaq	yookeb'	yooqeb'

The progressive formations in Q'eqchi' can make use of both intransitive and transitive verbs. In the case of intransitive verbs, the inflected form of *yook* combines with the preposition

37

chi and the unconjugated form of the infinitive to create complete sentences. For example:

- ***Yookin chi wa'ak***. « I am eating. »
- ***Yookin chaq chi wa'ak*** *naq xatk'ulun.* « I was eating when you arrived. »
- ***Yookeb' chi b'atz'unk*** *sa' xmu kab'l li kok'al.* « The children are playing in the hallway. »
- *Wulaj chi eq'la* ***yooqex chi b'eek*** . « You will be walking tomorrow morning. »
- *Ma* ***yooqeb' chi oyb'enink.*** « Will they be waiting ? »

In the case of transitive verbs, the inflected form of *yook* combines with the transitive form of the verb infinitive and an inflected form of *chi* to create complete sentences. However, whereas in the intransitive formation of the progressive the use of the preposition *chi* is obligatory, in transitive formation it is optional. First consider how base infinitives are changed into their transitive forms for the purpose of forming progressive tenses.

Transitive infinitives are formed differently for two main types of verbs—the first type consists of a verb stem with a single syllable and the second type ends in **"nk"** preceded by a long vowel. First consider formations for monosyllabic roots: these consist of dropping the ending of the intransitive infinitive such as **"ok"** or **"uk"** and then adding an active pronoun as a prefix to the root and the suffix **"b'al"** to the end. For example, the verb *sik'ok* (to seek) drops its ending to form the root *sik'*. In order to form a conjugated verb with the transitive meaning of "seeking me" the first person singular pronoun **"in"** and the suffix **"b'al"** enclose the root **"sik'"** to render *insik'b'al*. This process is repeated across all personal pronouns as shown in the following box:

Person	Pre-Consonant Pronoun	Verb Root "to seek" (sik'ok)	Transitive Infinitive Suffix
(1S)	in	sik'	b'al
(2S)	aa	sik'	b'al
(3S)	x	sik'	b'al
(1P)	qa	sik'	b'al
(2P)	ee	sik'	b'al
(3P)	e'x	sik'	b'al

If the verb stem begins with a vowel then the active pronouns for vowels are used as a prefix instead, as in the following inflections of the verb *ilok* (to see):

Person	Pre-Vowel Pronoun	Verb Root "to see" (ilok)	Transitive Infinitive Suffix
(1S)	w	il	b'al
(2S)	aaw	il	b'al
(3S)	r	il	b'al
(1P)	q	il	b'al
(2P)	eer	il	b'al
(3P)	e'r	il	b'al

Now consider the formation of transitive infinitves for the second type of verb—those that end in **"nk"** preceded by a long vowel. For example: *paab'aank* (to believe) and *ab'iink* (to hear). In this case the verb root is formed by dropping the final **"k"** of the intransitive infinitive and adding the suffix **"kil"**. The final vowel is also shortened. As with the first type, personal pronouns are added as prefixes to the verb root according to whether it begins with a consonant or a vowel, as shown in the following boxes.

Person	Pre-Consonant Pronoun	Verb Root "to believe" (paab'aank)	Transitive Infinitive Suffix
(1S)	in	paab'an	kil
(2S)	aa	paab'an	kil
(3S)	x	paab'an	kil
(1P)	qa	paab'an	kil
(2P)	ee	paab'an	kil
(3P)	e'x	paab'an	kil

Person	Pre-Vowel Pronoun	Verb Root "to hear" (ab'iink)	Transitive Infinitive Suffix
(1S)	w	ab'in	kil
(2S)	aaw	ab'in	kil
(3S)	r	ab'in	kil
(1P)	q	ab'in	kil
(2P)	eer	ab'in	kil
(3P)	e'r	ab'in	kil

Now consider various iterations using all of these transitive infinitives in conjunction with the inflected forms of *yook* and the particle *chi* (which can combine with the active pronoun and for simplicity be written as one word) to convey the different progressive tenses and moods, as shown and translated below:

PRESENT PROGRESSIVE

(Yo Xb'aanunkil)

- *Yookin chaawab'inkil.* « I am listening to you (singular). »
- *Yookat chixsik'b'al.* « You are looking for it (or him/her). »
- *Yookeb' cheerilb'al* sa' xmu kab'l. « They are looking at you (plural) in the hallway. »
- *Ma yookex chi xpaab'ankil* li raatin. « Are you believing what he is saying ? »
- *Yookin chi xtenq'ankileb'.* « I am helping them. »

FUTURE PROGRESSIVE

(Toj Tb'aanumanq)

- *Yooqat chi wilb'al.* « You will be seeing me. »
- *Yooqin chaasik'b'al.* « I will be looking for you. »
- *Yooqeb' cheerilb'al* wulaj chi eq'la. « They will be looking for you tomorrow morning. »
- *Ma yookex chi xpaab'ankil li raatin.* « Are you believing what he is saying ? »
- *Ma toj yooqin xtenq'ankileb'* li neb'a wi ninsach chi junil intumin. « Will I still be helping the poor if I lose all my money ? »

In the formation of the past progressive (also referred to as the past imperfect tense), the particle *chaq* is used in conjunction

41

with the inflected forms of *yook* in order to place the ongoing action in the past.

PAST PROGRESSIVE

(Ak B'aanunb'il)

- *Yookin chaq chaatenq'ankil.* « I was helping you. »
- *Yookin chaq chaasik'b'al.* « I was looking for you. »
- *Yookeb' chaq cheerilb'al* ewer chi eq'la. « They were looking for you yesterday morning. »
- Ma *yookex chaq xpaab'ankil* li raatin aj tzolonel. « Did you believe what the teacher was saying ? »
- *Yookin chaq rab'inkil* li ab'ib'aal aatin ewer jo'kan naq xink'e reetal naq wan jun nimla kub'enaq xtz'aq anaqwan. « I was listening to the radio yesterday and that 's how I found out there is a big sale today. »

COMMANDS

(Taqlahom)

There are a variety of ways to form commands from verbs in Q'eqchi' depending on whether they are intranstive or transitive in nature and also whether they are affirmative commands or negative commands. The basic types include the following:

- **Direct Commands**. Affirmative statements that convey an imperative mood of the desired action.

- **Exhortatives**. Exhortatives are not direct commands, but rather convey a desire for a given action to take place.
- **Conjugated Imperatives**. Sometimes the imperative mood of an action is conveyed using conjugated verb forms with the two future tense markers—« **ta** » (for near future) and « **chi** » for potential future.
- **Negative Commands**. Negative commands in Q'eqchi' take their own set of personal markers using inflected forms of « **mi** ».

These basic formations are as follows:

Direct Commands (Jolominb'il Taqlahom)		
Type (Xpaayil Ru)	**Form** (Chankatq Ru)	**Examples** (Xk'utb'al)
Intransitive (regular, singular)	Replace all final consonants of verb infinitive with **"n"**.	*Loq'ok* (to buy*)* → *Loq'on* (Buy!) *Hilank* (to rest) → *Hilan* (Rest!)
Intransitive (regular, plural)	Replace all final consonants of verb infinitive with **"nqex"**.	*Loq'ok* (to buy*)* → *Loq'onqex* (Buy!) *Hilank* (to rest) → *Hilanqex* (Rest!)
Intransitive (irregular)	Seven irregular forms that must be memorized. (Add **"qex"** for plural.)	*Xik* (to go*)* → *Ayu* (Go!) *Chaalk* (to come) → *Kim* (Come!) *Wa'ak* (to eat*)* → *Wa'in* (Eat!) *Waark* (to sleep) → *Warin* (Rest!) *Ajk* (to awaken*)* → *Ajen* (Wake up!) *Ok* (to enter) → *Okan* (Enter!) *Elk* (to leave*)* → *Elen* (Leave!)

Direct Commands (Jolominb'il Taqlahom)		
Type (Xpaayil Ru)	**Form** (Chankatq Ru)	**Examples** (Xk'utb'al)
Transitive (singular)	Verb root alone is used.	*Chupuk* (to put out*)* → *Chup* (Put it out!) *K'amok* (to bring) → *K'am* (Bring it!) *Numsink* (to pass) → *Numsi* (Pass it!)
Transitive (plural)	Add suffix **"omaq"** to verb root.	*Ab'iink* (to hear) → *Ab'iomaq* (Listen!) *K'ehok reetal* (to observe) → *K'ehomaq reetal* (Behold!)

With transitive commands the direct object of the action can be articulated using general pronouns, as in the following:

- *Ab'ihin.* « Listen to me. »
- *Elenqex. Q'axomaqo.* « Go! Leave us behind. »
- *Kim rik'in aajukub'. Numsihin junpak'al.* « Come with your boat. Take me to the other side. »

Exhortatives (Patz'b'il B'aanunk)		
Type (Xpaayil Ru)	**Form** (Chankatq Ru)	**Examples** (Xk'utb'al)
Intransitive (regular)	Replace final consonant **"k"** of verb infinitive with **"q"** and add suffix pronouns.	*Tijok* (to pray*)* → *Tijoqo* (Let us pray.) *Hilank* (to rest) → *Hilanq sa' tuqtuukilal.* (May he rest in peace.)

Exhortatives (Patz'b'il B'aanunk)		
Type (Xpaayil Ru)	**Form** (Chankatq Ru)	**Examples** (Xk'utb'al)
Intransitive (irregular)	A few verbs replace final consonant **"k"** of verb infinitive with **"aq"** and add suffix pronouns.	*Ok* (to enter) → *Okaqo* (Let us enter.) *Xik* (to go*)* → *Xikaqin* (Let me go.) Note: *xik* also has the unique forms **"yo'o"** and **"yo'qeb'"** (let's go).
Transitive (regular, vowel)	Add suffix **"aq"** to verb root and use active pronouns as prefixes to indicate subject.	***Ab'iink*** (to hear) *Wab'ihaq* → (Let me hear it.) *Aawab'ihaq* → (You should hear it.) *Rab'ihaq* → (Let him hear it.) *Qab'ihaq* → (Let's hear it.) *Eerab'ihaq* → (You should hear it.) *Rab'ihaqeb'* → (Let them hear it.)
Transitive (regular, consonant)	Add suffix **"aq"** to verb root and use active pronouns as prefixes to indicate subject.	***K'amok*** (to carry) *Ink'amaq* → (Let me carry it.) *Aak'amaq* → (You should carry it.) *Xk'amaq* → (Let her carry it.) *Qak'amaq* → (Let's carry it.) *Eek'amaq* → (Let you carry it.) *Xk'amaqeb'* → (They should carry it.)

Conjugated Imperatives (B'atz'unenb'il Taqlahom)		
Type (Xpaayil Ru)	**Form** (Chankatq Ru)	**Examples** (Xk'utb'al)
Intransitive & Transitive (regular)	Use near future tense markers in "**ta**" series.	***K'ehok*** (to put, place) *Taak'e li hu aran.* → (Put the book there.)
Intransitive & Transitive (regular)	Use future potential tense markers in "**chi**" series. The suffix "**aq**" is sometimes added to the conjugation.	***Kuyuk maak*** (to forgive) *Chaakuy inmaak.* → (Please forgive me; or, Pardon me.) *Chaakuyaq inmaak.* → (Please forgive me; or, Pardon me.)

Negative Commands (Mab'aanunb'il Taqlahom)		
Type (Xpaayil Ru)	**Form** (Chankatq Ru)	**Examples** (Xk'utb'al)
Intransitive	Use personal markers in the "**mi**" series. Drop final "**k**" from infinitive.	***Waark*** (to sleep) *Minwaar* → (May I not sleep.) *Matwaar* → (Don't sleep.) *Miwaar* → (May she not sleep.) *Mowaar* → (May we not sleep.) *Mexwaar* → (Don't sleep (pl).) *Me'waar* → (May they not sleep.)

Negative Commands		
(Mab'aanunb'il Taqlahom)		
Type (Xpaayil Ru)	Form (Chankatq Ru)	Examples (Xk'utb'al)
Transitive (regular, vowel)	Add personal markers in the "**mi**" series to the transitive verb root.	*Ab'iink* (to hear) *Miwab'i* → (May I not hear it.) *Maawab'i* → (May you not hear it.) *Mirab'i* → (May he not hear it.) *Miqab'i* → (May we not hear it.) *Meerab'i* → (May you not hear it (pl).) *Me'rab'i* → (May they not hear it.)
Transitive (regular, consonant)	Add personal markers in the "**mi**" series to the transitive verb root.	*Sak'ok* (to hit) *Minsak'* → (May I not hit him/her.) *Maasak'* → (Don't hit him/her.) *Mixsak'* → (May he not hit him/her.) *Miqasak'* → (May we not hit him/her.) *Meesak'* → (Don't hit him/her (pl).) *Me'xsak'* → (May they not hit him/her.)

PAST PARTICIPLES

(Mab'atz'unenb'il Numenaqil'uxk Xch'ool Aatin)

A participle is a form of a verb that is used in a sentence to modify a noun, noun phrase, verb, or verb phrase, and plays a role similar to that of an adjective or adverb. It is one of the types of nonfinite verb forms. A nonfinite verb is any of several verb forms that are not finite verbs; that is, they cannot serve as the root of an independent clause. Nonfinite verbs typically are not conjugated or inflected by grammatical tense.

In Q'eqchi' there are a number of verb forms that convey completed actions by the use of an altered verb form in conjunction with personal pronouns rather than through the use of the infinitive itself or its temporal conjugations. There are both verbal and adjectival applications of this form.

Past Participles (Mab'atz'unenb'il Numenaqil'uxk Xch'ool Aatin)		
Type (Xpaayil Ru)	**Form** (Chankatq Ru)	**Examples** (Xk'utb'al)
Intransitive	Add **"-enaq"** or **"-jenaq"** to the verb root and then a general pronoun to indicate the subject.	**Nume'k** (to pass) *Numenaqin* → (I have passed) *Numenaqat* → (You sg. have passed) *Numenaq* → (He/She has passed) *Numenaqo* → (We have passed) *Numenaqex* → (You pl. have passed) *Numenaqeb'* → (They have passed) **Adjectival Use** *Numenaq* → (passed)
Transitive	Use an active pronoun prefix to indicate the agent of the action and add an **"-om"** or **"-um"** suffix to the transitive verb root.	**K'ehok** (to give) *Ink'ehom* → (I have given) *Aak'ehom* → (You sg. have given) *Xk'ehom* → (He/She has given) *Qak'ehom* → (We have given) *Eek'ehom* → (You pl. have given) *Xk'ehomeb'* → (They have given) **Use as Possessed Noun** *Ink'ehom* → (the things I have given)

Following are a variety of illustrations of the use of both transitive and intransitive past participles in Q'eqchi':

- *Kalajenaqeb'.* « They have gotten drunk. »
- *Ma kamenaq li aaq.* « Has the hog died? »
- *Ak wanjenaqo El Estor.* « We have already been to El Estor. »
- *B'ar wan aaloq'om.* « Where are your purchases?»
- *Numenaq li b'eleeb'al ch'iich'.* « The bus is gone. »
- *Ma rab'ihom li chaab'il esil aayuwa'.* « Has your father heard the good news? »
- *Ak wilom ru li hu a'an.* « I have already read that book. »

PASSIVE VOICE

(Nume'k'uluk)

The passive voice is a grammatical construction in which the noun or noun phrase that would be the object of an active sentence appears as the subject of a sentence with a passive voice. For example, in English the following is an active sentence: "We made mistakes." In its passive reconstruction it would be" "Mistakes were made (by us)." It is used when the intent is to put the focus on the action itself, rather than the doers of the action (or when the agents of the action are not known). In Q'eqchi' there are a number of ways to form the passive voice, both conjugated and unconjugated, as described in the boxes below.

The regular passive voice in Q'eqchi' is a verbal construction in which transitive verbs take an intransitive conjugation with alternate verb endings. This construction closely approximates the meaning conveyed in the English passive voice.

Regular Passive Voice (Nume'k'uluk Ok Eechej)		
Type (Xpaayil Ru)	**Form** (Chankatq Ru)	**Examples** (Xk'utb'al)
Regular Passive (transitive verbs)	For verbs with a single syllable in the root and an "-**ok**" ending replace the ending with "-**e'k**" and conjugate normally.	*K'amok* (to carry) becomes *K'ame'k* (to be carried) *Xink'ame'* → (I was carried) *Xatk'ame'* → (You sg. were carried) *Xk'ame'* → (He/She was carried) *Xok'ame'* → (We were carried) *Xeek'ame'* → (You pl. were carried) *Xe'k'ame'* → (They were carried)
Regular Passive (transitive verbs)	For verbs multisyllable verbs the "-**nk**" ending is replaced with "-**k**" and the final vowel is long.	*Osob'tesink* (to bless) becomes *Osob'tesiik* (to be blessed) *Tinosob'tesiiq* → (I will be blessed) *Tatosob'tesiiq* → (You sg. will be blessed) *T-osob'tesiiq* → (He/She will be blessed) *To-osob'tesiiq* → (We will be blessed) *Texosob'tesiiq* → (You pl. will be blessed) *Te'osob'tesiiq* → (They will be blessed)

In the regular passive voice although the object of the action becomes the subject, it is possible to note the doer of the action by use of the preposition *"xb'aan"* (by). Following are several examples of sentences using the regular passive construction:

- *Xe'chape' laj elq'.* « The thieves were captured. »
- *Ink'a nakatile'.* « You (sg.) are not seen. »
- *Ma tink'ule'q xb'aan qawa Lu.* « Will I be received by Mr. Peter? »
- *X-osob'tesiik xb'aan aj K'ehol miis.* « She was blessed by the priest. »
- *Xe'kamsiik xb'aan li kaqsut-iq'.* « They were killed by the hurricane. »

The general passive voice is a verbal construction in Q'eqchi' which conveys that an action is done, but does not specify the doer of the action and cannot take the prepostion *"xb'aan"* to specify the agent. In this construction the suffix **"-maank"** is added to the transitive root of a verb. Because the agent is not known, onnly the third person forms tend to be used.

General Passive Voice (Nume'k'uluk Maa'ani Aj B'aanunel)		
Type (Xpaayil Ru)	**Form** (Chankatq Ru)	**Examples** (Xk'utb'al)
General Passive (transitive verbs)	For single and multi syllable transitive roots the verb ending with **"-maank"** and conjugate normally.	*Tz'iib'ank* (to write) *Natz'iib'aman* → (It is written) *Xtz'iib'aman* → (It was written) *Kitz'iib'aman* → (It was written anciently) *Ta'tz'iib'amanq* → (It will be written) *Chi'tz'iib'amanq* → (May it be written)

Following are several examples of sentences using the general passive construction:

- *Xk'utman chiqu chanru xb'aanunkil.* « We were shown how to do it. »
- *Wulaj wulaj li tuqtuukilal natz'iibaman chi ru li xch'ool.* « Everyday, peace is written on his heart. »
- *Maajoq'e tasachmaanq lix rahok.* « Her love cannot be destroyed.»
- *Chixjunileb' li xhuhil li tenamit che'tz'iib'amanq sa' xk'ab'a' a'an.* « All government contracts shall be drawn up in his name. »
- *Ma naoksiman li aatinob'aal Q'eqchi' sa' laa k'aleb'aal.* « Is Q'eqchi' used in your village? »

In Q'eqchi' there are also two ways to form the passive voice that make use of past particples (or unconjugated verb forms) as outlined in the box below.

Passive Voice with Participles (Nume'k'uluk Maa'ani Aj B'aanunel ut Mab'atz'unenb'il Numenaqil'uxk Xch'ool Aatin)		
Type (Xpaayil Ru)	**Form** (Chankatq Ru)	**Examples** (Xk'utb'al)
Passive Participle	Add suffix **"-b'il"** to the transitive root of short verbs or after the final **"-n"** of longer forms.	*K'ehok* (to give) *K'ehb'il* → (given) *Tz'aamank* (to request) *Tz'aamanb'il* → (requested) *B'atz'unenk* (to conjugate) *B'atz'unenb'il* → (conjugated) Note: This form can take the preposition *"xb'aan"* to indicate the agent.

Passive Voice with Participles (Nume'k'uluk Maa'ani Aj B'aanunel ut Mab'atz'unenb'il Numenaqil'uxk Xch'ool Aatin)		
Type (Xpaayil Ru)	**Form** (Chankatq Ru)	**Examples** (Xk'utb'al)
Repetitive Form	For any mono-syllabic verb root repeat the first consonant and add "**-o**" (or "**-u**" if root vowel is "**u**").	**Tehok** (to open) *Tehto* → (opened) **Patz'ok** (to ask about) *Patz'po* → (asked about) **K'utuk** (to show) *K'utk'u* → (shown) Note: This form only expresses the condition (like an adjective) and not the action itself and so it cannot take the preposition *"xb'aan"* to indicate the agent.

Following are several examples of sentences using these passive constructions:

- *Ma tehto li okeb'aal.* « Is the door opened ?»
- *Tz'aptz'o.* « It is shut.»
- *Chunchukin sa' li tem.* « I am seated on the bench.»
- *Tz'iib'anb'il xb'aan aj b'anonel.* « It was written by the doctor.»
- *K'ehb'ileb' chi k'anjelak.* « They are given to work (i.e., good workers). »
- *Anaqwan junelik xaqxookeb' li oxib' a'in: li paab'aal, li oyb'enink ut li rahok.* « And now abideth faith, hope, charity, these three. »

REFLEXIVE CONJUGATION

(B'atz'unenk Junaj B'aanunel ut K'ulunel)

A reflexive action is one in which the subject and the object are the same—that is, the doer of the action and the receiver are the same person. In Q'eqchi' this is conveyed through the transitive conjugation along with the preposition *"-ib'"* preceded by the relevant active personal pronoun, as outline in the box below.

Reflexive Conjugation	
(B'atz'unenk Junaj B'aanunel ut K'ulunel)	
Form (Chankatq Ru)	**Examples** (Xk'utb'al)
Conjugate transitive roots normally and add preposition **"-ib'** with personal pronouns preceding.	***Sak'ok*** (to hit) *Ninsak' wib'* → (I hit myself) *Naksak' aawib'* → (You sg. hit yourself) *Naxsak' rib'* → (He/She hits himself/herself) *Naqasak' qib'* → (We hit ourselves) *Nekesak' eerib'* → (You hit yourselves) *Neke'xsak' rib'* → (They hit themselves)
Pluralization of reflexive: formed with the phrase **"chi –ib'il –ib'"** as shown at right.	*Chiqib'il qib* → (we to ourselves) *Cheerib'il eerib'* → (you to each other) *Chirib'ileb' rib'* → (they to themsleves)

Following are several examples of sentences using the reflexive construction:

- ***Chi qilaq qib'.*** « May we see each other again soon.»
- ***Chaawil aawib'.*** « Take care of yourself.»

- *Li rahok ink'a' naxq'etq'eti rib'.* « Charity vaunteth not itself.»

- *Junxil neke'xcamsi rib' chirib'ileb' rib'.* « They used to kill each other.»

- *Tento taqara qib' chiqib'il qib.* « We must love each other. »

AGENTS

(Aj B'aanunel)

In Q'eqchi' there are several different ways to express the agent of an action—that is, who performs a given action commonly or as an occupation. Most forms are derived from verbs (either transitive or intransitive) and in all cases combine with the agentive particle *"aj"*. The two most common formations are described in the box below.

Agents (Aj B'aanunel)		
Type (Xpaayil Ru)	**Form** (Chankatq Ru)	**Examples** (Xk'utb'al)
Intransitive Agent	Add suffix **"-onel"** (sometimes **"-unel"** or **"-anel"**) to the transitive root of some verbs to form an intransitive agent.	*Tzolok* (to teach) *Aj tzolonel* → (teacher) *B'anok* (to cure) *Aj b'anonel* → (doctor) *Iqaank* (to carry) *Aj iqanel* → (porter) *Paab'ank* (to believe) *Aj paab'anel* → (believer) *B'ichank* (to sing) *Aj b'ichanel* → (singer)

Agents		
(Aj B'aanunel)		
Type (Xpaayil Ru)	**Form** (Chankatq Ru)	**Examples** (Xk'utb'al)
Transitive Agent	Add suffix "**-ol**" (sometimes "**-ul**") to the mono-syllabic transitive root of some verbs to form a transitive agent. Must be followed by a direct object.	***Ilok*** (to watch over) *Aj ilol tenamit* → (policeman) *Aj ilol xul* → (shepherd) ***Chapok*** (to grab) *Aj chapok kar* → (fisherman) ***Kamsiink*** (to kill) *Aj kamsihom aaq* → (hog butcher) *Aj kamsihom re* → (his killer)

ADVERBS

(Tz'aqob' Aatin)

Adverbs are words or phrases that modify verbs, adjectives, or other adverb or word group, expressing a relation of place, time, circumstance, manner, cause, or degree. Consider the following examples, in which the adverb is highlighted in bold text:

- *Kixtoq roq laj B'ex **ewer** sa' b'atz'unk b'olotz.* « B'ex broke his foot playing soccer **yesterday**. »
- ***Ink'a'** xwulak chi tzolok lix Mar.* « Mar did **not** come to study. »
- ***Jwal** kaw tz'aqal li hab' naq xsaqeew.* « It was raining **hard** this morning. »

56

Adverbs in Q'eqchi' can be usefully categorized as in the following table:

Adverbs (Tz'aqob' Aatin)		
Type (Xpaayil Ru)	**Function** (Xk'anjel)	**Examples** (Xk'utb'al)
Temporal (re hoonal)	Indicates the time that an action takes place.	*mixk (ma'laq), anaqwan, eq'la, jo'wan, hoon, toje', wulaj, jun xamaan, jun chihab', jun po, ewer, kab'ajer, oxejer, ewu, wa'leb', wulaj, kab'ej, oxej*
Negative (re q'etok)	Signifies actions that won't take place.	*i', moko, moko naru ta, maab'ay, maji', toj maji', maajaruj, ink'a', maachan, maajoq'e, maak'a', maamin, maajunwa, maajun*
Affirmative (re chaq'b'enk)	Signifies actions that will take place.	*us, ch'olch'o, jo'kan (jo'ka'an), tento, yaal, usaq, utan, heehe'*
Quantity (re k'ihalil)	Indicates the amount or size of an action	*nab'al, b'ab'ay, b'ayaq, xiikil, q'axal, jwal, b'itz'il, numtajenaq*
Locative (re na'ajej)	Indicates where an action takes place	*arin, aran, wa'ran, le', arin chaq, toj le', toj le' chaq, wili', we'kin*
Mode (re chan ru)	Indicates how an action is carried out.	*chaab'il, yib'ru, tojo'yaal, wilaq wan, ink'a' us, a'yaal re, jwal chaab'il*
Doubt (re k'a'uxl)	Indicates the uncertain nature of an action	*maare, tana, len, chankeb', chanchan, usan, ee, pe'yaal*

Adverbs (Tz'aqob' Aatin)		
Type (Xpaayil Ru)	**Function** (Xk'anjel)	**Examples** (Xk'utb'al)
Interrogative (re patz'ok)	Inquires about how an action will be carried out.	*b'ar, jo' nimal, jarub', ma, chan ru, k'a' ru, ani, aniheb', chan pe' ru, k'a' ru pe', k'a' ut, joq'e*
Manner (re chan ru xb'aanunkil)	Describes how an action will be carried out.	*junpaat, timil, timil timil, xyaalal, seeb', seeb' seeb', chi xjunil, ch'inqil, b'ab'ayqil*
Demonstrative (re k'utuk)	Indicates where an action will be carried out.	*wan le', a'in, a'an, wank, a'ineb', a'aneb', we', we'i, we'keb'*

AJ YEHONEL

(Adjetives)

Adjectives are words or phrases naming an attribute, and are added to or grammatically related to a noun to modify or describe it. They can indicate a wide variety of qualities including size, color, degree, etc. Examples of adjectives in Q'eqchi' include the following: *q'eq, chu, sa, ch'am, q'em, saq, q'es, kaq, rax, q'eel, ak', pejel, sak'a, nim, k'ach'in, saaj, josq', tuulan,* and the like. Consider the following examples, in which the adjective is highlighted in bold text:

- *Laj B'ex xsach lix **rax** b'olotz ewer.* « B'ex lost his **green** ball yesterday. »
- *Ink'a' xwulak li **nimla** tz'i' anaqwan.* « That **big** dog did not come today. »

- *Jwal **sa** li ki'il q'een xinwa'.* « The fruit I ate was so **delicious**. »

In Q'eqchi' many other types of words can be derived from adjectives. Consider the examples in the following table:

Derivation of Adjectives (Xpuktesinkil Rib' Li Aatin Aj Yehonel)			
Adjective (aj yehonel)	**Abstract Noun** (muhel k'ab'a'ej)	**Verb** (xch'ool aatin)	**Intensifier** (ka' yehok)
rax (green or blue)	xraxal (greenness)	xraxo'k (turned green)	rax rax (very green)
kaq (red)	xkaqal (redness)	xkaqo'k (turned white)	kaq kaq (very red)
chu (smelly)	xchuhil (stink)	xchuho'k (began to stink)	chuuchu (very smelly)
sa (delicious)	xsahil (deliciousness)	xsaho'k (became delicious)	saasa (very tasty)
ki' (sweet)	xki'al (sweetnes)	xki'o'k (became sweet)	ki' ki' (very sweet)
ch'am (deep)	xch'amal (depth)	xch'amo'k (deepened)	ch'am ch'am (very deep)
k'a (sour)	xk'ahil (sourness)	xk'aho'k (turned sour)	k'aak'a (very sour)
saq (white)	xsaqal (whiteness)	xsaqo'k (turned white)	saq saq (very white)
q'an (yellow)	xq'anal (yellowness)	xq'ano'k (turned yellow)	q'an q'an (very yellow)
q'em (good)	xq'emal (goodness)	xq'emo'k (became good)	q'em q'em (very good)
q'es (sharp)	xq'esnal (sharpness)	xq'esno'k (was sharpened)	q'es q'es (very sharp)

Derivation of Adjectives (Xpuktesinkil Rib' Li Aatin Aj Yehonel)			
Adjective (aj yehonel)	**Abstract Noun** (muhel k'ab'a'ej)	**Verb** (xch'ool aatin)	**Intensifier** (ka' yehok)
cha (gray)	xchahil (grayness)	xchaho'k (turned gray)	chaacha (very gray)
ke (cold)	xkehil (coldness)	xkeho'k (turned cokl)	keeke (very cold)

In the case of intensifiers, note that if the adjective ends with a consonant then it is written as two separate words, but if the adjective ends with a vowel then then the first vowel elongates and they are combined to form one word.

ADDITIONAL PARTS OF SPEECH

(Xkomon Chik Xk'ub'lal Aatinob'aal)

Additional Parts of Speech (Xkomon Chik Xk'ub'lal Aatinob'aal)		
Name (K'ab'a'ej)	**Function** (Xk'anjel)	**Examples** (Xk'utb'al)
Prepositions (aj tenq'anel)	A word modifying a noun or pronoun expressing a relation to another word or element in the clause (often in a spatial relationship).	*chi, sa', chi ru, rub'el, rik'in, re, toj, sa' xyanq, cho'q re, xb'aan, naq, a'yaal, sa' xb'een, chi rix*
Conjunctions (aj ch'utub'anel)	A word used to connect clauses or sentences or to coordinate words in the same clause.	*ut, jo', ab'aan, ab'aanan, xb'aan naq, malaj (malaq), xkun, wi', chi moko, usta*

Additional Parts of Speech (Xkomon Chik Xk'ub'lal Aatinob'aal)		
Name (K'ab'a'ej)	**Function** (Xk'anjel)	**Examples** (Xk'utb'al)
Articles (k'aj aatin)	A determiner that introduces a noun phrase and implies that the thing mentioned has already been mentioned, or is common knowledge, or is about to be defined	*li, jun, junaq*
Positionals (aj yehol wanjik)	In Q'eqchi' positionals are derived from verbs and are used to describe how things are positioned or situated. They can take personal marker suffixes (e.g., *xaqxokin* = "I am standing").	*xaqxo, wiq'wo, k'achk'o, salso, pechpo, k'utzk'u, peq'po, xulxu, q'e'q'o, an'o, k'itzk'o, chunchu, yokyo, pak'po, huphu, ch'a'ch'o, chok'cho*
Male Classifiers (xwinqilal aatin)	Used in conjunction with nouns to denote the male gender of the subject.	*ma', mama', qawa', qawa'chin, la, wa' aj/laj*
Female Classifiers (rixqilal aatin)	Used in conjunction with nouns to denote the female gender of the subject.	*xan, xa'an, qana', qana'chin, lix/ix, qa'a*

Q'EQCHI' SYNTAX

(Nawtus'aatin Q'eqchi')

Syntax refers to the arrangement of words and phrases to create well-formed sentences in a language.

LINGUISTIC TYPOLOGY

(Xpaayil Ru Aatinob'al)

In terms of linguistic typology, Q'eqchi' is a verb–object–subject (or verb–object–agent) language. This is commonly abbreviated as VOS (or VOA, in the case of ergative languages such as Q'eqchi'). For example, a VOS language is one in which most basic sentences arrange their elements in this order: *"Bit man dog."* This differs from English, which is a subject-verb-object (SVO) language, in which one would find instead: *"Dog bit man."*

SENTENCE FORMATION

(Xk'ub'lankil Li Raqal Aatin)

Consider the following examples of well-formed Q'eqchi' sentences:

- *Xsak' lix Pet laj Xiwan*. « Xiwan hit Pet. »
- *Na'aanilank rajlal kutan laj Xiwan*. « Juan runs every day. »
- *Xsik' ruutz'u'uj linna' wanab'*. « The mother of my older sister looked for her flowers. »
- *Xe'xkamsi chi ch'iich'*. « They killed it with a knife. »

- ***Ma a'in li kab'l wan wi' li qatumin.*** « Is this the house where our money is ? »
- ***Wankin chaawix.*** « I am behind you. »

TYPES OF SENTENCES

(Xpaayil Ru Raqal Aatin)

The above examples are sentences. A sentence is a set of words that is complete in itself and can stand alone in conveying meaning. Sentences typically contain a subject and a predicate consisting of a main clause and sometimes one or more subordinate clauses. There are a number of types of sentences—they can used to convey statements, questions, exclamations, or commands. Below are basic sentence types in Q'eqchi', with examples of each:

Sentence Type (Xpaayil Ru Raqal Aatin)	Examples (Xk'utb'al)
Affirmative Sentence (raqal aatin re yaal)	• *Wankeb' sa' tzoleb'aal li kok'al.* (The children are at school.) • *Xsak' laj Lix lix Mar.* (Maria hit Lix.) • *Yookin xtz'iib'ankil jun inhu sa' ulul ch'iich'.* (I am writing my paper on the computer.)
Negative Sentence (raqal aatin re q'etok)	• *Ink'a' naraj xyiib'ankil xk'anjel laj Lu' xkanab'aak xb'aan laj k'utunel.* (Lu' does not want to do the assignment the teacher left.) • *Moko yaal ta nakat-aatinak laa'at.* (It is not true that you are talking.)

Sentence Type (Xpaayil Ru Raqal Aatin)	Examples (Xk'utb'al)
Interrogative Sentence (raqal aatin re patz'ok)	• *B'ar xik aawe qawa' Lu'.* (Where are you going Mr. Lu?) • *K'a' ru k'aleb'aal wankat wi'.* (Which village are you in?) • *Ma sa laach'ool qawa' Kux.* (How are you doing Kux ?)

Q'EQCHI NUMBERS

(Ajl Q'eqchi')

Q'eqchi' words for the numbers 1 to 20 are typcially used in common speech in Q'eqchi'-speaking areas, with Spanish words for numbers used after that. However, the Q'eqchi' words for numbers beyond 20 are known and are sometimes used in formal publications and heard in speech (and are taught in bilingual education programs).

CARDINAL NUMBERS (0-100)

(Eb' li T'or'ajl)

(0.) maajun	zero.
(1.) jun	one.
(2.) wiib'	two.
(3.) oxib'	three.
(4.) kaahib'	four.
(5.) oob'	five.
(6.) waqib'	six.
(7.) wuqub'	seven.
(8.) waqxaqib'	eight.
(9.) b'eleeb'	nine.
(10.) lajeeb'	ten.
(11.) junlaju	eleven.
(12.) kab'laju	twelve.
(13.) oxlaju	thirteen.
(14.) kaalaju	fourteen.
(15.) o'laju	fifteen.
(16.) waqlaju	sixteen.
(17.) wuqlaju	seventeen.
(18.) waqxaqlaju	eighteen.
(19.) b'eleelaju	nineteen.
(20.) jun may	twenty.

(21.) jun xka'k'aal	twenty-one.
(22.) wiib' xka'k'aal	twenty-two.
(23.) oxib' xka'k'aal	twenty-three.
(24.) kaahib' xka'k'aal	twenty-four.
(25.) oob' xka'k'aal	twenty-five.
(26.) waqib' xka'k'aal	twenty-six.
(27.) wukub' xka'k'aal	twenty-seven.
(28.) waqxaq'ib' xka'k'aal	twenty-eight.
(29.) b'eleb' xka'k'aal	twenty-nine.
(30.) lajeeb' xka'k'aal	thirty.
(31.) junlaju xka'k'aal	thirty-one.
(32.) kab'laju xka'k'aal	thirty-two.
(33.) oxlaju xka'k'aal	thirty-three.
(34.) kaalaju xka'k'aal	thirty-four.
(35.) o'laju xka'k'aal	thirty-five.
(36.) waqlaju xka'k'aal	thirty-six.
(37.) wuqlaju xka'k'aal	thirty-seven.
(38.) waqxaqlaju xka'k'aal	thirty-eight.
(39.) b'elelaju xka'k'aal	thirty-nine.
(40.) ka'k'aal	forty.
(41.) jun roxk'aal	forty-one.
(42.) wiib' roxk'aal	forty-two.
(43.) oxib' roxk'aal	forty-three.
(44.) kaahib' roxk'aal	forty-four.
(45.) oob' roxk'aal	forty-five.
(46.) waq'ib' roxk'aal	forty-six.
(47.) wukub' roxk'aal	forty-seven.
(48.) waqxaq'ib' roxk'aal	forty-eight.
(49.) b'eleb' roxk'aal	forty-nine.
(50.) lajeeb' roxk'aal	fifty.
(51.) junlaju roxk'aal	fifty-one.
(52.) kab'laju roxk'aal	fifty-two.
(53.) oxlaju roxk'aal	fifty-three.
(54.) kaalaju roxk'aal	fifty-four.
(55.) o'laju roxk'aal	fifty-five.
(56.) waqlaju roxk'aal	fifty-six.

(57.) wuqlaju roxk'aal	fifty-seven.
(58.) waqxaqlaju roxk'aal	fifty-eight.
(59.) b'elelaju roxk'aal	fifty-nine.
(60.) oxk'aal	sixty.
(61.) jun xkaak'aal	sixty-one.
(62.) wiib' xkaak'aal	sixty-two.
(63.) oxib' xkaak'aal	sixty-three.
(64.) kaahib' xkaak'aal	sixty-four.
(65.) oob' xkaak'aal	sixty-five.
(66.) waqib' xkaak'aal	sixty-six.
(67.) wuqub' xkaak'aal	sixty-seven.
(68.) waqxaqib' xkaak'aal	sixty-eight.
(69.) b'eleb' xkaak'aal	sixty-nine.
(70.) lajeeb' xkaak'aal	seventy.
(71.) junlaju xkaak'aal	seventy-one.
(72.) kab'laju xkaak'aal	seventy-two.
(73.) oxlaju xkaak'aal	seventy-three.
(74.) kaalaju xkaak'aal	seventy-four.
(75.) o'laju xkaak'aal	seventy-five.
(76.) waqlaju xkaak'aal	seventy-six.
(77.) wuqlaju xkaak'aal	seventy-seven.
(78.) waqxaqlaju xkaak'aal	seventy-eight.
(79.) b'elelaju xkaak'aal	seventy-nine.
(80.) kaak'aal	eighty.
(81.) jun ro'k'aal	eighty-one.
(82.) wiib' ro'k'aal	eighty-two.
(83.) oxib' ro'k'aal	eighty-three.
(84.) kaahib' ro'k'aal	eighty-four.
(85.) oob' ro'k'aal	eighty-five.
(86.) waqib' ro'k'aal	eighty-six.
(87.) wuqub' ro'k'aal	eighty-seven.
(88.) waqxaqib' ro'k'aal	eighty-eight.
(89.) b'eleb' ro'k'aal	eighty-nine.
(90.) lajeb' ro'k'aal	ninety.
(91.) junlaju ro'k'aal	ninety-one.
(92.) kab'laju ro'k'aal	ninety-two.

(93.) oxlaju ro'k'aal	ninety-three.
(94.) kaalaju ro'k'aal	ninety-four.
(95.) o'laju ro'k'aal	ninety-five.
(96.) waqlaju ro'k'aal	ninety-six.
(97.) wuqlaju ro'k'aal	ninety-seven.
(98.) waqxaqlaju ro'k'aal	ninety-eight.
(99.) b'elelaju ro'k'aal	ninety-nine.
(100.) o'k'aal	one hundred.

DISTRIBUTIVE NUMBERS (1-20)

(Eb' li Jek'b'il Ajl)

1. junqjunq	every one.
2. ka'kab'	every other one.
3. ox'ox'	every third one.
4. kaaka	every fourth one.
5. o'otq	every fifth one.
6. waqitq	every sixth.
7. wuqutq	every seventh.
8. wajxaqitq	every eighth.
9. b'eleetq	every ninth.
10. lajeetq	every tenth.
11. junqtaqlaju	every eleventh.
12. kab'taqlaju	every twelfth.
13. oxtaqlaju	every thirteenth.
14. kataqlaju	every fourteenth.
15. o'taqlaju	every fifteenth.
16. waqtaqlaju	every sixteenth.
17. wuqtaqlaju	every seventeenth.
18. wajxaqtaqlaju	every eighteenth.
19. b'eletaqlaju	every nineteenth.
20. junmaytq	every twentieth.

ORDINAL NUMBERS (1-100)

(Eb' li Tusb'a'ajl)

(1st.) xb'een	first.
(2nd.) xkab'	second.
(3rd.) rox	third.
(4th.) xka	fourth.
(5th.) ro'	fifth.
(6th.) xwaq	sixth.
(7th.) xwuq	seventh.
(8th.) xwajxaq	eighth.
(9th.) xb'elee	ninth.
(10th.) xlajee	tenth.
(11th.) xjunlajuil	eleventh.
(12th.) xkab'lajuil	twelfth.
(13th.) roxlajuil	thirteenth.
(14th.) xkaalajuil	fourteenth.
(15th.) ro'lajuil	fifteenth.
(16th.) xwaqlajuil	sixteenth.
(17th.) xwuqlajuil	seventeenth.
(18th.) xwajxaqlajuil	eighteenth.
(19th.) xb'ele'lajuil	nineteenth.
(20th.) xjunmayil	twentieth.
(21st.) xjun xka'k'aalil	twenty-first.
(22nd.) xkab' xka'k'aalil	twenty-second.
(30th.) xlajee xka'k'aalil	thirtieth.
(40th.) xka'k'aalil	fortieth.
(50th.) xlajee roxk'aalil	fiftieth.
(60th.) roxk'aalil	sixtieth.
(70th.) xlajee xkaak'aalil	seventieth.
(80th.) xkaak'aalil	eightieth.
(90th.) xlajee ro'k'aalil	ninetieth.
(100th.) ro'k'aalil	hundredth.

OTHER NUMBERS

(Jalan Chik Ajl)

jun oq'ob'	four hundred.
kiib' oq'ob' xkab' xchuy	one million.
lajeeb' oq'ob'	four thousand.
lajeeb' syent	one thousand.
lajeek'aal	two hundred.
lajeek'aal rox oq'oob'	one thousand.
lajeek'aal xwaqxaq roq'ob'	three thousand.
maasumal'ajl	odd numbers.
o'k'aal xkab' roq'ob'	five hundred.
o'lajuk'aal	three hundred.
oob' chuy xwaq k'alab'	one million.
oob' oq'ob'	two thousand.
sumal'ajl	odd numbers.

II

Q'EQCHI' MAYAN
DICTIONARY

Molob'aal Aatin

Q'eqchi' ~ Inkles

A - a

a' *n.* leg.

a' *part.* [emphasis particle]. *Note:* Occasionally used with a noun in place of a definite article to provide emphasis or indicate one among many. **A' che' wan aran.** « That tree over there. »

a' ajb'an *conj.* that's why.

a' chik ut *conj.* however.

a' ut *conj.* but.

a' yaal aawe *phr.* it's up to you.

a'an *pron.* her, him. *Var:* ha'an.

a'an *pron.* he, she, that, it. *Var:* ha'an.

a'an a'an *pron.* that one.

a'an a'in *pron.* this one.

a'anaq *pron.* it will be that (him, her, it).

a'aneb' *pron.* they.

a'aq *pron.* it will be this.

a'in *pron.* this, this one. *Var:* ha'in.

a'ineb' *pron.* these.

a'wa'ran *pron.* that one. *Var:* a' wan aran.

a'wanle' *pron.* that one (over there). *Var:* a'wa'le'; a'wa'li'; a'wi'le'.

ab' *n.* swing.

ab' *n.* hammock.

ab'aj *n.* testicles, scrotum.

ab'ajil *n.* testicles, scrotum.

ab'an *conj.* but.

ab'anan *conj.* however, nevertheless.

ab'aqhu *n.* carbon paper.

ab'aal *n.* cherry, plum.

ab'en *n.* parcel, package.

ab'enak *v.* to ask for a favor.

ab'enank *v.* to commission, entrust.

ab'ib'aal *n.* hearing, sense of hearing.

ab'ib'aal *n.* earphones, headphones.

73

ab'ib'aal aatin *n.* radio (receiver).

ab'ib'aalson *n.* radio (receiver).

ab'ib'leb'aal aam *n.* stethoscope.

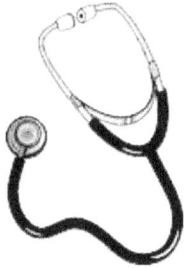

ab'ib'leb'aal yajel *n.* stethoscope.

ab'ib'leb'aal'ch'ool *n.* stethoscope.

ab'inel *n.* audience.

ab'ink *v.* to obey.

ab'ink *n.* hearing.

ab'ink *v.* to listen, hear.

ab'iresink *v.* to cause to hear, narrate (and divulge something).

ab'l *adj.* somebody else's, other people's. *Var:* ab'.

ab'lil aatinob'aal *n.* foreign language.

ab'lil poyanam *n.* foreigner.

ab'lilk'ayink *v.* to export.

ab'liltenamit *adj.* international.

achi *lang.* Achi (Baja Verapaz).

ach'ab'ank *v.* to liberate, free, let go.

ach'ab'alhu *n.* license.

ach'ab'ilal *n.* liberalism.

ach'abaak *n.* acquittal.

ach'ab'ank *v.* to cease.

ah *interj.* [utterance of understanding].

ahin jukxul *n.* reptile.

ahom *n.* aim, goal, objective. *Var:* ajom.

aj *part.* [gentilic particle], from. *Note:* Combines with place names to form demonyms. Used before place names when speaking about an individual's place of origin. **Aj Kob'an inna' inyuwa'.** « My parents are from Coban. » **Ma laa'at Aj Carcha.** « Are you from Carcha? »

aj *part.* [agentive particle]. *Note:* Used before nouns that imply an action to indicate the doer of the action or the profession or occupation of the doer. **Ma laa'at aj isihom ruuch e.** « Are you a dentist? »

aj *n.* mat, reed.

aj *part.* [adjectival particle]. *Note:* Used before some nouns to create an adjective which highlights a particular quality in the subject of a sentence. **Moko josq' ta li winq aran. A'an aj kuyanel.** « That man is not angry. He is calm. »

aj *part.* [masculine particle]. *Note:* Used before masculine names when speaking about an individual (not to them). **Aj Mek xk'ulun mixk.** « Mike arrived a little while ago. » *Var:* **laj.**

aj ab'ine'leb' *n.* crowd.

aj ab'l tenamit *n agt.* tourist.

aj ajlanel *n agt.* accountant.

aj am *n.* spider.

aj atawanel *adj.* greedy.

aj ateey *n agt.* atheist. *From:* Spanish 'ateo'.

aj awinel *n agt.* farmer.

aj aanilanel *n agt.* athlete, runner.

aj aatinanel *n agt.* announcer.

aj aatinanel rik'in yaj *n agt.* psychotherapist.

aj b'alaq' *n agt.* briber, extortionist.

aj b'anonel *n agt.* doctor, physician.

aj b'arat *phr.* where are you from?

aj b'atz'iil *n agt.* artist.

aj b'atz'unel *adj.* playful.

aj b'atz'unel *n agt.* athlete, sportsman.

aj b'atz'unel b'olotz oq *n agt.* soccer player, footballer.

aj b'atz'uneleb' *n.* team.

aj b'aanun re *adj.* guilty.

aj b'aanunel *n agt.* agent.

aj b'aanunel *n agt.* protagonist, subject.

aj b'e *n agt.* passer-by, migrant, traveler, pilgrim.

aj b'e *adj.* adventurous.

aj b'e *n agt.* tourist.

aj b'e chahim *n.* satellite.

aj b'e choxa *n agt.* astronaut.

aj b'ehenel *n agt.* navigator.

aj b'eresinel jukub' *n agt.* sailor, rower.

aj b'eresinelch'iich' *n agt.* pilot, driver, chauffeur.

aj b'esonel *n agt.* hairdresser.

aj b'eenel *n agt.* pedestrian.

aj b'eenel *n agt.* passenger.

aj b'eenel chi ru b'aqb'il k'aam sa iq' *n agt.* tightrope walker.

aj b'eenel sa' po *n agt.* astronaut.

aj b'eetaql *n agt.* messenger.

aj b'ichanel *n agt.* singer.

aj b'irom tumin *n agt.* accountant.

aj b'ironel *n.* calculator.

aj b'isonel na'leb' *n.* rate, ratio.

aj b'ojonel *n agt.* tailor.

aj b'ojonel ixq *n agt.* seamstress.

aj b'olotz *n agt.* ballplayer, soccer player, footballer.

aj b'olotz chakach *n agt.* basketball player.

aj b'onol xaab' *n agt.* shoeshiner.

aj b'ononel *n agt.* painter.

aj b'ononel kab'l *n agt.* housepainter.

aj b'oob' *n.* panther.

aj b'oox uch *n.* opossum.

aj b'uub'anel *n agt.* organizer.

aj chamalnawom *n agt.* scientist.

aj chapol'esil *n agt.*
camerman.

aj chaponel *n agt.* police,
policeman, police officer.

aj cheek *adj.* mature.

aj chi'resilnel *n agt.* adviser,
counselor.

aj cho'onel *n agt.* surgeon.

aj chupulxam *n agt.* fireman.

aj ch'e'ol b'aqlaq ch'iich' *n agt.*
cyclist.

aj ch'e'ol b'oq'ch'iich' iq' *n agt.*
astronaut.

aj ch'e'ol ch'iich' *n agt.* pilot,
driver, chauffeur.

aj ch'e'ol so'sol ch'iich' *n agt.*
aviator, airplane pilot.

aj ch'oolanel *adj.* responsible.

aj ch'uch' *n agt.* clown.

aj ch'upul xaml *n agt.* fire
brigade.

aj e re *n agt.* author.

aj elq' *n agt.* burglar, thief.

aj elq' *n agt.* kidnapper.

aj elq' karteer *n agt.*
pickpocket.

aj eechal k'uuleb'aal tumin *n
agt.* banker.

aj eek' *n agt.* magician.

aj ha'resinel *n.* solvent.

aj hiltesinel *n agt.* usher.

aj ilol chahim *n agt.*
astronomer.

aj ilol kamenaq *n agt.* coroner,
medical examiner.

aj ilol k'ila tasal hu *n agt.*
librarian.

aj ilol k'ula'al *n agt.* babysitter.

aj ilol mayer kab'k *n agt.*
archaeologist.

aj ilol okeb'aal *n agt.* janitor.

aj ilol tijob'aal *n agt.* sacristan.

aj ilol uutz'u'uj *n agt.* gardener.

aj ilol wakax *n agt.* cowboy,
cattleman, herder, herdsman.

aj ilol xna'aj ketomq *n agt.*
farmer.

aj ilol'uuch-e *n agt.* dentist.
Var: aj ilol ruuch e.

aj ilolketomq *n.* pastor
(animals), shepherd.

aj ilolk'anjel *n agt.* supervisor.

aj iloltenamit *n agt.* police,
policeman, police officer.

aj ilolyaj *n agt.* nurse.

aj ilom aj k'anjel *n agt.* supervisor.

aj ilom kamenaq *n agt.* undertaker.

aj ilom xul *n agt.* veterinarian.

aj ilom yaj *n agt.* paramedic.

aj ilonel *n agt.* spectator.

aj isihom jalam'uuch *n agt.* photographer.

aj isihom ruuch e *n agt.* dentist.

aj ixi'jeb' *n.* felines.

aj iiqanel *n agt.* pallbearer.

aj iiqom *n.* ferry.

aj iitz'in *n agt.* violinist.

aj jalom uuchinel *n agt.* sketch artist.

aj jalonel *n agt.* forger.

aj jek'ol preens *n agt.* newspaper boy.

aj jolominel *n agt.* authority.

aj jolominel b'atz'unk *n agt.* coach.

aj jolominel b'eeleb' *n agt.* captain.

aj jolominel k'aleb'aal *n.* mayor, town leader.

aj juch'unel *n agt.* voter.

aj juliis *adj.* Jewish.

aj jultikahonel *n agt.* prompter, commentator.

aj ka'aatin *n agt.* bilingual, polyglot.

aj kalajel *n agt.* alcoholic.

aj kamsinel *n agt.* assassin, murderer.

aj kanab'om esilhu *n agt.* letter carrier, mailman.

aj kaqal *adj.* envious.

aj kar *n agt.* fisherman.

aj kawaayach'iich' *n.* motorist.

aj kaxlanwahinel *n agt.* baker.

aj kayanel *adj.* curious.

aj kelonel *n agt.* hauler, carrier.

aj kolom *n agt.* hero.

aj kookox *n agt.* soldier.

aj kuyunel *adj.* calm.

aj kuutunel *n agt.* witness.

aj k'a'uxl *n agt.* thinker.

aj k'aleb'aal *n agt.* farmer, fieldworker.

aj k'alom *n agt.* farmer.

aj k'amol iiq *n agt.* porter, bellboy.

aj k'amolb'e *n agt.* guide, director.

aj k'anjel *adj.* hard-working.

aj k'anjel *n agt.* worker, laborer.

aj k'anjel re k'a' re ru *n agt.* craftsman.

aj k'anjel sa' chaq'rab' *n agt.* civil servant.

aj k'anjel sa' kab'l *n agt.* housewife.

aj k'anjel sa' kab'l *n.* maid.

aj k'anjel sa' so'sol ch'iich' *n agt.* flight attendant.

aj k'atol mayej *n agt.* Maya priest.

aj k'ay *n agt.* sales clerk, salesman, merchant.

aj k'ay ch'iich' *n agt.* ironmonger.

aj k'ay kar *n agt.* fishmonger.

aj k'ay ki'ilsaqb'ach *n agt.* ice cream vendor.

aj k'ay ki'tuux *n agt.* cotton candy vendor.

aj k'ay kok'toq' *n agt.* gum seller.

aj k'ay tib' *n agt.* butcher.

aj k'ay xe' ru che' *n agt.* vegetable seller.

aj k'ay xxe' pim *n agt.* grocer.

aj k'ay yib' aj b'an *n agt.* drug dealer.

aj k'ayinel *n agt.* merchant, salesman.

aj k'ayinel b'an *n agt.* pharmacist, chemist.

aj k'aak'alehom ketomq *n agt.* herdsman, herder.

aj k'aak'alenel *n agt.* police, policeman, police officer.

aj k'aak'alom *n agt.* security guard.

aj k'aak'anel *n agt.* keeper.

aj k'aak'anel *n agt.* ticket taker.

aj k'ehol esil *n agt.* journalist, reporter.

aj k'ehol kuult *n agt.* pastor (religious).

aj k'ehol miix *n agt.* priest.

aj k'ehol na'leb' *n agt.* counselor.

aj k'ehol purik *n.* airline.

aj k'ehonel tzakahemq *n agt.* waiter.

aj k'ihanel ajl *n.* coefficient.

aj k'ila'aatin *n agt.* polyglot.

aj k'oyoneleb' *n.* rodents.

aj k'ulul re *n agt.* receiver, recipient.

aj k'ulul ula' *n agt.* receptionist, secretary.

aj k'utunel *n agt.* teacher.

aj k'utunel b'e *n agt.* guide, director.

aj k'utunel re xnimal tzoleb'aal *n agt.* college professor.

aj k'uub'anel kab'l *n agt.* architect.

aj k'uub'anel poych'iich' *n agt.* mechanic.

aj k'uub'anel tzakahemq *n agt.* chef, cook.

aj k'uub'anelchaq'rab' *n.* representative, legislator.

aj letzolsimb'ha' *n agt.* plumber.

aj limoox *n agt.* beggar. *From:* limosna 'the offering or donation' (Spanish) (1).

aj loq'onel *n agt.* merchant.

aj maq'onel *n agt.* mugger, swindler.

aj maxxul *n.* primate.

aj mayab' *n.* Maya.

aj mayej *n.* Maya spiritualist.

aj maak *n agt.* sinner.

aj maak chi ru chaq'rab' *n agt.* delinquent.

aj maatan *n agt.* heir.

aj mesol ru xaab' *n agt.* shoeshiner.

aj mesunel *n agt.* street sweeper.

aj mitz-u *n.* Chinese.

aj molol'esil *n agt.* journalist, reporter.

aj mormon *adj.* Mormon.

aj mu's *n.* Ladino, foreigner. *Note:* Word adopted from other Mayan languages.

aj muqa'l *n agt.* swimmer.

aj muxunel *n agt.* rapist.

aj na'onel chaq'rab' *n agt.* attorney, lawyer.

aj naw'ajl *n agt.* mathematician.

aj nawal *n agt.* magician.

aj nawb'an *n agt.* pharmacologist.

aj nawcha'al'ixq *n agt.* gynecologist.

aj nawchahim *n agt.* astronomer.

aj nawch'oolej *n agt.* cardiologist.

aj nawhiik *n agt.* seismologist.

aj nawkomonil *n.* sociologist.

aj nawkomonyajel *n agt.* epidemiologist.

aj nawk'anjel *n agt.* professional.

aj nawk'anjel yajel *n agt.* medical professional.

aj nawk'uhil *n agt.* vulcanologist.

aj nawpoyanam *n agt.* anthropologist.

aj nawtijok *n agt.* pedagogue.

aj nawtuqch'ool *n agt.* psychologist.

aj nawtus'aatin *n agt.* lexicographer.

aj nawxul *n agt.* zoologist.

aj nawyu'amilal *n agt.* biologist.

aj naark *n agt.* drug trafficker. *Var:* **aj narko.** *From:* Spanish 'narcotraficante'.

aj num aatin *adj.* talkative.

aj numelb'e *n agt.* pedestrian.

aj numsihom k'aj' esil *n agt.* telegrapher.

aj numxinel *n agt.* swimmer.

aj okenel chi awab'ejink *n agt.* candidate.

aj ow *n.* fox.

aj pak'ol *n agt.* potter.

aj pak'onel *n agt.* potter, sculptor.

aj paab'anel *adj.* faithful, believing.

aj paab'anel *n agt.* adherent, believer.

aj paar *n.* skunk. *Var:* **paar xul.**

aj pech'ol che' *n agt.* woodcarver, carpenter.

aj pech'onel *n.* interviewer.

aj pech'onel *n agt.* sculptor.

aj peech' *n agt.* carpenter.

aj pitz' *n.* grasshopper.

aj pix *adj.* stingy, petty.

aj pleet *n agt.* fighter. *From:* Spanish 'pleito'.

aj poch'onel *n agt.* miller.

aj puch'unel *n agt.* laundress.

aj pukaatin *n.* broadcaster.

aj puub' *n agt.* soldier.

aj puub' *n agt.* security guard, armed guard.

aj q'an'isul *n.* American.

aj q'e *n agt.* fortune teller, spiritual guide.

aj q'em *adj.* lazy.

aj q'unb'esihonel xul   *n agt.* animal trainer.

aj q'unob'tesinel   *n agt.* conventioneer.

aj raholtenamit   *adj.* patriotic.

aj ramonel b'olotz   *n agt.* goalie, goalkeeper.

aj raqol chaq'rab'   *n agt.* judge.

aj raqol'aatin   *n agt.* judge, adjudicator.

aj santil paab'anel   *n agt.* saint.

aj se'   *adj.* amusing.

aj se' k'al   *n agt.* peasant.

aj setoneleb'   *n.* rodents.

aj seeb'alk'anjel   *n agt.* engineer.

aj seeb'alk'utb'esink   *n agt.* acrobat.

aj si'b'ich   *n.* serenade.

aj sik'onel xyib'al ru   *adj.* pessimistic.

aj takchi'   *n agt.* blackmailer.

aj taql'esil   *n agt.* sender.

aj taqlanel   *adj.* bossy.

aj taqlanel   *n agt.* dictator.

aj taqlanel re   *n agt.* sender.

aj tenamit   *n.* citizen.

aj tenol ch'iich'   *n agt.* blacksmith.

aj tenol ch'iich'   *n agt.* jeweller.

aj tenq'   *n agt.* barman, manservant.

aj tenq' re b'anok   *n agt.* nurse.

aj tenq' sa' li raxiik'   *n agt.* fireman.

aj tenq'anel   *n agt.* assistant.

aj tenq'anel risihom uuch e   *n agt.* dental assistant.

aj tik'ti'   *n agt.* liar.

aj tiikilal   *n agt.* saint.

aj tiikob'resinel'uuch-e   *n agt.* orthodontist.

aj tochonel   *n agt.* assailant.

aj tuqtuukilnel   *n agt.* pacifist.

aj tuqub'anel   *n agt.* referee.

aj tuqub'anel sa'   *n.* antacid, decongestant.

aj t'uyanel   *n agt.* trapeze artist.

aj tzilol'ix   *n agt.* researcher, investigator.

aj tzilonel   *n agt.* researcher, investigator.

aj tzolonel   *n.* teacher.

aj tz'ak   *n agt.* mason, bricklayer.

aj tz'alam   *n agt.* captive, prisoner.

aj tz'ilom k'a'uxl *n agt.* philosopher.

aj tz'ilonel *n agt.* detective.

aj tz'ilpoyanam *n agt.* census taker.

aj tz'iib' *n agt.* writer.

aj tz'iib' *n agt.* secretary, scribe.

aj tz'iib'ahom *n agt.* author.

aj tz'iib'anel esil *n agt.* reporter.

aj tz'uum xik' *n.* bat.

aj uch *n.* opossum.

aj uutz'u'ujinel *n agt.* decorator.

aj uutz'u'ujinel aatin *n agt.* poet.

aj wajb' *n agt.* band.

aj wajb' *n agt.* musician.

aj wajb'a'apuul *n.* trumpeter.

aj waklesihom ch'uut *n agt.* social worker.

aj xajonel *n agt.* ballerina, dancer.

aj xaqab'anel *n agt.* presenter.

aj xiw *adj.* shy, cowardly.

aj xiitinelch'iich' *n agt.* mechanic.

aj xoj *n.* wolf.

aj xokol mul *n agt.* garbage collector.

aj xokol tumin *n agt.* bank teller, teller.

aj xokol'al ixq *n agt.* midwife.

aj xokonel *n agt.* obstetrician.

aj yakonel *n agt.* shopkeeper, merchant.

aj yalol u chi awab'ejink *n agt.* politician.

aj yalonel *n agt.* warrior.

aj yehomb'aanuhem *n agt.* historian.

aj yehonel *n agt.* narrator.

aj yehonel'uxk *n agt.* commentator.

aj yib'anel eetalil aq' *n agt.* clothing designer, fashion designer.

aj yiib'ank xaqab'ank *n.* construction worker.

aj yiib'om ch'iich' *n agt.* mechanic.

aj yiib'om ha' *n agt.* plumber.

aj yiib'om q'ol *n agt.* jeweller.

aj yiib'om reloj *n agt.* watchmaker.

aj yiib'om saqen *n agt.* electrician.

aj yiib'om ulul ch'iich' *n agt.* computer programmer.

aj yiib'om xaab' *n agt.* shoemaker, cobbler. *Var:* aj yiib'ahom xaab'.

aj yo *n agt.* hunter.

aj yop *adj.* cowardly.

aj yoob'anel aatin *adj.* boastful.

aj yumb'eet *n agt.* fornicator.

aj'aj ru *adj.* alert.

ajaw *n.* king, lord.

ajawilxoy *n.* crown.

ajb'il *n.* request.

ajk *v.* to wake up. *From:* *aj 'wake up' (Yucatecan) (2).

ajl *n.* number, numeral.

ajlank *v.* to count.

ajleb'aal *n.* calculator. *Var:* ajlab'al.

ajleb'aal kutan *n.* calendar. *Var:* ajlab'al kutan.

ajleb'ilha' *n.* water meter.

ajlil *n.* numeration.

ajlilkomontoj *n.* tax identification number.

ajlilk'uultumin *n.* bank account.

ajok *n.* desire, attraction.

ajsi'baalb'ich *n.* serenade.

ajsib'aal hoonal *n.* alarm clock.

ajsib'aal u *n.* park.

ajsib'aal'u *n.* recreation, fun, recess.

ajsinel *n.* alarm clock.

ajsink u *v phr.* to entertain, enjoy.

ajsink u li tib'elej *v phr.* to exercise, play sports.

ajsink-u *n.* entertainment, diversion.

ajsiil *n.* protein.

Ak *sur. From:* ak' ('new') (B1).

ak anaqwan *adv phr.* right away.

ak xnume' chik *adv phr.* after.

aka' *adv.* immediately.

akateko *lang.* Akatek (Huehuetenango).

Akb'al *sur.*

ake' *adv.* shortly, soon. *Var:* a'ke.

ake' hoon *adv phr.* in a moment.

akoost *n.* August. *From:* Spanish 'agosto'.

Akte' *sur. From:* akte' (a thorny palm tree) (B1).

ak'il *adj.* new.

ak'o'k *v.* to renew.

ak'ob'resink *v.* to renew.

ak'ob'resink *adj.* renewable.

ak' *adj.* new.

ak'ach *n.* turkey.

ak'ach *n.* kettle.

ak'aatin *n.* neologism.

ak'chahim *n.* nova.

ak'il raaxiik' *n.* modern warfare.

ak'oresiil *adj.* recyclable.

al *adj.* unripe.

al *n.* son, child.

al *adj.* young.

al ixim *n.* sweet corn.

al po *n.* new moon.

alab' *n.* pair.

alab'metz'ew *n.* mitochondria.

alab'tesib'aal *n.* maternity ward.

alab'tesink *v.* to reproduce.

alal *n.* son. *From:* *alal 'child' (Ch'olan) (2).

alalch'iich' *n.* plumb.

alaleb' *n.* children.

alank *v.* to give birth.

alb'aak *n.* basil. *From:* Spanish 'albahaca'.

alib' *n.* daughter-in-law (of a man or woman).

alkohol *n.* alcohol (isopropyl). *From:* Spanish 'alcohol'.

alk'uula'al *n.* fetus.

almul *n.* basket. *From:* almud 'basket ?' (Spanish) (1).

alob'aal *n.* womb, uterus.

alpek'iich' *n.* key.

alfoombr *n.* rug, carpet. *From:* alfombra 'the rug' (Spanish) (1).

amamnak *v.* to feel itchy.

amapool *n.* poppy. *From:* Spanish 'amapola'.

amaq'il tenamit *n.* relatives.

amaq' *n.* clan.

amaq' tenamit *n.* crowd.

85

amaq'il *n.* society.

amaq'il loq'alil *n.* social studies.

amaq'il loq'alil *n.* social values.

amaq'kab'lk'a'uxl *n.* socio constructivism.

amb'ulaans *n.* ambulance. *From:* Spanish 'ambulancia'.

amiiw *n.* friend. *From:* Spanish 'amigo'.

amoch *n.* frog, toad. *From:* *amuch 'frog' (Yucatecan, Ch'olan, possible) (4).

an'o *adj.* leaning, sloping, inclining, at an angle.

anab' *n.* sister (older, of a male).

anab'ej *n sd.* older sibling. **wanab'** « my older sibling ».

anaqwan *adv.* now.

anaqwan *n.* today.

anaqwan q'e kutan *n.* nowadays.

anaqwan tz'aqal *adv phr.* immediately.

anaqwankil'uxk *n.* present tense.

anchal *adj.* all.

anchal ch'oolej *n.* excitement, enthusiasm.

anchal xch'ool *n.* passion.

anchal xmetzew *n.* elation.

ani *interr.* who?

ani aj e *interr.* whose? (singular).

ani aj ik'in *interr.* with whom?

aniheb' aj e *interr.* whose? (plural).

anis *n.* aniseed. *From:* Spanish 'anís'.

anum *n.* demon.

anum ch'iich' *n.* fax machine, fax.

anumal *n.* ghost.

anx *n.* garlic.

anyooj *n.* spectacles, glasses. *From:* anteojos 'glasses' (Spanish) (1).

apoostl *n.* apostle. *From:* Spanish 'apóstol'.

apusinel na'ajej *n.* fan.

apusink *v.* to inflate, blow up.

apuul *n.* fan.

apuunk *v.* to blow.

aq *n.* hay, grass. *From:* *ak, aq 'grass, hay' (Ch'olan) (2).

aq *part.* [indefinite or future particle]. *Note:* Used as a suffix on words to indicate a hypothetical, indefinite, desired or future state. **Usaq choq' qe xsik'b'al li yaal.** « It would be good for us to seek the truth. » **Ma wan junaq aapatz'om?** « Do you have any questions? »

aq ru ch'aat *n.* bedding.

aq'ab'ank *v.* to brake.

aq' *n.* uniform.

aq' *n.* vine.

aq' ch'ot ruq' *n.* vest.

aq' re atink *n.* swimsuit, bathing suit.

aq' re b'atz'unk *n.* sportswear.

aq' re puch'e'k *n.* laundry.

aq' re sa' aq'ej *n.* slip.

aq' re wark *n.* pyjamas.

aq'ej *n.* clothing.

aq'ink *v.* to dig.

aran *adv.* there.

aran tz'aqal *adv phr.* right there.

araaw *n.* Arabic numeral. *From:* Spanish 'arábigo'.

arb'eej *n.* pea, peas. *From:* Spanish 'arvejas'.

arin *adv.* here.

arin tz'aqal *adv phr.* right here.

arko *n.* arch. *From:* arco 'the arch' (Spanish) (1).

arkute' *n.* oak.

aros *n.* rice. *From:* arroz 'rice' (Spanish) (1).

aroow *n.* at symbol (@). *From:* Spanish 'arroba'.

arsob'iisp *n.* archbishop. *From:* Spanish 'arzobispo'.

artal *n.* altar. *From:* altar 'the altar' (Spanish) (1).

as *n.* brother (older).

as e *n.* cousin.

as itz'in *n.* neighbor.

asapran *n.* saffron. *From:* Spanish 'azafrán'.

asaron *n.* hoe. *From:* azadón 'the hoe' (Spanish) (1).

asb'ej *n sd.* brother (generic). **was** « my brother ».

asb'ej *n sd.* older sibling. **was** « my older sibling ».

aselk *n.* chard. *From:* Spanish 'acelga'.

asetuun *n.* olive. *From:* aceituna 'the olive' (Spanish) (1).

aseet *n.* oil. *Var:* **aseyt.** *From:* aceite 'the oil' (Spanish) (1).

Asij *sur. From:* 'asij' (a type of cicada.) (B1).

astz'iib' *n.* upper case, capital letter.

asuseen *n.* lily. *From:* Spanish 'azucena'.

asuukr *n.* sugar. *From:* azúcar 'sugar' (Spanish) (1).

asuukr utz'ajl *n.* sugarcane.

at *part.* [address particle, singular]. **At in qaawa', chinaatenq'a.** « Oh god, please help me. » *Note:* Used as a modifier to address an individual or being. It is used as a prefix and can modify a variety of singular nouns.

atawal *adj.* ambitious.

atawank *v.* to want.

atawank *n.* longing, temptation.

atib'aal *n.* pool, swimming pool.

atib'aal *n.* bathroom, shower.

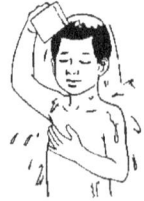

atink *v.* to bathe. *Var:* achink.

atiyach' *n.* bathing suit, swimsuit.

at'isb'ak *v.* to sneeze.

atz'am *n.* salt.

atz'am aapy *n.* celery salt. *From:* Spanish 'apio'.

atz'aminb'ilkaxlanwa *n.* French bread.

atz'um *n.* flower.

atz'umak *v.* to flower.

atz'umxox *n.* chickenpox.

awab'ej *n.* government.

awab'ej *n.* chieftain, president.

awab'ejilal *n.* government.

awab'ejink *v.* to rule, govern.

awas *n.* bad luck, taboo.

awasinel *n.* sorcerer, witch.

awinq *n.* plant.

awib'aal *n.* field.

awleb' *n.* stake.

awleb' *n.* digging stick, yamstick.

awleb'aal *n.* field.

awo *adj.* planted, sown.

awok *v.* to plant, sow.

awril *n.* April. *From:* Spanish 'abril'.

Ax *sur.* *From:* A tree, valuable for its hard red wood. (B1).

ay *interj.* [utterance of pain].

ay xkux na' *phr.* damn it.

ayi' *adv.* here.

ayin *n.* alligator. *Var:* ahin.

ayin kar *n.* shark.

ayin kaaq *n.* dinosaur.

aylok *v.* to cry out (in pain).

ayuunink rix *v phr.* to fast.
From: ayunar 'to fast' (Spanish) (1).

AA - aa

aaa *interj.* [utterance of pain or pity].

aajel *adj.* important, useful.

aakan *n.* agony.

aakanak *v.* to have difficulty breathing at night.

aakanak *v.* to have nightmares.

aak'ab' *n.* darkness. *Var:* ak'ab'.
From: *ahk'ab' 'night' (Yucatecan, Ch'olan, possible) (1).

aak'ab' *adj.* unknown, dark.

aal *adj.* heavy.

aalal *n.* weight.

aalank *v.* to weigh.

aalenk *v.* to induce, tempt.

aalom *n.* thing to be weighed.

aamej *n.* soul, spirit.

aanilak *v.* to run. *Var:* alinak.

aanilxaab' *n.* tennis shoes.

aapy *n.* celery. *From:* Spanish 'apio'.

aaq *n.* pig, hog, swine.

aaq kab' *n.* wild bee.

aaqam *sur. From:* agouti (dasyprocta) (Span 'cotuza') (B1).

aaqam *n.* agouti (dasyprocta).

aaqha' *n.* hippopotamus.

aatik'uul *n.* microphone.

aatin *n.* announcement.

aatin *n.* word.

aatinab'aal *n.* media, means of communication, communications.

aatinak *v.* to speak, talk, chat.

aatinak chi rix *v phr.* to opine, give one's opinion.

aatinak rik'in yaj *n.* psychotherapy.

aatinak-ib' *n.* monologue.

aatinamank *v.* to speak, talk.

aatinank *v.* to consult.

aatinank *v.* to have sexual relations.

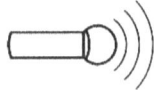

aatinob'aal *n.* microphone.

aatinob'aal *n.* language, tongue.

aatinob'aal ch'iich' *n.* telephone, phone.

aatinob'aal maay *n.* Mayan languages.

aatinob'aalil *adj.* idiomatic.

aatinom *n.* speech. *Var:* aatin.

B' - b'

B'a *sur.* *From:* Spanish 'taltuza' (a type of mole). (B1).

b'a *n.* gopher.

b'ab'ay *n.* baby.

b'ab'ay *pron.* a few, a little. *Var:* b'ayb'ay.

b'achal hab' *n.* rain with hail.

b'ach'al *n.* sprain. *Var:* b'ach'b'il.

b'ach'b'o *adj.* crooked.

b'akuun *n.* injection, shot, vaccination. *From:* vacuna 'the vaccination' (Spanish) (1).

b'ak'ok *v.* to tie.

b'alak' *adj.* dirty.

b'alam *n.* jaguar.

b'alamq'e *n.* sun god.

b'alaq xul *n.* zebra.

b'alaq' *n.* fraud, deceit.

b'alaq'ik *n.* bribery.

b'alaq'ik *v.* to lie (tell falsehoods).

b'alaq'ink *v.* to betray.

b'alent'ojiil *n.* screw.

b'alk *n.* sibling-in-law.

b'alk ixq *n.* sister-in-law.

b'alk winq *n.* brother-in-law.

b'alok *v.* to slide, slip.

b'alq'hu *n.* flipchart.

b'alq'usink *v.* to wring.

b'alq'usink *v.* to turn, turn around.

b'alq'usink *v.* to drop.

b'alxuk *n.* triangle.

b'an *n.* medicine, remedy.

b'an ha' *n.* sterilized water.

b'an re ixkej *n.* skin cream.

b'an re naq' u *n.* eye drops.

b'an re ojb' *n.* cough drops.

b'an re wark *n.* sleeping pills.

b'an uk'b'il *n.* syrup.

b'an xk'atom saq'e *n.* sunburn lotion.

b'anb'alil esil *n.* newspaper.

b'ane'k *n.* treatment.

b'anha' *n.* chlorine, bleach.

b'anleb'aal *n.* clinic, health center.

b'anok *v.* to cure, heal.

b'anol u *n.* ointment.

b'anpim *n.* herbicide.

b'antyox *phr.* thank you, thanks.

b'antyoxink *v.* to thank.

b'antz'ipxul *n.* insecticide.

b'anxxulelyajel *n.* antibacterial.

B'aq *sur. From:* b'aq ('bone'). (B1).

b'aq *n.* bone.

b'aq xtib'el *adj.* thin.

b'aqb'il k'aham ch'iich' *n.* chain.

b'aqch'iich' *n.* rebar.

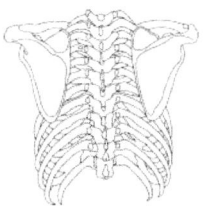

b'aqel *n.* skeleton.

b'aqel xb'een tel *n.* shoulder blade.

b'aqil b'an *n.* suppository.

b'aqil xuleb' *n.* vertebrate.

b'aqlaq ch'iich' *n.* bicycle.

b'aqlaq xul *n.* opossum.

b'aqsotz' *n.* rafter.

b'aqx *adj.* wet.

b'aqxul *n.* armadillo.

b'aq' *adj.* oval.

b'aq'al *n.* oval.

b'aq'b'o *adj.* oval.

b'aq'el'a' *n.* femur.

b'ar *interr.* where?

b'ar nakatchal *phr.* where do you come from?

b'ar rajlil laab'oqleb' *phr.* what's your phone number?

b'ar wan aatenamit *phr.* where are you from?

b'ar wan aawochoch *phr.* where do you live?

b'ar wan li tz'eqleb'aal *phr.* where is the toilet?

b'ar wan re *interr.* which?

b'ar wank *interr.* which? (singular). *Var:* **b'ar wan.**

b'ar wankat *phr.* where are you?

b'ar wankeb' *interr.* which? (plural).

b'aral *n.* cylinder.

b'arb'arink *v.* to roll.

b'arch'iich' *n.* screw.

b'arich' *adj.* thin.

b'arxab'on *n.* bar soap.

b'arxuk *adj.* rhomboid, diamond-shaped.

b'asb'il tasalhu *n.* pamphlet.

b'asok *v.* to fold.

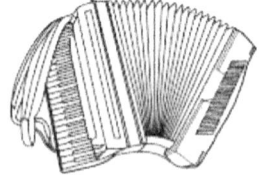

b'aswajb' *n.* accordion, concertina.

b'atb'a ib' *n.* coat.

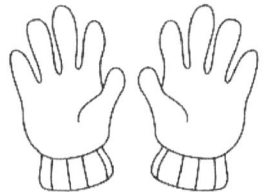

b'atb'a uq' *n.* glove.

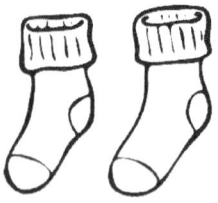

b'atb'al oq *n.* sock, stocking.

b'atb'een'aq *n.* knee guard, knee pad.

b'ateriiy *n.* battery. *From:* batería 'the battery' (Spanish) (1).

b'ateey *n.* feed tray.

b'atok *v.* to pack, wrap.

b'atxaqam *n.* mummy.

b'atz-aq' *n.* jersey, team jersey.

b'atz' *n.* monkey.

B'atz' *sur. From:* b'atz ('monkey'). (B1).

b'atz'il b'aanuhom *n.* artistic expression.

b'atz'iil *n.* art.

b'atz'ub'aal *n.* playing field.

b'atz'unenb'il *adj.* conjugated.

b'atz'unenk *v.* conjugate.

b'atz'unk b'aatal *n.* camisole.

b'atz'unk puub'ak *v phr.* to target shoot.

b'atz'unleb'aal *n.* stadium.

b'atz'uul *n.* toy, game.

b'axton *n.* walking stick. *From:* bastón 'stick used for walking or ceremonial purposes' (Spanish) (1).

b'ayaq *pron.* some.

b'ayeen *n.* whale. *From:* ballena 'the whale' (Spanish) (1).

b'ayjik *n.* delay.

b'ayk *adj.* extensive.

b'ayk *v.* to last.

b'ayok *v.* to delay, hold up, put off.

b'ayok ib' *v.* to waste time.

b'ayom *n.* debt.

b'aak *n.* cow. *From:* vaca 'the cow' (Spanish) (1).

b'aan *n.* cause.

b'aanu sa' xyaalal *phr.* take your time.

b'aanu usilal *phr.* please.

b'aanu usilal aatinan chi timil *phr.* please speak slowly.

b'aanu usilal tz'iib'a *phr.* please write it down.

b'aanu ye jun sutaq chik *phr.* please say that again.

b'aanunel *n.* subject.

b'aanunk *v.* to make, do.

b'aanunk *v.* to practice.

b'aanunk ib' *v phr.* to fake.

b'aark *n.* boat, ship. *From:* barco 'the boat' (Spanish) (1).

b'aas *n.* drinking glass. *From:* Spanish 'vaso'.

b'aatal *n.* clothing.

b'aayk *v.* to take (an amount of time).

b'e *n.* road.

b'e jolom *n.* hair part.

b'ech' *adj.* crooked. *From:* *b'ech' 'roll up' (Yucatecan, Ch'olan, possible) (2).

b'ehil *n.* method.

b'ehul *n.* formula.

b'ekleb' k'ix *n.* needle (sewing).

b'ekok *v.* to dig.

b'ekol ch'och' *n.* tractor.
Var: b'ekleb' ch'och'.

b'elahom iiq *n.* luggage tram.

b'elaal tzakahemq *n.* tray.

b'eleb'aal *n.* transport.

b'eleb'aal tem *n.* wheelchair.

b'eleb'aal tem *n.* wheel chair.

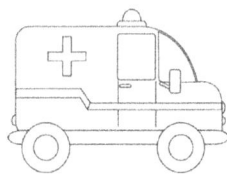

b'eleb'aal yaj *n.* ambulance.
Var: b'eeleb'yaj.

b'eleb'aalch'iich' *n.* bus.

b'eleb'poyanam *n.* bus.

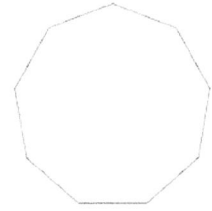

b'eleexuk *n.* nonagon.

b'entaan *n.* window. *From:*
ventana 'the window' (Spanish) (1).

b'eq *n.* tie, necktie.

b'esleb'aal *n.* barbershop.

b'estiiy *n.* dress. *From:* Spanish
'vestido'.

B'ex *nick.* Sebastián.

B'eeb' *sur.*

b'eeche' *n.* boardwalk.

b'eek *v.* to travel, walk.
Var: b'ehek.

b'eek chi ru ha' *v phr.* to sail.

b'eek chi tustu *v phr.* to
parade.

b'eek xb'aan choxach'och' *n.*
space travel.

b'eel *n.* veil. *Var:* b'elo. *From:*
velo 'the veil' (Spanish) (1).

b'eel *n.* sail. *Var:* b'ela. *From:*
vela 'the sail' (Spanish,
Portuguese, ?) (1).

b'eelom *n.* husband.

b'een'aqej *n.* knee pad, knee
patch.

b'eenelchahim *n.* satellite.

b'eenink *v.* to travel around,
travel.

b'eenink *v.* to invite.

b'eeresink *v.* to drive.

b'eeresink jukub' *v phr.* to row.

b'eeresink yib' aj k'ay *n.* drug
trafficking.

b'eetak'aak'alenel *n.* patrol.

b'eetak'aak'alenk *v.* to patrol.

b'eexam *n.* torch.

b'i' *conj.* well.

b'ich *n.* song. *Var:* b'ichk.

b'ich k'uula'al *n.* lullaby.

b'ichank *v.* to sing.

b'ichleb' *n.* songbook, hymnal.

b'ich'ok *v.* to peel, skin.

b'ihom *adj.* rich, wealthy.

b'ihomal *n.* wealth, riches.

b'ihomink *v.* to be rich.

b'ik'b'ik' *adj.* greasy.

B'in *sur.*

b'inaayr *n.* vinegar. *Var:* ninayr.
  From: Spanish 'vinagre'.

b'iqb'ilb'an *n.* ointment.

b'iqok *v.* to rub, handle.

b'iq'e'k *v.* to choke.

b'ir *n.* bandage.

b'irb'o *adj.* bandaged, wrapped.

b'irich *n.* penis.

b'irk *n.* clitoris.

b'irk *n.* vulva.

b'irleb'aal *n.* calculator.
  Var: b'irlob'aal.

b'isb'ametz'ew *n.* electric meter.

b'isb'il eetalil *n.* geometric figure, geometric shape.

b'isikleet *n.* bicycle. *From:* bicicleta 'bicycle' (Spanish) (1).

b'isketiiq *n.* degrees.

b'isleb' *n.* measuring tape.

b'isleb' *n.* scale.

b'isleb' iq' *n.* air gauge.

b'isleb' sek' *n.* measuring cup.

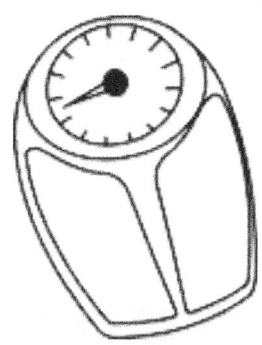

b'isleb'aal *n.* scale.

b'isleb'hab' *n.* rainfall meter.

b'isleb'hab' *n.* barometer.

b'isleb'hoonal *n.* chronometer.

b'isleb'tiq *n.* thermometer.

b'isok *v.* to weigh, measure.

b'isxuk *n.* protractor.

B'it *nick.* Victor. *Var:* B'itol.

b'itamin Se *n.* vitamin C.

b'itonk *v.* to carry (on head).
  From: *b'it 'to carry on head or shoulder' (Ch'olan) (2).

b'itonk'ot *n.* beetle.

b'itool *n.* head pad.

b'it'b'it'leb'aal *n.* beauty salon.

b'itzilch'iich' *n.* knife.

b'itzkiri' *n.* worm.

b'iin *n.* wine. *From:* vino 'the wine' (Spanish) (1).

b'iis'aal *n.* pound.

b'iismetz'ew *n.* amp meter.

b'o *n.* genitals (female).

b'ob' *n.* palm tree. *From:* b'ob' 'a certain plant with large leaves' (Yucatecan, Ch'olan, ?) (4).

b'oj *n.* fermented drink.

b'oj ha' tzakahemq *n.* vinegar.

b'ojleb' *n.* sewing machine.

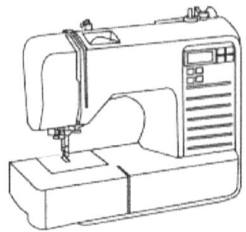

b'ojleb' ch'iich' *n.* sewing machine.

b'ojleb'aal *n.* sewing workshop.

b'ojok *v.* to sew.

b'ojok tiq'il *n.* suture.

b'ojom *n.* seam.

B'ol *sur.*

b'ola *n.* rolling pin. *Var:* b'ol.

b'olb'o *adj.* cylindrical.

b'olb'o *n.* cylinder.

b'olb'okiil ch'iich' *n.* metal tube, metal pipe.

b'ololch'iich' *n.* whistle (object).

b'olotz *n.* ball.

b'olotz chakach *n.* basketball.

96

b'olotz meex *n.* foosball table.

b'olotz oq *n.* soccer, soccer ball.

b'olotz sum uq'ib'k *n.* volleyball.

b'olotz-uq' *n.* basketball.

b'olsutaal'eek' *n.* axon.

b'omb'il eetalil *n.* painting.

b'omb'iiy *n.* light bulb. *From:* bombilla 'bulb' (Spanish) (1).

b'on *n.* paint.

b'on *n.* color.

b'onb'il ochoch *n.* painted house.

b'onb'il q'esnalna'leb' *n.* work of art.

b'onb'il u *n.* painted face.

b'onb'ilha' *n.* Kool-Aid. *Var:* b'omb'ilha'.

b'onkik' *n.* hemoglobin.

b'onleb' *n.* crayon, marker.

b'onleb' *n.* brush, paintbrush.

b'onok *v.* to dye, paint, stain.

b'onol *n.* color.

b'onxaab' *n.* shoe polish.

b'oqleb' *n.* telephone, phone.

b'oqleb' *n.* cell phone, cell (phone), cellular (phone).

b'oqleb'aal *n.* telephone, phone.

b'oqleb'aal *n.* doorbell.

b'oqleb'aal ch'iich' *n.* telephone, phone.

b'oqok *v.* to summon, call, invite.

b'oqok chi yaab' *v phr.* to whistle.

b'oq'ch'iich' iq' *n.* space capsule.

b'oq'leb'ch'iich' *n.* crowbar.

b'orb'il *adj.* erased.

b'oreeg *n.* lamb. *From:* borrego 'the lamb' (Spanish) (1).

b'orleb' *n.* eraser.

b'orok *v.* to erase, unwind, untie, unroll.

b'orok na'leb' *v phr.* to lose your train of thought.

b'ot *n.* ring.

b'otb'an *n.* capsule, caplet.

b'otb'il aq' *n.* skirt.

b'otb'il b'an *n.* capsule, caplet.

b'otb'il hu *n.* paper roll.

b'otb'okilsek' *n.* glass.

b'otonx *n.* button. *From:* botones 'the buttons' (Spanish) (1).

b'otwa *n.* taco.

b'ot'leb' *n.* bandage.

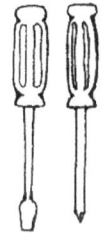

b'otz'leb' *n.* screwdriver.

b'ook *n.* steam. *From:* *b'ook 'the smell' (Yucatecan, Ch'olan, possible) (2).

b'ookatq *n.* gases.

b'ookha' *n.* methane.

b'ookhumha' *n.* kerosene.

b'ookil *adj.* gaseous.

b'ookilxaml *n.* propane.

b'ook-iq' *n.* oxygen.

b'ookol *n.* oxygen.

b'oolha' *n.* wave.

b'ools *n.* bag, purse. *From:* Spanish 'bolsa'.

b'oom *n.* bomb. *From:* bomba 'the bomb' (Spanish) (1).

b'oot *n.* boot. *From:* bote 'the boot' (Spanish) (1).

b'oot *n.* election. *From:* vota 'the vote' (Spanish) (1).

b'oot *n.* bucket, pail. *From:* Spanish 'bote'.

b'ootaxaab' *n.* boots.

b'ootib'k *n.* ballot.

b'oox *n.* pocket. *From:* *box 'round container' (Yucatecan, Ch'olan, possible) (2).

b'ooyx *n.* ox, yoke (of oxen). *From:* buey 'the ox' (Spanish) (1).

b'rookl *n.* broccoli. *From:* Spanish 'brócoli'.

b'ub' *n.* semen, ejaculate.

b'uch *n.* corn (prepared for grinding).

b'ujl *n.* fly (insect).

b'ujuk *v.* to beat, hit, strike.

b'ukleb'aal *n.* mixer.

b'ulux *adj.* dirty. *Var:* b'alux.

b'uqux *n.* bump.

b'uq' *n.* bun.

b'uq' *adj.* convex.

b'uq' ja'aj *n.* Adam's apple, goiter. *Var:* b'uq' ja'j.

b'uq' kux *n.* mumps.

b'uq'b'u *adj.* convex.

b'uq'ultzimitz *n.* camel.

b'urux *adj.* rough.

b'urux b'urux *adj.* thick.

b'ut *n.* flood.

b'utb'il paayil tib' aaq *n.* longaniza.

b'utb'il uuch e *n.* filling (dental).

b'utb'iltib' *n.* sausage, cold cuts.

b'utb'iltib' chorizo.

b'utb'iltib'aaq *n.* chorizo.

b'utuk *v.* to fill.

b'ut' *adj.* full. *From:* b'ut' 'full' (Yucatecan, Ch'olan, possible) (3).

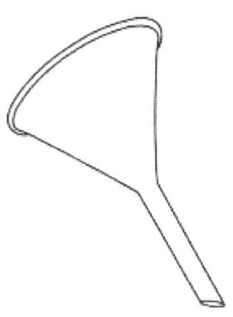

b'ut'leb' *n.* funnel.

b'ut'uk *v.* to stuff.

b'utzchahim *n.* comet.

b'ux *n.* syphilis.

b'uxo'k *v.* to be syphilitic.

b'uyuxink *v.* to pile up.

b'uuleb' *n.* raffle, lottery.

b'uuleb'aal *n.* lottery.

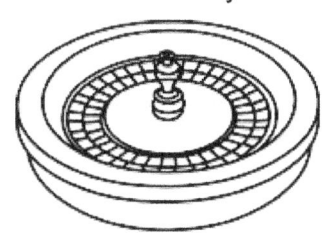

b'uulik *n.* raffle, lottery, gambling.

b'uulink *v.* to raffle.

b'uulink maatan *v phr.* to raffle a prize.

b'uulink tumin *v phr.* to raffle money.

b'uuluk *n.* lottery.

b'uur *n.* donkey, ass. *From:* burro 'donkey or ass' (Spanish) (1).

b'uuy *adj.* full.

b'uuy *n.* genitals (female).

b'yers *n.* Friday. *Var:* b'iyernes. *From:* viernes 'Friday' (Spanish) (1).

C - c

Cahabon *top.* [chi k'ajb'om] "place of abstinence or fasting". *Etym:* chi = by, among, in; k'ajb' = abstinence; om = permanently.

Camcal *top.* [k'aamk'al] "cornfield among vines". *Etym:* k'aam = string, thread; k'al = cornfield.

Caquipec Satex *top.* [kaqipek sa'teex] "red rocks of Sa'teex". *Etym:* kaq = red; pek = stone, rock; teex = teja (span).

Caralha *top.* [karaal ha'] "fishing hole". *Etym:* kar = fish; aal = place of action; ha' = water.

Carcha *top.* [karcha] "fish cooked in ashes". *Etym:* kar = fish; cha = ashes.

Coxopur Chichen *top.* [k'oxopur chi ch'en] "shrimp-like snail by the rocks". *Etym:* k'ox = shrimp; pur = snail; ch'en = stone (also 9th month of Mayan calendar).

Coban *top.* [kob'an] *Note:* No agreement exists on meaning.

Cruz Raxmax *top.* [kurus raxmax] "cross made of Raxmax wood". *Etym:* kurus = cross (Span); Raxmax = type of tree.

Ch - ch

cha *n.* ash.

cha'al *n.* organ, body part.

cha'alil *n.* organs.

cha'alil *n.* genitals.

cha'jleb'aal *n.* laundry room.

chab'il xch'ool *adj.* kind.

Chacalte Chichen *top.* [chakalte' chi ch'en] "chakalte' tree by Chich'en area". *Etym:* Chakalte' = type of tree.

chachib' *n.* skin rash.

Chahal *top.* [chi ha'al] "place of much water". *Etym:* chi = by, among, in; ha' = water; al = the quality or nature of the noun modified (ha').

chahim *n.* star.

chahim'eetalil *n.* asterisk.

chahimch'iich' *n.* satellite.

chahimch'iich' aj na'onel ru li ruchich'och' *n.* weather satellite.

chahimch'iich' re puktesink esil *n.* communications satellite.

chahimpek *n.* meteor.

chaj *n.* pine.

chajal *n.* worm.

chajb'a'e *n.* loudspeaker.

chajb'a'esil *n.* alarm.

chajb'a'esink *v.* to alarm.

chajok e *v phr.* to roar.

chajok e *v phr.* to shout.

Chajsel *top.* [chaqi seel] "place of dry gourds". *Etym:* chaqi = dry; seel = squash.

chakach *n.* basket.

chakalte' *n.* cedar.

chakeet *n.* jacket. *From:* Spanish 'chaqueta'.

chakmut *n.* pheasant.

chakow *n.* boar.

chakti' *n.* mojarra.

chak'aanil *n.* allergy.

chak'chotk *v.* to run.

chak'oq *n.* tripod.

chalchitan *lang.* Chalchitek (Huehuetenango).

chalen *prep.* from.

chalen *adv.* always.

chalen *adv.* since.

chalen anaqwan *adv.* starting today, from now on.

chalen chaq *adv.* since then.

chalen q'e kutan *n.* eternity.

chalik *n.* arrival.

chalk *v.* to come. *Var:* chaalk.

cham *adj.* deep.

Chama Conop *top.* [cham ha' k'onop] "K'onop trees by Cham Ha' area". *Etym:* K'onop = type of tree.

chamal *n.* depth.

chamal jul *n.* precipice.

chamal pim *n.* weeds.

Chamam *sur. From:* cha ('ashes'). (B3).

Chamelco *top.* [chameelk] "out of the depths". *Etym:* cham = deep; elk = to leave.

champa *n.* doorpost. *From:* jamba 'the doorpost' (Spanish) (1).

champa *n.* net.

champa *n.* woven shoulder bag.

champan *n.* champagne. *From:* French 'champagne'.

chan *part.* [citation particle, singular]. *Note:* Used when referring to what someone has said. **Tachalq li hab' wuulaj, chankin.** « It will rain tomorrow, I say. »

chan ru *interr.* how?

chan ru la weetalil sa' internet *phr.* what's your email?

chan ru li kutan *phr.* how's the weather?

chan ru nakaayaab'asi [ ] *phr.* how do you pronounce [ ]?

chan ru nayehman [ ] *phr.* how do you say [   ]?

chan ru wankat *phr.* how are you?

chan xaawil *phr.* hello, hi.

chanchan *adj.* like, similar.

chanchan aj wi' a'an *adj.* similar.

chanchanil eetalilatq *n.* similar figures.

chankatq ru *n.* form.

chankatq ru *n.* type. *Var:* chankatqru.

chankeb' *part.* [citation particle, plural]. *Note:* Used when referring to what someone has said. **"Ayuqex ut k'ehomaq chaq reetal chanru li na'ajej", chankeb'.** « And they said to them, "Go, search the land." »

chankilal *n.* gender, sex (gender), genre.

chap aawe *phr.* help yourself.

chapb'il *n.* hostage.

chapchookil ruuchil k'ab'a'ej *n.* dependent pronoun.

chapleb' *n.* nail.

chapleb' *n.* vise.

chapleb' aatin *n.* tape recorder.

chapleb' kar *n.* fishhook.

chapleb' saqen *n.* plug, socket, outlet (electrical).

chapleb'aal aatin *n.* tape recorder, tape player.

chapleb'aatin *n.* tape recorder, tape player.

chapleb'hu *n.* paper clip.

chapleb'ismal *n.* hair pin.

chapleb'jalam'u *n.* video camera, security camera.

chapleb'metz'ew *n.* plug, outlet.

chapleb't'ikr *n.* button.

chapok *v.* to arrest.

chapok *v.* to take, grasp, hold.

chapok aatin *v phr.* to record.

chapok b'e *v phr.* to leave, hit the road.

chapok kar *v phr.* to fish.

chapokhu *v.* to staple.

chapokmu *v.* to record a video.

chapteeleb' *n.* keychain.

chaq *part.* [time particle]. *Note:* Used when referring to things that happened in the past. **Numenaq chaq junmay chihab' naq ink'a ninchal kob'an.** « Twenty years have passed since I came to Coban. »

chaq *part.* [distance or motion particle]. *Note:* Used when referring to motion from there to here. **Kim chaq arin.** « Come over here. »

chaq re ru *adj.* ordinary, rough, crude.

chaqi *adj.* dry.

chaqi ch'och' *n.* desert.

chaqi ix *n.* dry skin.

chaqi'el *n.* thirst. *Var:* chaq'ieel; chaqi e.

chaqi'oqil *n.* rickets.

chaqihob' t'ikr *n.* towel.

chaqiq re *adj.* thirsty.

chaqiq we *phr.* I'm thirsty.

chaqi'eel *v.* to be thirsty.

chaqob'resink *v.* to dry. *Var:* chaqhiob'resink.

chaq' *adj.* ripe.

chaq' chi us *adj.* well done.

chaq'al ru *adj.* beautiful, pretty.

chaq'aliltz'iib' *n.* calligraphy.

chaq'b'enk *v.* to answer.

chaq'na' *n.* sister (older, of a female). *Var:* chaq'b'ej.

chaq'na' *n.* older sister.

chaq'na'b'ej *n sd.* older sibling. **inchaq'na'** « my older sibling ».

chaq'ok *v.* to answer, respond, reply.

chaq'om *n.* answer, echo.

chaq'rab' *n.* commandment, moral principle. *Var:* chaq'rab'il.

chaq'rab' *n.* law, justice.

chaq'rab'ink *n.* farewell.

chaq'rab'ink *v.* to say goodbye, bid farewell.

chatwarq chi us *phr.* sleep well (singular).

chawinik *n.* bee.

cha'al *n.* relative.

chaaab'il *phr.* great!

chaab' *n.* watering can.

chaab'aanu went *phr.* be careful.

chaab'il *adj.* good.

chaab'il *adv.* well.

chaab'il ch'iich' *n.* precious metal.

chaab'il xaab'anu *phr.* well done!

chaab'il xch'ool *adj.* noble.

chaab'il xtz'aq *n.* a good value.

chaab'ilob'resink *n.* paradigm.

chaab'iltz'iib' *n.* calligraphy.

chaacha *adj.* gray.

chaakuy inmaak *phr.* I'm sorry, forgive me.

chaalel *n.* future.

chaanumsi chi us li kutan *phr.* have a nice day.

chaanumsi chi us li xamaan *phr.* have a nice week.

chaayehaq we *phr.* let me know.

che' *n.* tree, wood.

Che' *sur. From:* che' ('tree'). (B1).

che'eb' *n.* trees.

che'k'aam *n.* vegetation.

che'wajb' *n.* wood drum.

chek' *adj.* stiff.

chek'chek' *adj.* very stiff.

chet-aq' *n.* skirt.

chexwarq *phr.* sleep well, good night (plural).

cheekel winq *n.* elder (male).

chi *prep.* to.

chi ch'inqil *adv phr.* little by little.

chi ixkej *n.* bottom.

chi jachal *adv.* fractionally, by fraction.

chi junaqlil *adv.* individually.

chi junil *adj.* all, everything. *Var:* chi xjunil.

chi kama'an *adv phr.* like that, thus.

chi kama'in *adv phr.* like this, thus.

chi lajetqil *adv phr.* by tens.

chi moko *conj.* neither.

chi nim *adv phr.* to the right.

chi ok'aalil *adj.* by the hundred.

chi qilaq qib' *phr.* see you later.

chi q'eq *n.* evening, night.

chi re ha' *n.* shore.

chi re xam *n.* kitchen, cookhouse.

chi rix *prep.* outside, behind, around.

chi rix *adj.* exterior.

chi rix *adv.* backwards.

chi rix chik *adv phr.* after.

chi ru *prep.* in front of, facing.

chi ru *adv.* onwards.

chi ru chi xjunil *prep.* above all.

chi ru li eq'la *adv phr.* in the morning.

chi ru li ewu *adv phr.* in the afternoon.

chi ru li hab' xnume' *adv phr.* last year.

chi ru li q'oqyin a'in *adv phr.* this evening.

chi ru li saqewk *adv phr.* in the early morning.

chi ru li xamaan chalk re *adv phr.* next week.

chi ru li xamaan xnume' *adv phr.* last week.

chi ru q'oqyin *adv phr.* at night, in the evening.

chi rub'elaj *prep.* before. *Var:* chi ru.

chi rub'el *adj.* down.

chi rub'el *prep.* under.

chi sa xch'oolil *adv phr.* with pleasure.

chi sa' *prep.* inside, between.

chi seeb' *adv phr.* soon.

chi timil *adv.* slowly.

Chi Toc *top.* [chi tok'] "among the flint rocks". *Etym:* chi = in, among; tok' = flint.

chi tz'e *adv phr.* to the left.

chi xjunil *adv.* rather, quite.

chi xk'atq *prep.* toward, next to.

chi'ajlil *adv.* mathematically.

chib'aat *n.* goat, lamb. *From:* Spanish 'chiva'.

Chicocom *top.* [chi kookom] "by the vines". *Etym:* kookom = type of vine.

Chicoj Raxquix *top.* [chi k'oj raxk'ix] "area of mask by Raxk'ix". *Etym:* k'oj = mask; Raxk'ix = type of thorn.

Chicuta La Union *top.* [chi kut ha'] "place where the water falls". *Etym:* kut = throw; ha' = water.

Chicuxab *top.* [chi k'uxhab'] "area of K'uxhab' grass". *Etym:* k'uxhab' = type of grass.

Chichaic *top.* [chi chahiq] "by the anthill". *Etym:* chahiq = type of winged ant.

Chichut *top.* [chi ch'ut] "by the ferns". *Etym:* ch'ut = type of fern.

chihab' *n.* year.

chik *adv.* more.

chik *adv.* again, already.

chik che' *n.* bush, shrub.

chikiriin *n.* cicada.

chikleb' *n.* fork.

Chilatz *top.* [chi laatz'] "narrow place". *Etym:* laatz' = narrow.

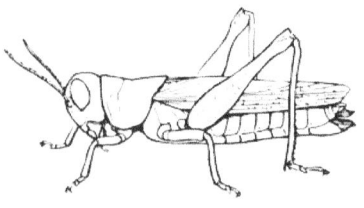

chili' *n.* grasshopper, cricket.

chimam *n.* priest.

Chinacocom *top.* [ch'ina kookom] "by the little vines". *Etym:* ch'ina = little; kookom = type of vine.

chinamiit *n.* gallery.

chinaakuy *phr.* excuse me, pardon me.

chinaakuy xatink'e chi oyb'enink *phr.* sorry to keep you waiting.

chinaakuy xinb'ayon chaq *phr.* sorry I'm late.

chinaawoyb'en b'ayaq *phr.* hang on a second, wait a minute.

chineetenq'aaaq *phr.* help!

Chinimlajoom *top.* [chi nimla joom] "place of the large gourd". *Etym:* nim = little; la == augmentative; joom = gourd.

Chio *top.* [chi o] "by the avocado plantation". *Etym:* o = avocado.

Chionon *top.* [chi honon] "by the bumblebees". *Etym:* honon = bumblebee.

Chipoc *top.* [chi poq] "sandy place". *Etym:* poq = type of sand.

chiqb'il *adj.* cooked.

chiqb'il tib' *n.* stew.

chiqleb' *n.* pans.

chiqleb' *n.* stove.

chiqok *v.* to cook.

chiqok tz'uum *v phr.* to tan.

chiq'chiq'ink *v.* to shake.

chiq'ch'ool *n.* amphetamine.

chiq'ok *v.* to shake.

Chiraxcaj *top.* [chi rax k'aj] "by the vine snakes". *Etym:* raxk'aj = flying serpent or vine snake.

Chiraxquen *top.* [chi raxq'een] "by the grasshoppers". *Etym:* raxq'een = grasshopper.

Chiretzaaj *top.* [chire tza'aj] "beside the Tza'aj trees". *Etym:* chi re = beside; tza'aj = type of tree.

Chirixpec Sacranix *top.* [chi rix pek sa' karaniix] "behind the cliff near Sa' Karaniix". *Etym:* chi rix = behind; pek = stone; karaniix = type of wild passion fruit (Span 'granadilla').

chirleb' *n.* watering can.

chirok *v.* to spread out.

chiron *n.* pork rind.

Chirre Mox Sejacoc *top.* [chi re mox se' ha' kok] "by the Moxl plantation near Se' Ha' Kok". *Etym:* chi re = beside; moxl = type of leaves used for wrapping; ha' = water; kok = turtle.

Chirremesche *top.* [chi re mesche'] "by the broom plantation". *Etym:* chi re = beside; mesche' = small broom made from twigs.

Chisec *top.* [chisek] "among navajuela plants". *Etym:* chi = among, in, or by; sek = herbaceous plant.

Chitay *sur.*

chix *interj.* [utterance of disgust].

Chibulvut *top.* [chi b'ulb'ut] "area of bubbling water". *Etym:* b'ulb'ut = bubbling or burbling.

chiin *adj.* orange.

chiin *n.* orange tree.

chiin *n.* orange.

cho'b'ol *n.* surgical scar.

cho'hix *n.* leopard.

cho'k'oj *n.* bat.

cho'leb' ch'och' *n.* plowed land, tilled land.

cho'ok *n.* operation.

cho'ok jul *n.* ditch, furrow.

cho'q re *prep.* for, to, in order to. *Var:* **cho'oq' re; chi'oq re.**

chocho' *n.* parrot.

chochtz'iib' *n.* floppy disk, diskette.

Chok *sur.*

Choko' *sur.*

chok'laak *v.* to crouch.

chok'ob'ank *v.* to crouch.

cholob'anel *n.* adjective.

cholok' *n.* breastbone.

Cholom *sur.*

choq *n.* cloud. *Var:* **choql.** *From:* *tyoq 'cloud' (Greater Tzeltalan)* (3).

choq ru *adj.* foggy.

choqlenk *v.* to burn.

choqlil tzoqchahim *n.* nebulous galaxy.

choqtin *n.* cassette. *Var:* **xochtin.**

choriis *n.* pork sausage. *From:* Spanish 'chorizo'.

choxa *n.* sky. *Var:* **choxaal.**

choxa *n.* heaven. *Var:* **choxaal.**

choxach'och' *n.* nature. *Var:* **ru choxach'och'.**

choxach'och' *n.* universe, cosmos.

choxahil wank *n.* paradise.

choxahilb'eeleb' *n.* space shuttle.

choy *n.* vulva.

choyok *v.* to end, finish.

Choval *top.* [ch'ob'al] "by the little holes". *Etym:* ch'ob' = small hole (Yucatec?); al = locative suffix.

chu *adj.* stinking, smelly.

chu' *n.* urine.

chu' ke *n.* dew.

chu'uk *v.* to urinate, pee, piss.

chuj *lang.* Chuj (Huehuetenango).

chumay *n.* cubit.

chun *n.* lime (stone).

Chun *sur. From:* chun ('lime'). (B1).

chunilb'an *n.* antibiotic, penicillin.

chunlan *phr.* have a seat.

chunlaak *v.* to sit. *From:* chum 'to sit' (Yucatecan, Ch'olan, possible) (4).

chunleb'aal *n.* chair.

chunleb'aal *n.* dental chair.

chunleb'aal *n.* desk, bench.

chunt'ikr *n.* cast.

chuntz'iib'l *n.* chalk. *Var:* chuntz'iib'.

chupchu *adj.* dull.

chupil *n.* worm.

chupleb' saqen *n.* light switch, power switch.

chupleb'xaml *n.* fire extinguisher.

chuplech *n.* breaker switch.

chupuk *v.* to extinguish, blow out.

chuq'ub' *n.* hiccough, hiccup.

chuq'ub'ak *v.* to hiccough, hiccup. *From:* chuq'ub' 'hiccoughs' (Q'anjob'alan) (4).

chut *n.* mole.

chu'ke *n.* dew.

chuub' *n.* saliva, spit.

chuub'ak *v.* to spit. *Var:* chuub'ank.

Ch' - ch'

ch'a'aj *adj.* difficult, hard.

ch'a'aj ru *adj.* annoyed.

ch'a'aj treek'a *adj.* uncomfortable.

ch'a'ajkil *n.* difficulty, problem.

ch'a'ajkilal *n.* annoyance.

ch'a'ch'o *adj.* wide open.

ch'a'jkilal *n.* court case.

ch'aj *adj.* clean.

ch'aj ch'aj *adj.* very clean.

ch'ajleb' *n.* sink.

ch'ajleb' sek' *n.* dishwasher.

ch'ajleb'aal sek *n.* dishwasher.

ch'ajleb'aal uq'b' *n.* sink. *Var:* ch'ajleb'aal uq'm.

ch'ajmich'aj *adj.* clean.

ch'ajok *v.* to wash.

ch'ajom *adj.* young.

ch'ajom *n.* boy, young man. *From:* *ch'ajom 'young man' (Yucatecan, Ch'olan, possible) (2).

ch'ajomal *n.* youth.

ch'am *adj.* sour, rancid.

ch'amb'ul *n.* fermented mush drink.

ch'amch'am *adj.* very fermented.

ch'amok' *v.* to ferment.

ch'anab'ank *v.* to cease.

ch'anaak *adj.* calm. *From:* *ch'an 'to become calm' (Ch'olan) (2).

ch'anaak *n.* silence.

ch'anch'o *n.* silence.

ch'antun *n.* fish net. *From:* *ch'antun 'fishnet' (Yucatecan, Ch'olan, possible) (4).

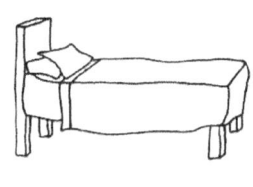

ch'aat *n.* bed.

ch'aat re junesal *n.* single bed.

ch'e'ok *v.* to fight.

ch'e'ok *v.* to touch, feel.

ch'eb'il jalam'uuchil *n.* digital camera.

ch'ejej *n.* tile.

ch'ejej *n.* crow.

ch'em samxul *n.* elephant.

ch'emna'yu'am *n.* prokaryotic cell.

Ch'en *sur. From:* ch'een ('mosquito'). (B1).

ch'epok *v.* to thresh.

ch'epok *v.* to pinch.

ch'ere'wajb' *n.* saxophone.

ch'een *n.* mosquito. *Var:* ch'en.

ch'i' *n.* bad omen.

ch'i'ch'i' *n.* agitation.

ch'i'ch'i'ink *v.* to bother.

ch'i'p *n.* last son.

ch'ich'i re *adj.* grumpy, impatient.

ch'ich'i' we *phr.* I'm in a bad mood.

ch'ich'i'il *n.* stress.

ch'ik ileb' *n.* contact lenses.

ch'ikb'ilb'an *n.* suppository.

ch'ik-ib' *n.* interference.

ch'ikok *v.* to measure.

ch'ilb'oqleb' *n.* cell phone, cell (phone), cellular (phone).

ch'ilb'oqleb' *n.* cell phone, cell (jail).

ch'ilonk *v.* to carry (in hand).

ch'ima *n.* guisquil (type of squash).

ch'imb' *n.* trap.

ch'imb'ul *n.* trap.

ch'imb'unk *v.* to trap.

ch'impo' *adj.* violent.

ch'in *adv.* little.

ch'ina *adj.* small. *Var:* ch'in; ch'inaj.

ch'ina al *n.* boy.

ch'ina b'an *n.* tablet, pill.
ch'ina b'e *n.* path, walkway.
ch'ina b'eleb'aal ch'iich' *n.* car.

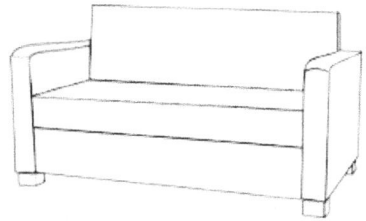

ch'ina chunleb' *n.* bench.
ch'ina ch'aat *n.* cot, stretcher.
ch'ina ch'iich' *n.* knife.
ch'ina elajinel *n.* turn signal.
ch'ina eetalil *n.* nametag.
ch'ina ha' *n.* spring, well (water).
ch'ina huhiljelool *n.* paper bag.
ch'ina ixqa'al *n.* girl.
Var: **ch'inaxqa'al.**
ch'ina iiqob'aal ch'iich' *n.* pickup truck.
ch'ina jukub' *n.* small boat.
ch'ina kawaay *n.* pony.
ch'ina kaxlan *n.* chick.

ch'ina kaaxukuutil lem *n.* streetlight.
ch'ina k'arch'iich' *n.* handsaw.
ch'ina k'arch'iich' *n.* hacksaw.
ch'ina k'iche' *n.* grove.
ch'ina k'uleb'aal *n.* service window.
ch'ina maal *n.* cleaver.
ch'ina meex *n.* night table.
ch'ina meex warib'aal *n.* night table, night stand.
ch'ina nima' *n.* creek.
ch'ina ochoch *n.* island.
ch'ina perk'anti' *n.* cobra.
ch'ina poy ch'iich' *n.* SUV (sport utility vehicle).

ch'ina ral simaj *n.* pinwheel.
ch'ina ruq' *n.* twig.

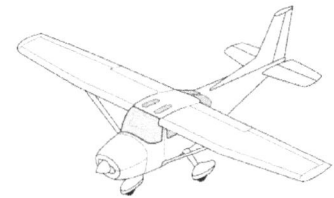

ch'ina so'sol ch'iich' *n.* light airplane.

111

ch'ina sursukil ch'iich' *n.* ring.

ch'ina tashu'esil *n.* magazine.

ch'ina teelom *n.* boy.

ch'ina tun *n.* wood drum.

ch'ina us *adj.* beautiful, pretty.

ch'ina wakax *n.* calf (of a cow).

ch'ina xch'ool *adj.* dejected.

ch'ina xukup *n.* crucifix.

ch'ina yax ch'iich' *n.* clip.

ch'inajelool *n.* briefcase.

ch'inank ch'ool *v phr.* to regret, be sorry.

ch'inank ch'ool *v phr.* to repent.

ch'inapuum *n.* gallon.

ch'inaak ch'ool *n.* frustration.

ch'inaaljuch' *n.* dash, hyphen.

ch'inkumb' *n.* pail.

ch'inqal *adv.* little by little.

ch'inq'ejuch *n.* hyphen, dash.

ch'int'ojiil *n.* tack, thumbtack.

ch'iq *adj.* ambitious.

ch'iqch'o xch'ool *adj.* unsatisfied.

ch'iq' rik'in k'a re ru *adj.* impatient.

ch'iich' *n.* iron.

ch'iich' *n.* metal. *Note:* Ch'iich' is said of anything metal, often with an additional descriptor for clarification of size, dimension or function.

ch'iich' *n.* armour.

ch'iich' *n.* car.

ch'iich' re setok *n.* cleaver.

ch'iich' sek' *n.* tin cup, tin plate.

ch'iich'tumin *n.* coin.

ch'iil *n.* piece.

ch'iilank *v.* to scold.

Ch'o *sur. From:* ch'o ('mouse'). (B1).

ch'o *n.* rat.

ch'och' *n.* land, soil. *From:* ch'och' 'earth, land' (Q'anjob'alan) (4).

ch'och' *n.* liver.

ch'och' *n.* floor.

ch'och' sek' *n.* plate.

ch'och' sutsu chi ha' *n.* island.

ch'och' uk'al *n.* clay pot, earthenware.

ch'och'el *n.* native country.

ch'och'el sululel *n.* culture.

ch'och'il b'e *n.* dirt path.

ch'och'ilha' *n.* island.

ch'ohib'aal *n.* mouse pad.

Ch'ok *sur.* *From:* choq ('cloud'). (B1).

Ch'oko'oj *sur.* *From:* cho'k'oj ('bat'). (1).

ch'ol *n.* chapter.

ch'ol *n.* part.

ch'ol *n.* furrow.

ch'ol ajl *n.* ordinal number.

ch'ol tul *n.* plantain.

ch'ol'aatin *n.* paragraph.

ch'ol'aatin *n.* sentence.

ch'ol'uutz'ujinb'il aatin *n.* verse.

ch'olch'o *adj.* certain.

ch'olch'o b'i'an *adv phr.* certainly.

ch'olch'o nak'anjelak *adj.* organized.

ch'olk'anjel *n.* process.

ch'olk'anjel tijok *n.* educational process.

ch'olk'anjelob'aal *n.* processor, central processing unit, CPU.

ch'olna'leb' *n.* orientation.

ch'olob'ank *v.* to swear (an oath), inform.

ch'olob'ank *v.* to solve, explain, order.

ch'olob'aal'aatin *n.* glossary.

ch'olob'aalna'leb' *n.* encyclopedia.

ch'olob'ihom *n.* predicate.

ch'olq'e *n.* calendar.

ch'olq'e maayab' *n.* Maya calendar. *Var:* ch'olkutan maayab'.

ch'oltz'iib' *n.* alphabet.

ch'olwinq *n.* caveman, troglodyte.

ch'olwinq *n.* unconverted (archaic).

ch'onpatz *n.* goose.

ch'op *n.* pineapple.

ch'oqom *n.* harvest. *Var:* ch'oqok.

ch'orti' *lang.* Chorti (Chiquimula, Zacapa).

ch'ot *adj.* short.

ch'ot b'estiiy *n.* miniskirt.

ch'ot t'ikr *n.* undershirt.

ch'otlepon *n.* shirt, t-shirt.

ch'otolal *n.* piece.

ch'otonel *adj.* last, final.

ch'otonik *n.* end (temporal).

ch'otwex *n.* shorts, briefs.

ch'ool *n.* heart.

ch'ool re *n.* hope.

ch'ool'aatin *v.* to paraphrase.

ch'oolch'oolkilal *n.* security.

ch'oolej *n.* soul, spirit.

ch'oolej *n.* heart.

ch'oolmetz'ew *n.* motor.

ch'oolyaab' *n.* phoneme.

Ch'ub' *sur. From:* ch'ub' ('wasp'). (B1).

ch'ub' *n.* wasp, hornet.

ch'uch'ib'k *v.* to joke.

ch'uch'ib'leb'aal *n.* circus.

ch'ukch'u xk'a'uxl *adj.* intelligent.

ch'um *n.* hunger.

ch'um ch'ool *n.* ardent desire.

ch'ume'k *v.* to be hungry.

ch'up *n.* belly button, navel.

ch'ut *n.* fern.

ch'utamil *n.* meeting, encounter.

ch'utb'aq cha'al *n.* bone tissue.

ch'utch'u *adv.* together.

ch'ut-eek' cha'al *n.* nerve tissue.

ch'utq'ooq cha'al *n.* fat tissue.

ch'uttenq' *n.* collection (of donations).

ch'utub'ank *n.* sum.

ch'utub'ank *v.* to join.

ch'utub'eetalil *n.* iconography.

ch'uyuk *v.* to pinch.

ch'uyuk *v.* to scratch.

ch'uyul *n.* piece.

ch'uukib'aal *n.* window.

ch'uukum *n.* elbow.

ch'uut *n.* set.

ch'uut *n.* group.

ch'uut aj wajb' *n agt.* musical group.

ch'uut awab'ejilal *n.* political party.

ch'uut chahim *n.* constellation.

ch'uut ich'mul *n.* nervous system.

ch'uut tumin *n.* savings account.

ch'uutal *n.* section.

ch'uutal tenamit *n.* United States.

ch'uutleb'aal *n.* meeting place, meeting hall.

ch'uutleb'aalkab'l *n.* meeting place, meeting hall.

ch'uutulal *n.* species.

ch'uuxul *n.* fauna.

E - e

e *n.* mouth.

e *n.* tooth.

e *n.* edge.

eb' *part.* [pluralization particle]. *Note:* Used preceding the definite article [li] to form plural; also as a suffix to pluralize nouns. **Ma xat-aatinak rik'in jun winq? Ink'a, xin'aatinak rik'in wiibeb'.** « Did you speak with one man? No, I spoke with two of them. »

eb' a'an *pron.* them, they. *Var:* **teb' a'an.**

eb' a'in *pron.* these.

eb' aj puub' *n.* army.

eb' li *art.* the (plural).

ech ajaatink *v phr.* to imitate.

ech alalb'ej *n.* sibling-in-law.

echanink *n.* victory.

echanink *v.* to earn.

echaalal *n.* partner.

ech-aatin *n.* close friend.

echb'enink *v.* to accompany.

echkab'al *n.* neighbor, inhabitant.

eh *interj.* [utterance of doubt or disagreement].

eh! *interj.* [utterance of surprise].

ek'ank ib' *n.* repentance.

ek'asink chi oq *v phr.* to pedal.

ela' *n.* remains.

elab'k *n.* success.

elab'k *v.* to succeed.

elajik *adj.* slow.

elektrisidad *n.* electricity. *From:* electricidad 'electricity' (Spanish) (1).

elepaant *n.* elephant. *From:* elefante 'the elephant' (Spanish) (1).

elik chi yaal *adv phr.* really.

elk *v.* to go out, leave.

elk *n.* departure.

elk sa' najtil tenamit *n.* international departures.

elk yal sa' xteep tenamit *n.* domestic departures.

elkleb'aal *n.* exit.

elkleb'aal sa' junpaat *n.* emergency exit.

elq' *n.* burglary, theft. *Var:* eelq'.

elq'ak *v.* to steal.

elq'ak sa' josq'il *n.* assault.

eneer *n.* January. *From:* Spanish 'enero'.

enhe' *adv.* yes.

eq'la *adj.* early.

eq'la *n.* morning.

eq'laaho'k *n.* sunrise.

ermiit *n.* temple. *From:* ermita 'holy place' (Spanish) (1).

esil *n.* announcement.

esil nayehman sa' li hu *n.* message (written).

esil sa' tz'iib' *n.* text message.

esil tz'iib'anb'il sa' li hu *n.* body text.

esilal *n.* guideline, notice, information.

esilal nawk'anjelahom *n.* information technology.

esilal re elk *n.* departing flights information.

esilalil *n.* bibliography.

esilank *v.* to announce.

esilhu *n.* letter, flyer, poster.

esilhu *n.* newspaper.

esilhu *n.* note.

esilk'anjel *n.* report.

esilnawom *n.* resumé, curriculum vitae, CV.

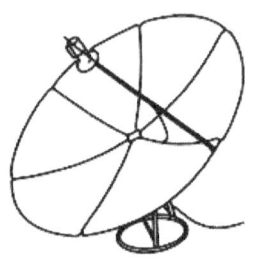

esilsek' chahimch'iich' *n.* satellite dish.

eskaleer *n.* ladder. *From:* escalera 'ladder, stairs' (Spanish) (1).

espinaak *n.* spinach. *From:* Spanish 'espinaca'.

estasion *n.* season. *From:* estación 'the season' (Spanish) (1).

estuuf *n.* stove. *From:* estufa 'the stove' (Spanish) (1).

eswaayr *n.* square. *From:* Spanish 'escuadra'.

etalink *v.* to copy.

ewer *n.* yesterday.

ewer chi q'eq *n.* last night, yesterday evening.

ewer eq'la *n.* yesterday morning.

eweraq *n.* a day ago.

ewu *adj.* late.

ewu *n.* afternoon.

ewuuk *n.* sunset.

ex *part.* [address particle, plural]. *Note:* Used as a modifier to address a group of people. It is used as a prefix and can modify a variety of plural nouns. **Ex was wiitz'in, ink'a' nink'oxla naq ak ta xweechani.** « Brothers and sisters, I do not consider myself yet to have taken hold of it. »

EE - ee

eeb' *n.* step. *From:* *e'ehb' 'the ladder' (Ch'olan) (2).

eeb' *n.* ladder. *From:* *e'ehb' 'the ladder' (Ch'olan) (2).

eeb' *n.* staircase.

eechaninb'il *n.* possessive.

eechanink *v.* to own, possess.

eechank *v.* to take possession of.

eechej *n.* resource.

eechej *n.* possessions.

eechej che'k'aam *n.* natural resources. *Var:* **eechel che'k'aam**.

eechej ch'och' *n.* natural resources.

eek' jalam'uuch *n.* moving picture, movie.

eek'ahom *n.* feeling, sentiment.

eek'aj ib' *v phr.* to know how to act.

eek'al uhej *n.* optic nerve.

eek'anb'iltz'iib' *n.* fable.

eek'ank *n.* noise.

eek'ank *v.* to guess.

eek'asink *v.* to move.

eek'asink rix u *v phr.* to blink.

eek'aal *n.* feeling, sentiment.

eek'ch'iich' *n.* X-ray machine.

eek'metz'ew *n.* motor.

eek'mu *n.* film, movie.

eek'ob'aal *n.* touch, sense of touch, feeling, tact.

eelelik *v.* to retreat, flee.

eeqaj *n.* substitute, retribution.

eeqaj *n.* namesake.

eeqajil *n.* backup copy.

eeqajink *v.* to represent.

eeqajsachomj *n.* voucher, travel allowance.

eetaj palaw *n.* Atlantic Ocean.

eetal *n.* symbol, sign.

eetal *n.* cursor.

eetal *n.* postage stamp.

eetalb'irok *adj.* algebraic.

eetalb'irool *n.* algebra.

eetalhu *n.* diploma.

eetalil *n.* nameplate, sign.

eetalil *n.* figure.

eetalil *n.* sticker.

0	1	2	3	4
5	6	7	8	9
10	11	12	13	14
15	16	17	18	19

eetalil ajl mayab' *n.* Mayan numbers.

eetalil hu *n.* play bill, advertising poster.

eetalil jalam u *n.* monument.

eetalil maak *n.* evidence.

eetalil patz'e'k *n.* monument.

eetalil xtz'uumal *n.* tattoo.

eetalil yaj *n.* patient chart.

eetalil yok'ol *n.* scar.

eetalilatq *n.* figures.

eetalilul *n.* symbolism.

eetalink *v.* to mark.

eetalkamenaq *n.* gravestone, headstone.

eetalkawyaab' *n.* accent mark.

eetalmu *n.* cinema, movie theater.

eetalnum'iq *n.* weather vane.

eetalpuk-ajl *n.* times, multiplication sign (x), multiplication symbol (x).

eetaltaql *n.* icon.

eetaltoj *n.* postage, stamp.

eetaltz'iib' *n.* glyph.

eetaal *n.* measuring tape.

eetil *n.* foolishness.

eetz'aal *n.* costume, disguise.

H - h

ha' *n.* water.

ha'ha' *n.* drain.

ha'il *n.* hydrogen.

ha'il ajtu'xul *n.* cetaceans.

ha'il tz'iib'leb' *n.* pen.

ha'ilyol *n.* nitroglycerine.

ha'ob'resink *v.* to melt, dissolve.

hab' *n.* rain.

hab' *n.* year.

hab'al q'e *n.* winter.

hab'ilhu *n.* birth certificate.

hab'ok *v.* to chew.

hach'lenk *v.* to bite.

hach'ok *v.* to bite.

halaw *n.* agouti (dasyprocta).

hasb'ak *v.* to whisper, mumble.

hay *n.* worm.

haye'k *v.* to approach.

hab'al *n.* rain.

hech'hotk *v.* to carry (in hand).

heleb' puch'um *n.* clothesline.

heleb'ank *v.* to hang out (clothing).

helhokil sek' *n.* plate. *From:* sek' 'plate' (approximate form) (Western Mayan) (2).

helhookil eetalilatq *n.* flat figures, plane figures.

helleb'aal *n.* clothesline.

helo *n.* plain.

helok *v.* to hang out (clothing).

helok *v.* to spread out, roll out.

hesok *v.* to refine.

heehe' *adv.* yes.

hi'b'ej *n sd.* son-in-law (of a man or woman). **inhi'** « my son-in-law ».

hi'om e *n.* parents-in-law.

hik'o *n.* early morning.

hilank *v.* to rest.

hilaal *n.* break, recreation.

hilaal *n.* pew, bench.

hilaal *n.* living room.

hilhookilna'yu'am *n.* homeostasis.

hilob'aal kutan *n.* day of rest.

hilob'aal k'iche' *n.* oasis.

hilob'eleb'aal ch'iich' *n.* bus station, terminal.

hilob'jukub' *n.* port.

hiltasib'aalch'iich' *n.* parking lot.

hirok *v.* to untangle.

hirok *v.* to sow.

hirook *adj.* disorganized.

hitb'arch'iich' *n.* screwdriver. *Var:* jitob'arch'iich'.

hitleb' kotox ch'iich' *n.* screwdriver.

hitok *v.* to untie, untangle, unravel. *From:* *hit 'to untie' (Ch'olan) (3).

hix *n.* jaguar, leopard, tiger, panther.

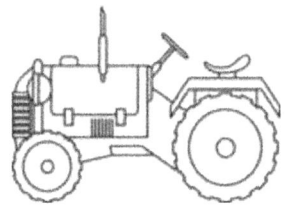

hixch'iich' *n.* tractor.

hiik *n.* earthquake.

hiil *n.* rest.

hiil *n.* kilometer.

ho'meet *n.* gallon.

hob'il *adj.* offended.

hob'ok *n.* insult.

homch'iich' *n.* metal tube.

hompaq' *n.* plastic tube.

homtol'iq' *n.* inner tube.

honon *n.* bumblebee.

hopleb' *n.* drill, hole punch.

hopleb'che' *n.* drill, hole punch.

hopleb'hu *n.* paper punch, hole punch.

hopleb'tz'ak *n.* drill.

hopo *adj.* hollow.

hopok *v.* to bore, drill.

hopolal *n.* hole.

hot'ok *v.* to gnaw, chew.

hoyal *n.* hose.

hoyok *v.* to pour, water, irrigate. *From:* *hoy 'to irrigate' (Yucatecan) (2).

hoon *adv.* today. *Var:* **hooni hoon.**

hoon chi q'eq *n.* tonight.

hoonal *n.* hour. *Var:* **honal.** *From:* jornal 'a day's wage' (Spanish) (2).

hoonal *n.* moment.

hoonalhilaal *n.* recreation, fun, recess.

hoonalil *n.* schedule. *Var:* **honalil.**

hu *n.* paper. *Note:* [hu] is said of anything made of paper, sometimes with an additional descriptor for clarification. **Eb' li tzolom neke'tz'iib' eb' li xtzolomil sa' li xtz'iib'leb'aal hu.** « The students write their assignments in their notebooks. »

hu *n.* book.
hu chi ru chaq'rab' *n.*
government identification, ID.

hu re li k'otak *n.* toilet paper.
hu xaqb'anb'il xwankil *n.*
IOU, promissory note.
Hub' *sur.*

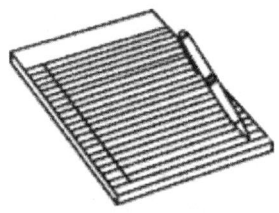

huhil *n.* paper.
huhil sut *n.* tissues, Kleenex.
huhilkub'ha' *n.* baptismal
certificate.
huhil-loq'om *n.* receipt,
invoice.
huhiltumin *n.* bills, banknotes.

hulaj *adv.* tomorrow. *Var:* wulaj.
hulaj chi eq'la *adv phr.*
tomorrow morning.
hulaj chi q'eq *adv phr.*
tomorrow evening.
hulaj ewu *adv phr.* tomorrow
afternoon.
hulak *n.* visit.
hulak *v.* to arrive, become.
Var: wulak.
hulak chi uhej *v phr.* to taste.
humb'ookilha' *n.* kerosene.
humb'ookilha' *n.* gasoline,
gas,
humuk *v.* to burn.
hupatz'om *n.* application,
written request.
huraqb'atzolok *n.* diploma,
title, credential.
hutojxoyiil *n.* community
beautification tax, city
improvement tax.
hutzuk *v.* to bend.
hutz'aam *n.* application,
written request.
hux *n.* whetstone.
huxaqalil *n.* government
identification, ID.

I - i

i' *adv.* no.

i' *interj.* [utterance indicating lack of interest].

ib' *part.* [reflexive particle]. *Note:* Used with verbs to indicate a reflexive action or one where the subject and the object are the same. **Chi qilaq qib'!** « See you soon! »

ib'oy *n.* armadillo.

ichaj *n.* grass.

ichaj tzakahemq *n.* salad.

ich'mul *n.* vein, artery.

ich' *n.* vein, artery.

ich' *n.* sinew, tendon.

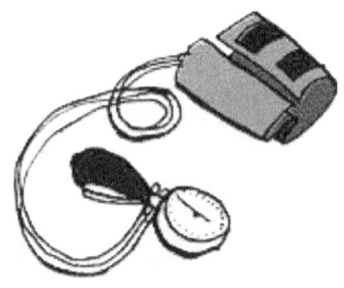

ich'leb'ch'iich' *n.* sphygmomanometer, blood pressure meter.

ich'mej *n.* nerve.

ich'mul *n.* sinew, tendon.

ich'mulb'an *n.* oral rehydration solution, ORS.

ih *interj.* [utterance of understanding].

Ik *sur. From:* ik ('chile'). (B1).

ik *n.* chili pepper.

ikan *n.* uncle, mother's brother.

ikan na' *n.* aunt. *Var:* ikanna'.

ikaq'b'ej *n.* sibling's child.

iklees *n.* church. *Var:* iglees. *From:* iglesia 'church' (Spanish) (1).

iko *n.* fig. *Var:* igo. *From:* higo 'the fig' (Spanish) (1).

ik'ek' *n.* early morning.

ik'oy *n.* guicoy (type of squash).

ilb'a'ixlem *n.* rear-view mirror.

ilb'ahoonal *n.* clock.
  Var: **ilob'aal hoonal.**
ilb'anumleb' *n.* traffic signal.
ileb' *n.* screen (TV).
ileb'aal *n.* sight, sense of sight, vision.

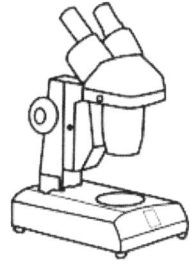

ileb'aalmitz' *n.* microscope.
ileb'aalmu *n.* cinema, movie theater.
iliii *phr.* look!
ilob'aal *n.* visor.
ilob'aal *n.* view.
ilob'aal chahim *n.* telescope.
ilob'aal hoonal *n.* wall clock.
  Var: **ileb'honal.**
ilob'aal mu *n.* video.
ilob'aal xsa'u *n.* sight, sense of sight, vision.
ilok *v.* to examine, check.
ilok *v.* to see, watch over.

ilok chi us *v phr.* to study.
ilok ib' *n.* sustainability.

ilok ru hu *v phr.* to read.

imul *n.* rabbit.
in *adj.* my. *Note:* Used as a prefix to nouns to convey possession. **Ma nakanaw b'ar wan inpunit?** « Do you know where my hat is? »
inkles *lang.* English. *From:* Spanish 'inglés'.
ink'a us *adj.* bad.
ink'a' *adv.* not.
ink'a' *adv.* no.
ink'a' b'i' *phr.* of course not.
ink'a' cham *adj.* shallow.
ink'a' ch'a'aj *adj.* easy.
ink'a' ch'olch'o *phr.* I'm not sure.

123

ink'a' ch'olch'o *adj.* obscure.

ink'a' jultik re *adj.* unconscious.

ink'a' jwal sa naweek'a *phr.* I don't feel very well.

ink'a' jwal us *phr.* not so well.

ink'a' k'i *pron.* few.

ink'a' na'ab'in *adj.* rebellious.

ink'a' na'aatinak *adj.* quiet.

ink'a' na'eek'an *adj.* introverted.

ink'a' na'oken *adj.* passive.

ink'a' na'oxloq'in *adj.* disrespectful.

ink'a' nahulak chi wu [ ] *phr.* I don't like [ ].

ink'a' nanawman k'a tb'aanu *adj.* unpredictable.

ink'a' naxk'ul inch'ool *phr.* I disagree.

ink'a' nin'aatinak sa' inkles *phr.* I don't speak English.

ink'a' nin'aatinak sa' q'eqchi' *phr.* I don't speak Q'eqchi'.

ink'a' ninnaw *phr.* I don't know.

ink'a' tuqtu xch'ool *n.* insecurity.

ink'a' t'e'b'il *adj.* uncombed.

ink'a' tz'aqal *adj.* incomplete.

ink'a' us *adj.* wrong.

ink'a' us xat-elq *phr.* too bad (for you)!

ink'a' us xna'leb' *adj.* dishonest.

ink'a' xq'ulub'ank *v phr.* to refuse.

ink'a' xsumenkil *v phr.* to deny.

inna' inyuwa' *n.* parents (my).

inseekt *n.* insect. *From:* insecto 'the insect' (Spanish) (1).

inup *n.* Ceiba.

Inupal *top.* [inupal] "among the Ceibas". *Etym:* inup = Ceiba; al = Span suffix indicating grove or plantation (as is 'cafetal')..

inwan b'i' *phr.* goodbye, bye.

iq' *n.* wind.

iq' *n.* air.

iq' xsa' *adj.* windy.

iq'ob'aal *n.* inner tube.

iq'xaml *n.* propane.

is *n.* sweet potato.

isb' *n.* blanket.

isb' *n.* poncho.

isib'aal tapon *n.* corkscrew.

isihob'aal jalam'uuch *n.* camera.

isink *v.* to take out, remove.

isink aq' *v phr.* to get undressed, undress.

isink b'aq *v phr.* to debone.

isink sa' re che' *v phr.* to notch.

isink xkehil *v phr.* to defrost.

isink xya'al tz'ejwal *v phr.* to ejaculate.

isk'i'ij *n.* mint, spearmint.

ismal *n.* hair.

it *n.* buttock, anus.

itza' *lang.* Itza (El Petén).

iwaan *n.* iguana. *From:* Spanish 'iguana'.

ix *n.* back.

ixajaw *n.* queen.

ixaqilb'ej *n sd.* wife. **wixaqil** « my wife ».

ixa'an *n.* grandmother.

ixi'ij *n.* nail, fingernail.

ixi'ij *n.* hoof.

ixi'jink *v.* to steal.

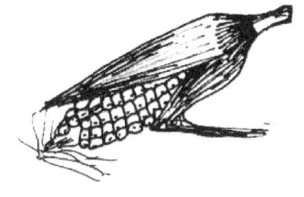

ixim *n.* maize, corn.

Ixim *sur. From:* ixim ('corn'). (B1).

iximaak *v.* to thresh. *Var:* **iximak.**

ixi'ij *n.* claw.

ixkej *n.* back.

ixkej *n.* touch, sense of touch, tact. *Var:* ixej; ixb'ej.

ixq *adj.* female.

ixq *n.* woman.

ixqa'al *n.* young woman. *Var:* xqa'al; qa'al.

ixqi aaq *n.* sow.

ixqi i *n.* granddaughter.

ixqilal *n.* femininity, females.

iyaj *n.* seed.

iyajib'aal *n.* chromosome.

iyajiil *n.* seedbed.

II - ii

iib'ej *n sd.* grandchild, grandson, granddaughter. **wii** « my grandchild ».

iimamb'ej *n sd.* great grandchild. **iimam** « my great grandchild ».

iiq *n.* suitcase, luggage, large bag.

iiqank *v.* to carry.

iiqaal *n.* backpack.

iiqaal *n.* cart, wheelbarrow.

iitz'inb'ej *n sd.* younger sibling (brother or sister). **wiitz'in** « my younger sibling ».

iitz'in ixq *n.* sister (younger, of a male or female).

iitz'in'e *n.* cousin (younger). *Var:* iitz'in we.

iitz'intz'iib' *n.* lower case letter.

J - j

ja'ajul *n.* voice.

ja'leb'aal *n.* kiosk.

ja'leb'aal'u *n.* park.

ja'leb'ch'ool *n.* park.

jachal *n.* piece.

jachb'il'ajl *n.* fraction.

jachinb'il chi *adj.* divided by.

jachkab'al *n.* divorce.

jachleb' *n.* saw.

jachleb'aal che' *n.* chainsaw.

jachlil'ajl *n.* fractional, mixed number.

jachok *v.* to cut down.

jachok *v.* to separate, divide.

jachok *v.* to halve, split.

jachok-ib' *n.* divorce. *Var:* jachoj ib'.

jachsirso *n.* semicircle.

jach'ok *v.* to bite.

jach'bil *adv.* separate, separated.

jahok u *v phr.* to entertain, amuse, distract.

jakalteka *lang.* Jakaltek [aka Popti] (Huehuetenango).

jal'iq' *n.* ozone.

Jalal *sur. From:* jal ('change'). (B3).

jalam u *n.* picture.

jalam'uuch *n.* film, movie.

jalam'uuch *n.* idol, holy image, statue.

jalam'uuch *n.* photo. *Var:* jalam'u.

jalam'uuchib'aal *n.* camera.

jalam'uuchib'k *v.* to take pictures.

jalam'uuchib'k *v.* to mark, trace.

jalam'uuchil taql *n.* postcard.

jalam'uuchink *v.* to sketch, draw.

jalam'uuchink *v.* to photocopy.

jalam'uuchleb' *n.* photocopier, copy machine, copier.

jalam'uuchleb'aal ch'iich' *n.* photocopier, copy machine, copier.

jalam'uuchu *n.* photocopy.

jalam'uuleb' *n.* camera.

jalan *adj.* other.

jalan aj e *adj.* somebody else's.

jalan chik *pron.* another.

jalb'a'metz'ew *n.* transformer.

jalb'ametz'ew *n.* adapter.

jalb'e *n.* path.

jalb'ehil saqen *n.* refraction, light refraction.

jalb'esiil'aatin *n.* dialect.

jalb'eetink *v.* to lend.

jalch'ool'aatin *n.* adverb.

jalch'ool'aatin kok'raq aatin *n.* adverbial phrase.

jaleb'aal *n.* hall.

jaljookil ru ajl *n.* algebra.

jaljookil ru aatin *n.* parable.

jaljookil'aatin *n.* refrain, saying, proverb.

jalmuqank *v.* to deny, hide. *Var:* jalmuqink.

jalok *v.* to change.

jalok *v.* to trade, barter.

jalok *v.* to lend.

jalok ru yaal *n.* forgery.

jalok ru yaal *v phr.* to forge.

jalok-aatin *n.* translation, interpretation.

jaltesink *n.* to change, transform, convert.

jamon *n.* ham. *From:* Spanish 'jamón'.

jap yahiil *n.* open syllable.

japink e *v phr.* to yawn.

jaqam *adj.* permanently open.

jaqleb' *n.* opener, key.

jaqok *v.* to open.

jaq'b'ab' *n.* perfume.

jaq'e'k *v.* to drown.

jaq'ilb'an *n.* air freshener.

jar *interr.* how much?

jarjar *interr.* how much for each?

jarjartk *interr.* how much each time?

jarjek'il *n.* denominator.

jarmayer *interr.* how long ago?

jarsut *interr.* how many times?

jarub' *interr.* how many?

jarub' chihab' wan aawe *phr.* how old are you?

jarwa *interr.* how many times?

jasmin *n.* jasmine. *From:* Spanish 'jazmin'.

jatz'uuchink *v.* to hate.

jay *adj.* thin. *From:* *jaay 'thin' (Yucatecan, Ch'olan, possible) (2).

jayab'aalb'e *n.* steering wheel.

jayal *n.* direction.

jayalihom *n.* aim, goal.

jayalink *v.* to point, aim.

jayaab' na'tz'iib' *n.* relaxed vowel.

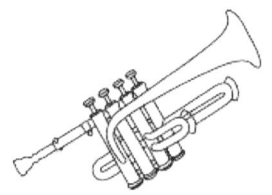

jayaab'wajb' *n.* horn, trumpet.

jayil'isb' *n.* sheet.

jayiltz'uumal'u *n.* retina.

ja'aj *n.* neck.

jeb'ib'aal *n.* divisor.

jeb'ok *v.* to subtract.

jeb'ok *n.* subtraction, remainder.

jeb'ok-ajl *n.* subtraction.

jech' *adj.* crooked.

jech'exink *v.* to carry (in hand).

jech'-uhil *n.* asymmetry.

jech'xuk *n.* corner, angle.

jekb'ametz'ew *n.* powerstrip, circuit board.

jek'b'il ajl *n.* distributive number.

jek'cha'alil chi rix *n.* exocrine gland.

jek'cha'alil chi sa' *n.* endocrine gland.

jek'inel *n.* distributor.

jek'ink *v.* to divide.

jek'iil *n.* numerator.

jek'muriil *n.* meiosis.

jek'ok *v.* to distribute, share. *Var:* **jek'ink**. *From:* *jek' 'break off, divide' (Yucatecan, Ch'olan, possible) (2).

jek'pojk'ok *n.* meiosis.

jelonk *v.* to carry (on shoulder).

jeqonk *v.* to approach.

jerink *n.* syringe. *From:* Spanish 'jeringa'.

jesok *v.* to chop.

ji *n.* oak.

ji'b'al e *n.* brush.

ji'ji' *adj.* smooth.

ji'leb' *n.* file, rasp.

ji'leb' *n.* sandpaper.

ji'leb' *n.* whetstone.

ji'leb' t'ikr *n.* iron (for clothing).

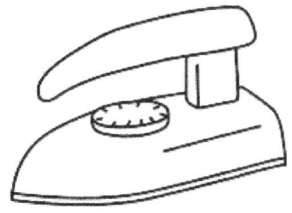

ji'leb'aal *n.* iron.

ji'leb'aal *n.* ironing board.

ji'leb'che' *n.* plane.

ji'leb'ch'iich' *n.* file, rasp.

ji'leb'-e *n.* toothbrush.

ji'leb't'ikr *n.* iron.

ji'leb'tz'ak *n.* trowel.

ji'lenk *v.* to scrub.

ji'ok *v.* to iron (clothing).

ji'ok *v.* to sand, file, smooth, plane, shave (wood).

jichok *v.* to grate, scrape.

jilb'il yaab' *n.* fricative.

jilix kawaay *n.* zebra.

jilok *v.* to rub, handle.

jilonk *v.* to approach.

jilosink *v.* to separate.

jilq'ank *v.* to snore.

jip *adj.* obstinate, stubborn, lazy.

jip *adj.* stupid, foolish, clumsy.

jipo'k *n.* infatuation.

jiqe'k *v.* to approach.

jiqok *v.* to advance.

jiq'e'k *v.* to choke.

jiq'jiq'ink ib' *v phr.* to whisper.

jiq'leb'aal b'an *n.* inhaler.

jiq'leb'mul *n.* vacuum cleaner.

jiq'ok ch'ool *v phr.* to breathe deeply.

jiq'ok iq' *v phr.* to breathe rapidly.

jisil t'ikr *n.* ribbon.

jiskotko tiwok *n.* annular eclipse.

jisleb' *n.* grater.

jisok *v.* to cut in strips.

jit *n.* prawns, shrimp. *From:* jit 'large shrimp' (Tzeltal) (3).

jitok *v.* to accuse.

jitom *n.* indictment.

jitonel *n.* plaintiff.

jitb'il *n.* defendant.

jit'aal *n.* buckle.

jit'iil *n.* screw.

jit'leb' *n.* nut (fastener), fastener.

jit'leb'wex *n.* belt.

jit'ok *v.* to tie.

jit'ok kotox ch'iich' *v phr.* to screw.

jitz'jitz' *n.* violin.

jiileb' *n.* plumb line.

jo' *adj.* like, similar.

jo' *adv.* according to.

jo' chan ru *adv phr.* in accordance with.

jo' chanru *adv.* naturally.

jo' ch'inal *interr.* what size?

jo' junelik *phr.* same as usual.

jo' k'ihal *interr.* how much?

jo' najtil *interr.* how far?

jo' nimal *interr.* how much?

jo' wan chik *phr.* see you soon.

jo' wanaq *adv.* later.

jo'kan *conj.* that's why.

jo'kan *adv.* so.

jo'kan *adv.* naturally.

jo'kan aj wi' *adv phr.* also, too.

jo'kan ajwi' tinye aawe *phr.* same to you.

jo'kan b'i' *adv phr.* then.

jo'kan b'i'an *adv phr.* definitely, absolutely.

jo'kan li wank *phr.* that's life.

jo'kan naq *conj.* that's why.

jo'kan tz'aqal *phr.* sure.

jo'kan tz'aqal *adv phr.* exactly.

jo'kanil *n.* inference.

jo'maajo' *adj.* ugly.

job' *adj.* empty.

job'che' *n.* trough.

job'enk *v.* to hollow out.

job'wajb' *n.* drum.

jochleb' *n.* rake.

jochleb'mul *n.* rake.

jochlenk *v.* to scratch.

jochok *v.* to scratch.

jochok *v.* to scrape. *From:* *joch 'to take off, peel off' (Yucatecan, Ch'olan, possible) (2).

jochok *v.* to steal.

jochok *v.* to pinch.

jochol *n.* scrape.

jochol *n.* scratch.

jochonel *n.* thief. *From:* joch-on-el 'the thief' (Ch'olan) (4).

johob'a mach *n.* razor.

johok *v.* to shave.

joj *n.* skin infection.

jok *adj.* stupid.

jok *adj.* lazy.

jokleb' *n.* spoon.

jokok *v.* to scrape, scoop.

jok' *n.* sling.

jok'ib'k *v.* to sling.

jole'k *v.* to slip, slide.

jolom *n.* head.

Jolom *sur. From:* jolom ('head'). (B1).

jolom ch'aat *n.* headboard.

jolom q'een *n.* garlic.

jolomb'ej *n.* headache.

jolomb'ej *n.* cold, flu.

jolomil *n.* chieftain.

jolomil na'leb' *n.* title.

jolomilal *n.* administration, board of directors.

jolomilal tzoleb'aal *n.* principal's office.

jolomilk'aleb'aal *n.* civic leadership committee.

jolomink *v.* to lead, direct.

Jolomna' *sur. From:* jolom na' ('head' and 'mother' or 'perhaps'). (B3).

jolomnib'aal *n.* principal's office.

jolool *n.* slide, chute, slippery place.

jomal *n.* playing field.

jonjoli *n.* sesame seeds. *From:* Spanish 'ajonjolí'.

joq'ank *v.* to snore. *Var:* jok'ank; joq'yank.

joq'e *interr.* when?

jorank *v.* to bake, toast.

jorank *v.* to bake.

jorb'ana'leb' *n.* riddle.

jorinb'il *adj.* baked, toasted.

jorinkleb' *n.* toaster.

jorleb'pek *n.* sledgehammer.

jorok *v.* to break.

jorol *adj.* broken.

josq' *adj.* violent, aggressive.

josq' *adj.* angry.

josq'il *n.* anger, fury, wrath.

josq'ok *n.* irritation.

jot'b'il *adj.* combed.

jot'ok *v.* to interrupt.

jot'ok *v.* to scrape.

jot'ok *v.* to injure.

jotz *n.* heron.

jotzleb' *n.* chisel, awl, scraper.

jotzleb' *n.* peeler.

jotzleb' tz'iib'leb' che' *n.* pencil sharpener.

jotzok *v.* to peel.

jotzok ru'uj *v phr.* to sharpen.

job'nil *n.* stomach. *From:* *job'nel 'entrails, belly' (Yucatecan, Ch'olan, possible) (2).

jookleb' *n.* hoe. *Var:* jokleb'.

jook' *n.* maracas.
jooleb' *n.* razor.
jooleb'mach *n.* razor.
joom *n.* gourd.

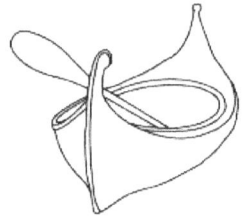

jukub' *n.* canoe, outrigger, boat.
Jukub' *sur. From:* jukub' ('canoe'). (B1).

joom *n.* basin.
joomuk'al *n.* pot.
joor *n.* oven. *From:* Spanish 'horno'.

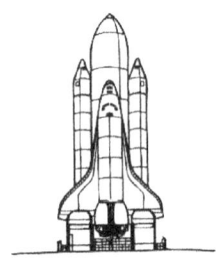

jukub' iq' *n.* space shuttle, spaceship.
jukub' re pleetik *n.* warship, battleship.

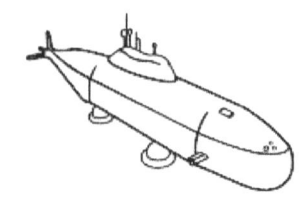

joob'aq *n.* owl.
ju'e'k *v.* to erode.
juch' *n.* signature.
juch' *n.* line.
juch'leb' *n.* ruler.
juch'uk *v.* to vote.
juch'uk *v.* to trace.

jukub' re rub'elha' *n.* submarine.
jukub'iiq *n.* ferry.
jukuch *adj.* long.
jukunk *v.* to crawl.
jukunk *v.* to pull.
jukxul *n.* reptile.

juk'uk *v.* to destroy, undo.

jul *n.* ditch, pit.

jul *n.* hole.

julel *n.* vacuole.

julel kamenaq *n.* grave.

juliis *n.* Jew.

julpek *n.* cave.

jultik uxk *n.* history.

jultikank *v.* to train, remember.

jultikaal *n.* form.

jultikleb' *n.* call button, buzzer.

jultikob'lhu *n.* agenda.

jultik'anjel *n.* agenda.

jumha'elch'iich' *n.* gasoline, gas,

jumpaat *adj.* brief. *Var:* **junpaat**.

jun *adj.* unique.

jun *art.* a, an.

jun aj wi' *adj.* only one, sole.

jun cheet *n.* a bunch.

jun chi aatin *adj.* gullible.

jun chik *adv.* another, one more.

jun jachal *n.* a half.

jun kaajachal *n.* a quarter.

jun ketzal *n.* one quetzal.

jun kuchaar *n.* a spoonful.

jun kutan rub'elaj *n.* the day before.

jun mooch' *n.* a handful.

jun nub'uk *n.* a mouthful.

jun oq'ob' *n.* four hundred.

jun q'aal *n.* an armful.

jun senta *n.* one cent, penny. *From:* Spanish 'centavo'.

jun surul *n.* a slice.

jun sut chik *adv phr.* again, once more.

jun suumal *n.* a pair.

jun toseen *n.* a dozen. *From:* Spanish 'docena'.

jun tuxtun *n.* fifty cents, half dollar.

jun tuub' *n.* a heap.

jun wa'leb' *n.* midday.

jun xka *n.* one fourth, a quarter.

jun xwaqxaqil *n.* one eighth.

jun'al iyaj *n.* monocotyledonous seed.

junaj *adj.* same.

junaj k'anjel *n.* linear function.

junaj tzoqchahim *n.* compact galaxy.

junajch'oolej *n.* democracy.

junajeetalb'irok *n.* monomial.

junajihom *n.* union.

junajil *n.* solidarity, unity.

junajink *v.* to globalize, generalize.

junajink *v.* to stir, mix.

junajroqil *n.* compass.

junaq *art.* a, an. *Note:* Indicates an indefinite, desired or future state of a modified noun. **Junaq kutan taanaw laa maayil k'ab'a'ej.** « Someday you will know your Mayan name. »

junaq *adj.* some.

junaqlil *n.* individual.

junaatal alalb'ej *n.* only child.

junaatalil *adj.* singular.

junelik *adv.* always.

junes *adj.* alone.

junes yo *adv phr.* frequently.

junesal *adj.* alone.

junesal *n.* isolation.

junesal *adj.* lonely.

junesal ruuchil k'ab'a'ej *n.* independent pronoun.

junesal'uxk *n.* intransitive (verb).

junesalil *adj.* independent.

junesalil *n.* independence.

juneet *adj.* same.

juneetil'aatin *n.* synonym.

juneetilk'ab'a' *n.* homonym.

junil na'tz'iib' *n.* short vowel.

junilna'yu'am *adj.* unicellular.

junkab'al *n.* family.
    Var: junkab'lal.

junlajuxuk *n.* hendecagon.

junmay kintal *n.* a ton.

junpak'alil *adj.* reversible.

junpak'alpalaw *n.* Europe.

junpaatil *n.* moment.

junpaatil'esil *n.* telegram.

junpaatilsachk *adj.* unconscious.

junq eechej *n.* per capita income.

junqalil *n.* unit, unity.

junqmayil *n.* base-twenty.

junq'aal uutz'u'uj *n.* flower bouquet, bouquet.

junrib' *adj.* unique.

junsut *adv.* once.

juntaq'eet *adj.* same.

juntaq'eetil *n.* equity, equality.

juntaq'eetil amaq'il *n.* social equality.

juntaq'eetil eetalil *n.* symmetric figure.

juntaq'eetil'aatin *n.* synonym.

$$9 + \frac{5x}{2} = 4$$

juntaq'eetin k'anjel'ajl *n.* equation.

juntaq'eetyaalalil *n.* synonym.

juntaalil *n.* loneliness.

juntuub' *adj.* abundant.

juntz'ap tiwok *n.* total eclipse.

junwa *adv.* one time, once.

junxaqalil t'ikr *n.* suit.

junxil *adj.* old, ancient.

junxil *adv.* before.

junxil chik *adv.* a long time ago.

jur aq' *n.* nightgown.

jur'ichaj *n.* chard.

juruch' *n.* spine, backbone, spinal column. *Var:* huruch'ix.

jurxaab' *n.* boot.

jus chahim *n.* shooting star.

jusk'aam *n.* cord, line.

jut aq' *n.* overcoat.

jut t'ikr *n.* overcoat.

jut-aq' *n.* dress.

jutzutzu *n.* fireworks, bottlerocket.

jutz' *adj.* pointed.

jutz' kar *n.* swordfish.

jutz' kaaxukuut *n.* pyramid (four-sided).

jutz' oxxukuut *n.* pyramid (three-sided).

jutz' ru'uj *adj.* pointed.

jutz'b'ojleb' *n.* needle (sewing).

jutz'che' *n.* spear.

jutz'-eetalil *n.* pyramid.

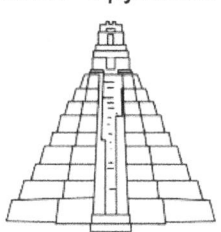

jutz'il na'aj *n.* pyramid (monument).

jutz'ju *n.* cone.

jutz'kutleb' *n.* needle (hypodermic).

jutz'leb' *n.* spear.

jutz'ochochilpek *n.* pyramid (monument).

jutz'un pemech *n.* mother-of-pearl.

juylek *v.* to beat, whip.

juyuk *v.* to row. *From:* *juy 'to move' (Ch'olan) (2).

juul *n.* July. *From:* Spanish 'julio'.

juun *n.* June. *From:* Spanish 'junio'.

juutz' *n.* cone.

jwal *adv.* very.

jwal *adj.* much.

jwal aajel *phr.* very important.

jwal ink'a us *adv phr.* worse.

jwal kach'in xkutum *n.* weak signal.

jwal laatz' wu *phr.* I've been busy.

jwal us *adv phr.* better.

jweews *n.* Thursday. *Var:* **jweeb's**. *From:* jueves 'Thursday' (Spanish) (1).

K - k

ka' *n.* molar.

ka' *n.* grinding stone.

ka' aj wi' *adj.* only, alone. *Var:* **ka'j wi'**.

ka' paay ru *n.* compound.

ka' paay ru k'ab'a'ej *n.* composite noun.

ka'aj wi a'an *phr.* nothing more, that's it, that's all.

ka'awb'il *n.* reforestation.

ka'awk *v.* to reforest, reseed.

ka'aatin *adj.* bilingual.

ka'ch'in chi ru *adv phr.* smaller than, younger than.

ka'ch'in roq *adj.* short.

ka'ch'in xteram *adj.* short.

ka'ch'olob'ank *n.* survey.

ka'eetalb'irok *n.* binomial.

ka'jultikank *v.* to emphasize, highlight.

ka'kab'iluxk *n.* transitive (verb).

ka'k'a'b'aink *v.* to rename.

ka'lach' *n.* scissors, shears.

ka'muluq'utiltz'uq *n.* quotes, quotation marks.

ka'na' *n.* stepmother.

ka'na'jilxul *n.* amphibian.

ka'oksink *v.* to recycle, reuse.

ka'pak'al u *adj.* hypocritical.

ka'pak'alil ru aatin *n.* antonyms.

ka'sutink *n.* repetition.

ka'sutink *v.* to reproduce.

ka'suut *n.* box.

ka't'oj *n.* rivet.

ka'tz'iib'ank *v.* to rewrite.

ka'tz'uq *n.* colon.

ka'wa *adv.* twice, two times.

ka'wahink *n.* repetition.

ka'xaqab'aal *n.* renown, fame.

ka'xik *n.* gold.

ka'xik *n.* earring.

ka'yab'aal ixkej *n.* rear-view mirror.

ka'yank *v.* to contemplate.

ka'yuwa' *n.* stepfather.

kab' *n.* caramel.

Kab' *sur. From:* kab' ('sweet'). (B3).

kab' *n.* candy, sweets.

kab' rix ch'ool *adv phr.* reluctantly.

kab'ej *n.* the day after tomorrow.

kab'ejer *n.* two days ago, day before yesterday.

kab'il kaxlan wa *n.* sweet roll.

kab'l najt xteram *n.* tower.

kab'lak *n.* construction site.

kab'lanb'il na'leb' *n.* constructivism.

kab'lank *v.* to build.

kab'yo'lajik *n.* resurrection.

kachiimp *n.* pipe. *From:* cachimba 'the pipe' (Spanish) (1).

kach'in *adj.* few.

kach'in *n.* baby.

kach'in *pron.* a few, a little.

kach'in *adj.* small.

kach'in chik (ma) *adv phr.* nearly, almost.

kach'in puub' *n.* handgun.

kach'in ru *adj.* narrow.

kach'in xteram *adj.* low.

kajunajink xna'tz'iib' *n.* diphthong.

Kak *sur.*

Kakaw *sur. From:* kakaw ('cacao'). (B1).

kakaw *n.* cocoa.

Kal *sur.*

kala' *n.* palm tree.

kalajenaq *adj.* drunk. *From:* *kal 'to get drunk' (Yucatecan, Ch'olan, possible) (2).

kalawx *n.* carnation. *From:* Spanish 'clavel'.

kalawx q'een *n.* clove spice.

kalha' *n.* alcoholic drink.

kalkab' *adv.* in peace.

kalon *n.* gallon. *From:* from Spanish 'galón'.

kaltesink *v.* to get drunk.

kama'an *adv.* like that.

kama'in *adv.* like this.

kamab'k *v.* to help.

kamab'k *n.* mutual help, volunteer work, assistance.

kamenaq *n.* carcass.

kamenaq *adj.* dead.

kamenaq *n.* corpse.

kamenaq xch'ool *n.* dejection.

kamenaq xch'ool *adj.* depressed.

kameey *n.* camel. *From:* camello 'the camel' (Spanish) (1).

kamij winq *n.* homicide.

kamiis *n.* shirt. *From:* camisa 'shirt' (Spanish) (1).

kamiis ixq *n.* blouse.

kamk *v.* to die.

kamk tojb'a maak *n.* death penalty.

kamna'aj *n.* morgue.

kampameent *n.* camp. *From:* campamento 'camp' (Spanish) (1).

kampaan *n.* bell. *From:* Spanish 'campana'.

kamsib'aal *n.* weapons.

kamsink *v.* to kill.

kamsink *v.* to murder.

kamsink chi uk'b'il *v phr.* to poison.

kamsink-ib' *n.* war.

kamsiik *n.* murder.

kamsiil *n.* weapons.

kamyon *n.* truck. *From:* Spanish 'camión'.

kamyoneet *n.* bus. *From:* camión 'the bus' (Spanish) (1).

Kan *sur.*

kanab'ank *v.* to put, place.

kanaleet *n.* oar. *From:* canaleta 'short, broad oar' (Spanish) (1).

kanaak *v.* to remain.

kanaak sa' yu'am *v phr.* to conceive.

kaneel *n.* cinnamon. *From:* Spanish 'canela'.

kanhub'aal *n.* briefcase.

kanser *n.* cancer.

kantaaw *n.* lock. *From:* candado 'the lock' (Spanish) (1).

kanteel *n.* candle. *Var:* **kandeel**. *From:* candela 'the candle' (Spanish) (1).

kanxam *n.* lamp, lantern, torch.

kape *n.* coffee. *From:* café 'coffee' (Spanish) (1).

kapiiy *n.* chapel, temple. *From:* capilla 'the chapel' (Spanish) (1).

kapiiy *n.* Protestant.

kapoteer *n.* peg. *From:* capotera 'peg ?' (Spanish) (1).

kapun *adj.* castrated.

kapuninb'il wakax *n.* ox.

kapunwakax *n.* ox.

kaq *adj.* red.

kaq ik *n.* turkey soup.

kaq kaq *adj.* scarlet.

kaq moyin *adj.* mauve.

kaq ra' *n.* frog.

kaq ru xch'ool *adj.* mean, selfish.

kaq saqin *adj.* pink.

kaqal *n.* envy, jealousy.

kaqcha *n.* firewood.

kaqcha *adj.* unfortunate, poor.

kaqchahim *n.* Venus, morning star. *Var:* kaqi chahim.

kaqchikel *lang.* Kaqchikel (Chimaltenango, Guatemala, Baja Verzpaz, Sacatepéquez, Sololá, Suchitepéquez).

kaqi atawank *n.* envy.

kaqi yajel *n.* fever, typhoid.

kaqiq'an *adj.* orange.

kaqjorin *adj.* bright red.

kaqkik' *n.* hemoglobin.

kaqkil mitz'kotkik' *n.* red blood cells.

kaqkoj *n.* mountain lion. *Var:* kaqkojl.

kaqlak *n.* menstruation, menses.

kaqlamj *n.* measles.

kaqlaaq' *n.* rainbow. *Var:* kaqla.

kaqpech'in *n.* inflamed, swollen.

kaqsut-iq' *n.* storm, hurricane.

kaqxe' *n.* radish.

kaqxot'ink *n.* red face.

kaqyajel *n.* AIDS.

kaqyojin *adj.* brown.

kaq'naab' *n.* lake, lagoon. *Var:* k'aqnab'; kaqnab'.

kaq'ok *v.* to blush, turn red.

kar *n.* fish.

karayool *n.* gladiola. *From:* Spanish 'gladiola'.

karetiiy *n.* wheelbarrow. *From:* Spanish 'carretilla'.

kareton *n.* cart, wagon. *From:* carretón 'cart' (Spanish) (1).

kareen *n.* chain. *From:* cadena 'the chain' (Spanish) (1).

kareet *n.* cart. *From:* Spanish 'carreta'.

karib'k *v.* to fish. *Var:* karab'k.

karil *n.* fish.

karink *v.* to fish.

karifuna *lang.* Garífuna (Izabal).

karneer *n.* sheep, ewe, ram. *From:* carnero 'the sheep' (Spanish) (1).

karton *n.* cardboard. *From:* from Spanish 'cartón'.

karwans *n.* chick peas, garbanzo beans. *From:* Spanish 'garbanzos'.

kastiiy *lang.* Spanish, Castilian. *From:* Spanish 'castellano'.

katoolk *n.* Catholic. *Var:* katolika.

Katun *sur.*

katunink *v.* to make war.

katz *n.* itch. *Var:* katzil.

katzkatz *n.* itch, tickle.

katzkatz aj ja'aj *n.* dry cough.

katzkatz kux *n.* cough.

kaw *adj.* loud.

kaw *adj.* strong.

kaw *adj.* hard.

Kaw *sur.*

kaw rib' *adj.* clever.

kaw rib' *adj.* brave, courageous, robust, energetic, vigorous.

kaw ru *adj.* solid.

kaw xch'ool *adj.* proud.

kaw xmetz'ew *adj.* strong.

kaw xyaab' *adj.* loud.

kawal *adj.* healthy.

kawalil chi ru raaxiik' *n.* disaster prevention, emergency preparedness.

kawaay *n.* horse, stallion. *From:* caballo 'the small horse' (Spanish) (1).

kawaaya ch'iich' *n.* motorcycle.

kawaayach'iich'inb'il *adj.* motorized.

kawaayink *v.* to ride (a horse).

kawb'aqel *n.* calcium.

kawil ch'ool *n.* optimism.

kawil hab' *n.* downpour, shower.

kawil k'aam *n.* hemp.

kawilal *n.* health.

kawresil *n.* stimulus.

kawresil-ib' *n.* self-esteem.

kawresinel ch'ool *n.* stimulant.

kawresink *v.* to exercise, get ready, prepare.

kawresink ch'ool *v.* to stimulate.

kawsik kaxaml *n.* electrical resistance.

kawub'l *n.* protein.

kawub'l kik' *n.* IV, intravenous line.

kawub'lb'an *n.* vitamin.

kawyaab' na'tz'iib' *n.* stressed vowel.

kawyaab'ink *v.* to stress.

kawyehink *n.* recital, recitation.

Kax *nick.* Lucas.

kax *part.* [foreign particle]. *Note:* [kax] or [kaxlan] is said of many things foreign, artificial or imported. **Ch'ina us li kaxpo'ot re li xMar.** « Maria's blouse is nice. » **Ma nakanaw aatinak sa' kaxlan aatin?** « Do you know how to speak Spanish? »

kax aaq *n.* hippopotamus.

kax'isk'i'ij *n.* celery.

kax'olb' *n.* lubricant, cooking oil.

kax'olb' poych'iich' *n.* motor oil.

01234 56789

kaxajl *n.* Arabic numeral.

kaxb'olol *n.* whistle (object).

kaxchaj *n.* flashlight.

kaxchampa *n.* briefcase.

kaxche'kenq' *n.* pea, peas.

kaxchixl *n.* rhinoceros.

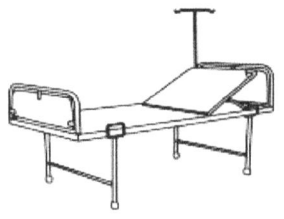

kaxch'aat *n.* hospital bed.

kaxch'i'kay *n.* artichoke.

kaxemel *n.* washbasin, washbowl.

kaxjoom *n.* washbasin, washbowl.

kaxjukin *n.* flamingo.

kaxjukub' *n.* motorboat.

kaxka' *n.* blender.

kaxkatras *n.* swan.

kaxkojl *n.* mixer.

kaxkukay *n.* otoscope.

kaxk'oyem *n.* cracker.

kaxlan *n.* chicken. *From:* Spanish 'Castellano'.

kaxlan aatin *lang.* Spanish, Castilian, foreign language. *From:* Spanish 'castellano'.

kaxlan b'oj *n.* alcohol, spirits.

kaxlan chiqleb' *n.* stove.

kaxlan is *n.* potato.
kaxlan pom *n.* incense.
kaxlan q'een *n.* pepper.
kaxlan tem *n.* wheel chair.

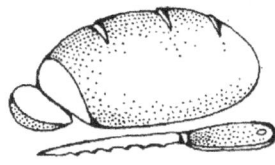

kaxlan wa *n.* bread.
kaxlan wahib'aal *n.* bakery.
kaxlan winq *n.* Ladino, foreigner.

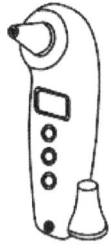

kaxlan xam *n.* otoscope.

kaxlan xamlel b'e *n.* traffic light.
kaxlan xut' *n.* hamburger.
kaxlanchi' *lang.* Spanish, Castilian, foreign language.
From: Spanish 'castellano'.

kaxlanha' *n.* soft drink, carbonated drink, soda.
kaxlankaq' *n.* false ceiling, sub ceiling.
kaxlank'uluj *n.* cake.
kaxlanq'ib' *n.* cooking oil.

kaxlant'usub' *n.* grape.
Var: **uub'**.
kaxlanuuq *n.* skirt. *Var:* **kax'uuq**.

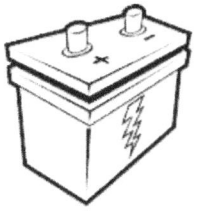

kaxmetz'ew *n.* battery. *From:* batería 'the battery' (Spanish) (1).
kaxmis *n.* marmot.
kaxmu *n.* television, TV.
kaxmu helleb' *n.* television.

kaxmu'eetalil *n.* computer screen, monitor, display.

kaxmuheb'aal *n.* tent.

kaxmuheb'aal ch'uch'ib'leb'aal *n.* circus tent.

kaxon *n.* crate. *From:* from Spanish 'cajón'.

kaxpatz xul *n.* penguin.
kaxpo'ot *n.* blouse.

kaxq'ooq' *n.* watermelon. *Var:* kaqiq'ooq'.
kaxsaq eknil *n.* flamingo.
kaxsaqenk *n.* electric light.

kaxsoq' *n.* backpack.
kaxsu *n.* thermos.
kaxsuk *n.* incubator.
kaxt *n.* seal, stamp. *Var:* kaaxt.
kaxtok' *n.* match.

kaxtzukxul *n.* stuffed animal, plush toy.
kaxtzuychampa *n.* plastic bag.
kaxukutinb'il *n.* grid.

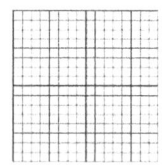

kaxukuutinb'ilhu *n.* graph paper.
kaxuk'a' *n.* soft drink.

kaxwakax *n.* buffalo, bison.
kaxwaal *n.* fan.

kaxxaml *n.* stove.

kaxxul *n.* beaver.

kaxxuxb' *n.* horn, trumpet.

kab' alal *n.* stepson.

kab'l *n.* house. *Var:* kab'.

ka' e *n.* molar.

ka' ralal *n.* stepdaughter.

ka'ta *adv.* twice, two times.

ka'yank *v.* to look, observe.

ka'b'ayaq *adj.* some.

kaajer *n.* four days ago.
Var: ko'ejer.

kaalt *n.* soup, broth. *From:* caldo
'soup or broth' (Spanish) (1).

kaan ru *adj.* mad.

kaan ru ixq *n.* prostitute.

kaanilb'an *n.* drug, narcotic.

kaans *n.* goose. *From:* ganso
(Spanish) (1).

kaaq *n.* storm, thunder.

kaax *n.* drawers. *From:* Spanish
'cajas'.

kaax *n.* trunk, box. *From:*
Spanish 'caja'.

kaaxtinb'il hu *n.* bond paper.

kaaxtink *v.* to seal, stamp.

kaaxukuut *adj.* square.

kaaxukuut *n.* square.

kaaxukuut *n.* painting.

kaaxukuutleb' *n.* square.

kaayehiil *n.* tetrasyllable.

ke *n.* cold.

ke *n.* ice.

ke *adj.* cold, chilly.

ke'b'il pix *n.* tomato sauce.

ke'b'il tib' *n.* ground meat.

ke'ek *v.* to grind.

ke'leb'aal *n.* windmill.

ke'leb'aal tib' *n.* meat grinder.

ke'ok *v.* to grind.

keb'il pix *n.* ketchup.

kehil chahim *n.* neutron star.

kehil ha' *n.* cold water.

kehilch'och' *n.* cold climate.

keho'k *v.* to freeze.

keho'ktib'elej *n.* hypothermia.

kehob'resib'aal *n.* freezer.

kehob'resilb'aal *n.* refrigerator, fridge.

Kej *sur. From:* kej ('deer'). (B1).

kej *n.* deer.

kelam *n.* longitude.

keleb'aal *n.* mill (grain).

kelkookil kaaxukuut *adj.* rectangular.

kelkookil soq' *n.* net.

kelkookil tem *n.* bench.

kelkookil tzuul *n.* hills, range, mountain range, mountain ridge.

kelkookilkaaxukuut *n.* rectangle.

kelk'arch'iich' *n.* saw. *Var:* k'arch'iich'.

kelo *phr.* pull.

kelonb'il *adj.* absorbed.

kelonk *v.* to absorb.

kelonk *v.* to pull. *From:* *kehl 'to pull' (Ch'olan) (2).

kem *n.* cloth.

kemleb' *n.* loom.

kemok *v.* to weave, braid, plait, knit.

kenq' *n.* kidney.

kenq' *n.* bean.

keresink *v.* to chill.

keresiil iq' *n.* air conditioner.

ketok *n.* victory.

ketok *v.* to beat, hit, strike.

ketomq *n.* livestock, farm animals. *Var:* ketomj.

ketomq *n.* fowl.

keehil siraal *n.* glacial zone.

keekehil siraalch'och' *n.* temperate zone.

146

keeleb'aal *n.* refrigerator, fridge.

keelsoq' *n.* net.

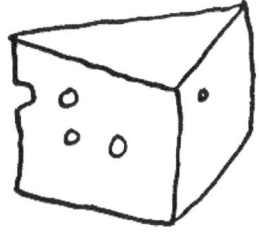

kees *n.* cheese. *From:* queso 'the cheese' (Spanish) (1).

ki' *adj.* sweet.

ki'b'ach *n.* ice cream.

ki'il ik *n.* chili pepper.

ki'il q'een *n.* fruit.

ki'il saqb'ach saa'us *n.* ice cream.

ki'ilsaqb'ach *n.* ice cream.

ki'tuux *n.* cotton candy.

kich'kich'ink *v.* to scrub.

kik' *n.* blood.

kik' ru *adj.* bloody.

kik' tz'iib' *n.* pen.

kik'che' *n.* rubber, latex.

kik'el *n.* blood.

kik'elej *n.* blood.

kik'sa' *n.* dysentery.

kik'xe' *n.* beet.

kilinb'il *adj.* fried.

kilinb'il kaxlan *n.* fried chicken.

kilinb'il paaps *n.* french fries.

kilinb'il tib' *n.* steak, beefsteak.

kira'sleb' *n.* watering can.

kis *n.* fart, flatulence.

kisik *v.* to fart, pass gas.

kitaar *n.* guitar. *From:* Spanish 'guitarra'.

kiib' kutan chi rix *n.* two days later.

kiib' oq'ob' xkab' xchuy *n.* one million.

kiib' oxib' *pron.* a few.

kiib'ank *v.* to split.

kiib'ank ch'ool *n.* doubt.

kiib'ch'oolink *v.* to regret, be sorry.

kiil *n.* kilo. *From:* from Spanish 'kilo'.

klaawx *n.* nail. *Var:* **kalawx**. *From:* clavos 'the nails' (Spanish) (1).

ko *n.* cheek. *From:* *ko:h (the cheek) (Western Mayan) (2).

ko' *n.* daughter. *From:* ko' 'grandmother; sister of the mother of the father' (Ch'olan) (2).

ko'ej *n.* in four days.

ko'xib' *adj.* brief.

kojl *n.* paddle.

kojlenk *v.* to row.

kojoj *n.* centipede.

kok *n.* tortoise, turtle.

kokakool *n.* Coca Cola, Coke.
   From: English 'Coca Cola'.

kokech *n.* guinea hen.

koko *adv.* immediately.

kokxul *n.* ladybug.

kok' ixim *n.* millet, sorghum.

kok' *adj.* small.

kok' aq' re ixq *n.* panties, underwear.

kok' aq' re winq *n.* underpants, underwear.

kok' che' *n.* plants.

kok' ch'iich' re wa'ak *n.* cutlery, silverware.

kok' kaxlan *n.* chick.

kok' kaxlan wa *n.* rolls.

kok' kuux *n.* pin.

kok' k'amk'ot *n.* small intestine.

kok' maak *n.* misdemeanor.

kok' neb'a' *n.* beggar.

kok' pim *n.* scrub, brush, bush.

kok' poch ob'en *n.* mini tamale.

kok' puub' *n.* pistol, revolver.

kok' q'an tz'ik *n.* canary.

kok' ru *adj.* narrow.

kok' ruhil hab' *n.* drizzle.

kok' samat *n.* cilantro.

kok' sut *n.* handkerchief.

kok' tenb'il ch'iich' *n.* jewelry.

kok' tumin *n.* coin.

kok' t'ikr *n.* gauze.

kok' tzelek xaab' *n.* ankle boot.

kok' utz' *n.* mosquito.

kok' xaab' *n.* sneakers.

kok' xul *n.* fairy, elf.

kok' xul *n.* insect.

kok' xul *n.* bird.

kok'ajil xsa' *n.* frequency.

kok'al *n.* children.

kok'alil *n.* childhood.

kok'anjel *n.* duty, chore.

kok'atq xsa' *adv phr.* often.

kok'awinq *n.* orchard, garden.

kok'cha'al *n.* organelle, inner cell components.

kok'k'aleb'aal *n.* hamlet, small village, collection of country houses.

kok'poli'n *n.* rolling pin.

kok'raq aatin *n.* phrase.

kok'sa' *adv.* often.

Kol *sur.*

kolb'a'ich'mulej *n.* meninges.

kolb'ach'ool *n.* snack, refreshment.

kolb'ajolom *n.* helmet.

kolb'eetank *v.* to preserve.

kolb'il che'k'aam *n.* ecological preserve.

kole'k *n.* protection.

koliplor *n.* cauliflower. *From:* Spanish 'coliflor'.

kolok *v.* to rescue, save.

kolok *n.* custody.

kolok *v.* to dodge, avoid.

kolok *v.* to defend, protect.

kolten *n.* bumper.

komon *n.* relative, partner, associate. *From:* común 'common' (Spanish) (1).

komon b'ichank *n.* choir.

komon sa' tzoleb'aal *n.* classmate.

komonil *n.* member.

komonil *n.* community.

komonilk'anjel *n.* cooperative.

komonilwank *n.* socialism.

komontenq' *n.* cooperation.

komontoj *n.* value-added tax, VAT.

konb'eent *n.* convent. *From:* Spanish 'convento'.

Konsep *nick.* Concepción.

kontineent *n.* mainland. *From:* continente 'the mainland or continent' (Spanish) (1).

konxik' *n.* clay frying pan.

kopmokooch *n.* cape.

koq'ok *v.* to drop.

koral *n.* fence. *From:* corral 'the fence, the space in front of the house' (Spanish) (1).

koral ch'iich' *n.* metal bars, cage.

koral ch'iich' *n.* bar (metal).

koral wakax *n.* pasture. *From:* corral, vacas 'corral, cows' (Spanish) (1).

korb'aat *n.* tie. *From:* Spanish 'corbata'.

kormaach *n.* partridge.

kordel *n.* fishing line. *From:* cordel 'the string' (Spanish) (1).

kordeer *n.* lamb. *From:* cordero 'the lamb' (Spanish) (1).

kosa *adj.* uncomfortable.

kosa xch'ool *adj.* disappointed, disillusioned.

kostiiy *n.* ribs. *From:* Spanish 'costillas'.

kotchapleb' *n.* button.

kotko *adj.* round.

kotko *n.* circle.

kotkookil b'atz'uul *n.* Ferris wheel.

koton is *n.* worm.

kototiil tzoqchahim *n.* spiral galaxy.

kotoxch'iich' *n.* nut (fastener), fastener.

kottzuj *n.* tambourine.

kotzko *adj.* cheap.

kotzko xtz'aq *n.* sale, bargain.

kotzok *v.* to loosen.

koxib' *adj.* a little.

koxtal *n.* sack. *From:* from Spanish 'costal'.

kook *n.* coconut. *From:* coco 'coconut' (Spanish) (1).

kootal *n.* silhouette.

kranaa *n.* pomegranate. *From:* Spanish 'granada'.

kranyon *n.* stallion. *Var:* **granyon**. *From:* grañón (possible) (Spanish) (1).

kristian *n.* person, people. *Var:* **kristiaan**; **kristyan**; **kristyaan**. *From:* Spanish 'cristiano'.

kristyaan *n.* Christian.

kristyaanil paab'aal *n.* Christian faith.

krus *n.* cross. *Var:* **kurus**. *From:* cruz 'the cross' (Spanish) (1).

Ku' *nick.* Domingo.

kub'enaq xtz'aq *n.* sale, bargain.

kub'enaq xtz'aq *adj.* inexpensive, cheap.

kub'eet *n.* bucket. *From:* Spanish 'cubeta'.

kub'iha' *n.* baptism.

kub'sa' *n.* womb, uterus.

kub'sib'aal ru'uj aq' *n.* tongue depresser.

kub'siil *n.* task, job, chore.

kuchaar *n.* spoon. *From:* Spanish 'cuchara'.

kuk *n.* squirrel.

kukb' *n.* water jar.

Kuk'ul *sur.* *From:* k'ul ('receive').
(B3).

kulantr *n.* coriander. *From:*
Spanish 'cilantro'.

kulb'ch'iich' *n.* steel.

kulb't'ojom *n.* steel nail.

kulku *adj.* silent, quiet.

kuluk *n.* worm, caterpillar.
From: *kuluk 'hairy worm'
(Yucatecan, Ch'olan, possible) (2).

kumb' *n.* spring, well (water).

kumb' *n.* barrel, cask.

kumb'i'uk'al *n.* bucket.

kun *n.* penis.

Kun *sur.*

kunutz' *n.* penis.

kuriit *n.* Band-Aid. *From:*
Spanish 'curita'.

kuruk *v.* to split, cut.

Kus *sur.*

kutan *adj.* clear.

kutan *n.* day, weather.
Var: kutank.

kutan *n.* time.

kutan chahim *n.* morning star.

kutaniru *adj.* transparent.

kutankil hab' *adj.* rainy.

kutanob'resink *v.* to develop
photos.

kutb'il b'an *n.* injection, shot.

kutleb' *n.* syringe.
Var: kutleb'b'an.

kutleb'mu *n.* overhead
projector, projector.

kutuk *v.* to inject.

kutuk *v.* to shoot, throw.

kutuk q'e'che' *n.* javelin throw.

kutuk suriil *n.* discus throw.

Kuwa' *sur.*

kux *n.* neck.

Kux *nick.* Marcos.

kuxb'ej *n.* cough, tuberculosis.

kuxil *n.* melody.

kuut *n.* bunch.

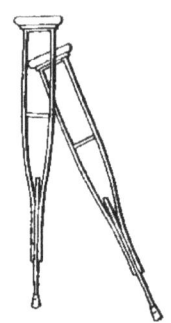

kuy *n.* pig.

kuyuk *v.* to tolerate.

kuyuk maak *v phr.* to forgive, acquit.

kuyuk sa' *n.* fast.

kuyuk sa' *v phr.* to fast.

kub'eek *v.* to go down.

kuuk *n.* wall.

kuukb'eleb'ch'iich' *n.* body work, metal carriage insert.

kuukch'iich' *n.* balcony.

kuukil tz'ak *n.* wall.

kuult *n.* church services. *From:* Spanish 'culto'.

kuutiil *n.* crutch.

kuutunk *v.* to lean.

kuux *n.* needle. *From:* Spanish 'aguja'.

kuux re karab'k *n.* fishhook.

kuuxink *v.* to sew.

kwaart *n.* room. *From:* cuarto 'the room' (Spanish) (1).

kweent *n.* bill. *From:* cuenta 'the bill or account' (Spanish) (1).

K' - k'

k'a *adj.* bitter.

k'a *n.* bile.

k'a *adj.* sour.

k'a' *interr.* what?

k'a' ru a'an *phr.* what is that?

k'a' ru a'in *phr.* what is this?

k'a' xja'lenkil *phr.* what a pity, what a shame.

k'a'aq re ru *n.* thing.

k'a'aq re ru li tenamit *n.* public services.

k'a'atq ru *n.* thing.

k'a'ej *n sd.* bile. **ink'a** « my bile ».

k'a'na *adj.* some.

k'a'ru *interr.* which?

k'a'ru *interr.* what?

k'a'ru aj e *interr.* for what?

k'a'ru aj ik'in *interr.* with what?

k'a'ru naraj naxye [ ] *phr.* what does [ ] mean?

k'a'ru xaaye *phr.* what did you say?

k'a'ru xk'ulman *phr.* what's the matter?, what happened?

k'a'ru yo *phr.* what is happening?

k'a'ru yookat *phr.* what are you doing? (singular).

k'a'ut *interr.* why?

k'a'ut naq ink'a' *phr.* why not?

k'a'ux *n.* mind.

k'a'uxl *n.* sorrow, grief.

k'a'uxl *n.* idea, thought.

k'a'uxlak *v.* to think, suspect.

k'a'uxlak *n.* anguish.

k'a'uxlal *n.* comment.

k'a'uxlal *n.* editorial.

k'a'uxlanb'il *n.* hypothesis.

k'a'uxlanb'il *adj.* hypothetical.

k'a'uxlanb'il k'atok *n.* arson.

k'a'uxlanb'ilal *n.* irrealism.

k'a'uxlanb'ilna'leb' *n.* imagination.

k'a'uxlil *n.* motto.

k'ab'a' *n.* name.

k'ab'a'atq *n.* noun.

k'ab'a'ej *n.* noun.

k'ab'a'ej *n sd.* name. **ink'ab'a'** « my name ». *From:* k'aab'a' 'name' (Yucatecan, Ch'olan, possible) (2).

k'ab'a'ej k'a'aqru *n.* common noun.

k'ab'a'ink *v.* to call (a name), name.

k'ab'a'na'jej *n.* toponym, place name.

k'achiik *v.* to crawl.

k'achleb' *n.* stapler.

k'achleb'aal sa' po *n.* lunar module, lunar capsule.

k'ahamch'iich' *n.* wire. *Var:* k'aamch'iich'; k'aham ch'iich'.

k'ahil ch'oolej *n.* pessimism.

k'aj *n.* flour.

k'aj atz'am b'an *n.* bath salts, effervescent salts.

k'aj nawcha'al *n.* particle physics.

k'aj sut *n.* gauze.

k'aj t'ikr *n.* gauze.

k'aj'aatin *n.* particle.

k'aj'esil *n.* telegram.

k'ajchahim *n.* meteor.

k'ajche' *n.* sawdust.

k'ajil kaxlanwa *n.* flour.

k'ajkab' *n.* sugar.

k'ajk'amonkmetzew *n.* trophy.

k'ajk'amontzolok *n.* title.

k'ajk'amunk *v.* to reward.

k'ajk'amunkil *n.* reward, recompense.

k'ajo' sununkil *adj.* fragrant.

k'ajob' *n.* dew.

k'ajol *n.* child.

k'ajolb'ej *n.* son (of god).

k'ajolink *v.* to beget.

k'ajpek *n.* gravel.

k'ajtesink *v.* to punish.

k'ajtz'iib' *n.* particle.

k'ajxul *n.* insect, bug.

k'ajyaab'aatin *n.* morpheme.

k'ak'naab' *n.* spring, well (water). *From:* k'ahk'-naab' 'the sea' (Yucatecan, Ch'olan, possible) (2).

k'al *n.* field, cornfield. *From:* k'al 'cornfield' (Tzeltal) (4).

k'aleb'aal *n.* countryside, field.

k'aleb'aal poy ch'iich' *n.* Jeep.

k'alomal *n.* goods.

k'amb'il esilhu *n.* parcel.

k'amb'olay *n.* oncilla, tiger cat.

k'amch'oolanink *n.* responsibility.

k'amk'otej *n.* intestines, guts.

k'amleb'aal *n.* briefcase.

k'amok *v.* to bring.

k'amok b'e *v phr.* to lead.

k'amok chaq *v.* to bring.

k'amolb'e *n.* administration, board of directors.

k'amom *n.* packet.

k'ams *n.* termites. *From:* *k'amas 'termite' (Yucatecan, Ch'olan, possible) (2).

k'anasink rix *v phr.* to boast.

k'anha' *n.* swamp.

k'anjel *n.* homework.

k'anjel *n.* work, profession, job.

k'anjelank *v.* to cultivate.

k'anjeleb'aal ruuch e *n.* dental instrument.

k'anjelob'aal *n.* tool, instrument. *Var:* k'anjeleb'aal.

k'anti' *n.* snake. *From:* *k'anti' 'yellow bearded snake' (Ch'olan) (4).

K'anti' *sur.* *From:* k'anti' ('snake'). (B1).

k'anti' kar *n.* eel.

k'anti' ra xmay re *n.* viper.

k'anti'ch'iich' *n.* train.
k'apok chi e *v phr.* to bite.

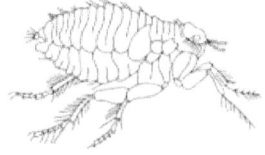

k'aq *n.* flea.
k'arhu *n.* sandpaper.
k'as *n.* account.
k'as *n.* debt.
k'as *n.* goal.
K'as *sur.*
k'asal *n.* minute.
k'asib'k *n.* loan.
k'asok *v.* to owe.
k'atal *n.* burn.
k'atb'il-eetalil *adj.* scanned.
k'atink *v.* to burn.
k'atk *v.* to burn.
k'atk'al *n.* scrub, brush.
k'atleb'aal pom *n.* incense burner.

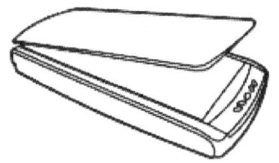

k'atleb'-eetalil *n.* scanner.
k'atok *v.* to burn.
k'atok oq *v phr.* to commit adultery.
k'atok-eetalil *v.* to scan.
k'atolch'iich' *n.* catalytic converter.
k'atom *n.* burn.
k'atom saq'e *n.* sunburn.
k'atq *n.* side.
k'atq jolom *n.* temples.
k'atzleb' *n.* pliers.
k'atzok *v.* to bite.
k'atz'leb'hu *n.* stapler.
　Var: **qatz'leb' hu.**
k'axkuk *n.* chinchilla.
k'axleb'hu *n.* stapler.
k'ay *n.* spice.
k'ayib'aal *n.* shop, store.
k'ayib'aal b'an *n.* pharmacy, drugstore, chemist.
k'ayib'aal b'an re ketomj *n.* veterinary store.
k'ayib'aal b'atz'uul *n.* toy store.
k'ayib'aal b'oleet *n.* ticket office.

k'ayib'aal kape *n.* cafe, cafeteria.

k'ayib'aal kaxlan wa *n.* bakery.

k'ayib'aal kok' tenb'il ch'iich' *n.* jewelry store.

k'ayib'aal k'anjelob'aal *n.* hardware store.

k'ayib'aal k'areru *n.* candy store.

k'ayib'aal saa'us *n.* fruit shop.

k'ayib'aal tasal hu *n.* bookstore.

k'ayib'aal tib' *n.* butcher shop.

k'ayib'aal uutz'u'uj *n.* florist, flower shop.

k'ayib'aal xaq ut xe' pim *n.* greengrocer.

k'ayib'aal xaab' *n.* shoe store.

k'ayib'aalhu *n.* bookstore.

k'ayib'aalhumb'ookilha' *n.* gas station.

k'ayihom rib' *n.* prostitute.

k'ayink *v.* to sell.

k'ayiil *n.* market.

k'aytesiil *n.* preschool.

k'aak'a *adj.* very bitter.

k'aak'aleb'aal *n.* control tower.

k'aak'aleb'aal ch'iich' *n.* police car.

k'aak'alenk *v.* to keep.

k'aal *n.* twenty-day period.

k'aalil *n.* base-twenty.

k'aam *n.* string, thread, vine.

k'aam *n.* fishing line.

k'aam keenq' *n.* green bean.

k'aamak *v.* to spin.

k'aamal pim *n.* creeper vine.

k'aamal sa' *n.* sash.
    Var: k'aamalsa'ej; k'aamasa'.

k'aamk'ot *n.* tripe.

k'aan *n.* latch, door-bolt.

k'e reetal li taab'aanu *phr.* watch out, look out.

k'ehal *n.* crowd.

k'ehob'a iq' *n.* air pump.

k'ehok *v.* to give, permit. *From:* k'eh 'to give (as a present or libation) (Tzeltal) (3).

k'ehok *v.* to serve.

k'ehok *v.* to put, place.

k'ehok aq' *v phr.* to get dressed.

k'ehok b'otonx *v phr.* to sew on buttons.

k'ehok chi ru saq'e *v phr.* to sun dry.

k'ehok chuq'ub' *v phr.* to hiccough, hiccup.

k'ehok eetal *v phr.* to take note of, notice, realize.

k'ehok eetal *v phr.* to observe.

k'ehok eetal *v phr.* to control.

k'ehok juch' *n.* endorsement.

k'ehok k'anjel *v phr.* to hire.

k'ehok k'as *v phr.* to win.

k'ehok limoox *v phr.* to give alms.

k'ehok numik *v phr.* to let through, cede way, give way.

k'ehok q'esnal *v phr.* to sharpen.

k'ehok sa' sahilal *v phr.* to release.

k'ehok sa' tzalam *v phr.* to imprison.

k'ehok sahil ch'ool *v phr.* to greet.

k'ehok tiq *n.* fever.

k'ehok xam *v phr.* to light.

k'ehok xiw *v phr.* to threaten.

k'ehok xiw *n.* threat.

k'ehok xtz'aqob' *v phr.* to add.

k'ehol numleb' *n.* traffic signal.

k'ehom uhej *n.* amusement.

k'eleb' iq' *n.* air pump.

k'erex *n.* zipper.

k'eelenk *v.* to preach.

k'i *n.* growth.

k'i *pron.* a lot.

K'i'ix *sur.*

k'iche' *lang.* K'iche (El Quiché, Huehuetenango, Quetzaltenango, Retalhuleu, Sololá, Suchitepéquez Totonicapán, San Marcos, Chimaltenango).

k'iche' *n.* mountain.

k'iche' *n.* woods, forest.

k'iche' aaq *n.* wild boar.

k'iche' ch'o *n.* dormouse.

k'iche' imul *n.* hare.

k'iche'b'aal *n.* jungle.

k'iche'b'aalik *v.* to travel through the mountains.

k'iche'b'aalik *v.* to travel through the forest.

k'ihal *adj.* many.

k'ihalatq *adj.* plural.
Var: k'ihalatqil.

k'iham *n.* abundance.

k'ila *pron.* a lot, many.

k'ila eetalb'irok *n.* polynomial.

k'ila poyanam *n.* crowd.

k'ila sek' *n.* crockery.

k'ila wakax *n.* herd of cattle.

k'ila'aatinob'aal *adj.* multilingual.

k'ila'u *n.* polygon.

k'ilab'atz'unk *n.* athleticism.

k'ilana'leb' *adj.* multicultural.

k'ilana'yu'am *adj.* pluricellular, multicellular.

k'ilapotz' puub' *n.* machine gun.

k'ilayehiil *n.* polysyllable.

k'ileb'aal *n.* toaster.

k'ileb'aal *n.* frying pan.

k'ileb'aal *n.* pan.

k'ilimb'il saa'us *n.* churro.

k'ilink *v.* to fry.

k'ilolb' *n.* frying pan.

k'ilpoyanimil *adj.* multiethnic, diverse.

K'im *sur. From:* k'im ('straw' or 'thatch'). (B1).

k'im *n.* hay, straw.

k'imal kab'l *n.* thatch.

k'imal kab'l *n.* straw hut.

k'imalch'iich' *n.* tin roofing sheet. *Var:* **k'imch'iich'**.

K'inich *sur.*

k'inich *n.* freckle.

k'ipitz'in *adj.* salty.

k'irnak *adj.* quiet.

k'irtesink *v.* to cure. *Var:* **k'irtasink**.

k'isis *n.* cypress.

k'isk'im *n.* lemon tea.

k'isk'is *n.* bad odor.

k'ix *n.* thorn, spine.

k'ix k'ahamch'iich' *n.* barbed wire.

k'ix uch *n.* porcupine.

k'ix'atz'um *n.* rose.

k'ixix *n.* worm.

k'ixkoot *n.* compass.

k'ixleb' *n.* screwdriver.

k'ixok *v.* to untie.

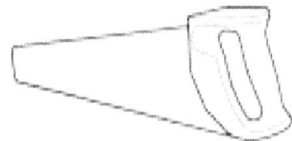

k'ixsetleb' *n.* saw.

k'iik *v.* to grow.

k'iila b'an *n.* medicine.

k'iilayehom b'aanuhom *n.* multiculturality, diversity.

k'o'al *n.* treasure, savings.

k'ob'b'il *n.* hole.

k'ob'leb' *n.* awl, drill.

k'ob'ok *v.* to bore.

k'ob'ok chi ch'iich' *v phr.* to stab.

k'ochkaq'l *n.* scaffolding.

k'ochlaak *v.* to land, alight. *Var:* k'ojlaak.

k'ochlaak sa' li po *n.* moon landing.

k'ochleb'aal *n.* airport.

k'ochleb'aal ch'iich' *n.* runway, landing strip.

k'ohaal *n.* piggy bank, money box.

k'oj *n.* mask.

k'ojarib' *n.* chair.

k'ojarib'aal *n.* throne.

k'ojkookilch'ool *adj.* satisfied.

k'ojk'o xch'ool *adj.* happy, content.

k'ojla xch'ool *adj.* pleased.

k'ojlajik *n.* beginning.

k'ojob' aach'ool *phr.* calm down.

k'okok *v.* to slice.

K'ol *sur.*

k'ol *adj.* male (of animals).

k'olok *v.* to shorten. *Var:* k'osok.

k'olwakax *n.* bull.

k'on tzoqchahim *n.* elliptical galaxy.

k'onk'o *adj.* crooked. *From:* k'on 'twisted' (Ch'olan) (2).

k'onk'okiltz'uq *n.* comma.

k'onk'ookil ch'iich' *n.* sickle, scythe.

k'onok *v.* to twist, bend. *From:* *k'ong 'to bend' (Ch'olan) (1).

k'onoljuch' *n.* curved line.

k'onon *n.* sunflower.

k'onop *n.* magnolia.

k'ontz'uq *n.* parentheses, brackets.

k'ontz'uq *n.* comma.

k'onx a' *n.* hip.

k'orechib'aal *n.* toaster.

k'orechkaxlanwa *n.* toast.

k'orechtul *n.* plantain chip.

k'orkik'xe' *n.* enchilada.

k'orleb' *n.* toaster.

k'osb'il *adj.* summarized.

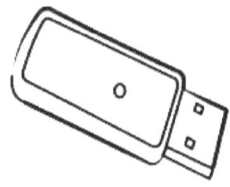

k'osleb' *n.* zip drive.

k'osok *v.* to reduce, shrink, trim.

k'osok *v.* to summarize.

k'ot uk' *n.* nit.

k'otak *v.* to defecate. *From:* k'ot 'to throw' (Q'anjob'alan) (4).

k'otleb'aal *n.* toilet, latrine.

k'ox *n.* prawns, shrimp.

k'oxib'k *v.* to shrimp, fish for shrimp.

k'oxlak *v.* to think.

k'oxlank *v.* to reflect.

K'oy *sur. From:* k'oy ('chewing gum'). (B1).

k'oy *n.* gum.

k'oylenk *v.* to chew.

k'ook' *n.* fatty meat.

k'ook' *n.* lard.

k'oopopo' *n.* toad.

k'oopopo' *n.* genitals (female).

k'ooq *adj.* slow.

K'u *sur. From:* k'u ('volcano'). (1).

k'u *n.* volcano.

k'ub' *n.* fireplace.

k'ub' *n.* gearshift.

k'ub' *n.* handle, lever.

k'ub'el *n.* fundamental.

k'ub'k'u *adj.* cooked.

k'ub'k'u *adj.* ready.

k'ub'lb'eeleb'aal na' yu'am *n.* endoplasmic reticulum.

k'uch *n.* hawk.

k'ucha'alk'anjel *n.* formula.

k'uhilpek *n.* gravel.

k'ukub'ank *v.* to crouch.

K'uk'ul *sur. From:* kuk ('squirrel'). (B3).

k'uk'umtz'iib' *n.* pen.

k'ul'esilal *n.* beeper.

k'ulb'a tz'aj *n.* apron.

k'ulb'ab'aq *n.* joint (bones).

k'ulb'aq'qax'ib' *n.* roundabout, traffic circle.

k'ulb'atz'iib' *n.* synaleph, linkage of syllables.

k'ulb'ayaab' *n.* articulation.

k'ulb'ilal *n.* consequence.

k'ulb'lem *n.* security door.

k'uleb'aal *n.* reception.

k'ulim *n.* bedbug. *Var:* k'ulin.

k'ultiq *n.* connection.

k'ulub' *n.* rights.

k'ulub'ank *v.* to accept, contemplate.

k'ulub'em *n.* rights.

k'uluk *v.* to get, receive.

k'uluk *n.* attack.

k'uluk *v.* to assist.

k'uluk ib' *v phr.* to meet.

k'ulul *n.* receiver.

k'ulunel *n.* receiver.

k'ulunk *v.* to come, arrive.

k'um *n.* gourd, squash, pumpkin.

k'unuch imul *n.* kangaroo.

k'unuk *v.* to bend.

k'urux *adj.* rough. *From:* *k'urux 'curly' (Ch'olan) (2).

k'utb'a numleb' *n.* traffic light.

k'utb'ahom *n.* theatrical production.

k'utb'aatal *n.* costume, disguise.

k'utb'esib'aal *n.* stage.

k'utb'esib'aal *n.* theater.

k'utb'esil *n.* proof.

k'utb'esink *v.* to perform, present.

k'utb'esink *v.* to demonstrate, motivate, signal.

k'utb'il *adj.* theatrical.

k'utleb' mu *n.* camera (television).

k'utleb'hu *n.* poster, sign.

k'utleb'ruuchich'och' *n.* geography.

k'utub' *n.* worm.

k'utuk *v.* to teach, show, indicate.

k'utuk b'e *v phr.* to lead.

k'utuk eetalil *v phr.* to make the sign of the cross.

k'utuk josq'il *n.* ferocity.

k'utul numeb'aal *n.* traffic light.

k'utunel ru'uj uq' *n.* index finger.

k'utunk *v.* to appear.

k'ux *n.* ear of corn.

k'uxch'iich' *n.* pliers, pincer.

k'uxuk *v.* to chew.

k'uxuk *n.* sandfly, midge, gnat.

k'uyum k'at *n.* electrical resistance.

k'uub'anb'il b'an *n.* oral rehydration solution, ORS.

k'uub'anb'il k'anjel *n.* program (TV).

k'uub'anb'il olb' *n.* butter.

k'uub'ank *n.* program (TV).

k'uub'ank *v.* to fix.

k'uub'ank *v.* to arm, set up, assemble.

k'uub'aak *adj.* cooked.

k'uub'aal sam *n.* pituitary gland.

k'uub'aal xeeb' *n.* sebaceous gland.

k'uub'ch'iich' *n.* machine.

k'uub'ch'iich'b'ojleb' *n.* sewing machine.

k'uub'ch'iich'kem *n.* loom.

k'uub'kutha' *n.* water pump.

k'uub'k'ay *adj.* industrial.

k'uub'leb'aal *n.* workshop.

k'uub'leb'aal *n.* kitchen, cookhouse.

k'uub'leb'chaq'rab' *n.* congress.

k'uub'poch'leb' *n.* mill (grain).

k'uub'suutaalkik' *n.* circulatory system.

k'uub'tz'iib'leb' *n.* typewriter.

k'uub'wank *n.* ecosystem.

k'uuk'um *n.* feather.

k'uul ru *adj.* sad, self-absorbed.

k'uul tumin *n.* bank account.

k'uulank *v.* to watch over.

k'uulank *v.* to save, memorize.

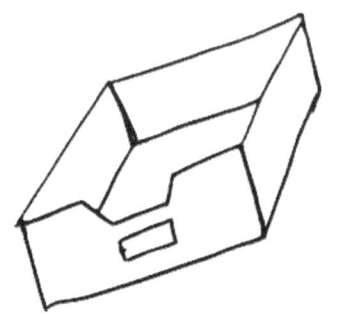

k'uulb'ahu *n.* in-box.

k'uulchob' *n.* drawer.

k'uuleb'aal *n.* warehouse.

k'uuleb'aaltiq *n.* thermos.

k'uuleb'aaltumin *n.* bank. *Var:* k'ulab'aal.

k'uuleb'jalam'uuch *n.* photo album.

k'uulhu *n.* file, archive.

k'uulmetz'ew *n.* accumulator, storage battery.

k'uut *n.* letterhead.

L - l

la *n.* nettle.

lab' *adj.* bad.

Laj *sur.*

Laj *nick.* Alejandro.

lajeb' ketzal *n.* ten quetzals.

lajeb' senta *n.* ten cents, a dime.

lajetqil *adj.* base-ten.

lajetqil *n.* tithing.

lajetqil *n.* unit of ten.

lajeeb' hab' *n.* decade.

lajeeb' oq'ob' *n.* four thousand.

lajeeb' syent *n.* one thousand. *From:* 10 ciento '10 hundred' (Spanish) (1).

lajeek'aal *n.* two hundred.

lajeek'aal rox oq'oob' *n.* one thousand. *Var:* lajeek'aal rox roq'ob'.

lajeek'aal xwaqxaq roq'ob' *n.* three thousand.

lajtesib'aalxul *n.* insecticide.

lakaam *n.* flag. *Var:* lakan.

lak'am *n.* shield. *Var:* lakam. *From:* lakam 'banner' (Yucatecan, Ch'olan, possible) (2).

lal *n.* semen, ejaculate.

lamb'a tu' *n.* bra, brassiere.

lampr *n.* lamp, lantern, torch. *From:* lámpara 'the lamp' (Spanish) (1).

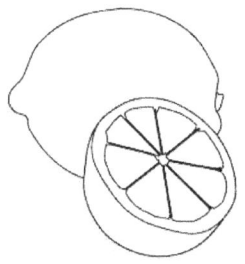

lamuunx *n.* lemon, citrus fruit. *Var:* lamuux; lamunx. *From:* limón 'the lemon' (Spanish) (1).

lan lan *adj.* humid.

lanb'aja'aj *n.* scarf.

lanb'alwa *n.* napkin. *Var:* lamb'awa.

lanleb' *n.* napkin.

lanok *v.* to wrap.

Lanquin *top.* [lamk'in] "where the sun sinks". *Etym:* lan = root of lanok (to cover or wrap); k'in = sun (Classic Mayan).

lantu' *n.* bra, brassiere.

lapok *v.* to kick.

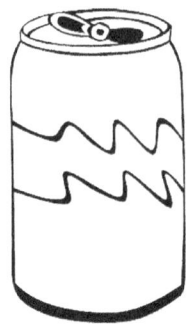

lapok chi oq *v phr.* to kick.

laq'ab'ank *v.* to join.

laq'ab'ank *n.* union.

laq'juch' *n.* parallel line.

laq'lo *adv.* together.

laq'lookil juch' *n.* parallel line.

Las *nick.* Lázaro.

latz-eetal *n.* sticker.

latzleb'ch'iich' *n.* electrode.

latzlut *n.* Siamese twins, conjoined twins.

latzok *v.* to seal.

latztz'in *n.* dextrine.

laa'in ajwi' *phr.* me too.

laan *n.* wool. *From:* lana 'wool' (Spanish) (1).

laas *n.* lasso. *From:* lazo 'the lasso' (Spanish) (1).

laasp re xtz'uumal e *n.* lipstick.

laat *n.* tin, can, canister. *From:* lata 'tin or can' (Spanish) (1).

laatz' *n.* strait.

laatz' *adj.* narrow.

laatz' ru *adj.* busy.

laatz'al *n.* occupation, commitment.

laaw *n.* key. *From:* llave 'the key' (Spanish) (1).

laa'at *pron.* you (singular). *Var:* at.

laa'ex *pron.* you (plural).

laa'in *pron.* I.

laa'o *pron.* we, us. *Var:* aa'o; ha'o.

le' *adv.* there.

leb'eb'nak *adj.* slow.

leb'lo *adj.* thick.

lechleb' *n.* lighter.

lechuuk *n.* lettuce. *From:* Spanish 'lechuga'.

lekleb' *n.* shovel. *Var:* lek.

lekleb' *n.* spoon, ladle. *Var:* lek.

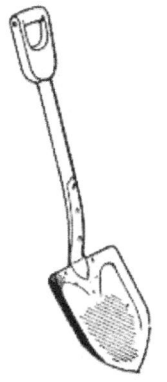

lemlotk *v.* to shine.

lekleb'ch'och' *n.* shovel.
lekok *v.* to draw water.
lem *n.* window pane.

lem *n.* mirror.
lem *n.* glass.

lem'u *n.* spectacles, glasses.
  Var: kaxlan lem; lem.
lemaal *n.* screen (TV).
lemaal'esil *n.* television or TV.
lemaal'ix *n.* rear-view mirror.
lemaank sa' muqmu *v phr.* to
  spy.

lemskaaq *n.* lightning bolt.
lemtz' *adj.* bright.
lemtz'b'on *n.* varnish.
lemtz'b'onik *v.* to varnish.
lemtz'ch'iich' *n.* aluminum.
lemtz'juch'leb'aal *n.*
  fluorescent marker.
lemtz'pek *n.* diamond.
lemtz'ti'kr *n.* silk.
lemtz'un xan *n.* tile.
len *part.* [citation particle,
  plural]. *Note:* Used when
  referring to what someone has
  said. **Laa'in aj q'an'isul len.**
  « I'm an American, they
  say. »
Len *nick.* Elena.
lep ch'iich' *n.* hood.
leplepb'aal *n.* pedal.

165

lepok *v.* to cover.

lepon *n.* shirt (woman's).

lep-punit *n.* visor.

let'ok *v.* to carve.

letzb'il b'an *n.* patch.

letzelhu *n.* sticker.

letzleb' *n.* glue, tape.
   Var: latz'leb'.

letzok *v.* to glue, tape.

letzool *n.* backpack.

Lex *nick.* Andrés.

leech *n.* milk. *From:* leche 'milk' (Spanish) (1).

leeleb'ak *v.* to dribble.

li *art.* the (singular).

li hab' chalk re *n.* next year.

li po a'in *n.* this month.

li po ak xnume' *n.* last month.

li po chalk re *n.* next month.

li xamaan a'in *n.* this week.

liklik *n.* hawk.

lil *adj.* used.

liq'lo *adj.* crooked.

liq'ok *v.* to bend.

liseens *n.* driver's license.
   From: licencia 'driver's license' (Spanish) (1).

lit'b'e *n.* brakes.

lit'leb'aal *n.* barrier.

lit'ob'l uuch e *n.* braces.

liib'r *n.* book. *From:* libro 'the book' (Spanish) (1).

Liik *nick.* Federico.

Liin *nick.* Marcelina.

Liin *nick.* Marcelino.

liitr *n.* liter. *From:* Spanish 'litro'.

liiwr *n.* pound. *From:* Spanish 'libra'.

Lo *nick.* Pablo.

lo'y *n.* friend. *Var:* looy.

lo'yil *n.* friendship.

lochleb' xaml *n.* match.

lochok *v.* to light. *Var:* lechok.

lochte'b'aal *n.* scaffolding.

lochte'ek *v.* to climb.

lokoch *n.* hook.

lokoch *n.* peg.

lokok *v.* to bend.

loktor *n.* physician, doctor.
   From: doctor 'physician or doctor' (Spanish) (1).

lolob' *adj.* vulgar.

lolob' aatin *n.* bad words.

lolom re *adj.* toothless.

loqlotk *v.* to boil.

loq' jun ut yal siib'il li xkab' *phr.* buy one get one free.

loq'al *n.* worthy, dignitary.

loq'al *adj.* valuable.

loq'al wankilal *n.* identity.

loq'alil *n.* worthiness, dignity.

loq'alil *n.* values.

loq'alil na'leb' *n.* cultural values.

loq'alil sutam *n.* ecological values.

loq'altenamit *adj.* civic.

loq'b'ilch'och' *n.* farm, plantation.

loq'-ilok *n.* identity.

loq'leb' *n.* money.

loq'leb'aal *n.* shop, store.

loq'leb'aal b'an *n.* pharmacy, drugstore.

loq'ok *v.* to buy, purchase.

loq'om *n.* purchase.

loq'onink *n.* adoration.

loq'onink *v.* to worship.

loq'oniik *v.* to take communion.

loq'tasalhu *n.* bible.

lotz re *v phr.* to stutter, stammer.

loob' *n.* wolf. *From:* lobo 'the wolf' (Spanish) (1).

look *adj.* mad. *From:* loco 'crazy' (Spanish) (1).

Lool *nick.* Lola.

loon *n.* canvas. *From:* Spanish 'lona'.

loonil wex *n.* jeans, blue jeans.

loor *n.* parrot. *From:* loro 'the parrot' (Spanish) (1).

loot' *n.* corner.

Lu' *nick.* Pedro.

lub'ik *n.* vertigo, dizziness.

lub'k *n.* fainting spell.

lub'k *v.* to tire, get tired.

lub'k chi ru saq'e *n.* sunstroke.

lub'k ch'oolej *n.* depression.

lub'lu *adj.* weak, tired. *Var:* lub'lub'. *From:* lub' 'tired' (Ch'olan) (4).

lub'luukin *phr.* I'm exhausted.

luhasib'aal *n.* heater.

lujuch *adj.* long.

lukleb' *n.* pegboard.

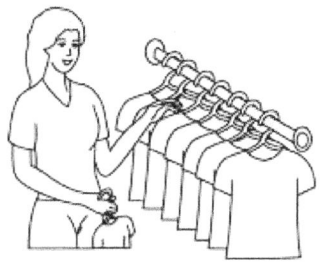

lukleb'aal *n.* clothes rack.

lukub'ank *v.* to hang.

lukum *n.* worm, earthworm.

lukub'al *n.* peg.

luk'luk' che' *n.* rattle.

luqaak *n.* polio.

Lus *nick.* Luz.

lut *n.* twins. *From:* *lut 'the twins' (Yucatecan, Ch'olan, possible) (2).

lut-al iyaj *n.* dicotyledonous seed.

luttz'uq *n.* colon.

luttz'uqyaab' *n.* dieresis.

luub' *adj.* wet.

luulu *adj.* mild, cool, lukewarm.

luuns *n.* Monday. *From:* lunes 'Monday' (Spanish) (1).

M - m

ma *part.* [negation particle]. **Makach'in naktinra.** « I love you a lot ('not a little'). »

ma *part.* [interrogative particle]. **Ma yaal a'an?** « Is that true? »

ma ak nakenaw eeru *phr.* do you know each other?

ma chan naxye *adv phr.* not even.

ma jun wa *adv phr.* never.

ma nakat-aatinak sa' inkles *phr.* do you speak English?

ma nakat-aatinak sa' q'eqchi' *phr.* do you speak Q'eqchi'?

ma ra xk'ul *phr.* is anything wrong?

ma relik chi yaal *phr.* are you sure?

ma sa laach'ool *phr.* how are you?

ma tawaj uk'ak *phr.* would you like a drink?

ma us wankat *phr.* are you OK?

ma wan b'ayaq aahoonal *phr.* have you got a minute?

ma yaal *phr.* really?

ma'laq *adv.* a while ago.

mach *n.* beard.

machb'onleb' *n.* brush.

majel *adj.* scarce.

makach'in *adj.* extensive.

makaan *n.* sword. *From:* macana 'the club' (Spanish) (1).

Makin *sur.*

mak'aam b'oqleb' *n.* cordless phone.

malaj *conj.* or.

malaj ut *conj.* or. *Var:* maraj ut.

malka'an *n.* widow. *Var:* xmalka'an.

mam *n.* rectum.

mam *n.* great grandchild.

mam *lang.* Mam (Huehuetenango, Quetzaltenango, San Marcos, Retalhuleu).

mama' *adj.* old.

mama' *n.* elder (male).

mama' *n.* grandfather.

mama' ayin *n.* crocodile. *Var:* ahin.

mama' kar *n.* shark.

mama' kaax *n.* steamer trunk.

mama' max *n.* gorilla.

mama' pimil t'ikr *n.* coat.

mama' rochochil aq'ej *n.* department store.

mama' tenamit *n.* city.

mama' jukub' *n.* ship.

mams *n.* firefly, lightning bug. *Var:* mans.

manawb'il *adj.* unknown.

maniiy *n.* peanut. *Var:* maniik. *From:* mani 'the peanut' (Spanish) (1).

mank *n.* mango. *Var:* maank. *From:* Spanish 'mango'.

mansaan *n.* apple tree.

mansaan *n.* apple. *From:* manzana 'apple' (Spanish) (1).

mansek' *n.* saucepan.

manteek *n.* grease, fat, butter. *From:* manteca 'lard' (Spanish) (1).

mandariin *n.* tangerine. *From:* Spanish 'mandarina'.

maqab' *n.* chest, torso, thorax.

maqs *n.* pumice.

Maqs *sur. From:* maqs ('pumice'). (B1).

maq'ok *n.* mugging.

maq'ok sa' b'alaq' *n.* swindle.

Mar *nick.* María.

marilb'ej *adj.* last.

markariit *n.* daisy. *From:* Spanish 'margarita'.

masleb' *n.* eraser.

masleb'ha' *n.* windshield wiper.

masleb'ix *n.* towel.

masleb'tz'ak *n.* mop.

Mat *nick.* Matilde.

matchoqin *phr.* shut up! (singular).

matk' *n.* dream.

matk'a'uxlak *phr.* think nothing of it, don't mention it, don't worry about it.

matk'ek *v.* to dream.

matq'ab' *n.* ring. *From:* matk'ab' 'ring' (Ch'olan) (4).

matz' *n.* mush, porridge.

max *n.* moth, weevil.

max *n.* monkey.

Max *nick.* Tomás.

Max *sur. From:* max ('monkey') (Span 'mico'). (B1).

maxel hal *n.* weevil.

maxelyu'am *n.* AIDS.

Maxena *sur.*

May *sur. From:* may ('tobacco' or 'poison'). (B1).

may *n.* cigarette, cigar.

may *n.* tobacco.

may *n.* poison.

mayab' *adj.* Maya. *Note:* Perhaps from original Mayan name for the Yucatan (ma'ya'ab) meaning "few, not many", or "we have none" referring to its sparse population or alternatively its lack of gold (as sought by the Spaniards).

mayalok *adj.* many.

mayej *n.* sacrifice.

mayejak *v.* to make an offering.

mayer *adv.* a long time ago.

mayer q'e *n.* Archean era, Archaeozoic era.

mayertz'iib' *n.* hieroglyphic, glyph.

mayertz'iib' maay *n.* Mayan glyph.

mayib'k *v.* to smoke.

mayonees *n.* mayonnaise, mayo. *From:* Spanish 'mayonesa'.

mayr *n.* nun. *From:* Spanish 'madre'.

mayta' *n.* bird guano.

maa'al'ixq *n.* sterile (woman).

maa'alwinq *n.* sterile (man).

maa'ani *pron.* no one. *Var:* **maani**.

maa'ani *adj.* absent.

maa'anihilk *n.* absence.

maa'us *adj.* bad.

maa'us *n.* demon.

maa'us aj winq *n agt.* the devil.

maab'ar *adv.* nowhere.

maachoyb'ach'uut *adj.* infinite.

maajaruj *adv.* never.

maajewank *n.* humiliation.

maaji' *adv.* not yet.

maajoq'e *adv.* never.

maajun *pron.* nothing.

maak *n.* machine. *From:* máquina 'the machine' (Spanish) (1).

maak *n.* guilt.

maak *n.* sin.

maak *n.* crime, fault.

maakonel *adj.* guilty.

maak'a' *phr.* not at all.

maak'a' *pron.* nothing.

maak'a' chi junwaakaj *adv phr.* nothing at all.

maak'a' chik *phr.* there is no more.

maak'a' ink'as chi rix *phr.* I don't mind.

maak'a' naraj wi' *adj.* insensitive.

maak'a' naraj wi' *adj.* indifferent, listless.

maak'a' naxch'e' *adj.* honest.

maak'a' naxye *phr.* you're welcome, it doesn't matter.

maak'a' nume'k *phr.* no entry.

maak'a' rusil *adj.* unuseful.

maak'a' xkuyum *adj.* ruthless, vicious.

maak'a' xk'as chi rix *adj.* irresponsible.

maak'a' xmaak *adj.* innocent, not guilty.

maak'a' xmetz'ew *adj.* weak.

maak'a' xna'leb' naxk'ut rib' *adj.* naive.

maak'a' xsa' *adj.* empty.

maak'a' xxutaan *adj.* rude, insolent.

maak'a' xyos *n.* atheism.

maak'a'il wara *n.* insomnia.

maak'e xloq'al *phr.* it's not worth it.

maal *n.* pancreas.

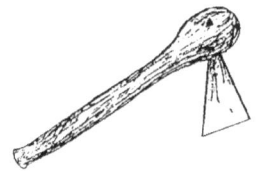

maal *n.* axe.

maal *n.* battle-axe.

maalajkch'uut *n.* infinite set.

maalay *pron.* nothing.

maare *adv.* probably.

maare *adv.* maybe, perhaps. *Var:* mare.

maare *adv.* suddenly.

maare jo'kan *phr.* I hope so.

maars *n.* March. *From:* Spanish 'marzo'.

maarts *n.* Tuesday. *From:* martes 'Tuesday' (Spanish) (1).

maaruuchich'och' *n.* extraterrestrial.

maasahil wank *n.* unhappiness.

maasumal'ajl *n.* odd numbers.

maatan *n.* gift, prize, surprise.

maatanej *n.* trophy.

maatzab' u *n.* eyebrow.

maausilanb'il *adj.* happy.

maawa' *phr.* it is not.

maawa' re ruchich'och' *n.* extraterrestrial.

maawa' rik'in *prep.* without.

maay *n.* May. *From:* Spanish 'mayo'.

maay *adj.* Maya.

maayil *adj.* Mayan, Maya.

maayil na'leb' *n.* Maya culture, Maya tradition.

Mek *nick.* Miguel.

mek'onk *v.* to embrace, hug.
From: mek' 'to embrace'
(Yucatecan, Ch'olan, possible) (1).

mel *n.* grandparents.

mel *n.* grandfather, great grandfather.

melon *n.* melon. *From:* Spanish 'melón'.

mem *adj.* mute.

mem'riiy *n.* quince. *From:* Spanish 'membrillo'.

mertyolaat *n.* iodine. *From:* Spanish 'mertiolate'.

Mes *sur. From:* mes ('wipe' or 'scrub'). (B1).

mes *n.* cat. *Var:* mis. *From:* mis 'call made to a cat' (Spanish) (3).

mesb'a lem *n.* windshield.

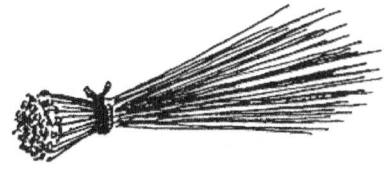

mesche' *n.* brush, handbroom.

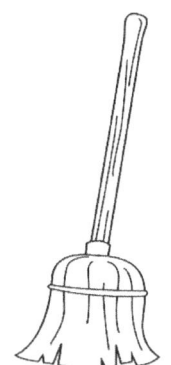

mesleb' *n.* broom.

mesleb' xaab' *n.* shoe brush.

mesok *v.* to shine, polish, wipe.

mesol lem *n.* squeejee, wiper.

mesunk *v.* to sweep.

met *adj.* dwarf.

met' tokan *n.* strawberry.

metz'ew *n.* energy.

metz'ew *n.* strength, force.

metz'ew ich'mulej elkik' *n.* systolic blood pressure.

metz'ew ich'mulej okik' *n.* diastolic blood pressure.

metz'ew kaxlan xaml *n.* electric energy.

metz'ewanb'il *adj.* catalytic.

metz'ewib'aalb'oqleb' *n.* charger, phone charger.

metz'ewil *n.* speed, velocity.

metz'ewil iq' *n.* atmospheric pressure.

metz'ewil'eeb' *n.* escalator.

metz'ewilpuch'leb' *n.* washing machine.

metz'ewilxaml *n.* electricity, electric current.

metz'kelob' *n.* magnetism.

meej *n.* Mexico.

meet *n.* glass, bottle, container. *From:* limeta 'bottle of wine' (Spanish) (1).

meetilsu *n.* liter.

meex *n.* table. *From:* mesa 'the table' (Spanish) (1).

meex re k'anjelak *n.* workbench.

meexil tz'iib' *n.* student desk.

meexwajb' *n.* piano.

meexwajb' *n.* speaker.

mi' *n.* vagina. *From:* mi' 'mother' (Q'anjob'alan) (2).

mich'ok *v.* to skin.

mich'mo *adj.* naked.

mich'ok ix *v phr.* to peel.

miercools *n.* Wednesday. *Var:* **myeers**. *From:* miércoles 'Wednesday' (Spanish) (1).

mikro oont *n.* microwave oven.

milmich' hu *n.* streamer.

min'isink *v.* to loot, sack, plunder.

minaach'ich'i *phr.* leave me alone.

minb'ilna'leb' *n.* ideological imposition.

minok *v.* to push.

minyamtesink *v.* to loot, sack, plunder.

misach sa' laach'ool *phr.* don't forget.

misik *n.* antenna (insect).

misik'ch'iich' *n.* antenna.

mitz *adj.* small.

mitzt'orotz *n.* marbles.

mitz' b'olotz *n.* marbles.

mitz'cha'al *adj.* microscopic.

mitz'jalam'u *n.* thumbnail photo.

mitz'jisb'ilis *n.* millimeter.

mitz'k'amk'ot *n.* ribosome.

mitz'k'icha'al *n.* microorganism.

mitz'meetil b'an *n.* vial.

mixk *adv.* a while ago.

mixpirik *n.* the day before a party.

miikisink *v.* to push.

miin *n.* centimeter.

miix *n.* mass. *From:* Spanish 'misa'.

Mo' *sur. From:* mo' ('macaw') (Span 'guacamaya'). (B1).

mo' *n.* macaw.

mo' *n.* rust, oxidation.

mo'onk *v.* to rust, oxidize.

mochiil *n.* backpack. *From:* Spanish 'mochila'.

mochleb' ismal *n.* hairnet.

mochmo *adj.* wrinkled.

mochok *v.* to fold.

mochox *adj.* wrinkled.

moch' *n.* fist.

moch'kar *n.* octopus.

moko a'an ta *adv phr.* nothing of the kind.

moko chaab'il ta *adv phr.* badly, poorly.

moko ch'a'aj ta *adj.* easy.

moko naxsume ta jo'yaal *adj.* unreliable.

moko us ta *phr.* out of order.

moko wan ta xloq'al *phr.* it doesn't matter, it's not important.

moko yaal ta *adj.* wrong, untrue.

moko yaal ta laak'a'uxl *phr.* you're wrong.

moko [ ] ta *adv phr.* not, no. *Note:* That which is inserted between 'moko' and 'ta' is negated. **A' kok' kab' a'an moko sa ta.** « That candy does not taste good. »

mokooch *n.* tarp, dropcloth.

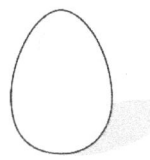

mol *n.* egg. *Var:* molb'.

molam *n.* association.

molb' *n.* testicles.

molob'ank *n.* addition.

molob'ank *v.* to gather, collect.

molob'aal aatin *n.* dictionary, lexicon.

molok *v.* to choose.

molok *v.* to gather.

molool *n.* sum.

mopan *lang.* Mopan (El Petén).

moqoj *n.* fathom.

moqon *adv.* after, afterwards, later.

moqon *n.* future.

moqonil'uxk *n.* future tense.

moqx *n.* popcorn. *Var:* **moqs**.

moq'mo *adj.* naked.

moronk *n.* blood sausage.

motor *n.* motor. *From:* motor 'the motor' (Spanish) (1).

motzo' *n.* worm. *From:* motzo' 'worm' (Ch'olan) (2).

motzo'ch'iich' *n.* trailer truck, semi truck, eighteen-wheeler, box truck.

moyileb' *n.* sunglasses.

moyk ru li saq'e *n.* eclipse.

moymo *adj.* dark.

moymo ru *adj.* dizzy.

moymo ru xtib'el *adj.* sullen.

moyok xutaan *v phr.* to hide one's shame.

moor *n.* drum.

moos *n.* servant, slave. *From:* mozo 'lad, manservant' (Spanish) (1).

moosil *n.* servitude, slavery. *From:* mozo 'lad, manservant' (Spanish) (1).

moot *n.* motorcycle. *From:* moto 'motorcycle' (Spanish) (1).

mu *n.* spirit.

mu *n.* sunshade.

mu *n.* parasol.

mu *n.* shadow, shade.

mu' *n.* seedbed.

mu'us *adj.* foreign.

muchkej *n.* cramp.

much' jukub' *n.* launch.

much'uk *v.* to break.

much'ul *adj.* broken.

muhej *n.* shadow (of animate being).

muhel *n.* spirit.

muhelil *n.* silhouette.

muheel *n.* umbrella.

muhil'esil *n.* fax.

muhilb'atijok *n.* virtual education.

muhilsik'leb' *n.* internet.

muhiltaql *n.* email.

muhul *n.* island.

mukuy *n.* pigeon, dove. *From:* *mukuy 'dove' (Yucatecan, Ch'olan , ?) (2).

mul *n.* garbage, trash.

mul *n.* litter.

mulel *n.* garbage, trash.

muluq'utchahim *n.* comet.

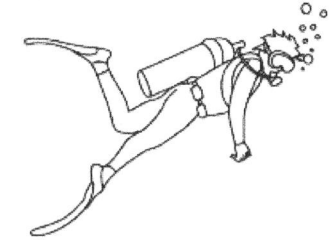

muqa'lik *v.* to dive, scuba dive. *Var:* **muqa'alik.**

muqb'aanunb'il *adv.* mysteriously.

muqb'il *adj.* cloudy, overcast.

muqlaak kutan *n.* eclipse.

muqlaak po *n.* lunar eclipse.

muqlaak saq'e *n.* solar eclipse.

muqleb'aal *n.* cemetery.

muqmukil aatin *n.* secret.

muqmukilna'leb' *n.* secret.

muqmuukil *adj.* mysterious.

muqmuukilal *n.* mystery.

muqpo *n.* lunar eclipse.

muqsaq'e *n.* solar eclipse.

muquk *v.* to bury, hide.

muquk poyanam *n.* kidnapping.

muqunk *v.* to sink, disappear.

murink *v.* to separate, segregate, break down, fragment. *Var:* xmurb'al.

musiq' *n.* respiration. *Var:* musiq'ak.

musiq'ab'aal *n.* respiratory system.

musiq'ak *v.* to breathe, respire. *From:* *mus iik' 'to breathe' (Yucatecan, Ch'olan, possible) (2).

musiq'ank *v.* to breathe. *From:* *mus iik' 'to breathe' (Yucatecan, Ch'olan, possible) (2).

musiq'ej *n.* spirit.

musmus *adj.* very fine.

musmus hab' *n.* mist.

musulman *n.* Muslim.

mut aq' *n.* shorts.

mutzuy *n.* centipede.

mutz' *adj.* blind.

mutz'mutz'ink *v.* to blink.

muxuk *n.* adultery.

muxuk *v.* to rape, violate.

muxuk *n.* rape, sexual assault, violation.

muxuk sumlajik *n.* adultery.

muy che' *n.* cedar.

muul *n.* mule. *From:* mula 'the mule' (Spanish) (1).

muult *n.* fine. *From:* multa 'the fine' (Spanish) (1).

N - n

na *part.* [equivocal particle]. *Note:* Used to express doubt or uncertainty about a preceding idea or notion. **Tinxik na sa' k'ayiil.** « Maybe I'll go to the market. »

na' uq'm *n.* thumb.

na'aj *n.* place.

na'aj b'onhu *n.* printer cartridge.

na'aj re muhenk *n.* garden shed.

na'aj re oyb'enink *n.* waiting room.

na'aj uutz'u'uj *n.* flower vase.

na'ajej *n.* location, place.

na'ajil *adj.* same.

na'ajink *v.* to live.

na'b'ej *n sd.* mother. **inna'** « my mother ».

na'chinb'ej *n.* godmother.

na'el *n.* product, result.

na'elk *n.* departures.

na'ilman xhuhil re najtil tenamit *n.* international check-in.

na'leb' *n.* advice.

na'leb' *n.* idea, intelligence, theme.

na'leb' xe'toon *n.* custom.

na'leb'ak *v.* to ponder, comprehend, understand.

na'leb'ank *v.* to reason.

na'leb'ank tz'iib' *v phr.* to edit, redact, write up.

na'leb'aal ch'iich' iq' *n.* space station.

na'leb'aal tasal hu *n.* encyclopedia.

na'lenk *n.* discovery.

na'link *v.* to recognize.

na'no ru *adj.* familiar.

na'ok *n.* to discover.

na'ok *v.* to know, be familiar with.

na'ol *n.* he who knows.

na'onel *n.* he who knows.

na'oxloq'in *adj.* respectful.

na'uuchik *v.* to dream.

na'wakax *n.* cow.

na'yu'am *n.* cells.

nab'anyoxin *adj.* thankful, grateful.

nache'ch'ot *adj.* extrovert.

nach' *adj.* near.

nach' rik'in *prep.* next to.

nach' xk'atq *adv phr.* near.

nach'a'ajko' *adj.* annoying.

nach'a'ajko' *adj.* upset.

nach'ilchahim *n.* Ursa Minor.

nach'o'k *v.* to approach.

nahulak chi wu [ ] *phr.* I like [ ].

naj xyanq *adv phr.* seldom.

najkutan *n.* afternoon.

najt *adj.* far.

najt kutan *adj.* late.

najt roq *adj.* long, tall.

najt xk'atq *adv phr.* far from.

najt xtenamit *n.* stranger.

najt xteram *adj.* tall, high.

najter *adv.* a long time ago.

najter *adj.* old, ancient.

najter na'leb' *n.* tradition.

najter q'e kutan *n.* former times, olden days.

najterilk'utb'esink *adj.* traditional.

najtil *n.* distance.

najtil pisk'ok *n.* long jump.

najtil poyanam *n.* stranger.

najtil t'uru' ak'ach *n.* ostrich.

najt-ileb' *n.* telescope.

najto'k *v.* to be late.

najunajin aatin *n.* conjunction.

nakatinjultika *phr.* I miss you.

nakayan *adj.* curious.

nakujkut *adj.* nosy.

nakuyuk *adj.* broad-minded.

nak'ab'a'iik *n.* subject.

nak'ulun *n.* arrivals.

nalemtz'un *adj.* shiny, golden.

namunta *adj.* arrogant, vain.

napaab'an *adj.* obedient.

naq *pron.* when, that.

naq ta ewuuq *adv phr.* at dusk.

naq ta saqewq *adv phr.* at dawn.

naq tk'e tuktu q'oqyin *adv phr.* at midnight.

naq tk'e waleb' *adv phr.* at noon.

naqk *v.* to begin.

naqk sa' ch'ool *v phr.* to remember.

naq' it *n.* testicles.

naq' kun *n.* testicles.

naraj *n.* manner.

narataw *adj.* ambitious.

nasach sa' xch'ool *adj.* forgetful.

nasach xch'ool *adj.* surprised, impressed.

nasaho inch'ool xnawb'al aawu *phr.* nice to meet you.

Nat *nick.* Natividad.

nataqlan *adj.* dominant.

nat'b'il uk'al *n.* pressure cooker.

nat'b'iltz'ap *n.* bottle cap.

nat'ich'mul *n.* blood pressure.

nat'leb' *n.* press, pressing machine.

nat'leb' *n.* latch, door-bolt.

nat'leb' okeb'aal *n.* lock, padlock.

nat'leb'hu *n.* paper clip.

nat'leb'ismal *n.* diadem, tiara, hairband.

nat'ok *v.* to press, tighten.

nat'yaab' *n.* glottal, glottalization.

natz'ilok chi us *adj.* meticulous.

naw'ajl *n.* mathematics, math.

naw'amaq'il *n.* social studies, sociology.

naw'amaq'ilchi' *n.* sociolinguistics.

naw'awk *n.* agriculture, agronomy.

naw'aatinob'aal *n.* linguistics.

naw'q'och *n.* kinesiology.

nawajlil *n.* numeracy.

nawal *n.* alter ego. **Laa'in wan we jun in nawal. A'an aj Pedro Amasoleil xk'ab'a'.** « I have an alter ego. His name is Peter Amasoleil. »

nawalil *n.* magic.

nawaaj *n.* razor. *From:* navaja 'knife' (Spanish) (1).

nawb'anok *n.* medicine.

nawb'ehil *n.* methodology.

nawcha'al *n.* physics.

nawcha'al'ixq *n.* gynecology.

nawchahim *n.* astronomy.

nawchaq'rab'ik *n.* legislation.

nawchi' *n.* linguistics.

nawch'oolej *n.* cardiology.

nawha'il *n.* hydrology.

nawhiik *n.* seismology.

nawil hu *n.* newspaper.

nawink *v.* to know.

nawkab'lank *n.* architecture.

nawkomonil *n.* sociology.

nawkomonyajel *n.* epidemiology.

nawk'ajyaab'aatin *n.* morphology.

nawk'anjel *n.* engineering.

nawk'anjelahom *n.* technology.

nawk'anjelil *n.* professionalism.

nawk'iche' *n.* botany.

nawk'iijikch'ool *n.* evolutionary psychology.

nawk'uhil *n.* volcanology.

nawk'utuk *n.* teaching.

nawk'uub'tzuul *n.* structural geology.

nawok chi yaal *n.* apprehension.

nawom *n.* knowledge.

nawom chi rix ajl *n.* math, mathematics.

nawom chi rix k'a re ru *n.* science.

nawom chi rix yu'am *n.* biology.

nawpoyanam *n.* anthropology.

nawpoyaatinob'aal *n.* ethnolinguistics.

nawq'ehil *n.* meteorology.

nawralab'aatinob'aal *n.* dialectology.

nawrub'elalink *v.* to diagnose.

nawso'solch'iich' *n.* aviation.

nawsutam *n.* science.

nawtijok *n.* pedagogy.

nawtuqch'ool *n.* psychology.

nawtuqch'oolil *adv.* psychologically.

nawtus'aatin *n.* syntax.

nawtus'aatin *n.* lexicography.

nawtzoltz'iib' *n.* literacy.

nawtz'iib'ak *n.* orthography.

nawxokok *n.* obstetrics.

nawxul *n.* zoology.

nawyajel *n.* pathology.

nawyaalal *n.* decipherment.

nawyaalalink *v.* to decipher.

nawyu'am *n.* biology.

nawyu'amilsutaal *n.* ecology.

naxik xch'ool *adj.* absent-minded.

naxiwak *adj.* terrified.

naxkuj rib' *adj.* cheeky.

naxk'e reeqaj naxk'ul *adj.* vindictive.

naxk'uula ra sa' xch'ool *adj.* spiteful.

naxtiw rib' li saq'e ut li po *n.* eclipse.

naxyoob' rib' *adj.* courageous.

nayeeman sa' li esilhu *n.* letter body.

nayl *n.* nylon. *From:* Spanish 'nylon'.

na' eechej *n.* aunt.

na'chin *n.* grandmother.

naab'al *adj.* abundant.

naab'al *pron.* much, a lot.

naab'al *pron.* enough.

naab'alil *n.* crowd.

naab'alwa b'antyox *phr.* thank you very much.

naaw *n.* turnip. *From:* Spanish 'nabo'.

naab'al honal *adj.* for a long time.

ne'b'aal *n.* entry platform.

neb'a *n.* patio.

neb'a ha' *n.* island.

neb'a' *n.* orphan.

neb'a' *n.* tramp, beggar.

neb'a' *adj.* poor.

neb'a'il *n.* poverty.

neb'a'irk *v.* to slowly go broke.

neb'a'o'k *v.* to go broke.

neb'aal *n.* yard, court, atrium.

neb'aal *n.* playground.

neb'aal *n.* field.

neb'aal kab'l *n.* front yard.

Nich *nick.* Dionisio.

nim *adj.* big.

nim chi ru *adv phr.* bigger than.

nim roq *adj.* long, tall.

nim ru *adj.* wide.

nim sa' xkux *adj.* hoarse.

nim xkelam *adj.* long.

nim xsa' *adj.* thick.

nim xteram *adj.* high, tall.

nim xteram *n.* height.

nim xtib'el *adj.* fat.

nima' *n.* river, stream.

nimajel *adj.* deductive.

nimal *n.* size, quantity.

nimal *n.* greatness.

nimaljuch' *n.* parentheses, brackets.

nimaljuch' *n.* parentheses.

nimalraqb'leb'aatin *n.* supreme court.

nimaltzoleb'aal *n.* university.

nimank *v.* to grow.

nimank ru *v phr.* to worsen.

nimank u *n.* praise.

nimb'e *n.* road.

nimk'uub'tzolok *n.* curriculum.

nimla b'e *n.* road.

nimla ch'aat *n.* double bed.

nimla ch'iich' *n.* sword.

nimla iiqob'aal ch'iich' *n.* box truck.

nimla kab'l *n.* building.

nimla kaqnab' *n.* lake.

nimla k'ayib'aal *n.* grocery store, supermarket.

nimla k'ayib'aal *n.* department store.

nimla k'ayib'aal tzakahemq *n.* restaurant.

nimla lek *n.* ladle.

nimla ochoch *n.* building.

nimla ramleb'aal t'ikr *n.* curtain.

nimla rokeb' palaw *n.* gulf.

nimla siinch *n.* belt. *From:* cincho 'belt' (Spanish) (1).

nimla tem *n.* easy chair.

nimla tenamit *n.* country, city.

nimla tijob'aal *n.* cathedral.

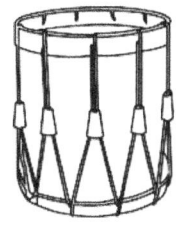

nimla tun *n.* drum, bass drum.

nimla t'ikr *n.* cloak, vestment.

nimla xna'ajkar *n.* fish tank.

nimlab'anleb'aal *n.* hospital.

nimlachahim *n.* planet.

nimlamaak *n.* offense.

nimlaraqalmetz'ew *n.* circuit breaker.

nimlawa'leb'aal *n.* restaurant.

nimnim *adj.* giant, tall.

nimob'eresink ib' *v phr.* to boast.

nimob'resink *v.* to amplify.

nimqi ixi'ij *n.* claw, talon.

nimqi kab'l *n.* buildings.

nimq'e *n.* party, fair. *Var:* ninq'e.

nimq'ehink *v.* to party.

nimroq *n.* length.

nimru'ajk'anjel *n.* professional.

ninb'anyoxi laa tenq' *phr.* thanks for your help.

ninnaw *phr.* I know.

ninqal *n.* size.

ninqank *v.* to grow.

ninqi che' *n.* forest.

ninqi seeb'alil *n.* macro competencies.

ninqi'ochoch *n.* building.

ninqilwank *n.* irresponsibility.

ninqilwankil *adv.* irresponsibly.

ninqiperhu *n.* poster.

ninqiwank *adj.* irresponsible.

ninqixox *n.* chickenpox, smallpox.

nispr *n.* medlar. *From:* Spanish 'nispero'.

nokal *n.* walnut tree. *From:* Spanish 'nogal'. *Var:* nohal.

noq' *n.* thread.

noq' *n.* cotton.

noq' re uuch e *n.* dental floss, floss.

nowyemr *n.* November. *Var:* **nob'yemb'r**. *From:* Spanish 'noviembre'.

nub'aal *n.* boundary, border, property line. *Var:* **nub'ajl**; **nub'aj**. *From:* nub' 'to join' (Ch'olan) (2).

nub'leb'aal *n.* plug, outlet.

nub'resink *v.* to rinse.

nub'un *adj.* cloudy.

nuchkawaay ch'iich' *n.* scooter.

nujab'resink *v.* to fill.

nujenakin *phr.* I'm full.

nujenaq *adj.* full.

num atz'am *adj.* very salty.

num'esil *n.* fax.

numay *n.* rickets.

numch'o *n.* cursor.

nume' sa' *n.* diarrhea.

nume'k *v.* to pass, cross.

nume'k'uluk *n.* passive voice.

nume'sa'xa'aw *n.* cholera.

nume'uxkb'il *n.* antipassive voice. *Note:* Antipassive voice refers to intransitive verb forms that have an active sense but no direct object.

numen laa'at xb'een wa *phr.* after you.

numenaqil'uxk *n.* past tense.

numilhu *n.* passport.

numjalam'uuch *n.* scanner.

numjip *adj.* stubborn.

numkawyaab' *adj.* supersonic.

numlab'al *n.* cruelty.

numleb' kaxlanxaml *n.* semiconductor.

numleb' yaab'ej *n.* Eustachian tube.

numleb'aal *n.* road, street, route, path, passage.

numleb'ha' *n.* canal.

numleb'yaab' xik *n.* inner ear.

numlentz' saqen *n.* meridian.

nums *n.* footprint.

nums'esilb'aal *n.* post office, telegrapher.

numsachk *adj.* absurd.

numsach'ool *n.* emotion.

numsaxch'ool *adj.* emotional.

numseeb' *n.* genius.

numseeb' xch'ool *n.* prodigy.

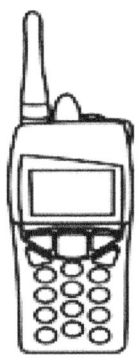

numsib'aal esil *n.* radio transmitter, walkie talkie.

numsib'aal k'aj' esil *n.* telegraph machine.

numsinb'il'eetalil *n.* X-ray.

numsinel *n.* conductor.

numsink *v.* to transmit.

numsink kutan *v phr.* to earn a living.

numsink-al *n.* miscarriage.

numsiilk'anjel *n.* radioactivity.

numtajenaq *adv.* too much.

numtaak *adj.* proud.

numt'ikt'ot-aam *n.* hypertension.

numxib'aal *n.* pool, swimming pool.

numxik *v.* to swim.

numxik *n.* swimming.
nuq'b'ilb'an *n.* tablet, pill.
nuq'uk *v.* to swallow. *From:* *nuq' 'throat' (Western Mayan) (4).
nuq'unk *v.* to sink.

nut'b'il yaab' *n.* fricative.
nut'leb'hu *n.* newsprint.
nuumel ula' *n.* client.
nwes *n.* nut. *From:* nuez 'the nut' (Spanish) (1).

O - o

o *n.* avocado.
o'k'aal ketzal *n.* one hundred quetzals.
o'k'aal xkab' roq'ob' *n.* five hundred.
o'laju xk'ak'aal senta *n.* twenty-five cents, a quarter.
o'lajuk'aal *n.* three hundred.

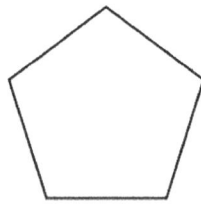

o'xukuut *n.* pentagon. *Var:* ho'xukuut; o'xuk.
ob'en *n.* tamale.
ob'iisp *n.* bishop. *From:* Spanish 'obispo'.
Och *sur.*
ochb'enb'il *adj.* accompanied.
ochb'enej *n.* accompanist.
ochb'eninb'il *adj.* together.

ochb'een *n.* companion. *Var:* ochb'en.
ochoch *n.* house.
ochoch pek *n.* cave.
ochochib'aal *n.* address.
ochochil *n.* habitation.
ochochnaal *n.* hotel.
ojb' *n.* flu, cough. *Var:* oj.
ojb'ak *v.* to cough.
ojob'an b'aanu usilal *phr.* cough please.
ok *v.* to begin, enter.
ok chi ha' *v phr.* to drown.
ok eechej *adj.* typical.
ok k'a'uxl *n.* distress.
ok we chi elk *phr.* I'm going out.
okan *phr.* come in (singular).
okanqex *phr.* come in (plural).
okeb'aal b'olotz *n.* goalposts. *Var:* okleb'aal b'olotz.
okenk *n.* opportunity.
okesink *v.* to drip.

okeb'aal *n.* door, gate, entry, entrance. *Var:* **okleb'aal**; **rokleb'aal**.

okox *n.* mushroom.

oksinb'il na'leb' *n.* pragmatism.

oksink nawk'anjelahom *n.* technology use.

oktuuwr *n.* October. *Var:* **oktuub'wr**. *From:* Spanish 'octubre'.

ok'aal hab' *n.* century.

ok'aalil *n.* hundred.

ok'aalil b'isleb' *n.* measure (by one hundred).

olb' *n.* lard, fat, grease, oil. *Var:* **q'olb'**.

olb'il b'an *n.* oil, ointment.

olb'lit'b'e *n.* brake fluid.

olb'xaqleb' *n.* brake fluid.

ons *n.* ounce. *From:* Spanish 'onza'.

oq uq' *n.* body parts.

oqech *n.* post, pole, beam, column.

oqechch'iich' *n.* metal beam.

oqej *n.* footprint.

oqil *n.* footprint.

oq'ej *n sd.* foot, feet. **woq** « my foot ».

oq'lok *v.* to howl.

oreek *n.* oregano. *From:* Spanish 'orégano'.

orkeet *n.* fork, pitchfork. *From:* horqueta 'pitchfork' (Spanish) (1).

orteens *n.* hortensia. *From:* Spanish 'hortensia'.

oso'jik *n.* end (temporal).

oso'k *v.* to run out, end.

osob'tesinb'il *adj.* holy, blessed.

osob'tesink *v.* to bless.

otoony *n.* autumn, fall (season). *From:* otoño 'autumn' (Spanish) (1).

ow *n.* raccoon. *Var:* **aj ow**.

ox ox *adv.* three by three.

ox'eetalb'irok *n.* trinomial.

ox'u *n.* pyramid.

ox'ukab'l *n.* pyramid (monument).

ox'ukab'l mayab' *n.* Maya pyramid.

oxej *adv.* in three days.

oxejer *adv.* three days ago.

oxichal *n.* group of three.

oxjach *adj.* in three parts, in thirds.

oxjachal *n.* one third.

oxjunajink xna'tz'iib' *n.* triphthong.

oxloq' *adj.* sacred.

oxloq' ilob' *n.* cultural identity.

oxloq'il *n.* respect.

oxloq'il hu *n.* prayer book.

oxloq'il na'aj *n.* altar.

oxloq'il na'leb' *n.* culture.

oxloq'ilal *n.* morality.

oxloq'inb'il *adj.* respected.

oxloq'ink *v.* to love, appreciate, respect.

Oxom *sur. From:* ox ('three'). (B3).

oxraqyehok *n.* trisyllable.

oxsut *adv.* three times.

oxtz'uq *n.* suspension points, ellipsis.

oxwa *adv.* three times.

oxwahink *v.* to cube.

oxxaala *n.* tripod.

oxxukuut *n.* triangle.

oyb'eb'aal *n.* waiting room.

oyb'enink *v.* to wait.

ob'eja *n.* lamb. *From:* oveja 'sheep' (Spanish) (1).

OO - oo

oob' chuy xwaq k'alab' *n.* one million.

oob' ketzal *n.* five quetzals.

oob' oq'ob' *n.* two thousand.

oob' senta *n.* five cents, nickel.

oont *n.* sling. *From:* honda 'sling' (Spanish) (1).

oor *n.* hour. *From:* hora 'the hour' (Spanish) (1).

oos *n.* bear. *From:* oso 'the bear' (Spanish) (1).

P - p

Pa' *sur.*

Pa'aw *sur. From:* aw ('sow'). (B3).

pachi' *n.* beetle.

pach'aya' *n.* grass, lawn.

pach'il ha' *n.* waterfall.

pach'lenk *v.* to splash.

pach'ok *v.* to splash.

pahal *n.* opening.

pahok jul *n.* ditch, furrow.

pahpo *adj.* open.

pajaj ha' *n.* waterfall.

pajink *v.* to pour.

pakun wakax *n.* ox.

pak'al *n.* side.

pak'alilch'och' *n.* continent.

pak'b'il *n.* pottery.

pak'b'il *adj.* earthen, made of clay.

pak'b'il ismal *n.* wig.

pak'b'il k'uula'al *n.* doll.

pak'b'il poyanam *n.* statue.

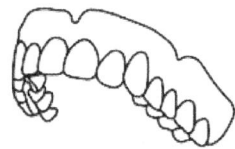

pak'b'il ruuch e *n.* denture.

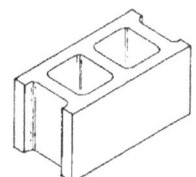

pak'b'il tzak *n.* clay brick, cinder block.

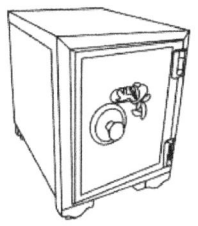

pak'b'il tz'ak *n.* safe.

pak'ok *v.* to mold, form, shape. *From:* pak' 'to shape' (Yucatecan, Ch'olan, possible) (2).

pak'ok aatin *v phr.* to lie (tell falsehoods).

pak'po *prep.* facing up.

pak'yu'amha' *n.* fountain.

palaw *n.* ocean, sea, lake. *From:* palaw 'sea' (Ch'olti') (3).

palaw kariiw *n.* Carribean sea.

palawhiik *n.* undersea earthquake.

paleet *n.* paddle, oar. *From:* paleta 'paddle' (Spanish) (1).

pam'iq' *n.* balloon.

pamamnak *v.* to float.

pamb'eeresinb'il *n.* blimp, dirigible, zeppelin.

Pana' *sur.*

panchool *n.* nettle. *From:* panchola ('a type of nettle' ?) (Spanish) (1).

panyal *n.* diaper. *From:* Spanish 'pañuelo'.

pap tz'unun *n.* large hummingbird.

papelseya *n.* birth certificate. *From:* papel de sello 'sealed document' (Spanish) (1).

papeer *n.* mumps. *From:* Spanish 'paperas'.

Paqay *sur.*

paqleb' *n.* pall.

paqmaal *n.* salamander.

paqonk *v.* to carry.

paqonk *v.* to raise, lift.

paq'al *adj.* broken.

paq'e'k *v.* to drown.

paq'e'k *n.* drowning.

paq'ek *n.* choking.

paraq'aq'a *n.* machine gun.

paraaw *n.* umbrella. *From:* Spanish 'paraguas'.

parenheitil b'iis *n.* degrees Fahrenheit.

parok *v.* to scratch.

parpotk *v.* to shiver, tremble.

pasaaj *n.* fare. *From:* Spanish 'pasaje'.

pastiiy *n.* pill, tablet. *From:* pastilla 'pill, tablet' (Spanish) (1).

pastor *n.* pastor. *From:* Spanish 'pastor'.

pat *n.* scale (reptilian).

pat *n.* corn (cutaneous).

pata *n.* guayaba.

pataal *n.* centipede.

patb' *n.* club.

pati kar *n.* fish scale.

patkik' *n.* coagulation (blood).

patux *n.* duck. *From:* pato 'duck' (Spanish) (1).

patux ha' *n.* heron.

patz'b'il *n.* request.

patz'leb' aatin *n.* interrogative.

patz'num *n.* turn signal.

patz'numleb' *n.* turn signal.

patz'ok *v.* to interrogate.

patz'ok *v.* to ask, beg, plead, survey, inquire.

patz'ok b'aanunk *v phr.* to exhort.

patz'ok limoox *v phr.* to ask for alms.

patz'om *n.* question.

paynum *adj.* fast.

payok *v.* to whisper sweetly.

payok *v.* to fall in love, entrust.

payom *n.* object of a suitor's affection.

payr *n.* priest. *From:* padre 'father, priest' (Spanish) (1).

paab'ajel *n.* confidant.

paab'ank *v.* to obey, believe.

paab'aal *n.* religion.

paab'aal *n.* faith.

paach *n.* baby bottle. *From:* pacha 'the rubber nipple' (Spanish) (1).

paachach *n.* cockroach, roach. *From:* pachajk 'insect said to resemble the cockroach' (Ch'orti') (2).

paak'ilal *n.* model, make.

paal *n.* shovel, spade. *From:* pala 'shovel, paddle' (Spanish) (1).

paaltil *n.* error.

paap *n.* pope. *From:* Spanish 'papa'.

paapa'x *n.* hut. *Var:* papa'ax.

paaps *n.* potato, sweet potato. *Var:* **paps**. *From:* papas 'potatoes' (Spanish) (1).

paast *n.* pasta. *From:* Spanish 'pasta'.

paattzim *n.* motorcycle.

paay *n.* type, class, variety.

paayil *n.* type, class, variety.

pe' *part.* [insistence particle]. *Note:* Used to supply additional emphasis to a declartive or interrogative. **Jo'kan pe'.** « That's the way it is. » **Pe' yaal?** « Is that really true? »

pechtokan *n.* strawberry.

pech'ok *v.* to carve. *From:* pech' 'to carve in wood' (Ch'olan) (2).

pejok *v.* to tear.

pek *n.* stone, rock.

Pek *sur. From:* pek ('stone'). (B1).

pek ha' *n.* ice.

pekal *n.* stone, rock.

pekark *v.* to harden, become hard.

pekb'ach *n.* ice.

pekil ha' *n.* reef.

pekil nima' *n.* river rock.

pekilha' ch'och' *n.* glacier.

pekilnimb'e *n.* dirt road, unpaved road.

pek'iich' *n.* lock.

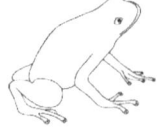

pelpel *n.* frog.

pemech *n.* shell.
Var: xpemechul rix.

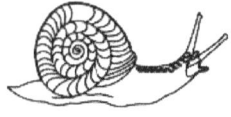

pemech *n.* snail.

pens *n.* pepper.

pepiin *n.* cucumber. *From:* Spanish 'pepino'.

per'uk'al *n.* saucepan.

pere'xaab' *n.* slipper. *Var:* per xaab'.

perejil *n.* parsley. *From:* Spanish 'perejil'.

pere'maal *n.* chameleon.

pereera *n.* birth certificate. *From:* fe de edad 'birth certificate' (Spanish) (1).

perees *n.* strawberry. *From:* Spanish 'fresa'.

pereex *n.* convict. *Var:* preex. *From:* Spanish 'preso'.

perhu *n.* card.

perhub'aal *n.* cardholder.

periood *n.* newspaper. *From:* periódico (Spanish) (1).

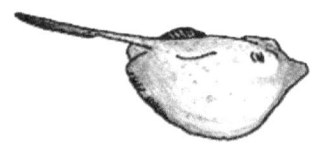

perkar *n.* ray, stingray.

perperink *v.* to pedal.

perpo *adj.* flat.

perxaab' *n.* sandal.

pes *adj.* dirty.

Pet *nick.* Petrona.

peteet *n.* spindle. *Var:* **pet'eet'**.

petrool *n.* petroleum. *From:* petróleo 'petroleum' (Spanish) (1).

pewreer *n.* February. *Var:* **peb'reer**. *From:* Spanish 'febrero'.

peech'ab'k *n.* carpentry.

peech'leb'aal *n.* woodshop.

peekem *n.* forehead.

peekem kun *n.* pubis.

peepem *n.* butterfly.

peer *n.* pear. *From:* Spanish 'pera'.

peeraj *n.* shawl.

peetaq *n.* cactus.

peex *n.* scale. *From:* Spanish 'pesa'.

pich' *n.* woodpecker.

pihamb'r *n.* cold cuts. *From:* Spanish 'fiambre'.

pikleb' *n.* pickaxe.

pikleb' *n.* fork.

pikleb' *n.* chisel.

pikok *v.* to dig. *From:* *pik 'to dig' (Ch'olan) (2).

pim *adj.* thick.

pim *n.* wild grass.

pim *n.* shrub, bush, weeds.

pimilhu *n.* cardboard.

pirich *n.* penis.

pirik' *n.* worm.

pirk' *n.* vulva.

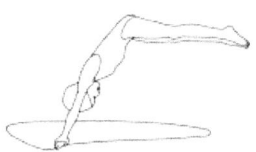

pisk'leb'aal *n.* diving board.

pisk'ok *v.* to jump, leap.

pitzk' *n.* spring (metal).

pitzok *v.* to jump, leap.

pitz'ok *v.* to squeeze, press.

pitz'leb' *n.* juice press.

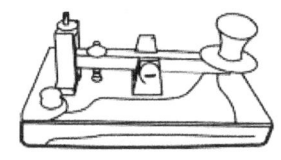

pitz'leb'taql *n.* telegraph.

pitz'pitz' *adj.* salty.

Pix *sur.* *From:* pix ('tomato'). (B1).

pix *adj.* stingy.

pix *n.* tomato.

pixcal *n.* sacristan.

pixilk'a'uxl *n.* egocentrism.

pixlenk *v.* to tangle.

piyok *n.* thief.

piitza *n.* pizza. *From:* English 'pizza'.

plastiik *n.* plastic. *Var:* **plaas**. *From:* plástico 'plastic' (Spanish) (1).

platiiy *n.* saucer. *From:* platillo 'saucer' (Spanish) (1).

plaat *n.* silver. *From:* plata 'silver' (Spanish) (1).

pleet *n.* battle, war. *From:* pleito 'fight' (Spanish) (1).

pleetik *n.* combat.

po *n.* month.

po *n.* moon. *From:* *poy'a 'moon' (Mixe-Zoquean) (3).

po *n.* wages, monthly pay. *From:* *poy'a 'moon' (Mixe-Zoquean) (3).

po'jik *n.* anger.

po'lem *n.* ruins, abandoned house. *Var:* polem. *From:* *po'lem 'abandoned house or ruin' (Ch'olti') (2).

po'lem kab'l *n.* hut, cabin.

po'ok *v.* to undo, break down.

po'ok ch'ool *v phr.* to displease.

po'ot *n.* blouse (typical Mayan).

Po'ow *sur. From:* po' ('rot'). (B3).

poch'leb' *n.* mill (grain).

pohol *n.* month.

pojel *n.* pus.

pojk *n.* pus. *Var:* poj.

pojkun *n.* gonorrhea.

pojk'ok *n.* mitosis.

polook' *n.* thorax.

pom *n.* incense.

pomaat *n.* ointment. *From:* Spanish 'pomada'.

pomb'il *adj.* roasted, grilled.

pomb'il paaps *n.* baked potatoes.

pomb'il tib' *n.* roast beef.

pomleb' *n.* grill, roasting pan.

pomleb'aal *n.* oven.

pomleb'aal tzakahemq *n.* microwave oven.

pomok *v.* to broil, grill, roast, fry.

popti *lang.* Popti [aka Jakaltek] (Huehuetenango).

Poq *sur. From:* poq ('powder'). (B1).

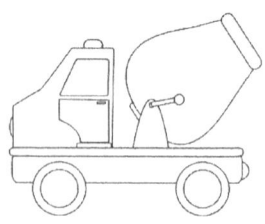

poq re tz'akab'ak *n.* cement.

poqb'an *n.* talcum powder, talc.

poqilsunob'l *n.* talcum powder, talc.

poqlenk *v.* to register.

poqomam *lang.* Poqomam (Escuintla, Guatemala, Jalapa).

poqomchi' *lang.* Poqomchi (Alta Verapaz, Baja Verapaz, El Quiche).

poqs *n.* dust.

poqsiyajink *n.* pollination.

poqsiyaal *n.* pollen.

poqsxaml *n.* gunpowder, powder.

poqxab'on *n.* detergent.

porha' *n.* rash, blister.

pormon *n.* chisel, awl.
Var: **formon.** *From:* formón 'awl or chisel' (Spanish) (1).

porselaan *n.* porcelain. *From:* Spanish 'porcelana'.

pos *n.* lung.

pospo'oy *n.* lung. *Var:* **pospoy.**

pospo'ykar *n.* gills.

potreer *n.* pasture, meadow, paddock. *From:* potrero 'pasture' (Spanish) (1).

potzkaxlanwa *n.* rolls.

potzpotz *adj.* soft.

potztem *n.* couch, sofa.

potzt'ikr *n.* towel.

potzwex *n.* sweatpants, sweats.

potzxaab' *n.* tennis shoes.

potz'b'aqib'k *n.* boxing.

potz'ok *v.* to strike, hit, beat.

poxe'k *n.* blister.

poy *adj.* light (in weight).

poy ch'iich' *n.* bus.

poy'al *n.* doll.

poyanam *n.* human.

poyanam *n.* person, people.

poyanam wan aatin chirix *n.* suspect.

poyanamb'iltz'ak *n.* statue.

poyanamilal *n.* ethnic group.

poyanimil *n.* humanity.

poyanimil nawyu'am *n.* human biology.

poyb'atz'uul *n.* marionette, puppet.

poyte' *n.* raft. *From:* pooyte' 'raft' (Yucatecan, Ch'olan, possible) (2).

poyte'ib'k *v.* to raft.

po'ok *v.* to destroy.

poolok'il *n.* rib.

Poop *sur.* *From:* poop ('straw mat'). (B1).

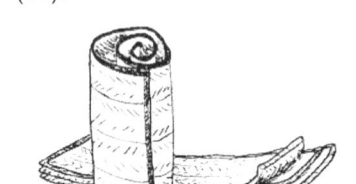

poop *n.* mat.

poopirk *v.* to rule, govern, reign.

poopol *n.* court.

poopol kab'l *n.* city hall.

poos *n.* match. *From:* fósforo 'the match' (Spanish) (1).

preex *n.* captive, prisoner. *Var:* **pereex**. *From:* preso 'captive' (Spanish) (1).

preexil *n.* captivity. *Var:* **pereexil**. *From:* preso 'captive' (Spanish) (1).

primab'eer *n.* spring (season). *From:* primavera 'spring' (Spanish) (1).

priim *n.* dawn, early morning. *From:* prima 'first canonical hour' (Spanish) (1).

pu'ak *n.* money, metal. *Var:* pu'aq; pwaq.

pu'akink *v.* to work metal.

puchha' *n.* blister.

puchil *n.* anemia. *Var:* puchilk.

puchirk *v.* to become anemic.

puch'leb' *n.* washbasin, washbowl.

puch'leb'aal ch'iich' *n.* washing machine.

puch'uk *v.* to wash.

puch'uk *v.* to menstruate.

puj *n.* belly.

pujha'nel ch'iich' *n.* fire truck.

pujkik' *n.* hemmorhage.

pukchahim *n.* supernova.

pukhub'aal *n.* print house, printer's, publisher.

pukleb'hu *n.* printer.

pukleb'hu *n.* mimeograph.

pukta'esil *n.* propaganda.

puktahil'ajl *n.* multiplication.

puktasib'aal *n.* radio (transmitter).

puktasib'aal aatin *n.* loudspeaker.

puktasib'aal esil *n.* media, means of communication.

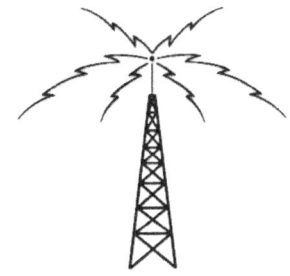

**puktasib'aal kab'l najt
xteram** *n.* radio tower.

puktasib'aalhu *n.* photocopier,
copy machine, copier.

puktasib'aalhu *n.* printer,
imprint.

puktasinb'il *adj.* published.

puktasinb'il *adj.* multiplied.

puktasinel *n.* multiplier.

puktasink *v.* to edit.

puktasink *v.* to multiply.

puktasink ajl *v.* to multiply.

puktasink chi *phr.* multiplied
by.

puktasink esil *v phr.* to publish.

puktasink ib' *v phr.* to square.

puktasiil *n.* printer.

puktasiil *n.* multiplication.

puktaal *n.* multiple.

pukyaab' *n.* microphone,
speaker.

puk'um *n.* piñata.

puk'xaar *n.* jug, pitcher.

pulaat *n.* dish. *From:* Spanish
'plato'.

pulseer *n.* bracelet. *From:*
pulsera 'the bracelet' (Spanish) (1).

pumb'uul *n.* raffle, lottery.

pumb'uul *n.* revolving drum.

pumleb'ha' *n.* water tank.

pumleb'yaab' *n.* stereo.

pumpuri' *n.* beetle.

pumpuukil ha' *n.* lake, pond,
lagoon.

pumuk *v.* to throw.

punit *n.* hat, cap.

puq'b'il *n.* milkshake.

puq'b'il paaps *n.* mashed
potatoes.

puq'b'il pix *n.* tomato sauce.

puq'leb' *n.* blender, mixer.

pur *n.* penis.

pur *n.* snail.

Purahub *top.* [pur ha'
hub"] "edible snails". *Etym:*
pur = snail or snail-like; hub' =
snail (Yucatec).

puraq' *n.* space suit.

purik *v.* to fly.

purik aq' aj b'eenel sa' po *n.* space suit.

purux *adj.* rough.

putul *n.* papaya.

Putul *sur. From:* tul ('plantain'). (B3).

putzputzb'an *n.* talcum powder, talc.

putz'b'il *n.* sauce.

putz'b'il pix ik *n.* hot sauce, picante sauce, salsa.

putz'ink *v.* to liquify.

puxink *v.* to shake.

puyuch' *n.* parakeet.

puub' *n.* firearm, gun, rifle.

puub' che' *n.* blowgun.

puub' tzuul *n.* volcano.

puub'ak *v.* to shoot.

puub'ank *v.* to shoot.

puub'b'on *n.* paintgun.

puub'xaml *n.* blowtorch.

puukalche'k'aam *n.* flora.

puukalil *n.* generation.

puukalxul *n.* fauna.

puukchahim *n.* asteroid.

puulesink *v.* to throw.

puut *n.* prostitute. *From:* Spanish 'puta'.

puutink *n.* prostitution.

puutzink *v.* to spray.

puutz'leb'aal *n.* nebulizer, spray.

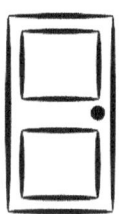

pweert *n.* door, gate. *From:* puerta 'the door' (Spanish) (1).

Q - q

qachok *v.* to bite. *Var:* qatzok.

qana' *n.* lady.

qapo'lem *phr.* our rustic abode, our abandoned house, our ruins.

qapok *v.* to chop.

qawa' *n.* sir.

qaana' *n.* goddess.

qaawa' *n.* god, lord.

qeel *adj.* used, old.

qeer *n.* furrow.

qirok *v.* to scrape.

qishumha' *n.* diesel.

qixb' *n.* burp.

qixb'ak *v.* to burp.

qoch *n.* crow.

qoorank *v.* to snore.

Q' - q'

q'a *n.* bridge.

Q'a'al *sur. From:* al ('young boy'). (B3).

q'ab'anb'il *n.* defendant.

q'ab'ank *v.* to accuse.

q'ab'ankil *n.* accusation.

q'ajel ix *adv phr.* backwards.

q'ajk *v.* to return, come back, go home.

q'ajsink *v.* to give back.

q'alnak *v.* to carry (under the arm).

q'alunk *v.* to embrace, hug.

q'alunk ib' *v phr.* to hug each other.

q'an *adj.* ripe.

Q'an *sur. From:* q'an ('yellow'). (B1).

q'an *adj.* yellow.

q'an ch'iich' *n.* bronze, copper.

q'an kaqin *adj.* orange.

q'an pwaq *n.* gold, yellow gold. *Var:* q'anpuhak; q'anpuhaq.

q'an tu'lay aj imul *n.* guinea pig.

q'an yaj *n.* bloating, intestinal gas.

q'anb'uyin *adj.* yellowish.

q'anch'ik' *adj.* copper.

q'anch'iich' *n.* horn, trumpet.

q'anch'ub' *n.* yellow hornet.

q'anich'iich' *n.* gold. *Var:* q'an ch'iich'.

q'anil *n.* hepatitis.

q'anjob'al *lang.* Qanjobal (Huehuetenango).

q'anjorin *adj.* golden.

q'anmalaw *adj.* yellowish.

q'anmuch'iich' *n.* rhodium.

q'anq'an *adj.* brilliant.

q'antzoq'i *adj.* yellowish.

q'anxe' *n.* carrot.

q'anyajel *n.* hepatitis.

q'ap *n.* green bean, string bean.

q'aqt *n.* dice.

q'axal *adv.* more.

q'axal chaab'il *adj.* right (correct).

q'axal q'un *adj.* mild, meek.

q'axal us *adj.* good, very good.

q'axleb'aal *n.* footbridge, walkway, gangway, catwalk.

q'axok *v.* to cross, pass, overtake, leave one behind.

q'axtesink *v.* to present, give.

q'axtesink *v.* to return.

q'axtesink ib' *v phr.* to surrender, give up.

q'aajenaq *adj.* spoiled.

q'aak *n.* infection. *Var:* q'a'k.

q'aal *n.* fathom.

q'aaneq *adj.* rotten.

q'aayajel *n.* cancer.

q'e *n.* era, eon.

q'e'q'o *adj.* horizontal.

q'ehink *v.* to guess, predict.

q'ehink chi ru *v.* to prognosticate.

q'ekutan *n.* era, eon.

q'em *n.* dough, cornmeal.

q'em ha' *n.* cornmeal drink.

q'emalk'uub' *adv.* artistically.

q'emkun *adj.* lazy.

q'emkunal *n.* laziness.

q'emrasink *v.* to knead.

q'emtu' *n.* cheese.

q'emya'altu' *n.* cheese.

q'eq *adj.* black.

q'eq aj am *n.* tarantula.

q'eqchi' *lang.* Q'eqchi' (Alta Verapaz, Baja Verapaz, Isabal, Peten, Belize).

q'eqhilk'anjel *n.* schedule.

q'eqi che' *n.* ebony tree.

q'eqil b'iin *n.* red wine.

q'eqitz'aakalb'e *n.* asphalt, tar.

q'eqmoyin *adj.* purple.

q'eqmoyin *adj.* brown.

q'eq'i ch'ejej *n.* black crow.

q'eq'ookil eetalil *n.* equator.

q'eq'ookil juch' *n.* horizontal line.

q'es *adj.* pointed, sharp.

q'es ru *adj.* rough.

q'esyaxch'iich' *n.* tongs.

q'etok *v.* to break, fold.

q'etok *v.* to negate.

q'etok aatin *v.* to break one's word, disobey.

q'etq'et *adj.* proud.

q'etq'etil *n.* bitterness.

q'etq'etil *adj.* negative.

q'eel *adj.* old.

q'eem *n.* fertilizer. *Var:* q'em.

q'een *n.* leaf.

q'ichok *v.* to tear.

q'ichok e *v phr.* to shout. *From:*
q'ich 'to open the mouth to laugh'
(Q'anjob'alan) (3).

q'inixtz'iib' *n.* cursive.

q'inolaatin *n.* preposition.

q'irok *v.* to tear.

q'ix *adj.* hot.

q'ix ha' *n.* hot water.

q'ixaml *n.* stove.

q'ixleb'aq' *n.* jacket.

q'ixnal *n.* heat.

q'ixt'ikr *n.* sweater, jacket.

q'iil *n.* time.

q'ochb'il noq' ch'iich' *n.* coil.

q'och-eetalil *n.* film.

q'ochleb'aal *n.* gym,
gymnasium.

q'ochleb'tzolom *n.* physical
education.

q'ochok *v.* to wrap.

q'ochq'och *adj.* elastic.

q'ochq'och *adj.* soft.

q'ojyin *adj.* dark.

q'ojyin *n.* night, evening.
Var: **q'oqyin.**

q'ol *n.* jewel.

q'ol *n.* chain.

Q'ol *sur. From:* q'ol ('bead' or
'necklace'). (B1).

q'ol *n.* sap.

q'ol *n.* necklace.

q'ol *n.* pearl, bead.

q'ol is *n.* body hair, peach
fuzz.

q'ol'uq' *n.* bracelet.

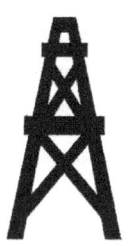

q'olch'och' *n.* oil, petroleum.

q'olok *v.* to harvest.

q'olom *n.* harvest.

q'olxulkar *n.* dolphin.

q'oq *n.* pain, sadness.

q'otch'och'ilpalaw *n.*
Mediterranean Sea.

q'ot-eetalil *n.* parabola.

q'otleb'ch'iich' *n.* wrench, crescent wrench.

q'otok *v.* to turn.

q'otol *n.* shackle.

q'otonk *v.* to turn around.

q'otq'o *adj.* curved, twisted.

q'otq'o *adj.* round, circular.

q'otq'ookil sek' *n.* bedpan.

q'oyok *v.* to scratch, scrape.

q'oyol *n.* scratch.

q'ooch *n.* roll.

q'ooqil ik'e *n.* aloe vera.

q'oot *adj.* curved, twisted.

q'oot *n.* curve.

q'un *adj.* weak.

q'un *adj.* humble, tender.

q'un *adj.* soft, smooth.

q'un xch'ool *adj.* gentle, peaceful, attentive.

q'unal *n.* fondness.

q'unb'esink *v.* to campaign.

q'unil *n.* tenderness.

q'unil t'ikr *n.* flannel.

q'unixholob'oob' *n.* mango.

q'unleb' *n.* sandpaper.

q'unq'un ru *adj.* fine.

q'unuk *v.* to hold.

q'uq' *n.* quetzal.

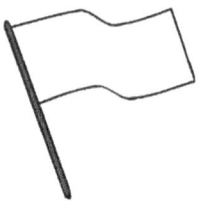

q'uq'il t'ikr *n.* flag.

q'urq'utk *v.* to growl, grunt.

q'usuk *v.* to scold, warn, reprimand.

q'usunel *n.* teacher.

q'ut *n.* adobe.

q'uusank *v.* to snore.
   Var: q'usank.

R - r

ra *adj.* painful.

ra chu' *n.* urinary pain.

ra re *adj.* acidic.

ra xch'ool *adj.* sad, gloomy.

ra' che' *n.* forked branch.

ra'al *n.* trap.

ra'alenk *v.* to trap.

ra'leb'kar *n.* fishhook.

rab'in ajwal *n.* princess.

rab'inkil *v.* to tune in.

rachhab' *n.* precipitation.

rachok *v.* to splash.

rachrotk *v.* to drip.

rahil *n.* pain.

rahil ch'ool *adj.* sad.

rahil ch'oolej *n.* grief.

rahil ch'oolejil *n.* sadness, gloom.

rahil jolom *n.* headache, migraine.

rahil kutan *n.* holy week, Easter.

rahil ruuch a' *n.* leg pain.

rahil ruuch e *n.* toothache.

rahil sa' xik *n.* earache.

rahil sa'ej *n.* stomach ache.

rahil u *n.* conjunctivitis.

rahil xalaa'it *n.* backache.

rahilal *n.* pain, difficulty. *Var:* raylal.

rahink *v.* to want.

raho'k *v.* to hurt, suffer.

raho'k xch'ool *v phr.* to get sad, sadden.

rahob'k *n.* disappointment.

rahob'tesink wank *n.* vulnerability.

rahok *v.* to love.

rahok *n.* love.

rahom *n.* love.

rahro *adj.* beloved.

raj *part.* [conditional particle]. *Note:* Used to indicate a desired, hypothetical, or probable action **Laa'in raj aj b'anonel, a'ut xinkanab' li tzolok naq xkam inyuwa'.** « I would have been a doctor, but when my father died I stopped studying. »

rajb'al ru *n.* need, necessity.

rajikab'aal *n.* rebirth.

rajikru *v.* to be reborn.

rajlal *adv.* always.

rajlal naab'al *adv phr.* more and more.

rajlal rajlal *adv phr.* frequently.

rajlal xamaan *adv phr.* every week.

rajleb' tij *n.* rosary.

rajlil *n.* number, page number.

rajlil b'oqleb' *n.* phone number.

rajlil ketom *n.* grade, score.

rajlilb'eleb'ch'iich' *n.* license plate.

rajliltoj *n.* tax identification number.

rajom *n.* mission.

rajtziil *n.* enemy.

rajb'al *n.* intention.

rak'ach tzuul *n.* roadrunner.

ral chaq'na' *n.* niece, nephew.

ral chib'aat *n.* baby goat, kid.

ral kawaay *n.* foal, colt. *From:* Spanish 'caballo'.

ral kaxlan *n.* chick.

ral punitch'iich' *n.* little bell.

ral wakax *n.* calf (of a cow), bull calf.

ral we *n.* nephew.

ral yuk *n.* baby goat, kid.

ralab'aatinob'aal *n.* dialect.

ralal ikan *n.* niece.

ralal xk'ajol *n.* descendants.

ralch'och' *n.* indigenous, Maya. *Var:* ral ch'och'. *Note:* Literally 'son of the land'. Term the Q'eqchi' use to refer to themselves. (Aj Q'eqchi' traditionally refers to a speaker of the Q'eqchi' language, not a tribe or ethnicity.)

ralch'och'il *n.* ethnicity.

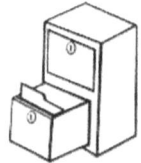

ralmeex *n.* drawer. *From:* Spanish 'mesa'.

ralpuub' *n.* gas dispenser.

ralsaq'e *n.* planet.

ralteeleb' *n.* latchkey.

raltoj *n.* bonus, award.

raltumin *n.* interest.

ralyu'amej *n.* embryo.

ramb'al ru yajel *n.* first aid.

ramb'atz'aj *n.* smock, apron.

ramch'iich' *n.* shutters.

ramleb' *n.* railing.

ramleb' *n.* bedrail.

ramleb' *n.* curtain.

ramleb' saqen *n.* curtain, drape, blind.

ramleb'aal lem *n.* stained glass.

ramleb'ch'iich' *n.* balcony.

ramok *v.* to catch, block, prevent.

rampalaw *n.* marines.

ramro' *adv.* sometimes.

ramtzelek *n.* shin guard.

ranab' xyuwa' *n.* father's sister.

ranok chi noq' *v phr.* to stitch.

ranq' *n.* hymen.

rant'in *n.* sling.

ranumal q'ojyin *n.* fairy, elf.

Rap *nick.* Rafael.

raq xtasalil'iq' *n.* exosphere.

raqal *n.* part, article.

raqal'aatin *n.* sentence.

204

raqal'aatin *n.* phrase.

raqalil li paab'aal *n.* article of faith.

raqalilk'utb'esink *n.* scene.

raqalk'a'uxl *n.* paragraph.

raqaltz'iib' *n.* verse.

raqalyalb'a'ix *n.* survey, questionnaire.

raqan *n.* trunk (fruit bearing).

raqaxink *v.* to separate.

raqaxinkil *n.* diagram.

raqb'a' aatin *n.* judgment.

raqb'ametz'ew *n.* electric switch, switch, interruptor.

raqe'k *v.* to cease.

raqik *n.* end (temporal).

raqik *adj.* last.

raqink *v.* to chop.

raqleb' saqen *n.* power switch, light switch.

raqleb'aatin *n.* court.

raqleltz'uq *n.* period.

raqmetz'ew *n.* electricity.

raqmetz'eweb' *n.* escalator.

raqok *v.* to finish, end.

raqok *v.* to cross.

raqok aatin *n.* trial, justice.

raqok aatin *v phr.* to judge, adjudicate.

raqok aatin chi rix *v phr.* to convict, condemn.

raqonel chaq'rab' *n.* jury.

raqro juch' *n.* perpendicular line.

raqtz'aqob'l *n.* suffix, ending.

raqtz'uq *n.* period.

raqyanq *n.* semicolon.

raq'kaaq *n.* lightning.

raq'xam *n.* flame. *Var:* raq'xaml.

raq' aj b'anonel *n.* hospital gown.

raq' aj b'eenel sa' po *n.* space suit.

raq' qaawa' *n.* cloak, vestment.

raq' yaj *n.* hospital robe.

raq'metz'ewanb'il eeb' *n.* escalator.

raq'xaab' *n.* tongue (of a shoe).

rarehilpoq *n.* sulphur.

raschaq'rab' chi rix tojb'amaak *n.* penal code.

rastriiy *n.* fork, pitchfork, rake. *From:* rastrillo (Spanish) (1).

rataw chi us *adj.* excited.

ratz'amilq'olch'iich' *n.* nitrate.

rawimal ch'och' *n.* natural resources.

rax *adj.* green.

rax *adj.* unripe.

rax *adj.* raw.

Rax *sur. From:* rax ('green' or 'blue'). (B1).

rax ch'iich' *n.* lead (metal).

rax ch'och' *n.* pasture.

rax ju'in *adj.* blue. *Var:* raxrax; rax.

rax moyin *adj.* navy blue.

rax moyin *adj.* dark green.

rax muhel *n.* good luck.

rax q'u'in *adj.* blue.

raxjo'in *adj.* sky blue.

raxki' *n.* pear.

raxkihob' *n.* malaria. *Var:* raxkehob'.

raxk'aj *n.* flying serpent, vine snake.

raxk'urin *adj.* light (not dark).

raxmo'in *adj.* greenish.

raxmo'in *adj.* bluish.

raxmoyinil tzoqchahim *n.* blue galaxy.

raxonb'an *n.* fertilizer.

raxpan *n.* toucan.

raxpotz'in *adj.* cerulean, sky blue.

raxq'een *n.* grasshopper.

raxtint *n.* bruise.

raxtint *adj.* violet.

raxtul *n.* graft.

raxtz'o'in *adj.* blue.

raxwak' *n.* broccoli.

ray *n.* radio. *From:* radio 'the radio' (Spanish) (1).

rab'in *n.* daughter.

ra'l kar *n.* fish trap.

raanil *n.* speed, velocity.

raap *adj.* wet.

raapal *n.* verse, stanza.

raasa *adj.* difficult.

raatik'aamch'iich' tenamit *n.* public telephone.

raatinul *n.* idiolect.

raatinxcha'alil aatinib'aal *n.* variant form.

raaxiik' *n.* war, battle.

raaxiik' *n.* quarrel.

re *prep.* of, from.

re *adv.* for.

re b'e *n.* fence gate.

re b'isok tiq *n.* thermometer.

re chajok sa' e *n.* toothbrush.

re chajok tiqil *n.* disinfectant.

re ch'ool *n.* breast, bust, chest.

re ha' *n.* beach.

re kab' *n.* door, gate.

re kotzok siip *n.* anti-inflammatory.

re kotzok xrahil *n.* analgesic.

re kubsink rahil *n.* sedative.

re lanok tiq'il *n.* bandage.

re maqab' *n.* chest.

re palaw *n.* coast, seashore.

re raxkehob' *n.* cold tablets.

re tenamit *adj.* public.

re tenamit *n.* outskirts.

re t'ikr *n.* lace.

re wartesink *n.* anesthesia.

re wotz'ok *n.* anti-itch cream.

re xch'ool wex *n.* fly (of pants).

re xkotzb'al xrahil *n.* painkiller.

re xkub'sinkil xrahil *n.* painkiller.

re xmay *n.* antibiotic.

re'ok *v.* to tear.

reb'e *n.* sidewalk. *Var:* re b'e; reeb'e.

rehil loq'alil *n.* personal values.

rek' *adj.* all.

rek' *adj.* well done.

rela' *n.* rest, remains.

rela' t'ikr *n.* scrap of cloth.

releb' iq' *n.* north. *Var:* releb'aal iq'; releb'l iq'.

releb' saq'e *n.* east. *Var:* releb'aal saq'e; releb'l saq'e.

releb'aal ha' *n.* fountain.

releb'aalsib' *n.* exhaust pipe.

releb'tz'ajha' *n.* drain.

releb'aal sib' *n.* chimney.

releb'sib' *n.* chimney.

reloj *n.* clock. *From:* reloj 'the clock or watch' (Spanish) (1).

remolaach *n.* beet. *From:* Spanish 'remolacha'.

remrem *adj.* sour, brackish.

rep'ix *n.* scale.

repok *v.* to splash.

repolmu *n.* overhead projector, projector.

repom *n.* overhead projector, projector.

repom *n.* lightning.

repom kaaq *n.* thunderstorm.

repooy *n.* cabbage. *From:* Spanish 'repollo'.

repsaqenk *n.* flash.

req'ok *v.* to lick.

resil yu'amej *n.* biography.

resilal b'aanuhom *n.* history.

resilal wank *n.* history.

resilal yajel *n.* medical record.

retal *conj.* until.

retal *adv.* finally, always.

rexb'een *prep.* with.

reepri *n.* refrigerator, fridge.
  From: Spanish 'refrigeradora'.

reetal jach'ajl *n.* division symbol (/).

reetal molam ajl *n.* plus sign (+), addition symbol (+).

reetal puktasiil *n.* times, multiplication sign (x), multiplication symbol (x).

reetalil *n.* pattern.

reetalil *n.* example.

reetalil b'an *n.* prescription.

reetalil b'aq *n.* X-ray plate.

reetalil b'e *n.* traffic sign.

reetalil b'eleb'aal ch'iich' *n.* license plate.

reetalil ch'och' *n.* map.

reetalil iyajil *n.* family tree.

reetalil kik' *n.* blood test.

reetalil k'uub'ank *n.* recipe.

reetalil ochoch *n.* address.

reetalil patz'omq *n.* question mark (?)

reetalil ru chi ch'och' *n.* globe.

reetalil tiq'ilal *n.* scar.

reetalil tzolom *n.* diploma.

reetalil tz'aqob'tz'iib' *n.* punctuation mark.

reetalil tz'iib'aal *n.* email address.

reetalil xaab' *n.* shoe mold, shoetree.

reetalil xyo'lajik *n.* birth certificate.

reetalilk'utb'ch'oolejil *n.* asterisk.

reetalilruuchich'och' *n.* world map.

reetaljeb'ok-ajl *n.* minus sign (-).

reetaljek'ajl *n.* division symbol (/).

reetalsachb'ach'oolej *n.* exclamation point (!).

reetaltamok-ajl *n.* plus sign (+), addition symbol (+).

reetaltenamit *n.* patriotic symbols.

Rik *nick.* Ricardo.

rik'in *prep.* with, through. *Var:* ruk'in.

rik'in *adj.* near.

rik'ok *v.* to blink.

rilb'al *n.* form, structure.

rilb'al xtoq'ob'al *n.* compassion.

rilom aj b'anonel *n.* check-up.

rin *n.* rubber.

rininink *v.* to carry (in hand).

rinok *v.* to stretch.

rinrin *n.* elastic band.

rinrin *adj.* elastic.

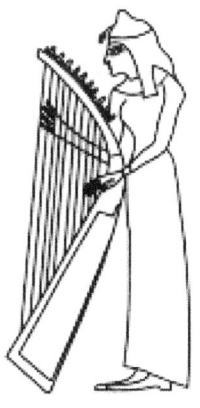

rinwajb' *n.* harp.

rismal jolom *n.* hair.

rismal u *n.* eyelash.

rismal xul *n.* feather.

rismal xxik' *n.* feather.

rit oq *n.* heel.

rit telb' *n.* elbow.

rit uq'b' *n.* elbow.

rit xaab' *n.* heel (of a shoe).

rix *n.* case, sheath.

rix *n.* bark.

rix *n.* husk.

rix che *n.* bark.

rix esilhu *n.* envelope.

rix ja'aj *n.* nape of the neck.

rix kok *n.* turtle shell.

rix kux *n.* nape of the neck.

rix sok jolom *n.* pillowcase.

rix taqlhu *n.* envelope.

rix u *n.* eyelid. *Var:* rix'uhej.

rix uq'm *n.* back of the hand. *Var:* rix uq'b'.

rix xul *n.* skin, hide.

rixch'iich' *n.* case, sheath, scabbard.

riximul kaxlan wa *n.* wheat.

rixkil paab'aal *n.* nun.

rixnaq'puub' *n.* shell, bullet casing.

rixxnaq'puub' *n.* bullet shell.

riil *adj.* slow.

riiqankil *n.* suspender.

riiqk'uula'al *n.* placenta.

ro' na'aj *n.* fifth grade.

ro' q'ekutan *n.* Cenozoic era.

ro' ralsaq'e *n.* Jupiter.

ro'ilpo *n.* May.

ro'wahink *v.* to raise to the fifth power.

Rob' *nick.* Roberto.

rochoch aj titz'ol toj *n.* toll booth.

rochoch aaq *n.* pigpen.

rochoch kab' *n.* beehive, apiary.

rochoch ketomq *n.* farm.

rochoch ruuchilawab'ej *n.* state capital, state house, departmental government.

rochoch tz'ik *n.* aviary.

rochoch xul *n.* zoo.

rochochil ab'lil tenamit *n.* embassy.

rochochil aj k'uub'anel chaq'rab' *n.* congress.

rochochil aj puub' *n.* barracks.

rochochil awa'b'ejink *n.* national palace.

rochochil b'oqleb' *n.* call center.

rochochil esilhu *n.* post office.

rochochil hal *n.* granary.

rochochil ilob'aal mu *n.* cinema, movie theater.

rochochil k'anjel *n.* workshop.

rochochil k'utb'esink *n.* arts center.

rochochil li yiib'leb'aal xaab' *n.* shoe workshop, shoemaker's, cobblery.

rochochil ruk'a' poych'iich' *n.* gas station.

rochochil tasal hu *n.* bookcase.

rochochil tasal hu *n.* library.

rochochil tumin *n.* bank.

rochochil tz'ik *n.* birdhouse.

rochochil yaj *n.* hospital.

rochochil'awab'ej *n.* palace.

rochochilmolam *n.* office.

rokeb' iq' *n.* south.
  Var: rokeb'aal iq'; rokeb'l iq'.

rokeb' palaw *n.* bay.

rokeb' saq'e *n.* west.
  Var: rokeb'aal saq'e; rokeb'l saq'e.

rokeb' xlaawil kab'l *n.* door lock.

rokeb'aal b'eleb'aal ch'iich' *n.* driveway.

rokeb'aal saqen *n.* window, skylight.

rokeb'l sib' *n.* oven vent.

roksinkil naw'aatinob'aal *n.* applied linguistics.

rok'ox *adj.* crooked.

romeer *n.* rosemary. *From:* Spanish 'romero'.

romok *v.* to prevent.

ron *n.* rum. *From:* Spanish 'ron'.

roq *n.* paw.

roq *n.* end piece, handle, grip.

roq *n.* tree trunk.

roq *n.* wheel.

roq ab'yayala *n.* South America.

roq ch'aat *n.* footboard.

roq ha' *n.* stream, brook.

roq ha' *n.* ditch.

roq ha' *n.* river.

roq ha'il tzaj *n.* drain.

roq poy ch'iich' *n.* wheel, tire.

roq ruq'm *n.* limbs.

roq saq'e *n.* sunshine.

roq taq'a *n.* plain, prairie.

roq tz'ik *n.* erection.

roq waj *n.* cornstalk.

roq wex *n.* pant leg.

roq xwinkil atz'um *n.* filament (flower).

roq-atz'um *n.* style (flower).

roqb'e *n.* street.

roqechal q'uq'il t'ikr *n.* flagpole.

roqechal xmukab'l *n.* pillar.

roqechil k'at *n.* electric tower.

roqel *n.* origin, factor.

roqil *n.* rhythm.

roqkaxlan xam *n.* electric current.

roqtaq'a *n.* basin, catchment area, watershed.

roq' *n.* stem.

roq'roq' *adj.* soft.

roso'jik *adj.* last.

rosob' *adj.* last.

rosojik k'ay *n.* clearance sale.

rox kawil yaab' *n.* stress on third to last syllable.

rox na'aj *n.* third grade.

rox q'ekutan *n.* Paleozoic era.

rox tasal'iq' *n.* mesosphere.

roxch'otonel *adj.* antepenultimate, third to last. *Var:* **roxch'otol**.

roxilpo *n.* March.

Room *nick.* Rómulo.

room *adj.* blunt. *From:* romo 'blunt' (Spanish) (1).

roopilch'iich' *n.* cable.

roos *n.* rose. *From:* Spanish 'rosa'.

roos *n.* rose bush. *From:* Spanish 'rosal'.

ru *n.* fruit.

ru *n.* side.

ru *adj.* similar.

ru a' *n.* thigh.

ru almeentr *n.* almonds. *From:* Spanish 'almendras'.

ru aq' *n.* pattern (clothing).

ru chaj *n.* cone.

ru che' *n.* fruit.

ru choxa *n.* atmosphere.

ru ch'aat *n.* mattress, blanket, bedding. *Var:* **ruuch'aat**.

ru ch'och' *n.* floor.

ru ch'oolej *n.* moods.

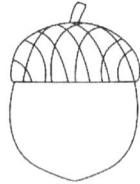

ru ji *n.* acorn.

ru meex *n.* desk mat.

ru meex *n.* tablecloth.

ru oq *n.* instep.

ru peetaq *n.* fruit of the cactus.

ru sa' *n.* abdomen.

ru taq'a *n.* valley.

ru tzelek *n.* shin.

ru tzoleb'aal *n.* class.

ru tzolom *n.* course, subject.

ru tz'ak *n.* wall.

ru tz'ak *n.* floor.

ru tz'amb'a *n.* ceiling.

ru tz'iib'leb' *n.* key (of keyboard).

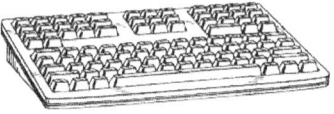

ru ululch'iich' *n.* keyboard.

ru ut xe' pim *n.* vegetables.

ru warib'aal *n.* bedspread, comforter.

ru xaml *n.* charcoal.

ru'uj *n.* top.

ru'uj *n.* snout.

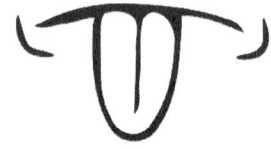

ru'uj aq' *n.* tongue.

ru'uj atz'um *n.* stigma (flower).

ru'uj ch'och' *n.* peninsula.

ru'uj puub' *n.* cannon.

ru'uj tu' *n.* nipple, teat.

ru'uj tu' *n.* aureola.

ru'uj tzuul *n.* summit, peak.

ru'uj uq' *n.* finger. *Var:* ru'uj uq'b'.

ru'uj uq'b' *n.* fingerprint.

ru'uj xkaalam e *n.* chin.

ru'uj'aq' yaab' *n.* alveopalatal.

rub'aarb' *n.* rhubarb. *From:* Spanish 'ruibarbo'.

rub'el *prep.* under.

rub'el e *n.* jaw, chin.

rub'el kab'l *n.* basement.

rub'elal xraqik *adj.* penultimate, second to last.

rub'elal'aj'ookil *n.* subconscious.

rub'rub' *adj.* sour.

rueed *n.* wheel. *From:* rueda 'the wheel' (Spanish) (1).

ruhan *n.* power.

ruhib'e *n.* cobblestone.

ruhil *n.* cover, cover page.

ruhiltz'ak *n.* rug, carpet.

ruk' *n.* relative.

ruk'a ch'iich' *n.* gasoline, gas, diesel, fuel.

ruk'a'il lit'olb' *n.* brake fluid.

rululil *n.* hard disk.

rumuk *v.* to throw.

Rup *nick.* Ruperto.

rupelhu *n.* kite.

rupik *v.* to fly. *Var:* rupupik.

rupkuk *n.* flying squirrel.

ruqb'e *n.* path.

ruq' *n.* branch.

ruq' che' *n.* branch. *Var:* ruq'b' che'.

ruq' ch'aat *n.* bed crank.

ruq' ka' *n.* pestle.

ruq' nima' *n.* tributary.

ruq'b' *n.* sleeve.

ruq'b'chaq'rab' *n.* decree, order, ruling.

ruq'b'e *n.* avenue.

ruq'b'ich'och' *n.* peninsula.

ruq'il *n.* branch, extension, outlet. *Var:* ruq'b'il.

ruq'm aq' *n.* cuff.

ruq'wajb' *n.* drumstick, hammer.

rusilal *n.* benefit.

rusos *n.* waterfall.

rub'elaj *adv.* before.

ruuch *n.* productivity.

ruuch che'k'aam *n.* vegetable.

ruuch e *n.* tooth, teeth.
   Var: uuch e.
ruuch e *n.* beak.

ruuchich'och' *n.* world, Earth.
ruuchiha' *n.* hydrosphere.
ruuchil ab'l tenamit *n.*
   ambassador.

ruuchil k'ab'a'ej *n.* pronoun.
   Var: ruuchik'ab'a'ej;
   uuchilk'ab'a'ej.
ruuchilawab'ej *n.* governor,
   ruler, delegate.
ruujik *v.* to cease.
ruutaq'a *adj.* flat.
ruutz'u'ujil aq' *n.* adornment,
   accessory, decoration.
ruutz'u'ujil ru b'e *n.* flower
   carpet.
ruutz'u'ujinkil *n.* crown
   (dental).
ruutz'uujil kab'l *n.* flower bed.
ruuxam *n.* embers, coals,
   charcoal.

S - s

sa *adj.* comfortable.
sa *adj.* tasty, delicious, rich.
sa *adj.* pleasing.
sa inch'ool chi rab'inkil *phr.*
   happy to hear it.
sa na'aatinak *adj.* friendly.
sa naxye *phr.* sounds good.
sa xch'ool *adj.* content, glad,
   happy.

sa' *prep.* to, through, in, inside,
   at, by. *Var:* se'.
sa' *n.* belly.
sa' *n.* stomach.
sa' *n.* bottom.
sa' a'an *adv phr.* there, over
   there.
sa' ixq *n.* womb, uterus.
sa' jumpaat *adv phr.*
   immediately, quickly.

sa' jun chik *adj.* next.

sa' jun sut *adv phr.* ever.

sa' junesal *adj.* alone.

sa' junpaat jo'naxk'e rib' *phr.* as soon as possible.

sa' junq sut *adv phr.* sometimes.

sa' kab'l *n.* room.

sa' komonil *adj.* together.

sa' kuxej *n.* throat.

sa' k'ilawank *adj.* intercultural.

sa' laanim *adv phr.* to your right.

sa' laatz'e *adv phr.* to your left.

sa' memil *n.* mime.

sa' najter q'e kutan *adv phr.* anciently.

sa' nim *adj.* right (spatial).

sa' oq *n.* sole.

sa' roq xaab' *n.* sole (footwear).

sa' ruq' aq' *n.* cuff.

sa' taqb'eet *adv.* inductively.

sa' tel *n.* armpit. *Var:* sa' talb'; sa' telb'.

sa' tzoltz'iib' *adv.* alphabetically.

sa' tz'e *adj.* left. *From:* *tz'eh 'left' (Ch'olan) (2).

sa' uleb'aal *n.* eyewear shop.

sa' uq' *n.* palm (of the hand).

sa' xb'een *prep.* over, above, on top.

sa' xka'yab'aal *prep.* in front of.

sa' xk'ab'a' *prep.* through.

sa' xmaak *prep.* through.

sa' xsal *adv phr.* backwards.

sa' xse'enkil *adj.* funny, entertaining.

sa' xyanq *prep.* between.

sa' xyaalal *adj.* wary.

sa' xyi *n.* middle.

sa' yaal na'aatinak *adj.* realistic.

sa' yi *n.* waist.

sa' yu'am *adj.* pregnant.

sa'ej *n.* diarrhea.

sa'ej *n.* bowels.

sa'ej *n.* stomach ache.

sa'iltz'aqob'l *n.* infix.

sa'in *adv.* here.

sab'esink *v.* to clean up.

sachalkil *n.* error.

sachaamil xch'ool *adj.* surprised, astonished.

sachb'ach'ool *n.* emotion.

sachb'ach'oolej *n.* amazement, astonishment.

sachb'ach'oolej *adj.* magical, miraculous.

sachb'ach'oolej *n.* miracle.

sachenaq ru *adj.* confused, puzzled.

sachenaq xch'ool *adj.* amazed.

sachik *v.* to use up.

sachjik *n.* mistake.

sachk *v.* to get lost, go astray, disappear.

sachk *v.* to confuse.

sachk *n.* error.

sachk sa' ch'ool *v phr.* to forget.

sachleb' *n.* eraser.

sachok *v.* to destroy.

sachok *v.* to erase.

sachok *v.* to lose.

sachok *v.* to spend.

sachom *n.* budget. *Var:* **sachomq.**

sachom *n.* bill, tab, expense.

sachomj *n.* economics.

sachomj junkab'lal *n.* home economics.

sachso *adj.* absent.

sachsookin *phr.* I am lost.

sahil *n.* flavor.

sahil *n.* liking.

sahil ch'ool *adj.* happy.

sahil ch'oolej *n.* peace.

sahil ch'oolej *n.* greeting.

sahil ch'oolejil *n.* happiness, contentment.

sahil ch'oolejil choq' aawe *phr.* congratulations!

sahil ch'oolejil choq' aawe sa' laakutan *phr.* happy birthday.

sahil ch'oolejil choq' aawe sa' ralankil *phr.* Merry Christmas.

sahil ch'oolib'k *v phr.* to greet.

sahil wank *n.* harmony (social).

sahilal *n.* affection.

sahilank *n.* delight, pleasure, enjoyment. *Var:* **saylank.**

sahilwank *n.* democracy.

sahilyaab' *n.* harmony (musical).

sahob'k'utleb'aal *n.* staging, set.

sahob'resink ch'ool *v phr.* to please.

Sakb'a *sur.*

sakil *n.* seed.

Sakil *sur. From:* sakil (the seed of plants like melons or squashes). (B1).

sakil k'um *n.* pumpkin seed.

Sakul *sur. From:* saq ('white'). (B3).

sak'a *adj.* diligent.

sak'ahil *n.* diligence. *Var:* **sak'ahal.**

sak'lemb'ilb'olotz *n.* volleyball.

sak'ok *v.* to beat, hit, strike.

sak'ok aatin *n.* murmurs, offensive words, slurs.

salab'ank *v.* to recline.

salam *adj.* diagonal.

salb'a *n.* dandruff. *Var:* **sakb'a.**

Salchicha *top.* [sa' chi chaj] "among the pines". *Etym:* chaj = pinetree.

salchiich *n.* sausage, hot dog. *From:* salchicha 'the sausage' (Spanish) (1).

salso *adj.* reclined.

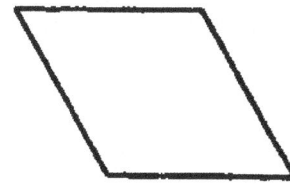

salsookil kaaxukuut *n.* rhombus, diamond.

saltul *n.* mamey, pouteria sapota.

sam *n.* nasal mucus.

Sam *sur. From:* sam ('snot'). (B1).

samahi' *n.* sand. *Var:* **samayib'.**

samat *n.* wild cilantro.

samxul *n.* elephant.

sanahoor *n.* carrot. *From:* Spanish 'zanahoria'.

sank *n.* ant.

santil hu *n.* bible. *From:* Spanish 'santo'.

santil musiq'ej *n.* holy spirit.

sandiiy *n.* watermelon. *From:* Spanish 'sandía'.

sapsapink ib' *n.* despair.

saq *adj.* white.

saq b'alam *n.* tiger cat.

saq ru *adj.* clean.

saqb'ach *n.* hail, ice.

saqb'ach ha' *n.* snowcone, shaved ice.

saqb'achleb'aal *n.* freezer.

saqb'e *n.* Milky Way.

saqb'et *n.* pallor.

saqb'etin *adj.* pale.

saqb'in *n.* weasel.

saqb'yino'k *n.* fainting spell.

saqb'yino'k *v.* to fainting.

saqch'iich' *n.* aluminum.

saqen *adj.* light (not dark).

saqen *n.* light.

saqen *adj.* light, clear.

saqen ru *adj.* transparent.

saqenb'aal *n.* lamp. *Var:* **saqen.**

saqenk'im *n.* ceiling light, transparent roof panel, skylight.

saqenlem *n.* glass.

saqi aq' *n.* clean laundry.

saqi b'iin *n.* white wine.

saqi ch'iich' *n.* silver.

saqi ismal *n.* gray hairs.

saqi kar *n.* sardines.

saqi pek *n.* marble.

saqi pwaq *n.* silver, white gold. *Var:* **saqpuhak; saqpuhaq.**

saqi tul *n.* plantain.

saqihix *n.* white orchid, monja blanca.

saqijoj *n.* cyst.

saqikaq *adj.* pink.

saqikil *n.* heron.

saqirax *adj.* cerulean, sky blue.

saqjorin *adj.* whitish.

saqjuy *n.* mush, porridge.

saqkil mitz'kotkik' *n.* white blood cells.

saqkirin *n.* anemia. *Var:* **saq kirink.**

saqkirin *adj.* pale.

saqleb' *n.* leper. *Var:* **saqlep.**

saqleb' *n.* disinfectant.

saqleb' rix *adj.* leprotic.

saqlep *n.* skin spots (white).

saqmot *n.* cauliflower.

saqmoy *adj.* colorless.

saqmuch'iich' *n.* palladium.

saqonaqilchahim *n.* galaxy.

saqoonak *n.* cave.

saqpotz'in *adj.* very white.

saqpotz'in *adj.* silver.

saqpuk'in *adj.* very white.

saqwak' *n.* cauliflower.

saqxe' *n.* turnip.

saqxul *n.* fly (insect).

saq'e *n.* sun.

saq'ehil *n.* drought, dry spell.

saq'ehil *n.* summer.

saq'ehil kutan *n.* sunny.

Saramilche Chichen *top.* [sa' ramil che' chi ch'en] "wooden trenches by the Chich'en area". *Etym:* ram = blockage or barrier; il = adjectival suffix; che' = wood or tree.

sarampyon *n.* measles. *From:* Spanish 'sarampión'.

Sarxoch *top.* [sa' sarxoch] "among the Sarxoch birds". *Etym:* sa' = in or among; Sarxoch = type of bird in Q'eqchi'.

sas *adj.* thick.

sasalxab'on *n.* shampoo.

sasob'resink *v.* to thicken.

satuurn *n.* Saturn. *From:* Spanish 'Saturno'.

Sawi' *sur.*

Sayaxche *top.* [sa' yaxche'] "by the forked tree". *Etym:* sa' = in, among, by; yaxche' = the claw of the tree.

sayi' *n.* plantain.

sabaan *n.* savannah. *From:* sabana 'the savannah' (Spanish) (1).

sa' e *n.* gums.

sa' u *n.* eye.

sa' u'uj *n.* nostril.

sa' xk'atq *prep.* beside.

saa'us *n.* fruit.

saa'us *n.* candy.

saab' *n.* swamp.

saab' ha' *n.* marsh, swamp.

saaj *adj.* young.

saaj al *n.* boy.

saaj ixqa'al *n.* girl.

saajil poy ch'iich' *n.* minivan.

saak' *n.* grasshopper.

saan *n.* wound, sore.

saant *n.* saint. *From:* Spanish 'santo'.

saapunk *v.* to catch.

saasa *adj.* tasty.

saasa xch'ool *adj.* satisfied.

saaseb' *n.* liver.

saaw *n.* Saturday. *From:* sábado 'Saturday' (Spanish) (1).

se' *n.* smile.

se'ek *v.* to laugh, smile.

se'eel winq *n.* clown.

se'se' ru *adj.* light-hearted.

se'se'il ch'oolej *n.* sense of humor.

seb' *n.* clay.

Seb' *sur. From:* seb' ('clay'). (B1).

seb'esink *v.* to threaten.

seb'ooy *n.* onion. *From:* cebolla 'the onion' (Spanish) (1).

sekch'iich' *n.* knife.

sektiyemr *n.* September. *From:* Spanish 'septiembre'.

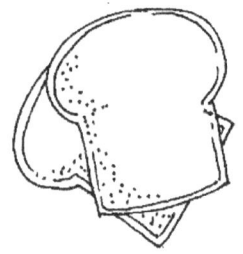

sek' *n.* cup, dish, bowl. *From:* sek' 'plate' (approximate form) (Western Mayan) (2).

sek' re kape *n.* coffee cup.

Senahu *top.* [se' nahuq'] "among the nahuq' plants". *Etym:* chi = by, among, in; nahuq' = type of plant.

sepiiy *n.* brush. *From:* cepillo 'the brush' (Spanish) (1).

serees *n.* cherry. *From:* Spanish 'cereza'.

sero *n.* zero. *From:* cero 'zero' (Spanish) (1).

seruch *n.* saw. *From:* Spanish 'serrucho'.

serwees *n.* beer. *Var:* serb'ees. *From:* cerveza 'beer' (Spanish) (1).

Sesec Yalpur *top.* [se' sek' xya'al pur] "among the vessels near the snail waters". *Etym:* sek' = cup or bowl; xya'a = water of; pur = snail.

setb'ilkaxlanwa *n.* sliced bread.

setinb'il tib' *n.* ground meat.

setleb' *n.* scissors, shears.

setleb' ixi'ij *n.* nail clippers.

setleb' pach'aya' *n.* lawnmower.

setleb' uutz'u'uj *n.* pruning shears.

setok *v.* to mow.

setok *v.* to saw.

setok *v.* to trim, cut.

setok chi kaaxukut *v phr.* to dice.

setok chi kok' *v phr.* to chop.

setok tib' *v phr.* to mince.

seb'aad *n.* barley. *From:* cebada 'the barley' (Spanish) (1).

seeb' *adj.* light (in weight).

seeb' *adj.* audacious.

seeb'ajch'iich' *n.* aluminum.

seeb'al rib' *n.* involuntary reflex.

seeb'alil *n.* competence, capability.

seeb'altz'iib' *n.* stenography, shorthand.

seeb'ch'oolil *n.* acrobatics.

seel *n.* gourd, squash.

seelapan *n.* toucan. *Var:* selepan; seleepan.

seelxul *n.* armadillo.

seer *n.* bee. *From:* cera 'bee's wax' (Spanish) (1).

seeraq' *n.* story, tale, chat, message.

seeraq' *n.* legend.

seeraq'ik *v.* to speak, talk, tell stories, narrate. *Var:* saaraq'ik; saraq'ik; seraq'ik.

seet *n.* silk. *From:* seda 'the silk' (Spanish) (1).

seeb'ank *v.* to hurry.

sht *interj.* [utterance seeking recognition].

sht! *interj.* [utterance of disapproval].

si *n.* gift.

si' *n.* firewood.

Si' *sur. From:* si' ('firewood'). (B1).

sib' *n.* smoke.

sib'ha' *n.* carbohydrates.

sib'tehenk *v.* to smoke.

sihink *v.* to share.

sihokna'leb' *v.* to suggest.

sij *n.* cricket.

sijb' *n.* arrow.

sik *n.* paralytic.

sik *adj.* lame, paralyzed.

siksotk *v.* to shiver.

sik'ok ib' *v phr.* to earn.

sik'l *n.* cigarette, cigar.

sik'leb' aatin *n.* dictionary, lexicon.

sik'lik *v.* to smoke.

sik'mank'a'uxl *n.* ideal.

sik'ok *v.* to look for, seek.

sik'ok maak *v phr.* to sin.

sik'ok u *v phr.* to choose.

sik'ok-eetalil *n.* iconography.

sik'ok-u *n.* election, choice.

simb' *n.* bamboo.

simb'ch'iich' *n.* pipe (metal).

simb'plaast *n.* pipe (plastic), PVC.

simb'tz'uum *n.* hose.

sink *n.* zinc.

sip *n.* tick.

sipakapense *lang.* Sipakapa (San Marcos).

sipook *n.* swelling, inflammation.

sipres *n.* cypress. *From:* Spanish 'cipres'.

siq'il *adj.* crooked.

siq'ok *v.* to twist.

siril *n.* circle.

sirk'arch'iich' *n.* electric saw. *Var:* **surk'arch'iich'**.

sirso *n.* circle. *Var:* **surso**.

sirweel *n.* plum. *From:* Spanish 'ciruela'.

Sis *sur.*

sis *n.* white-nosed coati.

sisanb'iltib' *n.* grilled meat.

sisank *v.* to roast, fry.

sisib'aaltib' *n.* barbeque stall.

siwan *n.* cave, abyss.

siyab'aal *n.* biotope.

siyaak *v.* to be born. *From:* *sih 'to be born (Yucatecan, Ch'olan, possible) (5).

sib'eel *n.* carbon.

sib'j *n.* charcoal.

siip kaxlan wa *n.* French bread.

siipilal *n.* swelling, inflammation. *Var:* **siip**.

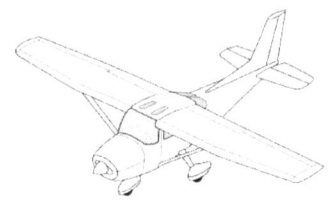

so'sol ch'iich' *n.* airplane.

sob'e'k *v.* to sink, fall.

sob'ok *v.* to crush, grind, dent.

sob'olal *n.* dent.

sob'sob'k'uub' *n.* sponge.

sob'yajel *n.* cancer.

soch *n.* shell, sea snail.

sok jolom *n.* pillow, cushion.

sok xb'een'aq *n.* knee pad, knee patch.

sok xul *n.* nest.

sokink *v.* to nest.

sol *n.* husk (grain), plaque.

solel *n.* scale.

soldaa *n.* soldier. *Var:* **sola.** *From:* soldado 'soldier' (Spanish) (1).

somenkil *n.* oath.

son *n.* music. *From:* son 'music' (Spanish) (1).

soq' *n.* net bag, rope net.

soq' re karab'k *n.* fish net.

soq'ch'iich' *n.* chicken wire.

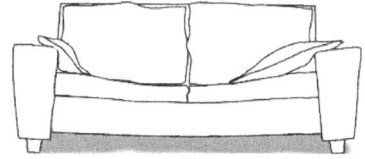

soq'il chunleb' *n.* couch, sofa.

soq'keep *n.* beret, cap.

soq'punit *n.* beret.

sote'k *v.* to remove.

sotlaak *v.* to lie down.

sotz' *n.* bat.

sowen *adj.* jealous. *Var:* **sowem.**

sowenal *n.* jealousy.

sowenk *n.* jealousy, zeal.

so'sol *n.* vulture. *Var:* **so'sool.** *From:* sosool 'vulture' (Yucatecan, Ch'olan, possible) (2).

soop *n.* soup. *From:* Spanish 'sopa'.

sooto'y *n.* digestive system.

sooyom *n.* intestines, guts.

Sub' *sur.* *From:* sub (a thorny tree). (B1).

sub'e'k *v.* to sink. *From:* *suhp' 'to sink' (Ch'olan) (2).

sub'inch'iich' *n.* nail.

sujen *n.* frost. *Var:* **sujew.**

sujew *n.* mist, fog.

suk *n.* nest. *From:* sik 'house construction' (Ch'olan) (2).

sukhu *n.* book bag, school bag.

sulem *n.* light bulb.

sulul *n.* mud.

sulutz *n.* marrow.

sum ajlil *n.* binary system.

sum na'tz'iib' *n.* long vowel.

sumal *n.* pair.

sumal'ajl *n.* even numbers.

sumal'aq' *n.* change of clothes.

sumchi'ib'k *v.* to exchange (words).

sumch'a'ajkilal *n.* equation.

sumenk *v.* to answer, respond, reply.

sumenk *v.* to assist.

sumenk aatin *n.* oath.

sumenk ru aatin *v phr.* to promise.

sumenk-ib' *adj.* reciprocal.

sumlajik *n.* wedding.

sumlaak *v.* to marry.

sumlaak chi ru chaq'rab' *n.* civil marriage.

sumsihink *v.* to exchange (gifts).

sumsuukil *n.* married man, married woman.

sumwank *n.* covenant.

sumyaab' *n.* echo.

Sun *sur.*

sunob'l *n.* perfume.

sunob'resiil *n.* cosmetics.

sununk *adj.* fragrant.

sununkil b'an *n.* ointment.

sununkil b'ook *n.* lotion, perfume.

sununkil k'ol *n.* incense.

sununkil pim *n.* herbs.

supq'een *n.* vegetable.

suq *n.* mosquito.

suq *n.* fly (insect), sandfly, midge, gnat.

suq'iik *v.* to come back.

sur chapleb'aal *n.* CD-ROM, compact disk, disk, CD.

surb'ich *n.* record, album, CD.

surb'ichleb'aal *n.* record player.

surchoch *n.* disk.

surjachleb'che' *n.* electric saw.

sursu *n.* wheel.

sursu *adj.* round, circular.

sururu *n.* top.
sururu *n.* propeller.
sururub'atz'uul *n.* top.
sut *n.* handkerchief, rag.

sut *n.* sling.
sut *n.* time.
sutam *n.* environment, area.
  Var: **suutaal.**
sutisink *v.* to spin.
sutq'isinb'il *n.* repatriate.
sutq'iik *v.* to repatriate, revert, return.
sutrib' *n.* rotation.
sutrix *n.* revolution.

sutruuchich'och' *adv.* internationally.
sutruuchich'och'ink *v.* to internationalize.
sutuxink *v.* to surround.
sutz'uj *n.* cedar.
sutz'ujl *n.* mahogany.
suwajb' *n.* guitar.

suunal *n.* boyfriend, girlfriend.
suunuhom *n.* boyfriend, girlfriend.
suurisink *v.* to flip.
suurk *n.* furrow. *From:* surco 'the furrow' (Spanish) (1).
suut *n.* furrow.
suut ha' *n.* whirlpool.
suutalnawom *n.* cosmology.
suutilal *n.* orbit.
sweer *n.* IV, intravenous solution.

T - t

ta *part.* [doubt particle]. *Note:* Used to indicate doubt or rhetorical nature of a question. **Ma ink'a' ta a'in li b'e sik'b'il ru inb'aan?** « Is this not the path that I have chosen? » *Var:* **ta b'i'**.

ta *n.* fur.

ta'ok *n.* to discover.

tachweel *n.* tack, thumbtack. *From:* Spansish 'tachuela'.

tach'to *adj.* flat. *From:* tach' 'be flat' (Ch'olan) (2).

tahu *n.* folder, binder.

takchi' *n.* bad advice.

takchi' *n.* blackmail.

taks *n.* taxi.

talanch'iich' *n.* bell.

tam *n.* hay.

tamb'aha' *n.* washbasin, washbowl.

tamb'or *n.* drum. *From:* tambor 'drum' (Spanish) (1).

tamleb'aal metz'ew *n.* battery.

tamleb'aalha' *n.* barrel, cask.

tamok-ajl *n.* addition, total, sum.

tana *adv.* maybe, perhaps.

tap *n.* crab.

tap re nima' *n.* crayfish.

tapon *n.* stopper. *From:* from tapón (Spanish).

taqb'eetil *adj.* inductive.

taqe'k *v.* to go up, climb, mount.

taqe'k chi rix kawaay *v phr.* to ride, go horseback riding, mount a horse.

taqe'q *prep.* up.

taqe'q *adv.* above.

taqe'q q'eq'ookot eetalil *n.* Tropic of Cancer.

taqik *n.* time.

taql *n.* post, mail.

taqlahom *n.* command, order, commandment.

taqlank *v.* to send.

taqlank *v.* to rule, govern.

taqlank *v.* to command, order.

taqlankil *n.* mission, mandate.

taqleb' *n.* scaffolding, platform.

taqleb'aal *n.* steps.

taqleb'aal *n.* scaffolding, platform.

taqleb'aal *n.* ladder.

taqlhu *n.* document.

taqlil *n.* assignment, errand, commission.

taqlilk'ay *n.* export, exportation.

taqsink *v.* to rise, raise.

taqsiil *n.* jack.

taq'a *n.* valley, plain, prairie.

taq'a *adv.* below.

taq'a *prep.* down.

taq'a q'eq'ookot eetalil *n.* Tropic of Capricorn.

taq'eetil *n.* likeness.

taq'eetink *n.* analogy.

tarjeet postal *n.* postcard.
From: tarjeta postal 'postcard' (Spanish) (1).

tarjeet re b'oqleb' *n.* phone card.

tas *n.* division, level.

tasal *n.* shelf.

tasal hu re ula' *n.* appointment book, visitor log.

tasal ruuchich'och' *n.* tectonic plates.

tasalhu *n.* book.

tasl *n.* screen (dividing).

tat re *v phr.* to stutter, stammer.

tawajenaq *adj.* tired, weary.

tawajenaqin *phr.* I'm tired.

tawasink *v.* to injure.

tawilna'leb' *n.* refrain, saying, proverb.

tawloq'aal *n.* civilization.

tawok *v.* to appear.

tawok *v.* to get, find.

tawok u *v phr.* to meet.

tawok u *v phr.* to understand.

tawok xyaalal *v phr.* to understand.

tawrib' oxxukuut *n.* congruent triangle.

taxaq *part.* [utterance indicating hope or a wish]. Us taxaq wi yaal a'an. « I hope that's true. »

tayarin *n.* noodles. *From:* Spanish 'tallarines'.

taab' *n.* tumpline, head strap.

taab'leb'aal b'ich *n.* tape player.

taaqenk *v.* to follow, pursue.

taaqinel *n.* guard.

taas *n.* cup. *From:* taza 'the cup' (Spanish) (1).

taat *n.* father.

te *n.* tea. *From:* té 'tea' (Spanish) (1).

teb'elal *n.* swelling.

teb'es *adj.* thick.

teb'tookil hu *n.* cardboard.

tehok *v.* to open.

tehok ru *n.* to discover.

tehto *adj.* open. *Var:* teeto.

teken ch'iich' *n.* truck.

tektiteko *lang.* Tektitek (Huehuetenango).

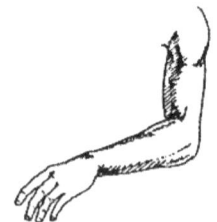

tel *n.* arm. *Var:* telb'.

teleb'ision *n.* television. *From:* televisión 'television' (Spanish) (1).

teleef *n.* telephone, phone. *From:* teléfono 'the telephone' (Spanish) (1).

telnak *v.* to carry (in hand).

telonk *v.* to carry (on shoulder).

tem *n.* chair, bench.

temb'il *n.* blow.

tenamit *n.* village, town. *From:* tena:mitl 'wall' (Nahuatl) (1).

tenamitil *n.* people.

tenamitil teepal *n.* urban center.

teneb'anb'il sa' junkab'lal *n.* family chores.

teneb'anb'ilkamk *n.* death penalty.

teneb'aal *n.* obligation.

teneb'ankil sa' xb'een *v phr.* to convict.

Teni' *sur.* *From:* ten ('hammer'). (B3).

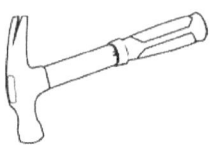

tenleb' *n.* hammer, mallet.

tenok *v.* to beat, hit, strike. *From:* *ten 'to hammer, flatten' (Ch'olan) (2).

tenok *v.* to crush, grind. *From:* *ten 'to hammer, flatten' (Ch'olan) (2).

tenok chi che' *v phr.* to beat up.

tenq' *n.* scholarship.

tenq' *n.* task, job, chore.

tenq'ank *v.* to help, protect.

tenq'aal *n.* help, assistance.

tenq'aal *n.* cooperation.

tento tinxik *phr.* I've got to go.

terq'usink k'ab'a' *n.* praise.

terto xtz'aq *adj.* expensive.

testiig *n.* witness. *From:* testigo 'the witness' (Spanish) (1).

Teyul *sur.*

te'elch'ool *n.* widower.

teeb'il xk'a'uxl *v phr.* to consider.

teeleb' *n.* key.

teeleb' *n.* opener. *Var:* teheleb'.

teeleb' laat *n.* can opener.

teeleb' meet *n.* bottle opener, corkscrew.

teeleb'ha' *n.* faucet, water tap.

teelom *adj.* male (of humans).

teelom *n.* man. *From:* *tehlom 'young man' (Ch'olan) (2).

teelom i *n.* grandson.

teep *n.* batch.

teep *n.* part.

teep *n.* district, neighborhood, sector, canton.

teepalpoopol *n.* municipality.

teeto xk'a'uxl *adj.* considerate.

ti'ok *v.* to bite.

tib' *n.* meat. *Var:* chib'.

tib' *n.* flesh.

tib'el wa *n.* food, meal.

tib'elej *n.* muscles, flesh.

tib'elej *n.* thigh.

tichk'ok *v.* to trip.

tihok u *v phr.* to choose.

tij *n.* doctrine.

tij *n.* prayer.

tijb'a'ajsiil *n.* physical education.

tijb'ab'atz'il *n.* art education.

tijb'ab'ich *n.* music education.

tijb'ajunesal *n.* distance education.

tijb'apoyanam *n.* adult education.

tijb'il *adj.* educated.

tije'k *v.* to be indoctrinated.

tijob'aal *n.* church, chapel, temple.

tijok *v.* to pray.

tijok *v.* to indoctrinate.

tijok *v.* to educate.

tijok chi rix kawilal *n.* health education.

tijok chi rix loq'ok *n.* consumer finance.

tijok sa' ka'aatinob'aal *n.* bilingual education.

tijom *n.* pupil, student.

tikb'il *n.* challenge.

tikib'ank *v.* to begin.

tikil che' *n.* ruler.

tikkehil kutan *n.* spring (season).

tiklajik *n.* beginning.

tiklaak *v.* to begin.

tikok *v.* to challenge.

tikok *v.* to attack.

tikonel *n.* challenger.

tikto *adv.* soon, immediately.

tiktz'aqob'l *n.* prefix.

tik'ti' *n.* lie, falsehood.

tik'ti'ink *v.* to lie (tell falsehoods).

tilin *n.* bell.

timil *adj.* slow.

tin *n.* worm.

tiq *adj.* hot.

tiq *adj.* warm.

tiq *n.* fever.

tiqam *n.* continuation.

tiqb'al *n.* dress.

tiqb'al *n.* clothing, clothes.

tiqilal *n.* link (in a chain).

tiqkaxlan xaml *n.* proton.

tiqkehil *n.* temperature.

tiqob' *n.* sweat.

tiqob'ak *v.* to perspire. *Var:* tiqob'ank.

tiqok *v.* to add.

tiqok ib' *v phr.* to put on.

tiqwal *n.* steam. *From:* tikwal 'heat' (Ch'olan) (3).

tiqwal ha' *n.* hot water.

tiqwal kakaw *n.* hot chocolate.

tiqwal saq'e *adj.* hot.

tiqwal siraalch'och' *n.* tropics, sun belt.

tiqwalch'och' *n.* hot climate.

tiqwasink *v.* to heat.

tiqwok' *n.* arousal.

tiq'eek *n.* accident.

tiq'ilal *n.* wound, sore. *Var:* tiiq'; tiq'il.

tisyemr *n.* December.
Var: risyemr; risymb'r. *From:*
Spanish 'diciembre'.

titz'e'k *n.* appeal.

titz'jenaq *adj.* bored.

titz'k *v.* to bore.

titz'ok *n.* interview.

Tiul *sur.*

tiwb'il *n.* bite.

tiwok *v.* to eat, bite.

tiwok posaq'e *n.* eclipse.

tixeer *n.* scissors, shears.
From: tijera 'scissors' (Spanish) (1).

tixk *v.* to grow old.

tixl *n.* tapir. *Var:* tis.

tixto toj *conj.* until.

tiburon *n.* shark. *From:* tiburón
'the shark' (Spanish) (1).

tiik *adj.* straight.

tiik *adj.* smooth.

tiik ru *adj.* serious.

tiik xch'ool *adj.* faithful, just,
righteous.

tiikal *n.* direction.

tiikal juch'leb' *n.* ruler.

tiikalil *n.* ethics, values.

tiikaljuch' *n.* straight line.

tiikalxaqab'aal *n.* plumb.

tiikil juch'ul *n.* straight line.

tiikil kaxlanxaml *n.* electron.

tiikil k'ayib'aal *n.* duty free
shop.

tiikil loq'alil *n.* ethics, values.

tiikil'aatin *adj.* colloquial.

tiikilal *n.* honesty.

tiikilwank *n.* justice.

tiikink *v.* to push. *Var:* tiikisink.

tiikis *phr.* push.

tiikisib'aal *n.* pedal.

tiikob'resink *v.* to season.

tiik-uhil *n.* symmetry.

tiimbr *n.* postage, stamp. *From:*
timbre 'postage stamp' (Spanish)
(1).

tiiqeltz'uq *n.* period.

tiix *n.* elder, old man, old
woman. *From:* *ti'ix 'old woman'
(Ch'olan) (2).

tiix *adj.* old.

tiixil ch'ajom *n.* confirmed
bachelor.

tiixil po *n.* full moon.

tk'a'uxlaq *adj.* thoughtful.

tk'ul ach'ool *adj.* charming.

to' *n.* loan.

to'aatin *n.* borrowed word.

to'chi' *n.* linguistic borrowing,
borrowed word.

to'nink *v.* to borrow.
   Var: **to'onink**.

to'nink *v.* to lend, loan.
   Var: **to'onink**.

tob'b'ak *v.* to fall.

tob'ok *v.* to let go.

toch'ok *n.* hurt, harm.

toch'ok *n.* assault.

toch'ok *v.* to play (instruments).

toch'ok *v.* to assault.

toch'ol *n.* injured party.

toch'ool *adj.* hurt.

toj *n.* tax, tribute, VAT.

toj *conj.* until, still.

toj *adj.* more.

toj al *adj.* unripe.

toj chi ru awab'ej *n.* taxes.

toj eq'la *adv.* earlier.

toj le' *adv phr.* over there.

toj rax *adj.* rare.

toj reetal *adv phr.* at last, finally.

toj ruch... *phr.* there still are...

toj wan... *phr.* there still are...

toja' *conj.* until now, just now.

toja' yaal *phr.* that depends.

tojaq *adv.* since.

tojb'a maak *n.* punishment.

tojb'il b'oqleb' *n.* payphone.

toje' *adv.* a moment ago, recently.

toje' *adj.* recent.

tojhuil b'oqleb' *n.* prepaid phone card.

tojl *n.* ticket.

tojl *n.* fine.

tojleb' re maak *n.* bail.

tojleb'aal *n.* box office, ticket window.

tojleb'aal maak *n.* hell.

tojleb'aal maak *n.* penalty, punishment.

tojleb'hu *n.* check.

tojmaak *n.* fine.

tojok *v.* to pay.

tojok maak *v phr.* to serve a sentence.

tojok maak *n.* sentence.

tokan *n.* blackberry, mulberry.

tokxaml *n.* match.

tok' *n.* flint.

Tok' *sur. From:* tok' ('flint'). (B1).

tolb'ech'iich' *n.* wheel, tire.

tolche' *n.* piece.

tolokok *n.* lizard. *Var:* **toolok**; **tookok**. *From:* *to:loki, *tohloki 'izard' (Nahuatl) (2).

toltem *n.* wheel chair.

toltol *n.* cart, wheelbarrow.

tomiin *n.* Sunday. *Var:* **domiin**; **romink**. *From:* domingo 'Sunday' (Spanish) (1).

Tomtem *top.* [toon tem] "trunk of the Tem tree". *Etym:* toon = trunk; Tem = type of tree..

tonq' *n.* quail.

topleb' *n.* spear.

toqb'ilpuub' *n.* shotgun.

toqok *v.* to break, split.

toqol *n.* fracture.

toqol a' *n.* broken leg.

toqolal *adj.* broken. *Var:* **toqol**.

toq' *n.* gum.

toq'ob' ru *adj.* poor.

toq'ob'al u *n.* pity, compassion.

torniiy *n.* screw. *From:* tornillo 'the screw' (Spanish) (1).

torol'ichaj *n.* cabbage.

toronj *n.* grapefruit. *From:* Spanish 'toronja'.

tos e *n.* speech impairment.

tool *n.* tire.

toon *n.* tree trunk, stump.

toon xik *n.* temples.

toor *n.* bull. *From:* from Spanish 'toro'.

toor *n.* tower. *Var:* **tore**. *From:* torre 'tower' (Spanish) (1).

traamp *n.* fish trap. *From:* trampa 'the trap' (Spanish) (1).

traaw *n.* liquor, shot. *From:* Spanish 'trago'.

tren *n.* train. *From:* tren 'the train' (Spanish) (1).

triiw *n.* clan. *From:* tribu 'the clan' (Spanish) (1).

triiw *n.* wheat. *From:* trigo 'the wheat' (Spanish) (1).

trompeet *n.* horn, trumpet. *From:* trompeta 'trumpet' (Spanish) (1).

tu' *n.* teat.

tu' *n.* breast, bust.

tu'ej *n sd.* breast, bust. **intu'** « my breast ».

tu'resink *v.* to nurse.

tu'uk *v.* to breastfeed.

tu'unel *n.* mammal, mammalian.

tu'unil *n.* baby bottle.

Tucuru *top.* [chitukur] "among the owls". *Etym:* chi = by, among, in; tukur = owl (K'iche', Poqomchi', Kaqchikel).

tuntun *n.* drum.

tuntunkil choq *n.* fog.

tuntuukir t'ikr *n.* towel.

tuntz'oq *n.* raven.

Tupil *sur.*

tupus roq *adj.* short.

tuq *n.* spring, well (water). *Var:* tuqb'.

tuqb'ametz'ew *n.* thermostat, regulator, controller.

tuh *adj.* dark.

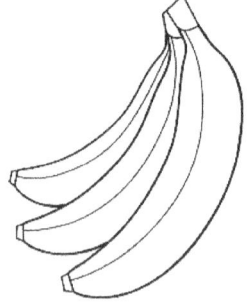

tul *n.* banana. *Var:* q'un tul.

tul *n.* banana tree.

tulux ch'iich' *n.* helicopter.

tumin *n.* money.

tumin re uuchil *n.* ransom.

Tun *sur.* *From:* tun (a hollow wooden musical instrument). (B1).

tun is *adj.* hairy.

tuqb'isleb' *n.* scale.

tuqb'iis *n.* level.

tuqlaaltz'iib' *n.* orthography.

tuqleb' *n.* level.

tuqleb' *n.* correcting fluid, White Out.

tuqtiq *n.* radiator.

tuqtu q'ojyin *n.* midnight.

tuqtu ru *adj.* easy-going.

tuqtu waleb' *n.* noon.

tuqtu xch'ool *adj.* content.

tuqtutz'iib' *n.* orthography.

tuqtuukil *n.* balance, equilibrium.

tuqtuukil k'a'uxl *n.* logic.

tuqtuukilal *n.* peace.

tuqub'ank *v.* to balance, reform.

tuq'ixq *n.* virgin, young woman. *Var:* **t'ujixq.**

turans *adj.* peach.

turans *n.* peach. *Var:* **lorans.** *From:* Spanish 'durazno'.

turunhut tz'ik *n.* quail.

turux *adj.* rough.

tusb'a'ajl *n.* ordinal number.

tusb'ehul *n.* methodological steps.

tusb'ich *n.* score, sheet music.

tusb'il che' son *n.* marimba.

tusb'il chunleb'al *n.* bleachers, stands.

tusb'ilche'wajb' *n.* marimba.

tusche'wajb' *n.* marimba.

tusch'iich'wajb' *n.* lyre.

tusilb'eek *n.* parade.

tusk'anjel *n.* plan.

tusk'anjel komonil *n.* community projects.

tusk'anjelank *v.* to plan.

tusleb' aatin *n.* glossary.

tusleb'aal aatin *n.* vocabulary.

tusleb'aal k'ay *n.* shelves.

tusleb'hu *n.* paper collator.

tusna'leb' *n.* index.

tusnaw *n.* logic.

tustu ru *adj.* organized.

tusub'ank *v.* to order, arrange.

tusuk *v.* to order, arrange.

tusul *adj.* organized.

tutz'tu *adj.* giant, tall.

tuwaay *n.* towel. *From:* toalla 'the towel' (Spanish) (1). *Var:* **tohaay.**

Tux *sur.*

tux kaxlan *n.* hen.

tuxil noq' *n.* cotton swab. *Var:* **tuux noq'; tuuxil noq'.**

tuxim *n.* onion.

tuxl *n.* scabies.

tuub'ank *v.* to memorize.

tuul *n.* magic.

tuulan *adj.* humble, quiet, peaceful.

tuulan *adj.* mild, meek.

tuulan palaw *n.* Pacific Ocean.

tuulanel *n.* sorcerer, witch.

tuulux *n.* dragonfly.

Tuut *sur.*

twaj ru *phr.* I'm in a hurry.

twulaq chi ru *adj.* delighted.

tyox *n.* god. *Var:* **yos.** *From:* dios 'God' (Spanish) (1).

T' - t'

t' *interj.* [utterance indicating a minor failure].

t'ane'k *n.* defeat, fall, rendition.

t'ane'k *v.* to fall.

t'anleb'aalha' *n.* waterfall.

t'anliik *v.* to fall sick.

t'anruche' *n.* shelf.

t'aqresink *v.* to wet, irrigate.

t'aqt'aq *adj.* damp, wet, humid.

t'e'b'il *adj.* combed.

t'i'ok *v.* to kick.

t'i'ok *v.* to pound.

t'ikr *n.* clothing, cloth.

t'ikr loon *n.* denim.

t'ikr re chaqob'resink uq *n.* hand towel.

t'ikr re maqab' *n.* baby bib.

t'ikt'o *adj.* thick.

t'ilb'a'u'ji'aq *n.* tongue twister.

t'ilob'aal *n.* anchor.

t'ilru'uj'aq *n.* tongue twister.

t'inis *n.* heavyset person.

t'inis *adj.* fat. *Var:* t'initz.

t'initz *n.* wild horse.

t'int'ookil patux *n.* goose.

t'iw *n.* eagle.

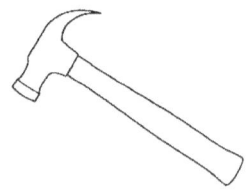

t'ojleb' *n.* hammer.

t'ojoch *adj.* bald.

t'ojok *v.* to hammer.

t'ojom *n.* nail.

t'ojt'o *adj.* bald.

t'oklal *n.* knot.

t'ok' *n.* knot. *Var:* tok'.

t'omt'o re *adj.* toothless.

t'onos *adj.* fat.

t'ont'on xyaab' *adj.* clamorous.

t'oqb'on *n.* wax seal.
t'oqtzak *n.* mayonnaise, mayo.
t'oqx *adj.* wet.
t'oq't'ookil b'an *n.* ointment.
t'or'ajl *n.* cardinal number.
t'orlemtz' *n.* marbles.
t'orol *n.* grain.
t'orol pens *n.* peppercorn.
t'ort'o *adj.* spherical, round.

t'ort'o *n.* sphere.
t'ort'ookil *adj.* spherical.
t'ort'ookil tib' *n.* meatballs.
T'ot' *sur.*
t'ot' *n.* snail.
T'ox *sur.*

t'uj *adj.* spotless.
t'ujleb'aal *n.* beauty salon.
t'upuy *n.* headband, headdress. *From:* t'upuy 'the headband' (Ch'olti') (2).
t'urt'u *adj.* naked.
t'uru' xjolom *adj.* bald.
t'usam *n.* nakedness.
t'ust'u *adj.* naked.

t'usub' *n.* grape. *Var:* uub'.
t'uyub'ank *v.* to hang up.
t'uuyleb' *n.* hammock, swing. *Var:* t'uyleb'.

Tz - tz

tza *n.* demon, devil.
tza'aj *n.* perymenium tuerkheimii. *Note:* tasiscobo (Spanish)
tzak *n.* prey. *From:* tzak 'to take or look for' (Ch'olan) (5).

tzakahem *n.* food, meal. *Var:* tzakahemq; tzekeem.

tzakank *v.* to eat, feed.
 Var: **tzekank.**

tzakib'k *v.* to win.

tzakib'k *v.* to hunt.

tzakink *v.* to earn.

tzaksu *n.* eggplant.

Tzalam *sur. From:* tzalam
 ('prison'). (B1).

tzapliik junelik *n.* life
 sentence.

tzaqal jun *adj.* whole.

tzaqal winq *n.* indigenous,
 Maya. *Note:* Literally 'authentic
 man'. Term the Q'eqchi' use to
 refer to themselves. (Aj
 Q'eqchi' traditionally refers to a
 speaker of the Q'eqchi'
 language, not a tribe or
 ethnicity.)

tzelam *n.* edge.

tzelek *n.* pimple.

tzelek xaab' *n.* boot.

tzemok *v.* to covet.

tzentzejer *n.* woodpecker.

Tzib' *sur.*

Tzib'oy *sur.*

tzilb'a'ix *n.* analysis.

tzilinch'iich' *n.* bell.

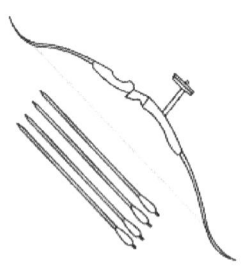

tzimaj *n.* bow and arrow.
 Var: **simaj.**

tzimitz *n.* horse.

tzinb'ak *v.* to sound, ring.

tzinb'ank *v.* to sound, toll.

tzintzin *n.* guitar.

tziib'aak *v.* to search.

tziitzib' *n.* snail.

tzo' *adj.* male (of birds).

tzo' pu' *n.* peacock.

tzo'xul ha' *n.* beer. *Note:* 'El gallo' is a popular brand of beer in Guatemala. The bottles have a rooster logo on the front.

tzojtzoj *n.* baby rattle.

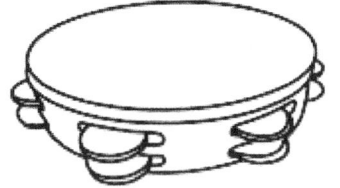

tzojtzojch'iich' *n.* tambourine.

tzol *n.* furrow. *From:* *tzohl 'line, row' (Yucatecan, Ch'olan, possible).

tzol *n.* row, line.

tzoleb' *n.* doctrine.

tzoleb'aal *n.* school, academy.

tzoleb'aal xb'een na'aj *n.* elementary school.

tzolil *n.* row, line.

tzoljalam'uuch'ink *n.* visual arts, plastic arts.

tzolok *v.* to teach.

tzolok *v.* to learn, study.

tzolom *n.* pupil, student.

tzolom chi rix ululch'iich' *n.* computer science.

tzolom k'anjel *n.* lesson.

tzolomil *n.* assignment, course.

tzolomilchoxach'och' *n.* natural sciences.

tzolomilkomon *n.* social studies.

tzolomilk'uub' *n.* home economics.

tzoltzo *adj.* lined up.

tzoltzookiltzuul *n.* hills, range, mountain range, mountain ridge.

tzoltz'iib' *n.* alphabet.

tzoltz'iib'ak *v.* to become literate.

tzoltz'iib'ank *n.* literacy.

tzolyiib'ahom *n.* industrial arts.

tzonok' *n.* worm.

tzoqchahim *n.* galaxy.

tzoqtzokilchahim *n.* constellation.

tzo' kaxlan *n.* cock, rooster.

tzo'xul *n.* cock, rooster.

tzub'pajha' *n.* water pump.

tzujtzuj *n.* maracas.

tzukinb'il ru *adj.* disorganized.

tzuklenk *v.* to tangle.

tzuul *n.* mountain, hill.

tzukxul *n.* sheep.

tzuultaq'a *n.* mountain spirit.

Tz' - tz'

tz'ab'ok *v.* to light.

tz'ahok *v.* to soak.

tz'aj ru *adj.* dirty. *Var:* tz'ajn; tz'aj.

tz'ajn *n.* grime, dirt, filth, muck.

tz'ajtz'otk *adj.* full.

tz'ak *n.* wall. *From:* *tz'ahk 'wall' (Ch'olan) (1).

tz'akal'ochoch *n.* terrace.

tz'akalb'e *n.* pavement.

tz'ak-eetalil *n.* stela.

tz'akkab'l *n.* masonry.

tz'akleb' *n.* trowel.

tz'aktz'um *n.* loroco (edible herb).

tz'alam *n.* prison, jail, iron bars.

tz'alam *n.* garden-house.

tz'alam *n.* cage.

tz'alam re ji'ok aq' *n.* ironing board.

tz'alamche' *n.* board.

tz'alamche' re setok *n.* cutting board.

tz'alamch'aat *n.* crib, cradle.

tz'alamch'iich' *n.* machete.

tz'amb'a *n.* ridgepole, beam. *From:* tz'am 'beam' (Western Mayan) (3).

tz'amb'ahilch'iich' *n.* chassis.

tz'ap yehiil *n.* closed syllable.

tz'apb'al oq *n.* sock, stocking.

tz'apb'al re *n.* cap.

tz'apil *n.* cap.

tz'apleb' *n.* lock.

tz'apleb' *n.* cover, lid, top.

tz'apleb' *n.* zipper.

tz'apok *v.* to shut, close, cover.

tz'apok *v.* to lock up.

tz'apokeb'ch'iich' *n.* security door, metal door.

tz'aptz'o *adj.* closed.

tz'aptz'ookil uk'al *n.* pressure cooker.

tz'apxik *adj.* deaf.

tz'apyaab' *n.* occlusive.

tz'apyaab'il *adj.* deaf.

tz'aqal *adj.* enough, sufficient, complete.

tz'aqal *phr.* that's enough.

tz'aqal re ru *adj.* clear.

tz'aqal re ru naraj *adj.* strict.

tz'aqal ru *adj.* positive.

tz'aqal'ajk'anjel *n.* professional.

tz'aqalil hab' *n.* legal adult.

tz'aqalna'yu'am *n.* eukaryote.

tz'aqob' *n.* adjustment, complement.

tz'aqob' aatin *n.* adverb.

tz'aqob'resink *v.* to adjust, complement, modify.

tz'aqtaanank *v.* to condemn.

tz'aab'il kaxlan wa *n.* French toast.

tz'aab'il ki'ik q'een *n.* fruit slices.

tz'aak *n.* beeswax.

tz'aamank *v.* to ask for, request.

tz'aamank limoox *v phr.* to ask for alms. *From:* Spanish 'limosna'.

tz'e *adj.* left. *From:* tz'eh 'left, left hand' (Ch'olan) (2).

tz'ej *n.* thigh, flesh.

tz'ejwal *n.* penis, genitals (male).

tz'ejwalej *n.* body. *Var:* tz'ejwal.

tz'eqink *v.* to waste.

tz'eqleb'aal *n.* toilet.

tz'eqok *n.* defeat.

tz'eqok *v.* to fail.

tz'eqok *v.* to lose (a game).

tz'eqok *v.* to throw.

tz'eqok ib' *v phr.* to defecate.

tz'eqok ib' *v phr.* to lose (a possession).

tz'eqok kik' *n.* bleeding, loss of blood, blood loss.

tz'eqok k'ula'al *n.* miscarriage.

tz'eqtananb'il *adj.* humiliated, rejected.

tz'eqtanank *n.* contempt.

tz'eqtanaank *n.* rejection.

tz'eqtaanank *v.* to reject. *Var:* tz'eqtanank.

tz'eeqel *adj.* disposable.

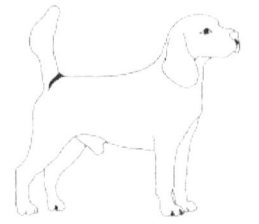

tz'i' *n.* dog.

Tz'i' *sur. From:* tz'i' ('dog'). (B1).

tz'i' e *n.* tusk.

tz'i' k'iche' *n.* wild cardamom.

tz'i' k'iche' *n.* wolf.

tz'i' pim *n.* coyote.

tz'i' tzuul *n.* coyote.

tz'i'b'eetal *adj.* abject, vile.

tz'i'ej *adj.* immoral.

tz'i'ej aatin *n.* obscenity.

tz'i'ej na'leb' *n.* immoral practices.

tz'i'ha' *n.* seal.

tz'ib' *adj.* reddish-gray.

tz'ik *n.* bird, fowl.

tz'ik *n.* penis.

tz'ikib' *n.* coitus.

tz'ilb'a'ix *n.* examination, exam, test.

tz'ilb'akax'olb' *n.* oil filter.

tz'ileb' *n.* strainer, colander, sieve.

tz'ileb' olb' *n.* oil filter.

tz'ileb' rix yajel *n.* lab, laboratory. *Var:* tz'ileb'aal yaj.

tz'ileb'aal *n.* lab, laboratory. *Var:* tz'ileb'aal yaj.

tz'ilok *v.* to sieve, strain. *From:* tz'iil 'to sieve or strain' (Mopan) (4).

tz'ilok ib' *n.* self-test.

tz'ilok ib'ink *v phr.* to self-test.

tz'ilok maak *n.* justice.

tz'ilok-ix *v.* to test, examine, investigate, research.

tz'ilol *n.* vacuole.

tz'ilool'ix *n.* examination, exam, test.

tz'ilpoyanam *n.* census.

tz'iltz'otk *v.* to drip.

tz'in *n.* manioc bread.

tz'in *n.* cassava, manioc.

tz'iray *n.* cricket.

tz'iraych'iich' *n.* call button, buzzer.

tz'iib' *n.* writing, letter.

tz'iib'ak *v.* to write, take notes.
tz'iib'anb'il esil *n.* newspaper.
tz'iib'anb'ilhu *n.* document.
tz'iib'leb' *n.* keyboard.
tz'iib'leb' *n.* pen.

tz'iib'leb' che' *n.* pencil.
tz'iib'leb' ch'iich' *n.* typewriter.
tz'iib'leb'aal *n.* office.
tz'iib'leb'aal che' *n.*
  blackboard, chalkboard.

tz'iib'leb'aalhu *n.* notebook.
tz'iib'leb'che' *n.* blackboard,
  chalkboard.

tz'iib'leb'meex *n.* desk.
tz'iib'leb'on *n.* pen.
tz'iib'uuchil *n.* ideograph.
tz'ob'ay *n.* namesake.
tz'ob'leb' *n.* extracter.
tz'okaak *v.* to be hungry.
tz'okaaq *adj.* hungry.
Tz'ub' *sur. From:* tz'ub' ('kiss').
  (B1).

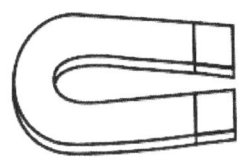

tz'ub'ch'iich' *n.* magnet.

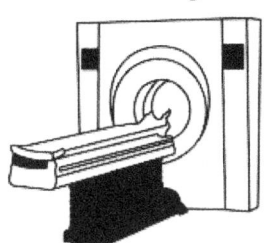

tz'ub'ch'iich'b'il eek'ch'iich'
  n. MRI machine, magnetic
  resonance imaging.
tz'ub'il *adj.* absorbed.
tz'ub'leb' *n.* straw.

tz'ub'pajha' *n.* fire truck.

tz'ub'uk *v.* to suck, absorb.

tz'ub'uk u *v phr.* to kiss.

tz'uleb' *n.* ribbon.

tz'uluk *n.* plait, braid.
Var: **tz'ulum**. *From:* *tz'ul 'to weave (mat arch)' (Ch'olti') (2).

tz'unun *n.* hummingbird.

tz'unun *n.* sparrow.

tz'upq'een *n.* praying mantis.

tz'uq *n.* point.

tz'uq *n.* period, apostrophe.

tz'uq aatin *n.* accent mark.

tz'uq kawyaab' *n.* accent mark.

tz'uqb'il b'an re sa' u *n.* eye drops.

tz'uqleb' b'an *n.* eyedropper.

tz'uqluk *v.* to drip.

tz'uqresink *v.* to soak.

tz'uqtz'um *n.* anteater.
Var: **tz'uqtz'un; tz'uqtz'uum**.

tz'uqux *n.* suspension points, ellipsis.

tz'utujil *lang.* Tz'utujil (Sololá, Suchitepéquez).

tz'uy tz'iib'esil *n.* beeper.

tz'uyink *v.* to groan.

tz'uyte'ek *v.* to howl.

tz'uytz'utk *v.* to growl, grunt.

tz'uywajb' *n.* organ.

tz'uum *n.* whip.

tz'uumal *n.* leather. *Var:* **tz'uum**.

tz'uumal *n.* tissue.

tz'uumal *n.* hide.

tz'uumal e *n.* lips.

tz'uumalej *n.* skin.
Var: **tz'uumal**.

tz'uumil chakeet *n.* fur coat.

tz'uuq *adj.* wet.

U - u

u *prep.* in front.

u *n.* fruit.

u *n.* face, forehead.

u'uj *n.* nose.

u'ujej *n.* nose.

uch ch'o *n.* mouse, rat.

uhej *n.* face.

ujinb'ilyaab' *n.* nasal, nasalization.

uk'al *n.* pot.

uk' *n.* flea.

uk' *n.* louse.

uk'a' *n.* drink.

uk'ak *v.* to drink.

uk'alpunit *n.* helmet.

uk'b'il b'an *n.* cough syrup.

uk'leb'aal *n.* spring.

uk'leb'aal *n.* water fountain, drinking fountain.

uk'leb'aal ha' *n.* water well.

uk'leb'aal kape *n.* cafe, cafeteria.

uk'leb'lem *n.* cup, glass, drinking glass.

uk'metz'ewilb'an *n.* oral rehydration solution, ORS.

ula' *n.* visit.

ula' *n.* visitor, guest.

ula'ak *v.* to visit.

ula'anink *v.* to receive visitors.

ula'ank *v.* to visit.

ulul *n.* brain. *From:* ulul 'marrow, brains' (Ch'olti') (5).

ulul ch'iich' *n.* computer or PC.

ululil xokleb' *n.* floppy disk, computer disk.

uq'm *n.* hand. *Var:* **uq'b'**. *From:* uuq' ooq ooq' uuq 'handle' (Ch'olan) (3).

uq'e'k *v.* to erode.

uq'e'k *n.* fault (geologic), erosion.

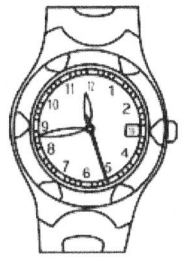

uq'mil k'uthoonal *n.* watch, wristwatch.

uq'miltz'iib' *n.* manuscript.

uq'mink *v.* to steal.

uq'ul *n.* landslide.

uq'un *n.* mush, porridge.

uq'unil b'an *n.* cream, ointment.

uq'unink *v.* to liquify.

uq'unleb'aal *n.* blender.

us *adv.* quite, rather, well.

us *adj.* good.

us *adv.* yes.

us chat-elq *phr.* good luck!

us li naraj *adj.* positive.

us maak'a naxye *phr.* it's OK.

us naq nawil *phr.* it's OK.

us raj *phr.* that's interesting, I'd love to.

us ta *conj.* although, though.

us wankin b'antyox *phr.* I'm fine thanks.

us'elk *adj.* outstanding.

usaq b'i' *phr.* of course.

usaak *v.* to improve, get better.

usaak wakliik *n.* development.

usil k'a'aq re ru *n.* raw materials.

usilal *n.* favor.

usilalch'ool *adj.* generosity.

usilanb'il *adj.* happy.

usilk'ulunk *adj.* welcome.

usilk'ulunk cho'q eere *phr.* welcome to all of you.

ustaanankil *n.* validation.

ut *conj.* and.

utwchx *adv.* etcetera, etc., and so forth, and on and on. *Note:* Derived from 'ut' (and), 'w' (first letter of 'wank', to exist or be), 'ch' (first letters of 'chik', more), and 'x' (first letter of 'xcomon', all other companions).

utz' *n.* mosquito.

utz' *n.* fly (insect).

utz'ajl *n.* sugarcane.

utz'aal *n.* sugarcane.

utz'leb'aal *n.* smell.

utz'leb'aal *n.* smell, sense of smell.

utz'uk *v.* to smell, sniff.

utz'uk *n.* smell.

utz'uk u *v phr.* to kiss.

uxb'il b'aanunb'il *n.* history.

uxk *v.* to become, happen.

uxtanank *n.* charity.

uy *interj.* [utterance indicating a close call].

uyaluy *interj.* [utterance indicating danger].

UU - uu

uuch eleb'aal *n.* dental clinic, dentist office.

uuchilej *n.* representative.

uuchilink *v.* to represent.

uuchininkil *n.* representativity.

uul *n.* cliff, precipice.

uul *n.* ravine, gully.

uul *n.* landslide.

uul ch'och' *n.* cliff.

uul pek *n.* cliff.

uuq *n.* skirt (typical indigenous).

uut *n.* wild dove.

uutz'u'uj *n.* candle.

uutz'u'jinb'il aatin *n.* poem.

uutz'u'jinb'ilkaxlanwa *n.* cake.

uutz'u'jinb'ilraq *n.* rhyme.

uutz'u'jinb'iltz'iib' *n.* poetry.

uutz'u'uj *n.* flower.

uutz'u'ujinb'il eetz'unk *n.* costume, disguise.

uutz'u'ujinb'il saa'us *n.* piñata.

uutz'u'ujink *v.* to decorate.

uuw *n.* grape. *From:* Spanish 'uva'.

W - w

wa *n.* tortilla.

wa *n.* acne.

wa *n.* clay.

wa *n.* meal.

wa re eq'la *n.* breakfast.

wa re ewu *n.* supper.

wa re wa'leb' *n.* lunch.

wa'ak *v.* to eat.

wa'al *n.* food.

wa'leb' sek' *n.* cup, plate.

wa'leb'aal *n.* dining room.

wa'leb'aal *n.* restaurant, diner.

wa'lem *n.* pasture.

wa'ok *v.* to eat.

wa'tesink *v.* to perform rituals.

wa'tesiik *v.* to receive rites.

wach'iil *n.* tamarind.

wahi' *phr.* here it is.

waj *n.* cornfield.

wajb' *n.* musical instrument.

wajb'ak *v.* to play instruments.

wajb'ak *n.* music, concert.

wakax *n.* cow, cattle. *From:* vaca 'the cow' (Spanish) (1).

wakax kab'l *n.* kiosk.

waklesinelch'ool *adj.* motivating.

waklesink *v.* to raise, lift.

waklesink naw'aatinob'aal *n.* linguistic development.

wakliik *n.* progress.

wakliik *v.* to rise, get up.

wakliik *v.* to progress.

wakliikil *n.* progressivity.

waltatyox ixq *n.* goddaughter.

waltatyox winq *n.* godson.

wan *adj.* present.

wan aj eechal re *adj.* owned.

wan aj eere *adj.* private.

wan b'ayaq rusilal *phr.* not bad.

wan le' *pron.* that, that one (over there).

wan naq *adv phr.* sometimes.

wan rusil *adj.* useful.

wan xna'leb' *adj.* wise, smart, intelligent.

wanjik *n.* ecology.

wank *v.* to live, reside, be.

wank e *v phr.* to have.

wank sa' ilb'il *adj.* on parole, on probation.

wank sa' raqb'a aatin *adj.* on trial.

wank sa' xyaalal *n.* safety.

wankil *n.* pride.

wankil *adj.* holy.

wankil *n.* power.

wankil *adj.* clever.

wankil *adj.* brave.

wankilal *n.* kingdom.

wankilal saq'e *n.* solar system.

wankin sa' wochoch *phr.* I'm at home.

waqib' *n.* half dozen.

waqib' ru *n.* six-pack.

waqlajuk'aam *n.* lot, plot, terrain. *Note:* From 'Sixteen cords," or the size corresponding to the unit of measure called "manzana" in Guatemala.

waqxaqxuk *n.* octagon.

waqxaqxuk-u *n.* octahedron.

waqxuk *n.* hexagon.

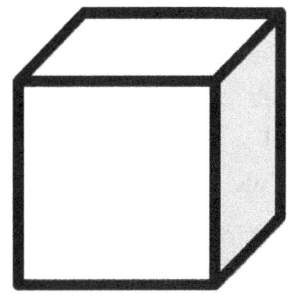

waqxukuut *n.* cube.
Var: waxaqxukuut.

wara *n.* sleepiness.

warb'etaal *n.* boarding house.

warib' *n.* bed.

warib'aq *n.* pyjamas.

warib'aal aq *n.* pyjamas.

waril *n.* guest.

warib'aal *n.* bedroom, dormitory.

wark *v.* to sleep.

warom *n.* owl.

wartesiilb'an *n.* anesthesia.

wax ru *adj.* mad. *From:* wax "mad' (Ch'olti') (2).

wax ru *n.* rabies.

wax'ilom *n.* hallucination.

waxerk *n.* anger.

waa *adj.* viscous.

waal *n.* fan. *From:* *wahl 'the fan' (Yucatecan, Ch'olan, ?) (2).

waalesink *v.* to fan.

waalunk *v.* to blow, fly.

we'ej *adj.* scarce. *Var:* wi'ej.

we'ej *n.* hunger, famine. *From:* *wi'ij ('hunger' ?) (Yucatecan) (3).

we'ejil *n.* scarcity.

we'ejink *v.* to go hungry.

wechelal *n.* piece. *Var:* wechel.

wech' re *adj.* fussy.

wech'ok *n.* description. *Var:* xwech'b'al rix.

wech'ok *v.* to describe.

wej *adv.* in four days.

wenb'enk ib' *v.* to brag, boast, show off.

wex *n.* trousers, pants.

wex ch'ot roq *n.* shorts.

wex re loon *n.* jeans, blue jeans.

wi *conj.* if.

wi' chik *adv phr.* again.

wiheb' *n.* grandchildren.

wilix *n.* sparrow.

winq *n.* man.

winqilal *n.* manhood, masculinity, males.

winqilal *n.* bravery.

wiq'laak *v.* to kneel.

wiisk *n.* whiskey. *From:* English 'whiskey'.

woch ichaj *n.* lettuce.

wohok *v.* to bark.

wojok *v.* to beat, strike, hit.

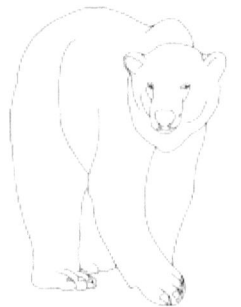

wonxul *n.* bear.

woqx *n.* foam, bubble.

woqx re joohok *n.* shaving cream.

woqxeel *n.* ebullience, boiling point.

woqxink *v.* to boil.

woqxink chi timil *v phr.* to simmer.

woqxkum *n.* lava.

woq'laak *v.* to sit.

wosleb' *n.* radiator.

wosol *n.* chill. *Var:* woso.

wote'ek *v.* to howl. *Var:* wute'ek.

wotz *pron.* both.

wotzb'aanuhem *n.* interculturality.

wotzok *v.* to share.

wotz'ok *n.* itch.

wotz'okil *n.* itch.

wotz'otz' *n.* tickle.

wotz'otz'ink *v.* to tickle.

wuqchahim *n.* Ursa Major.

wuqub'ix *adv.* in seven days.

wuqxuk *n.* heptagon. *Var:* **wuqxukuut**.

wuq'ix *n.* week.

X - x

x'am *n.* spider.

x'am ja'aj *n.* asthma. *Var:* **amja'aj**.

x'el *n.* product, result.

xa'aw *n.* vomit.

xa'awilk'u *n.* eruption. *Var:* **xxa'aw k'u**.

250

xa'awku *n.* lava.

xa'b'eetal *adj.* ugly.

xa'n wakax *n.* cow.

xa'nch'o *n.* mouse.

xa'wak *v.* to vomit.

xa'wil ru *adj.* disgusting.

xab'on *n.* soap. *From:* jabón 'the soap' (Spanish) (1).

xab'onink *v.* to wash with soap.

xajleb' *n.* dance. *Var:* xajl.

xajleb'aal *n.* disco, nightclub.

xajok *v.* to dance.

xam *n.* lamp, lantern, torch.

xam *n.* fire. *Var:* xaml.

xamaan *n.* week. *From:* semana 'the week' (Spanish) (1).

xaml *n.* electricity.

xamlt'or *n.* ionosphere.

xampu *n.* shampoo. *From:* English 'shampoo'.

xamxul *n.* firefly.

xan *n.* brick, adobe.

xanxiiwr *n.* ginger.

xaq *n.* leaf. *Var:* xxaq.

Xaq *sur. From:* xaq ('leaf'). (B1).

xaqab'ank *v.* to elect, vote, name, propose, nominate.

xaqab'ank *v.* to raise.

xaqab'ank *v.* to assemble.

xaqab'ank aatin *n.* contract.

xaqal *n.* posture.

xaqalch'ool *n.* attitude.

xaqam *adj.* standing.

xaqamkaaxuk *n.* rhombus, diamond.

xaq-aatin *n.* contract.

xaqchaj *n.* needle (of a tree).

xaqch'iich' *n.* license plate.

xaqleb' *n.* brakes.

xaqleb'aal ch'iich' *n.* bus stop.

xaqleb'jukub' *n.* dock.

xaqleb'jukub' *n.* port.

xaqliik *v.* to rise, stand.

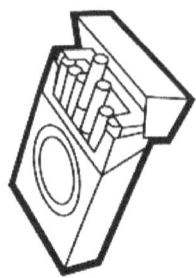

xaqmay *n.* cigarette.

xaqxo *adj.* vertical.

xaqxo jalam'uuch *n.* still life.

xaqxookil juch' *n.* vertical line.

xaq'ab'ank *v.* to detain, stop.

xartin *n.* pan, frying pan. *From:* sartén 'the pan' (Spanish) (1).

xawak *n.* vomit.

xaxaq lawrel *n.* bayleaf. *From:* Spanish 'laurel'.

xayaw *n.* annatto.

xa'an aaq *n.* sow.

xa'an imul *n.* hare, rabbit.

xa'an kaxlan *n.* hen.

xaab' *n.* shoe.

xaab'ank *v.* to kick.

xaal che' *n.* forked branch. *From:* xaal che' 'forked branch' (Yucatecan, Ch'olan, possible) (2).

xaal it *n.* back.

xaaqalhu *n.* government identification, ID.

xaaqalil *n.* posture.

xaaqilalk'utuk *adj.* masterly.

xaar *n.* mug.

xaar *n.* jug, pitcher. *From:* jarro 'jug' (Spanish) (1).

xaaril ha' *n.* water jug.

xb'ak'b'al wex *n.* belt.

xb'alb'a *n.* hell, underworld. *Var:* b'alb'a; xib'alb'a.

xb'anil xxulil awimq *n.* insecticide.

xb'anol *n.* spice, seasoning.

xb'anol suq *n.* bug spray, insecticide.

xb'anol tzakahemq *n.* condiment.

xb'aqel jolom *n.* skull, cranium.

xb'aqel xukuy *n.* rib.

xb'arxukil *n.* coordinate.

xb'asalal *n.* pant cuff.

xb'asb'al *n.* fold.

xb'asb'al sa' xyi *n.* crease.

xb'atz'iilal *adj.* artistic.

xb'ay chaq *adj.* delayed.

xb'aalil *n.* axle.

xb'aan *prep.* through.

xb'aan naq *conj.* because.

xb'aanunkil *n.* action, execution, practice.

xb'aanunkil mayejak *v phr.* to worship.

xb'aar li qaawa' *n.* gladiola.

xb'aatal ja'aj *n.* scarf.

xb'e ch'o *n.* rafter.

xb'e ha' *n.* channel.

xb'e li po *n.* date. *Var:* xb'epo.

xb'e ruuchich'och' *n.* orbit.

xb'e'chahim *n.* orbit. *Var:* xb'eechahim.

xb'ehil k'anjel *n.* career.

xb'ehil ru k'anjel *n.* bureaucracy, agenda.

xb'ehil sib' *n.* chimney.

xb'ehul *n.* method.

xb'ehul k'osok *n.* synthesis.

xb'ehul k'utuk *n.* teaching methods.

xb'ehul k'utuk xkab'aatinob'aal *n.* second language acquisition.

xb'ehulk'utuk *n.* study guide.

xb'ele' ralsaq'e *n.* Pluto.

xb'eleb'aal ha' *n.* hose.

xb'eleb'aal poyanam *n.* crosswalk.

xb'elehilpo *n.* September.

xb'eeleb'aal yaj *n.* wheelchair.

xb'eelil *n.* wheel.

xb'een *n.* remains.

xb'een *n.* surface.

xb'een alal *n.* first-born.

xb'een aq *n.* knee. *Var:* xb'een oq.

xb'een aatinob'aal *n.* mother tongue.

xb'een che' *n.* attic.

xb'een kab'l *n.* roof.

xb'een kutan *n.* Monday.

xb'een na'aj *n.* first grade.

xb'een ochoch *n.* rooftop terrace.

xb'een pojk'ok *n.* prophase.

xb'een q'ekutan *n.* Precambrian era.

xb'een ralsaq'e *n.* Mercury.

xb'een tasal iq' *n.* atmosphere, troposphere.

xb'een tasal kab'l *n.* ground floor.

xb'een tel *n.* shoulder.

xb'een tzuul *n.* summit, peak.

xb'een wa *adv phr.* first of all, in the first place.

xb'een waleb' *n.* afternoon.

xb'een'e *n.* palate, soft palate.

xb'een'e yaab' *n.* velar.

xb'een'e yaab' *n.* palatal.

xb'eenil aj tij *n.* priest.

xb'eenil awab'ej *n.* president.

xb'eenil poopol *n.* mayor.

xb'eenil tijonel *n.* director.

xb'eenil tzoleb'aal *n.* principal.

xb'eenilpo *n.* January.

xb'eeresib'aal k'ula'al *n.* baby walker.

xb'iisul b'an *n.* dose.

xb'onilkaaxt *n.* ink pad, stamp pad.

xb'otb'al chi chunt'ikr *v phr.* cast.

xb'ook iq *n.* oxygen.

xb'ookil-iq' *n.* oxygenation.

xb'oolpuub' *n.* cannon.

xb'ooxil saqb'ach *n.* ice bag, icepack.

xb'ooxil tiqwal ha' *n.* hot-water bottle.

xcha'al *n.* elements.

xcha'al seeraq' *n.* moral (to a story).

xcha'al uutz'u'uj *n.* flower petal.

xcha'aleb' b'eleb'aal ch'iich' *n.* car parts.

xcha'alil aatinob'aal *n.* dialectal variety.

xcha'alil li tib'elej *n.* body parts.

xcha'alil ruuchich'och' *n.* geography.

xchakachil aq' *n.* laundry basket.

xchakachil b'aq *n.* rib.

xchakachil mul *n.* wastebasket, trash can, garbage can.

xchamal taq'a *n.* abyss.

xchamal xb'onol *n.* color tone.

xchampa aj kanab'om esilhu *n.* mailbag.

xchapliikroqruq'b' *n.* mortgage.

xchaqijik *n.* dendrite.

xchaq' *adj.* like.

xchaq'al u *n.* beauty.

xchaq'na' na' *n.* mother's sister.

xchaq'rab' li tenamit *n.* constitution.

xchaq'rab'il *n.* rules.

xche' kaqixaml *n.* infrared light.

xche' saq'e *n.* ultraviolet light.

xche'e'b'al *n.* keyboard.

xche'el ab'aj *n.* penis.

xche'el kab' *n.* beehive.

xche'el kaxolb' ch'iich' *n.* dipstick.

xche'el lep ch'iich' *n.* hood support.

xche'el li b'otb'il hu *n.* paper towel dispenser, roll paper dispenser.

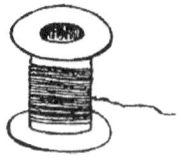

xche'el noq' *n.* bobbin, spool.

xche'el noq' *n.* cotton tree.

xche'el pim *n.* stem, stalk.

xche'el tiikob'aal b'e *n.* steering wheel.

xche'elhu *n.* papyrus.

xchi hab' *n.* age.

xchu' ke *n.* snow. *Var:* xchu'i keh.

xch'ajom *n.* erosion.

xch'ajom ajwal *n.* prince.

xch'ajom hab' *n.* alluvial erosion.

xch'ajom iq' *n.* wind erosion.

xch'ajom saqb'ach *n.* glacial erosion.

xch'e'b'al *n.* steering wheel.

xch'i'pul uq'mej *n.* pinkie finger.

xch'ina ch'iich'ul *n.* buckle.

xch'ina kawaay palaw *n.* seahorse.

xch'och palaw *n.* island.

xch'och'il *n.* climate.

xch'olch'ookil amaq'il *n.* social security.

xch'olch'ookilal *n.* legibility.

xch'olob'ankil *n.* introduction, presentation.

xch'ool *n.* nucleus.

xch'ool ch'iich' *n.* motor.

xch'ool nataqlank re *n.* free will, free agency.

xch'oolaatin *n.* verb.

xch'oolaatin juntaq'eetil *n.* thesaurus.

xch'oolil *n.* axis.

xch'uylal *n.* segment.

xch'uut aj b'ichk *n.* choir.

xch'uutamil *n.* academy.

xch'uutulal *n.* module.

xch'uutulal chahim *n.* constellation.

xch'uutulal ilob' *n.* ethnicity.

Xe' *sur. From:* xe' ('root'). (B1).

xe' *n.* root, bulb, trunk. *Var:* xxe'.

xe' ru che' *n.* vegetable.

xe' toon *n.* ancestors.

xe'k'a'uxl *n.* metaphysics.

xe'nawom *n.* philosophy.

xe'nawomil *adv.* philosophically.

xeb'ok _v._ to pinch. _From:_ *xeb' 'to pinch' (Yucatecan, Ch'olan, possible) (2).

xelexkaxlanwa _n._ cupcake.

xeq'el _adj._ gored.

xeq'ok _v._ to stab. _From:_ *xeq', xek' 'to stab or pierce' (Ch'olan) (2).

xerek' winq _n._ young men.

xerok _v._ to split.

xe'xke rib' _v phr._ to surrender.

xeek' _n._ palm tree. _From:_ *xeek'el 'a type of palm or palm tree' (Western Mayan) (2).

xeel _n._ remains.

xeer _n._ saw. _From:_ sierra 'the saw' (Spanish) (1).

xhelam _n._ latitude.

xhesb'al _n._ refinement.

xhilob'aal b'eleb'aalch'iich' _n._ parking meter.

xhoplalil _n._ black hole.

xhopolal _n._ opening.

xhoonal asjsink-u _n._ recreation, fun, recess.

xhoonalil _n._ schedule.

xhuhil li aatik'aam ch'iich' _n._ telephone bill.

xhuhil li ha' _n._ water bill.

xhuhil li k'uulank _n._ deposit receipt.

xhuhil li saqen _n._ electric bill.

xhuhil loq'om _n._ receipt, invoice.

xhuhil purik _n._ plane ticket, boarding pass.

xhuhil purik _n._ airfare.

xhuhil resil kamk _n._ burial notice.

xhuhil tojok _n._ payroll.

xhuhil tojok _n._ payment plan.

xhuhilk'uluk _n._ receipt, invoice.

xhuhiltoj _n._ IOU, promissory note.

xhuhiltumin _n._ check.

xhuhuil'esil _n._ recipe book.

xhuhul b'an _n._ prescription.

xhuhul esil _n._ newspaper.

xhuhul raq _n._ syllabary.

xhuhul tenamit _n._ government identification, ID.

xhuhul uutz'u'jinb'il aatin _n._ poetry collection.

xhuhultojb'amaak _n._ sentence.

xhumalilche' _n._ shaving.

Xi' _sur._

xib'enk _v._ to threaten.

xib'esink _n._ fright.

xik _v._ to go.

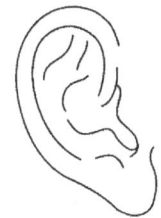

xik *n.* ear.

xik aak'a'uxl *n.* caring.

xik so'sol ch'iich' *n.* airplane wing.

xikelyaab' *n.* earphones, headphones.

xikenaq xch'ool *adj.* in love.

xikin i *n.* great-grandchild.

xikin mama' *n.* great-grandfather.

xikin xa'an *n.* great-grandmother.

xik' *n.* wing, fin.

xik' *n.* feather.

xik' aj aatin *n.* dirty words.

xik' ilok *n.* hate, hatred, disgust, disdain.

xik' naxye *adj.* noisy, sensational, controversial.

xik' ru *adj.* strange.

xik'jukub' *n.* rudder.

xik'onel *n.* enemy.

xik'sotz' *n.* umbrella.

xik'uchink *v.* to hate.

xileet *n.* razor blade. *From:* French "Gillete".

xilik' *n.* fairy, elf.

xinka *lang.* Xinca (Santa Rosa, Jutiapa).

xintaw ru *phr.* I understand.

xintitz' *phr.* I'm bored.

xiw *n.* fear, fright, dread. *From:* xiw 'to fear' (Q'anjob'alan) (3).

xiw xiw *adj.* dangerous.

xiwajenaq *adj.* scared, afraid, alarmed. *Var:* **xuwajenaq**.

Xiwan *nick.* Juan.

xiwxiw *n.* danger.

xiwxiwil *n.* insecurity.

xiyab' *n.* comb, hairbrush.

xiikil *adj.* a lot.

xiikil *pron.* much.

xiik' *n.* gully, ravine.

xiiqank *v.* to nod off.

xiitink *v.* to mend, darn.

xiitink tiq'il *n.* suture.

xiitleb' b'an *n.* bandage, Band-Aid.

xiitleb'ch'iich' *n.* soldering iron.

xjachalal *n.* part.

xjalalik ru *n.* catalysis.

xjalam'uuchil *n.* X-ray.

xjalanil *n.* variable.

xjalanil ru aatin *n.* dialect.

xjalob'aatinob'aal *n.* variant
form.

xjalpaq'il *n.* antonym.

xjartawahil *n.* frequency.

xjayal xb'e *n.* airline.

xjayalihom tijok *n.*
educational aims.

xjayalil *n.* address. *Var:* xjayal.

xjaar uutz'u'uj *n.* vase.

xjech'lal *n.* angle.

xjek'inkil *n.* division.

xjek'iil *n.* quotient.

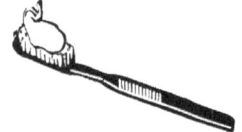

xji'b'al ruuch e *n.* toothbrush.

xjis'ich'mul xikej *n.* auditory
nerve.

xjolom ab'yayala *n.* North
America.

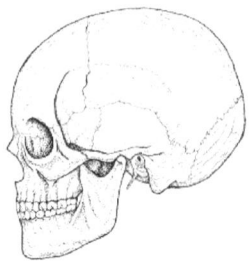

xjolom kamenaq *n.* skull.

xjolom muluq'util tz'uq *n.*
semicolon.

xjolomil awab'ejilal *n.*
cabinet (presidential).

xjolomil tzoleb'aal *n.*
principal.

xjolomiltenamit *n.* capital.

xjotzb'al ru'uj *v phr.* to
sharpen (a point).

xjuch' li nataqlan re *n.*
signature of sender.

xjul taq'a *n.* abyss.

xjultikankil *n.* formulation.

xjunes tz'ej *adj.* boneless.

xjunlajuhilpo *n.* November.

xjunpak'alil (li...) *prep.*
opposite.

xjuntaq'eetil xwinqul *n.*
gender equality.

xka na'aj *n.* fourth grade.

xka pojk'ok *n.* telophase.

xka q'ekutan *n.* Mesozoic era.

xka tasal'iq' *n.* thermosphere.

xka'awb'il *adj.* reforested.

xka'ha'resinkil *n.* rehydration.

xka'oksinkil *n.* recycling,
reuse.

xkab' alal *n.* stepson.

xkab' kawil yaab' *n.* stress on
second to last syllable.

xkab' na' *n.* stepmother.

xkab' na'aj *n.* second grade.

xkab' na'aj tzoleb'aal *n.* high
school.

xkab' rab'in *n.* stepdaughter.

xkab' tasal iq' *n.* stratosphere.

xkab' yuwa' *n.* stepfather.

xkab'aljuhilpo *n.* December.

xkab'awa'b'ejil *n.* vice president.

xkab'aatinob'aal *n.* second language.

xkab'il awab'ej *n.* vice president.

xkab'ilpo *n.* February.

xkab'kutan *n.* Tuesday.

xkab't'or *n.* metasphere.

xkakutan *n.* Thursday.

xkawil roq ha' *n.* rapids.

xkax'olb' poych'iich' *n.* oil, motor oil.

xkaxon aj b'onol xaab' *n.* shoeshiner kit.

xkaxonil esilhu *n.* mailbox, post office box, PO Box.

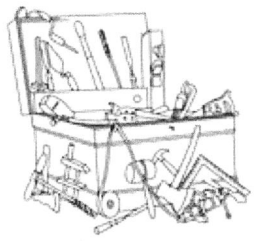

xkaxonil k'anjeleb'aal *n.* toolbox.

xka' alalb'ej *n.* stepdaughter.

xkaalam e *n.* jaw. *Var:* kalam e.

xkaapo *n.* April.

xkaatanal tzolok *n.* university level.

xkem aj am *n.* spider web.

xko it *n.* hip.

xko rit *n.* buttocks, butt.

xko uhej *n.* cheekbones.

xkok' xch'al xul *n.* menudo.

xkolb'al rix junkab'al *n.* family services.

xkolb'al rix li loq'laj che'k'aam *n.* resource conservation.

xkolb'al ru'uj uqb' *n.* thimble.

xkomon rib' *n.* accomplice, accessory.

xkoral k'ula'al *n.* crib, cradle.

xkoxtalil li esilhu *n.* mailbag.

xkukil li puutzink *n.* fumigation pump, fumigator.

xkumb'il ruk'a' poych'iich' *n.* gas pump.

xkuntz'i' *n.* eye inflammation.

xkutankil yo'lajik *n.* date of birth, birthday.

xkutum b'oqleb' *n.* cell phone signal.

xkux aq' *n.* collar.

xkux oq *n.* ankle. *Var:* xkuxb' oq.

xkux ruq' aq' *n.* shirt cuff.

xkux uq'b' *n.* wrist. *Var:* xkux uq'm.

xkux uq'b' ch'iich' *n.* handcuffs.

xkuxb'il *n.* sound, noise.

xk'aj ariin *n.* flour (wheat).

xk'ot xik *n.* earwax.

xk'a'uxlankil *n.* reflection (thought).

xk'ab'a' li nataqlan re *n.* name of sender, sender.

xk'ab'a' li taak'ulu'q re *n.* name of recipient, addressee, recipient.

xk'ab'a'il *n.* proper noun.

xk'aj aatin *n.* article.

xk'aj hu *n.* confetti.

xk'anjel *n.* function.

xk'anjelankil li ch'och' *n.* farming.

xk'anjelob'aal aj b'anonel *n.* surgical instruments.

xk'atq xraqik *n.* terminal side (of an angle).

xk'atq xtiklajik *n.* initial side (of an angle).

xk'atqil *n.* latitude.

xk'aamal *n.* suspender.

xk'aamal *n.* belt, strip, drive belt.

xk'aamal b'oqleb'aal *n.* phone line.

xk'aamal kaxmu *n.* cable television.

xk'aamal sa' aj puub' *n.* policeman's belt.

xk'aamal saqen *n.* extension cord.

xk'aamal uuq *n.* drawstring (for a skirt).

xk'aamal xaab' *n.* shoelace.

xk'eb'al xhuhul tojleb' *v phr.* to write a check.

xk'ihal b'eleb'aalch'iich' *n.* traffic.

xk'ilul kaxlan wa *n.* bread pan.

xk'ix *n.* thorn.

xk'ob'lal *n.* hole.

xk'oslal *n.* summary.

xk'ot oq' *n.* calf (of the leg).

xk'otchahim *n.* meteorite.

xk'ub'ankil ru chaq'rab' *n.* bill (legislative).

xk'ub'lal ich'mul ak re *n.* parasympathetic autonomic nervous system.

xk'ub'lal ich'mul yal jo' *n.* autonomic nervous system.

xk'ub'lal ich'mulej xtaq rib' *n.* autonomic nervous system.

xk'ub'lal xsa' *n.* operating system.

xk'ub'laltzolok *n.* curriculum.

xk'ub'laal tojb'a maak *n.* prison system, corrections.

xk'ub'leb'aalchaq'rab' *n.* legislative system.

xk'uhil *adj.* volcanic.

xk'ulb'al xtz'aq *v phr.* to charge.

xk'ulub'poyanam *n.* human rights, civil rights, rights.
Var: xk'ulub'eb' poyanam.

xk'utb'al *n.* example, demonstration.

xk'utum xaml *n.* reflection (light).

xk'uyb'al *n.* tolerance.

xk'uub'lalraqleb'aatin *n.* judicial system.

xk'uub'laltojb'amaak *n.* penitentiary system, prison system, corrections.

xlajehilpo *n.* October.

xlanb'al xb'een'aq *n.* knee pad, knee patch.

xlanlanil *n.* humidity.

xlaawil ha' *n.* water tap, faucet.

xlek aj tz'ak *n.* trowel.

xlem u *n.* iris (eye).

xlemtz' xaab' *n.* shoe polish.

xlemtz'iil u *n.* cornea.

xlemul kaxmuhel *n.* screen (TV).

xlemul kaxmuhel *n agt.* movie screen, silver screen.

xlemul k'ayib'aal *n.* glass cabinet, display case.

xlokochil t'ikr *n.* hanger.

xloq'al *n.* value, price.

xlub'ik li ch'ool *n.* heart attack, infarct.

xma'al ixq *n.* barren woman.

xmach u *n.* mustache.

xmajolil *n.* height.

xmama' t'iw *n.* condor.

xmama' wakax *n.* bull.

xmama'il uq'mej *n.* thumb.

xmap oq *n.* ankle, shin.

xmar *n.* end (spatial).

xmar *n.* edge.

xmar choxa *n.* obsidian.

xmaril kawil yaab' *n.* stress on last syllable.

xmaxel *n.* virus.

xmaak naq *conj.* because.

xmaal kaaq *n.* obsidian.

xmaatanil li yalok u *n.* trophy.

xmesul cho'ok *n.* operating table.

xmetz'ew ich'mulej elkik' *n.* systolic blood pressure.

xmetz'ew k'a'aq ru *n.* potential energy.

xmetz'ew raalal *n.* gravity.

xmetz'ew tiik *n.* kinetic energy.

xmetz'ew xyi li ruchich'och' *n.* gravity.

xmeexul li peech'ab'k *n.* work bench. *Var:* xmeexul li peech'b'k.

xminb'al ru *n.* rape.

xmisik' kaxmu *n.* television antenna.

xmisik' puktasib'aal *n.* radio antenna.

xmola *n.* sum.

xmolam aj kolonel *n.* rescue unit.

xmolamil aj k'utunel *n.* faculty, teaching staff, educators.

xmolamil aatinob'aal *n.* linguistic community.

xmolamil b'atz'unk *n.* team.

xmolamil k'iila tenamital *n.* United Nations.

xmu che' *n.* shade (under trees).

xmu kab'l *n.* hallway.

xmu mama' k'ayib'aal *n.* mall entrance.

xmurinkil rib' *n.* mitosis.

xn'aj alaal *n.* ovary.

xn'aj sek' *n.* sideboard.

xn'aj xchahil may *n.* ashtray.

xna' kar *n.* whale.

xna' k'anti' *n.* viper.

xna' k'anti' *n.* salamander.

xna' sijb' *n.* bow.

xna' tumin *n.* account.

xna' wechb'een *n.* mother-in-law.

xna'aj aj aatinanel *n.* recording studio.

xna'aj aj ilol tenamit *n.* police station.

xna'aj aj k'ehol esil *n.* information office.

xna'aj ajsink u *n.* recreation center.

xna'aj aq' *n.* dresser, chest of drawers, wardrobe.

xna'aj atz'am *n.* salt shaker.

xna'aj b'an *n.* medicine cabinet.

xna'aj b'an *n.* first aid kit.

xna'aj b'ar wi' wan li taak'ulu'q re *n.* address of recipient.

xna'aj b'eleb'aal ch'iich' *n.* bus station.

xna'aj b'eleb'aal ch'iich' *n.* garage.

xna'aj cha *n.* ashtray.

xna'aj chu *n.* bladder.

xna'aj elaat *n.* freezer.

xna'aj esil *n.* billboard.

xna'aj esilhu *n.* mailbox.

xna'aj eetalil *n.* dashboard.

xna'aj ha' *n.* watering hole.

xna'aj ha' *n.* water tank.

xna'aj ha' re atink *n.* bathtub.

xna'aj hal *n.* granary.

xna'aj hu *n.* bookcase.

xna'aj hu *n.* trash can, wastepaper bin.

xna'aj hu *n.* folder, binder.

xna'aj huhil tumin *n.* wallet.

xna'aj iq' *n.* air compressor, compressor.

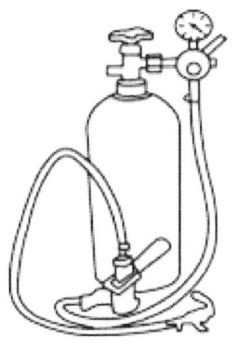

xna'aj iq' *n.* oxygen tank.

xna'aj iiq *n.* trunk.

xna'aj kab' *n.* beehive.

xna'aj kamenaq *n.* morgue.

xna'aj kampaan *n.* bell tower.

xna'aj kanteel *n.* candlestick.

xna'aj kape *n.* coffee maker.

xna'aj kape *n.* coffee pot.

xna'aj ketomq *n.* corral.

xna'aj kok'awinq *n.* orchard, garden.

xna'aj kuux *n.* pin cushion.

xna'aj k'a re ru *n.* locker, cubby.

xna'aj k'a'aq re ru *n.* utility room.

xna'aj k'aj kab' *n.* sugar bowl.

xna'aj k'aj pens *n.* pepper shaker.

xna'aj k'anjeleb'aal *n.* workshop.

xna'aj k'ay *n.* display shelves.

xna'aj k'ila xul *n.* zoo.

xna'aj k'ula'al *n.* baby room.

xna'aj k'uleb'aal *n.* cellar.

xna'aj k'utleb'aal *n.* art gallery.

xna'aj lemal eetalil *n.* videocassette.

xna'aj li k'anjel *n.* workplaces.

xna'aj mul *n.* wastebasket, trash can, garbage can.

xna'aj murinb'il sa us *n.* salad bowl.

xna'aj nimqal yaj *n.* ICU, intensive care unit.

xna'aj payas *n.* circus.

xna'aj puch'um *n.* wash basin (clothing).

xna'aj punitch'iich' *n.* bell tower.

xna'aj puub' *n.* holster.

xna'aj qaawa' *n.* altar.

xna'aj so'sol ch'iich' *n.* airport, hangar.

xna'aj taks *n.* taxi stand.

xna'aj taql *n.* mailbox.

xna'aj tasal hu *n.* library.

xna'aj tiiq' *n.* scar.

xna'aj tumin *n.* purse.

xna'aj tzakahemq *n.* pantry.

xna'aj tzolok *n.* study.

xna'aj uutz'u'uj *n.* flowerbed, flower garden.

xna'aj uutz'u'uj *n.* vase, flowerpot.

xna'aj xab'on *n.* soap dish.

xna'aj xam *n.* cookhouse.

xna'aj xam *n.* fireplace.

xna'aj xb'eenil *n.* principal's office.

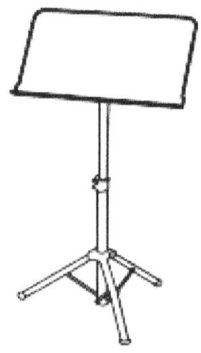

xna'aj xhu b'ich *n.* music stand, easel.

xna'aj xokleb' *n.* floppy disk, computer disk.

xna'aj yiib'ank xaqab'ank *n.* construction site.

xna'ajeb' cheek *n.* nursing home.

xna'ajil tz'iib'ahom k'ab'a'ej *n.* civil registry.

xna'ajkar *n.* fishbowl.

xna'ajleb'aalxul *n.* zoo.

xna'ajtasalhu *n.* bookcase.

xna'ajtz'uq *n.* abscissa.

xna'b'iisaalob' *n.* gram.

xna'chin inna' *n.* great-grandmother.

xna'chin inyuwa' *n.* great-grandfather.

xna'leb'ankil k'anjel *n.* job orientation.

xna'leb'il *n.* policy, theme.

xna'leb'il *adj.* thematic.

xna'leb'il nawaatinob'aal *n.* language policy.

xna'tz'iib' *n.* vowel.

xna'tz'iib'eb' *n.* vowels.

xna'yu'am *n.* cell (biological).

xnajtil roq *n.* longitude.

xnaq' u *n.* eye.

xnaq' uhej *n.* eye.

xnaq' *n.* seed.

xnaq' kakaw *n.* cocoa bean.

xnaq' puub' *n.* cartridge, magazine.

xnaq' saqen *n.* light bulb.

xnaq' telb' *n.* forearm.

xnaq' u *n.* face.

xnaq'puub' *n.* bullet.

xna' ixaqil *n.* mother-in-law (of a man).

xna' kawaay *n.* mare.

xna' b'eelom *n.* mother-in-law (of a woman).

xna'aj aros *n.* rice paddy.

xna'aj wakax *n.* stable, stall.

xneb'a' rix kab'l *n.* back yard.

xnimal *n.* size, dimension.

xnimal neb'aal *n.* plaza, square.

xnimal raqb'a chaq'rab' *n.* supreme court.

xnimal roq *n.* length.

xnimal ru *n.* width.

xnimal ru tzoleb'aal *n.* university.

xnimal winq *n.* hero.

xnimalpalaw *n.* ocean, sea.

xnoq'inkil li akuux *v phr.* to thread a needle.

xnumik poyanam *n.* crosswalk.

xnumleb' iyajiil *n.* fallopian tube.

xnumsinkil *n.* radiation.

xo't' *adj.* blind.

xojb' *n.* coyote.

xokaq'ab' *n.* rainbow.

xokch'oolej *n.* concentration.

xokleb' *n.* fork.

xokleb' *n.* cassette.

xokleb' *n.* file.

xokleb' hu *n.* folder, binder.

xokleb' mu *n.* video camera.

xokok *v.* to keep.

xokok *n.* harvest.

xokok *v.* to file, save.

xokok *v.* to pick up.

xokxoxch'ool *adj.* concentrated.

Xol *sur. From:* xolb' ('flute'). (B1).

xolb' *n.* flute. *From:* xool 'stick or flute' (Yucatecan, Ch'olan, possible) (2).

xolb'ak *v.* to play the flute.

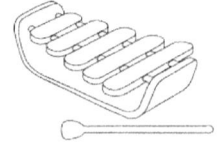

xolb'ch'iich' *n.* xylophone.

xolib'k *v.* to play the flute.

xolk'ok *v.* to drown.

xolol *n.* throat.

xoq'jaw *n.* queen.

xoral *n.* field, plot, terrain.

xoralwakax *n.* corral.

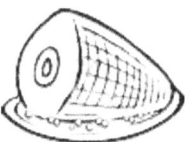

xorb'il tib' *n.* ham.

xorok *v.* to make tortillas.

xoronikpo *n.* full moon.

xotonk *v.* to confess. *Var:* **xootonk.**

xox *n.* spot, blemish.

xoy *n.* cover page, decoration, adornment.

Xoy *sur. From:* xoy (a certain weed, also an adornment). (B1).

xoyk'uluj *n.* cake.

xoob' *n.* gill. *Var:* **xob'.**

xookilch'iich' *n.* anchor.

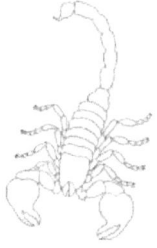

xook' *n.* scorpion.

xook'il ch'iich' *n.* tow truck.

xootonib'aal maak *n.* confessional.

xootonink *v.* to confess.

xpaayil kawub'l *n.* enzyme.

xpaayil tenamitil *n.* ethnic group.

xpemechil palaw *n.* sea shell.

xpisk' ha' *n.* waterfall.

xpoqsil kaxlanwa *n.* flour.

xpuchleb'aal tenamit *n.* laundromat.

xpuktasinkil *n.* edition, publication.

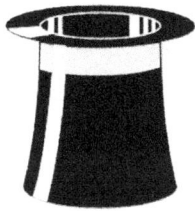

xpunit aj eek' *n.* magician's hat.

xputz't'ikr *n.* rag.

xq'ehil *n.* season.

xq'ehinkil *n.* omen.

xq'anal mol *n.* yolk.

xq'ehil hilaal *n.* vacation.

xq'ehil kutan *n.* calendar.

xq'ehinkil *n.* prediction.

xq'emal ru li ch'och' *n.* fertilizer.

xq'emal ruuch e *n.* toothpaste.

xq'emulch'och' *n.* fertilizer.

xq'esnal *n.* sharpness.

xq'ootil xik *n.* cochlea.

xra'al ch'o *n.* mousetrap.

xrab'in we *n.* niece.

xrajikraxil *n.* photosynthesis.

xramb'al xxulel yajel *n.* antivirus.

xramleb' ilob'aal *n.* balcony.

xraqalil *n.* unit.

xraqik *n.* outcome.

xraqik hab'alq'e *n.* autumn, fall (season).

xraqilal li aatinob'aal *n.* parts of speech.

xraqilal xsa' *n.* delivery truck.

xraqlil xsa' tz'alam *n.* cell (jail), jail cell.

xraqman ru *adj.* cancelled.

xrabin iitz'in *n.* niece (from a younger sibling).

xrab'in as *n.* niece (from an older sibling).

xrepom kaaq *n.* lightning bolt, bolt of lightning. *Var:* **xrepoom kaaq.**

xrepom palaw *n.* wave.

xrepomkaaq *adj.* electrocuted.

xsa' *adj.* area, contents.

xsa' ja'aj *n.* throat.

xsa' oq *n.* sole.

xsa' ruhil *n.* surface area.

xsa' tzoleb'aal *n.* classroom.

xsa' uq'b' *n.* palm (of the hand). *Var:* xsa' uq'm.

xsa' xaab' *n.* insole.

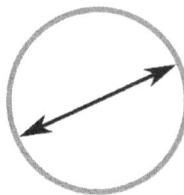

xsa'kotko *n.* diameter.

xsahob' ru *n.* adornment.

xsahob' tzakahemq *n.* spice, seasoning.

xsahob'resinkil *n.* illustration.

xsak'om tiqkaxlanxaml *n.* positive electric charge.

xsak'om tiikil kaxlanxaml *n.* negative electric charge.

xsal *adj.* reversed.

xsaqal kaxlan *n.* chicken breast.

xsek'ul tz'aj *n.* bedpan, chamber pot.

xsik ke *n.* shiver, chill, shudder.

xsiraal taq'eq *n.* arctic circle.

xsiiptz'ub' kaxlan wa *n.* yeast.

xsok b'itom *n.* head pad.

xsok oq *n.* carpet.

xsokel ru ch'aat *n.* mattress.

xsokilkar *n.* fish net.

xsol rix *n.* scale.

xsu oq *n.* calf (of the leg). *Var:* su oq.

xsulutzil b'aq *n.* marrow.

xsum *n.* accomplice.

xsum aam *n.* boyfriend, girlfriend, soul mate.

xsum ch'ool *n.* boyfriend, girlfriend.

xsum k'ab'a'ej *n.* surname, last name, patronym.

xsumalil *n.* minimal pair.

xsumenkil *n.* validation.

xsununkil sa' tel *n.* deodorant.

xsutq'isinkil chi rix *adj.* reversible.

xta *n.* wrap, wrap-around.

xta a' *n.* knee-high stocking.

xta b'aatal *n.* underwear.

xta jolom *n.* cap.

xta oq *n.* sock, stocking.

xta ru ch'och' *n.* rug.

xta ru sa'ej *n.* apron.

xta uq' *n.* glove. *Var:* xta uq'b'; xta uq'm.

xta xaab' *n.* sock, stocking.

xtameex *n.* tablecloth.

xtap palaw *n.* crab.

xtaqe'qil ruuchich'och' *n.* north pole.

xtaql li qaawa' *n.* angel.

xtaql xch'ool *n.* free will, free agency.

xtaql xch'ool li tyox *n.* god's will.

xtaq'ahil ruuchich'och' *n.* south pole.

xtasal xhuhil tumin *n.* savings passbook, checkbook.

xtasalal *n.* division.

xtasalil *n.* module.

xtasalil tzolok *n.* teaching module.

xtasalil xsa' tzoleb'aal *n.* classrooms.

xta-uuq *n.* underskirt, petticoat, slip.

xtawb'il li manawb'il *v phr.* to work out, make clear.

xtaab'il *n.* belt, strip.

xtaab'il xsa' *n.* fan belt.

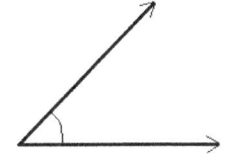

xtehelal *n.* angle.

xtehelal xkux *n.* bust, cleavage.

xtehelal xkux *n.* low neck.

xtehelem'u *n.* pupil (eye).

xtenamitil *n.* nationality.

xtenamitil ilob' *n.* national identity.

xtenq' aj b'anonel *n agt.* nurse.

xtenq'ankil *n.* help, assistance.

xteram *n.* degrees.

xteeb'al ha' *n.* faucet, water tap.

xteepal tenamit *n.* district, neighborhood, sector, canton.

xtib' jolom *n.* worry, preoccupation.

xtib' jolom *n.* headache.

xtib'el ak'ach *n.* turkey.

xtib'el aaq *n.* pork.

xtib'el kaxlan *n.* chicken.

xtib'el kej *n.* venison.

xtib'el ru'uj aq' *n.* tongue.

xtib'el wakax *n.* beef.

xtib'el xtoon ruuch e *n.* gums, gum tissue.

xtib'l sa'ej *n.* colic.

xtij tenamit *n.* pledge of allegiance.

xtijb'al *n.* education.

xtiklajik *n.* start, beginning, origin.

xtiklajik li yajel *n.* symptoms, disease onset.

xtiklajik xb'arxukil *n.* coordinate origin.

xtiqb'al aatin *n.* preposition.

xtiqwal *n.* calorie.

xtiqwalil *n.* temperature.

xtiwom xul *n.* insect bite.

xtoch'ol b'eleeb'aal ch'iich' *n.* car accident.

xtojb'al relik *n.* stamp, postage.

xtok' *n.* knot. *Var:* **t'oklal.**

xtoltolil b'an *n.* medicine cart.

xtoltolil ki'il saqb'ach saa'us *n.* ice cream cart.

xtorol ru uutz'u'uj *n.* bud.

xtoon telb' *n.* forearm.

xtoonal li ab'ib'aal aatin *n.* radio studio.

xtoonal ruq'b' *n.* tree trunk.

xtumb'choxa *n.* planet.

xtuqlajik q'e *n.* equinox.

xtuqlal'aatinob'aal *n.* grammar.

xtuqub'ankil *n.* reform.

xtusb'al xsa' *n.* pleat.

xtuslal'ich *n.* central nervous system.

xtusulal aatin *n.* dictionary, lexicon. *Var:* **xtuslal aatin.**

xtusulal ruuchich'och' *n.* solar system.

xtuxmel *n.* sprout, shoot.

xtu' wakax *n.* udder.

xtuulanil *n.* humility.

xt'ikrul wa *n.* napkin.

xt'oram ruuchich'och' *n.* globe.

xt'oy oq' *n.* calf (of the leg).

xtzakahemq ch'och' *n.* fertilizer.

xtzolb'al *n.* learning.

xtzoq saq'e *n.* Milky Way.

xtzuumal xna'yu'am *n.* cell membrane.

xtz'akeb' xe'toon *n.* ruins.

xtz'alam xul *n.* animal cage.

Aawe

xtz'apb'al surb'ich *n.* album cover.

xtz'aq *n.* value, price.

xtz'aq *n.* grade.

xtz'aqalil *adj.* complementary.

xtz'aqob' wa' *n.* dessert.

xtz'aqob'cha'al *n.* gland.

xtz'aqob'l *n.* complement.

xtz'aqob'l ajsiil *n.* carbohydrates.

xtz'aqob'l esilal *n.* additional information.

xtz'ik ha' *n.* seagull.

xtz'iral ch'och' *n.* crevice.

xtz'iib'ankil li yo'lajik *n.* birth registry.

xtz'iib'ul *n.* rule, norm.

xtz'iib'ul aatinob'aal *n.* linguistic norms.

xtz'iib'ul b'ich *n.* verse.

xtz'uq junajroqil *n.* cardinal directions.

xujanb'iltib' *n.* pork rinds.

xujsaa'us *n.* cookie.

xujwahiltib' *n.* tostada.

xujxuj *adj.* dry.

xuk *n.* corner. *From:* xuhk' 'corner' (Yucatecan, Ch'olan, possible) (2).

Xuk *sur. From:* xuk ('corner' or 'angle'). (B1).

xukub' *n.* horn. *From:* *xukub' 'the horn' (Ch'olan) (2).

xukub'k'ix *n.* safety pin, pin.

xukup *n.* cross.

xukuy *n.* rib.

xul *n.* animal.

xul aj al *adj.* mischievous, naughty.

xul e *n.* cavity.

xul iiqanel *n.* donkey, ass, mule, beast of burden.

xul k'iche' *n.* game.

xulab' *n.* Venus.

xulel xikej *n.* eardrum, tympanic membrane.

xulil *adj.* mischievous, naughty.

xulil'aatin *n.* flirtatious remark, flattering compliment.

xulkab' *n.* bee.

xulk'aq *n.* chigger.

xulk'ukil nima' *n.* waterfall.

xulub'ank *v.* pour.

xulum *n.* broken tooth.

271

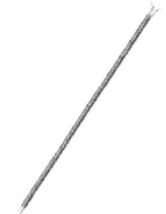

xuq' *n.* walking stick, baton.
Var: **xuq'y; xuq'l.** *Note:* A symbol of authority in Q'eqchi' local government.

xuq'l *n.* club, billy club.

xutaan *n.* shame, embarrassment.

xutaanal *adj.* ashamed, embarrassed.

xutaanaq *adj.* ashamed, embarrassed.

xut'uk *v.* to wrap.

xuxb' *n.* whistle (sound).

xuxb'ak *v.* to whistle.
Var: **xuxb'ank.** *From:* xuxub' 'to whistle' (Yucatecan, Ch'olan, possible) (2).

xwah kar *n.* bait.

xwalub'aal kab'l *n.* ceiling fan.

xwankilal b'aanunel *n.* executive power.

xwankilal chaq'rab'inel *n.* legislative power.

xwankilal raqonel *n.* judicial power.

xwaq na'aj *n.* sixth grade.

xwaq po *n.* semester.

xwaq q'ekutan *n.* Anthropozoic era, Anthropocene.

xwaq ralsaq'e *n.* Saturn.

xwaqkutan *n.* Saturday.

xwaqxaq ralsaq'e *n.* Neptune.

xwaqxaqpo *n.* August.

xwaresib'aal k'ula'al *n.* cradle.

xwaxil rumetz'ew *n.* adrenaline.

xwech'b'al xtz'aq *v phr.* to bargain, haggle.

xwuq ralsaq'e *n.* Uranus.

xxab'onil ruuch e *n.* toothpaste.

xxanil b'e *n.* cobblestone street.

xxaq *n.* leaves.

xxaq atz'um *n.* sepal.

xxaq pim *n.* fern.

xxaq xcha'al uutzu'uj *n.* flower petal.

xxaqeb' *n.* leaves.

xxaqleb'aal jukub' *n.* dock.

xxaqlin *phr.* stop it!

xxaqliik aamej *n.* heart attack.

xxaal b'e *n.* crossroads. *Var:* xxaali b'e.

xxaali it *n.* back. *Var:* xxala it.

xxaaril kape *n.* coffee pot.

xxaaril te *n.* teapot.

xxe'il *n.* roots.

xxe'ilal *n.* etymology.

xxeeb'ul pim *n.* margarine.

xxib'enkil k'al *n.* scarecrow.

xxik *n.* handle.

xxik aq' *n.* loop.

xxuk *n.* angle.

xxuk b'e *n.* street corner, corner.

xxuk e *n.* chin.

xxulel kik'el *n.* red blood cells.

xxulel palaw *n.* seafood.

xxulel yajel *n.* bacteria.

xya'al *n.* juice.

xya'al b'eleb'aal *n.* gasoline, gas, diesel, fuel.

xya'al chiin *n.* orange juice.

xya'al ch'iich' *n.* gasoline, gas, diesel, fuel.

xya'al ch'op *n.* pineapple juice.

xya'al e *n.* dribble, drool.

xya'al ik *n.* broth.

xya'al kab' *n.* honey.

xya'al lamunx *n.* lemonade.

xya'al mansaan *n.* apple juice, cider, apple cider.

xya'al pix *n.* tomato juice.

xya'al pix *n.* salsa.

xya'al puktasiilhu *n.* ink, printer ink.

xya'al tib' *n.* gravy.

xya'al tu' *n.* breast milk, mother's milk.

xya'al tu' *n.* milk.

xya'al u *n.* tear.

xya'alna'yu'am *n.* cytoplasm.

xyach'winq *n.* underwear, brief.

xyajel kik' *n.* leukemia.

xyajel pospo'oy *n.* tuberculosis, TB.

xyajelil *adj.* pathological.

xyajelpospo'oy *n.* bronchitis.

xyajelxnaq'ja'aj *n.* tonsillitis.

xyalojikeb' li saq'e ut li po *n.* eclipse.

xyampi ha' *n.* island.

xyanq tzuul *n.* gorge, canyon.

xyaab' b'ich *n.* note, musical note.

xyaab' kaaq *n.* thunder.

xyaab'asinkil *n.* pronunciation.

xyaab'kuxil *n.* intonation.

xyaab'tz'iib' *n.* consonant.

xyaalal *n.* truth, righteousness.

xyaalalil *n.* reality, meaning.

xye ab'yayala *n.* North America.

xye so'sol ch'iich' *n.* airplane tail, tail wing.

xyeb'al *n.* communication.

xyehok maak *n.* confession.

xyeeb'al *n.* conference.

xyi *n.* retina.

xyi *n.* waistband.

xyi *n.* center.

xyi ab'yayala *n.* Central America, Mesoamerica.

xyi aq' *n.* belt.

xyi tenamit *n.* downtown.

xyich'ool xna'yu'am *n.* cell nucleus, nucleus.

xyihil ru'uj uq' *n.* middle finger.

xyihil xk'ub'lal ich'mulej *n.* central nervous system.

xyihil xk'ub'lal ich'mulej *n.* neuron.

xyikutb'il aatin *n.* interjection.

xyik'utb'esink *n.* set, stage.

xyirib' *adj.* concentric.

xyuch'inkil xsa' *n.* gather.

xyuwa' b'eelomej *n.* parents-in-law.

xyuwa' ixaqilb'ej *n.* parents-in-law.

xyuwa'il ayin *n.* crocodile.

xyuwa'il paqmaal *n.* chameleon.

xyuwa'il xul *n.* lion.

xyuwa'ilb'iis *n.* a ton.

xyuwa' ixaqil *n.* father-in-law (of a man).

xyuwa' b'eelom *n.* father-in-law (of a woman).

xyuutzakahemq *n.* spice, seasoning.

Y - y

ya'al *n.* sap. *From:* ya'al 'sap' (K'iche'an) (4).

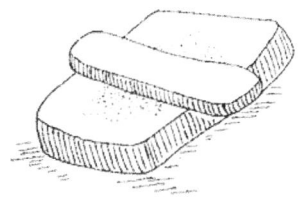

yab'ok *v.* to crush, grind.

yab'yab' *adj.* soft.

yach' *n.* underwear, brief, panty.

yach'yo *adj.* naked.

yaj *n.* patient.

yaj *adj.* sick, ill.

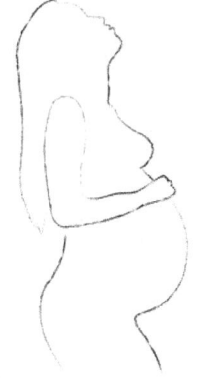

yaj aj ixq *adj.* pregnant.

yajel *n.* sickness, illness, disease.

yajel nab'onok *n.* epidemic.

yajel naxb'on rib' *n.* epidemic.

yajel qatib'el *n.* health problems.

yajelil *n.* sickness, illness, disease.

yajerk *v.* to get sick, sicken.

yajti'ox *n.* idiot.

yak *n.* lynx, fox.

yakonel *n.* merchant.

yak'ach *adj.* giant.

yak'ach *adj.* high, tall.

yak'achkej *n.* giraffe.

yal *adj.* only.

yal b'ayaq nin'aatinak sa' kastiiy *phr.* I only speak a little Spanish.

**yal b'ayaq nin'aatinak sa'
q'eqchi'** *phr.* I only speak a
little Q'eqchi'.

yal ch'uch'ib'k we *phr.* just
kidding, just joking.

yal k'a' naxb'aanu *adj.*
restless.

yal maatoch' *adj.* sensitive.

yal naxkuti rib' *adj.* impulsive,
rash.

yal sa' re naxik *adj.* talkative.

yal ta k'a' *pron.* nothing.

yal yalok re *adj.* insecure.

yal'ajot'onel *n.* adventurer.

yalaq *conj.* whichever.

yalaq ani *pron.* whoever.

yalaq b'ar *conj.* wherever.

yalaq b'ar wan *conj.* whatever.

yalaq chan ru *conj.* however.

yalaq chi b'ar *prep.*
everywhere.

yalaq joq'e *conj.* whenever.

yalaq k'a'ru *conj.* whatever.

yalaalt'ikt'ot-aam *n.*
hypotension.

yalb'a'ix *n.* examination,
exam, test.

yalb'ek *v.* to rehearse.

yaleb'aal *n.* taste, sense of
taste.

Yalib'at *sur.*

yaljot'ok *n.* adventure.

yalok *v.* to rehearse.

yalok *n.* war, battle.

yalok *v.* to fight.

yalok *v.* to try, taste, savor.

yalok ch'ool *v phr.* to give it a
shot.

yalok hu *v phr.* to bet.

yalok hu *n.* lottery.

yalok ix *n.* to test, assess.

yalok ix *n.* quiz.

yalok q'e *n.* effort.

yalok xsahil *v phr.* to taste.

yam *n.* zero.

yamch'uut *n.* empty set.

yamresink *v.* to empty.

yamyo *adj.* empty.

yamyo ru *adj.* unoccupied.

yamyo ruhil kutan *adj.*
cloudless, clear.

yamyookil ch'uut *n.* empty
set.

yanq *n.* space, interval.

yanqil *n.* intermediate point.

yanqxuk *n.* angle.

yatz'leb' *n.* juicer, juice press.

yatz'ok *v.* to milk.

yatz'ok *v.* to squeeze, wring.

yax *n.* tongs. *From:* *yax 'the crab'
(Ch'olan) (2).

yax *n.* claw, pincer. *From:* *yax
'the crab' (Ch'olan) (2).

yaxch'iich' *n.* pliers.

Yaxkal *sur. From:* yax ('pincers'). (B3).

ya'al *n.* soup.

yaab' *n.* cry.

yaab' *n.* sound, noise.

yaab' aatin *n.* stress.

yaab' kux *n.* phonetics.

yaab'ak *v.* to cry, shriek.

yaab'ak *v.* to peep.

yaab'ank *v.* to vocalize.

yaab'asink *v.* to recite, dictate, pronounce.

yaab'aal *n.* siren, ring (phone).

yaab'aal *n.* speaker.

yaab'aatin *n.* phonetics.

yaab'aatin *n.* accent, accentuation.

yaab'ich *n.* melody.

yaab'il *adj.* resonant, loud.

yaab'kuxink *n.* to sound, intone.

yaab'k'ab'a'il *n.* onomatopoeia.

yaal *phr.* that's true.

yaal *n.* truth.

yaal *adj.* true.

yaal laak'a'uxl *phr.* you're right.

yaal winq *n.* indigenous, Maya. *Note:* Literally 'true man'. Term the Q'eqchi' use to refer to themselves. (Aj Q'eqchi' traditionally refers to a speaker of the Q'eqchi' language, not a tribe or ethnicity.)

yaalt'ikr *n.* shirt.

yaaw *n.* tap, faucet. *From:* llave 'the key' (Spanish) (1).

ye *n.* tail.

ye chi timil *phr.* speak slowly.

ye wi'chik *phr.* say again, repeat that.

yehiil *n.* syllable.

DIEGO DE LANDA'S MAYA ALPHABET.

yehiileb' *n.* syllabary.

yehok *v.* to say, communicate.

yehok aatin sa' chaq'rab' *n.* witness statement.

yehok aatin sa' chaq'rab' *v phr.* to testify.

yehok maak *v phr.* to plead guilty.

yehokb'aanunk *n.* campaign.

yehol'esilal *n.* bulletin, news.

yehom *n.* testimony.

yehom *n.* language, narration.

yehom'uxb'il *n.* history.

yeksyon *n.* injection, shot. *From:* inyección 'the injection' (Spanish) (1).

yenyookil patux *n.* swan.

yeq *adj.* crippled, lame. *Var:* **yeeq**.

yeqo'k *v.* to limp.

yeq'ok *v.* to kick.

yeeb'il *adj.* verbal.

yeechi'ink *v.* to offer.

yeechi'ink *n.* commercial, ad, advertisement.

yees *n.* plaster. *From:* Spanish 'yeso'.

yi *n.* half.

yi *n.* middle.

yi *n.* waist.

yib' aj poyanam *n.* bad guy.

yib' ru *adj.* ugly, bad. *Var:* **yib'i ru**.

yib' yib' *adj.* revolting.

yib'ob'aal ru *adj.* dirty.

yib'ok *v.* to be disgusted.

yib'onik sa' sa'ej *n.* stomach acid.

yijach *n.* half.

yijachal *n.* half.

yik'ti'ink *v.* to lie (tell falsehoods).

yiib'anb'il *adj.* arranged.

yiib'anel *n.* artist, artisan.

yiib'ank *v.* to make, fix, build, construct.

yiib'ank ch'a'ajkilal *n.* solution (to a problem).

yiib'ank ch'a'ajkilal *v phr.* to solve equations.

yiib'ank sa' ru t'ikr *v phr.* to sew buttonholes, sew eyelets.

yiib'ank xaqab'ank *n.* construction.

yiib'ej *n.* waist. *Var:* yihej.

yiib'ej *n.* middle. *Var:* yib'ej.

yiib'ejilch'och' *n.* Central America, Mesoamerica.

yiib'leb'aal *n.* workshop.

yiib'na'leb' *adj.* negative.

yiisirso *n.* semicircle.

yiitoq *n.* waist, torso.

yo *part.* [progressive particle]. *Note:* Used like a verb to indicate that something is alive, happening, or ongoing in nature. **Ma yo li hab' chi kaw?** « Is it raining hard? »

yo hab' *adj.* rainy.

yo i roq *v phr.* to flow.

yo inch'ool chi royb'eninkil *phr.* I'm looking forward to it.

yo ink'a'uxl *phr.* I'm worried.

yo inyajel *phr.* I feel sick.

yo rix *adj.* moody, ill-tempered.

yo wix *phr.* I'm in a bad mood.

yo xiw *adj.* scared, afraid.

yo xjosq'il *adj.* furious.

yo xk'a'uxl *adj.* worried.

yo xsik *adj.* edgy.

yo xwara *adj.* sleepy.

yo'lajik *n.* birth.

yo'laak *v.* to be born, exist, give birth.

yo'laak xka'wa *v phr.* to be reborn.

yo'lhu *n.* birth certificate.

yo'o *phr.* let's go, come on. *Var:* yo'qeb'.

yo'oon ru *adj.* enough.

yo'ooo *phr.* come on!

yo'yo *adj.* alive.

yo'yook *v.* to be alive.

yo'yookilal *n.* nonperishable.

yoch *n.* wrinkles.

yohob'k *v.* to hunt.

yok *n.* step.

yoklaak *v.* to lie down.

yokob'ank *v.* to lie down.

yokos *adj.* crooked.

yokosink *v.* to twist.

yok'ok *v.* to cut, chop.

yok'ok si' *v phr.* to chop wood.

yok'ol *n.* cut.

yok'olal *n.* injury, wound, sore.

yole'k *v.* to slide, slip.

yolk'ok *v.* to slide, slip.

yolojch'iich *n.* robot.

yolojilb'aq *n.* human skeleton.

yolojilb'aq *n.* skeleton.

yolq'em *n.* lard, fat, grease, oil.

yolyol *adj.* slippery, slick.

yolyol *adj.* smooth.

yoq'ok *v.* to knead.

yotolal *n.* scar.

yotom *n.* scar.

yotyot *adj.* hard.

yot'e'k sa'ej *n.* constipation.

yot'ek ch'oolej *n.* dismay.

yot'ik *n.* anxiety.

yot'o'k *v.* to repent.

yot'ok ch'ool *v phr.* to regret, be sorry.

yotzotznak *adj.* loose.

yo'leb'aal ha' *n.* fountain.

yo'lejeb'ha' *n.* fountain.

yo'nink *v.* to hope.

yo'rahil *n.* handicapped.

yoob' *n.* invention.

yoob'anb'il *adj.* invented.

yoob'ank *v.* to begin, invent.

yoob'ank aatin *n.* gossip, rumor.

yoob'aal aatin *n.* neologism.

yoob'kink *n.* improvisation.

yoob'k'a'aq *n.* author, inventor. *Var:* **yoob'k'a'aj.**

yoob'k'a'uxl *n.* myth.

yoob'k'ab'a' *n.* nickname.

yook *n.* gallon.

yook *v.* to happen. *Note:* Infinitive form from which the particle "yo" is derived, which indicates the ongoing (or progressive) nature of an action. Can be inflected with personal markers to form past imperative, present progressive, and future progressive tenses.

yootzan *adj.* loose.

yooy *n.* fish net, fishing net. *From:* yoyo (Spanish) (2).

yu'am *n.* life.

yu'am ch'iich *n.* robot.

yu'amej *n.* life.

yu'amil *n.* pregnancy.

yu'amil *n.* life expectancy.

yu'aminb'il *n.* customs.

yu'k *v.* to progress.

yu'leb'yaab' *n.* amplifier.

yu'uk *v.* to stretch.

yu'uk ichmul *n.* muscle tear.

yu'uk ru *v.* to amplify, expand.

yu'yuukil k'a'uxl *n.*
paraphrase.

yuk *n.* goat. *Var:* **kaxlan yuk**.
From: *yuuk 'brocket deer'
(Yucatecan) (2).

yuki'q'een *n.* cocktail.

yulb'ilb'an *n.* pomade.

yulb'ilb'on *n.* nail polish.

yulenb'il molb' *n.* scrambled
eggs.

yulenk *v.* to whisk.

yum *n.* son (of a mother).

yumb'eetak *v.* to fornicate.

yumej *n.* son (of a mother).

yunta *n.* yoke. *From:* yunta 'the
yoke' (Spanish) (1).

yupus *n.* anus.

yuqyuqink *v.* to blink.

yuq'uq'nak *adj.* ripe.

yuq'yuq' *adj.* soft.

yutkux *n.* tie, necktie.

yutleb' *n.* hair tie, hair band.

yutleb'ch'iich' *n.* clamp.

yutuk *v.* to wrap.

yut'ismal *n.* hair pin.

yuwa'b'ej *n sd.* father. **inyuwa'**
« my father ».

yuwa'b'ejeb' *n.* parents.

yuwa'chin *n.* grandfather.

yuwa'chinb'ej *n.* godfather.

yuwa'chinb'ejeb' *n.*
grandparents.

yuuk'ink *v.* to stir.

yuuk'isib'aal *n.* carburetor.

yuul *n.* mix.

yuuleb' *n.* mixer, beater.

yuulink *v.* to dilute, blend.

III

ENGLISH ~ Q'EQCHI'
REVERSAL INDEX

Tusna'leb' Aatin
Inkles ~ Q'eqchi'

•••

A - a

a   *art.* **jun**
           art. **junaq**

a day ago *n.* **eweraq**

a few   *pron.* **b'ab'ay**
           pron. **kach'in**
           pron. **kiib' oxib'**

a little   *pron.* **b'ab'ay**
           pron. **kach'in**
           adj. **koxib'**

a long time ago *adv.* **junxil chik**
           adv. **mayer**
           adv. **najter**

a lot   *pron.* **k'i**
           pron. **k'ila**
           pron. **naab'al**
           adj. **xiikil**

a moment ago, recently
           adv. **toje'**

a while ago *adv.* **ma'laq**
           adv. **mixk**

abandoned house *n.* **po'lem**

abdomen   *n.* **ru sa'**

abject   *adj.* **tz'i'b'eetal**

above   *prep.* **sa' xb'een**
           adv. **taqe'q**

above all *prep.* **chi ru chi xjunil**

abscissa   *n.* **xna'ajtz'uq**

absence   *n.* **maa'anihilk**

absent   *adj.* **maa'ani**
           adj. **sachso**

absent-minded *adj.* **naxik**
           xch'ool

absolutely *adv phr.* **jo'kan b'i'an**

absorb   *v.* **kelonk**
           v. **tz'ub'uk**

absorbed   *adj.* **kelonb'il**
           adj. **tz'ub'il**

absurd   *adj.* **numsachk**

abundance *n.* **k'iham**

abundant   *adj.* **juntuub'**
           adj. **naab'al**

abyss   *n.* **siwan**
           n. **xchamal taq'a**
           n. **xjul taq'a**

academy   *n.* **tzoleb'aal**
           n. **xch'uutamil**

accent   *n.* **yaab'aatin**

accent mark *n.* **eetalkawyaab'**
           n. **tz'uq aatin**
           n. **tz'uq kawyaab'**

accentuation *n.* **yaab'aatin**

accept   *v.* **k'ulub'ank**

accessory *n.* **ruutz'u'ujil aq'**
           n. **xkomon rib'**

accident   *n.* **tiq'eek**

accompanied *adj.* **ochb'enb'il**

accompanist *n.* **ochb'enej**

accompany *v.* **echb'enink**

accomplice *n.* **xkomon rib'**
　　　n. **xsum**

according to *adv.* **jo'**

accordion *n.* **b'aswajb'**

account *n.* **k'as**
　　　n. **xna' tumin**

accountant *n agt.* **aj ajlanel**
　　　n agt. **aj b'irom tumin**

accumulator *n.* **k'uulmetz'ew**

accusation *n.* **q'ab'ankil**

accuse *v.* **jitok**
　　　v. **q'ab'ank**

Achi *lang.* **achi**

acidic *adj.* **ra re**

acne *n.* **wa**

acorn *n.* **ru ji**

acquit *v phr.* **kuyuk maak**

acquittal *n.* **ach'abaak**

acrobat *n agt.* **aj
　　　seeb'alk'utb'esink**

acrobatics *n.* **seeb'ch'oolil**

action *n.* **xb'aanunkil**

ad *n.* **yeechi'ink**

Adam's apple *n.* **b'uq' ja'aj**

adapter *n.* **jalb'ametz'ew**

add *v phr.* **k'ehok
　　　xtz'aqob'**
　　　v. **tiqok**

addition *n.* **molob'ank**
　　　n. **tamok-ajl**

addition symbol (+)
　　　n. **reetaltamok-ajl**
　　　n. **reetal molam ajl**

additional information
　　　n. **xtz'aqob'l esilal**

address *n.* **ochochib'aal**
　　　n. **reetalil ochoch**
　　　n. **xjayalil**

address of recipient *n.* **xna'aj
　　　b'ar wi' wan li
　　　taak'ulu'q re**

address particle (plural) *part.* **ex**

address particle (singular)
　　　part. **at**

addressee *n.* **xk'ab'a' li
　　　taak'ulu'q re**

adherent *n agt.* **aj paab'anel**

adjectival particle *part.* **aj**

adjective *n.* **cholob'anel**

adjudicate *v phr.* **raqok aatin**

adjudicator *n agt.* **aj raqol'aatin**

adjust *v.* **tz'aqob'resink**

adjustment *n.* **tz'aqob'**

administration *n.* **jolomilal**
　　　n. **k'amolb'e**

adobe *n.* **q'ut**
　　　n. **xan**

adoration *n.* **loq'onink**

adornment *n.* **ruutz'u'ujil aq'**
　　　n. **xoy**
　　　n. **xsahob' ru**

adrenaline *n.* **xwaxil
　　　rumetz'ew**

adult education
    n. **tijb'apoyanam**

adultery *n.* **muxuk**
    n. **muxuk sumlajik**

advance *v.* **jiqok**

adventure *n.* **yaljot'ok**

adventurer *n.* **yal'ajot'onel**

adventurous *adj.* **aj b'e**

adverb *n.* **jalch'ool'aatin**
    n. **tz'aqob' aatin**

adverbial phrase
    n. **jalch'ool'aatin
    kok'raq aatin**

advertisement *n.* **yeechi'ink**

advertising poster *n.* **eetalil hu**

advice *n.* **na'leb'**

adviser *n agt.* **aj chi'resilnel**

affection *n.* **sahilal**

afraid *adj.* **xiwajenaq**
    adj. **yo xiw**

after *adv phr.* **ak xnume'
    chik**
    adv phr. **chi rix chik**
    adv. **moqon**

after you *phr.* **numen laa'at
    xb'een wa**

afternoon *n.* **ewu**
    n. **najkutan**
    n. **xb'een waleb'**

afterwards *adv.* **moqon**

again *adv.* **chik**
    adv phr. **jun sut chik**
    adv phr. **wi' chik**

age *n.* **xchi hab'**

agenda *n.* **jultikob'lhu**
    n. **jultik'anjel**
    n. **xb'ehil ru k'anjel**

agent *n agt.* **aj b'aanunel**

agentive particle *part.* **aj**

aggressive *adj.* **josq'**

agitation *n.* **ch'i'ch'i'**

agony *n.* **aakan**

agouti (dasyprocta) *n.* **aaqam**
    n. **halaw**

agriculture *n.* **naw'awk**

agronomy *n.* **naw'awk**

AIDS *n.* **kaqyajel**
    n. **maxelyu'am**

aim *n.* **ahom**
    n. **jayalihom**
    v. **jayalink**

air *n.* **iq'**

air compressor *n.* **xna'aj iq'**

air conditioner *n.* **keresiil iq'**

air freshener *n.* **jaq'ilb'an**

air gauge *n.* **b'isleb' iq'**

air pump *n.* **k'ehob'a iq'**
    n. **k'eleb' iq'**

airfare *n.* **xhuhil purik**

airline *n.* **aj k'ehol purik**
    n. **xjayal xb'e**

airplane *n.* **so'sol ch'iich'**

airplane pilot *n agt.* **aj ch'e'ol
    so'sol ch'iich'**

airplane tail *n.* **xye so'sol ch'iich'**

airplane wing *n.* **xik so'sol ch'iich'**

airport *n.* **k'ochleb'aal**
n. **xna'aj so'sol ch'iich'**

Akatek *lang.* **akateko**

alarm *n.* **chajb'a'esil**
v. **chajb'a'esink**

alarm clock *n.* **ajsib'aal hoonal**
n. **ajsinel**

alarmed *adj.* **xiwajenaq**

album cover *n.* **xtz'apb'al surb'ich**

album, CD *n.* **surb'ich**

alcohol *n.* **kaxlan b'oj**

alcohol (isopropyl) *n.* **alkohol**

alcoholic *n agt.* **aj kalajel**

alcoholic drink *n.* **kalha'**

Alejandro *nick.* **Laj**

alert *adj.* **aj'aj ru**

algebra *n.* **eetalb'irool**
n. **jaljookil ru ajl**

algebraic *adj.* **eetalb'irok**

alight *v.* **k'ochlaak**

alive *adj.* **yo'yo**

all *adj.* **anchal**
adj. **chi junil**
adj. **rek'**

allergy *n.* **chak'aanil**

alligator *n.* **ayin**

alluvial erosion *n.* **xch'ajom hab'**

almonds *n.* **ru almeentr**

almost *adv phr.* **kach'in chik (ma)**

aloe vera *n.* **q'ooqil ik'e**

alone *adj.* **junes**
adj. **junesal**
adj. **ka' aj wi'**
adj. **sa' junesal**

alphabet *n.* **ch'oltz'iib'**
n. **tzoltz'iib'**

alphabetically *adv.* **sa' tzoltz'iib'**

already *adv.* **chik**

also *adv phr.* **jo'kan aj wi'**

altar *n.* **artal**
n. **oxloq'il na'aj**
n. **xna'aj qaawa'**

alter ego *n.* **nawal**

although *conj.* **us ta**

aluminum *n.* **lemtz'ch'iich'**
n. **saqch'iich'**
n. **seeb'ajch'iich'**

alveopalatal *n.* **ru'uj'aq' yaab'**

always *adv.* **chalen**
adv. **junelik**
adv. **rajlal**
adv. **retal**

amazed *adj.* **sachenaq xch'ool**

amazement
n. **sachb'ach'oolej**

ambassador *n.* **ruuchil ab'l tenamit**

ambitious *adj.* **atawal**
     adj. **ch'iq**
     adj. **narataw**

ambulance *n.* **amb'ulaans**
     n. **b'eleb'aal yaj**

American *n.* **aj q'an'isul**

amp meter *n.* **b'iismetz'ew**

amphetamine *n.* **chiq'ch'ool**

amphibian *n.* **ka'na'jilxul**

amplifier *n.* **yu'leb'yaab'**

amplify *v.* **nimob'resink**
     v. **yu'uk ru**

amuse *v phr.* **jahok u**

amusement *n.* **k'ehom uhej**

amusing *adj.* **aj se'**

an *art.* **jun**
     art. **junaq**

analgesic *n.* **re kotzok xrahil**

analogy *n.* **taq'eetink**

analysis *n.* **tzilb'a'ix**

ancestors *n.* **xe' toon**

anchor *n.* **t'ilob'aal**
     n. **xookilch'iich'**

ancient *adj.* **junxil**
     adj. **najter**

anciently *adv phr.* **sa' najter q'e kutan**

and *conj.* **ut**

and on and on *adv.* **utwchx**

and so forth *adv.* **utwchx**

Andrés *nick.* **Lex**

anemia *n.* **puchil**
     n. **saqkirin**

anesthesia *n.* **re wartesink**
     n. **wartesiilb'an**

angel *n.* **xtaql li qaawa'**

anger *n.* **josq'il**
     n. **po'jik**
     n. **waxerk**

angle *n.* **jech'xuk**
     n. **xjech'lal**
     n. **xtehelal**
     n. **xxuk**
     n. **yanqxuk**

angry *adj.* **josq'**

anguish *n.* **k'a'uxlak**

animal *n.* **xul**

animal cage *n.* **xtz'alam xul**

animal trainer *n agt.* **aj q'unb'esihonel xul**

aniseed *n.* **anis**

ankle *n.* **xkux oq**
     n. **xmap oq**

ankle boot *n.* **kok' tzelek xaab'**

annatto *n.* **xayaw**

announce *v.* **esilank**

announcement *n.* **aatin**
     n. **esil**

announcer *n agt.* **aj aatinanel**

annoyance *n.* **ch'a'ajkilal**

annoyed *adj.* **ch'a'aj ru**

annoying *adj.* **nach'a'ajko'**

annular eclipse *n.* **jiskotko tiwok**

another   *pron.* **jalan chik**
          adv. **jun chik**

answer   *v.* **chaq'b'enk**
          v. **chaq'ok**
          n. **chaq'om**
          v. **sumenk**

ant   *n.* **sank**

antacid   *n.* **aj tuqub'anel sa'**

anteater *n.* **tz'uqtz'um**

antenna   *n.* **misik'ch'iich'**

antenna (insect)   *n.* **misik**

antepenultimate
          adj. **roxch'otonel**

Anthropocene   *n.* **xwaq q'ekutan**

anthropologist   *n agt.* **aj nawpoyanam**

anthropology   *n.* **nawpoyanam**

Anthropozoic era   *n.* **xwaq q'ekutan**

antibacterial   *n.* **b'anxxulelyajel**

antibiotic   *n.* **chunilb'an**
             n. **re xmay**

anti-inflammatory   *n.* **re kotzok siip**

anti-itch cream   *n.* **re wotz'ok**

antipassive voice
             n. **nume'uxkb'il**

antivirus   *n.* **xramb'al xxulel yajel**

antonym   *n.* **xjalpaq'il**

antonyms   *n.* **ka'pak'alil ru aatin**

anus   *n.* **it**
          n. **yupus**

anxiety   *n.* **yot'ik**

apiary   *n.* **rochoch kab'**

apostle   *n.* **apoostl**

apostrophe   *n.* **tz'uq**

appeal   *n.* **titz'e'k**

appear   *v.* **k'utunk**
          v. **tawok**

apple   *n.* **mansaan**

apple cider   *n.* **xya'al mansaan**

apple juice   *n.* **xya'al mansaan**

apple tree   *n.* **mansaan**

application   *n.* **hupatz'om**
              n. **hutz'aam**

applied linguistics   *n.* **roksinkil naw'aatinob'aal**

appointment book   *n.* **tasal hu re ula'**

appreciate   *v.* **oxloq'ink**

apprehension   *n.* **nawok chi yaal**

approach   *v.* **haye'k**
           v. **jeqonk**
           v. **jilonk**
           v. **jiqe'k**
           v. **nach'o'k**

April   *n.* **awril**
          n. **xkaapo**

apron   *n.* **k'ulb'a tz'aj**
          n. **ramb'atz'aj**
          n. **xta ru sa'ej**

Arabic numeral *n.* **araaw**
    n. **kaxajl**

arch *n.* **arko**

archaeologist *n agt.* **aj ilol mayer kab'k**

Archaeozoic era *n.* **mayer q'e**

archbishop *n.* **arsob'iisp**

Archean era *n.* **mayer q'e**

architect *n agt.* **aj k'uub'anel kab'l**

architecture *n.* **nawkab'lank**

archive *n.* **k'uulhu**

arctic circle *n.* **xsiraal taq'eq**

ardent desire *n.* **ch'um ch'ool**

are you OK? *phr.* **ma us wankat**

are you sure? *phr.* **ma relik chi yaal**

area *n.* **sutam**
    adj. **xsa'**

arm *v.* **k'uub'ank**
    n. **tel**

armadillo *n.* **b'aqxul**
    n. **ib'oy**
    n. **seelxul**

armed guard *n agt.* **aj puub'**

armful *n.* **jun q'aal**

armour *n.* **ch'iich'**

armpit *n.* **sa' tel**

army *n.* **eb' aj puub'**

around *prep.* **chi rix**

arousal *n.* **tiqwok'**

arrange *v.* **tusub'ank**
    v. **tusuk**

arranged *adj.* **yiib'anb'il**

arrest *v.* **chapok**

arrival *n.* **chalik**

arrivals *n.* **nak'ulun**

arrive *v.* **hulak**
    v. **k'ulunk**

arrogant *adj.* **namunta**

arrow *n.* **sijb'**
    n. **tzimaj**

arson *n.* **k'a'uxlanb'il k'atok**

art *n.* **b'atz'iil**

art education *n.* **tijb'ab'atz'il**

art gallery *n.* **xna'aj k'utleb'aal**

artery *n.* **ich'**
    n. **ich'mul**

artichoke *n.* **kaxch'i'kay**

article *n.* **raqal**
    n. **xk'aj aatin**

article of faith *n.* **raqalil li paab'aal**

articulation *n.* **k'ulb'ayaab'**

artisan *n.* **yiib'anel**

artist *n agt.* **aj b'atz'iil**
    n. **yiib'anel**

artistic *adj.* **xb'atz'iilal**

artistic expression *n.* **b'atz'il b'aanuhom**

artistically *adv.* **q'emalk'uub'**

arts center *n.* **rochochil k'utb'esink**

as soon as possible *phr.* **sa' junpaat jo'naxk'e rib'**

ash *n.* **cha**

ashamed *adj.* **xutaanal**
  adj. **xutaanaq**

ashtray *n.* **xn'aj xchahil may**
  n. **xna'aj cha**

ask *v.* **patz'ok**

ask for *v.* **tz'aamank**

ask for a favor *v.* **ab'enak**

ask for alms *v phr.* **patz'ok limoox**
  v phr. **tz'aamank limoox**

asphalt *n.* **q'eqitz'aakalb'e**

ass *n.* **b'uur**

ass, mule *n.* **xul iiqanel**

assailant *n agt.* **aj tochonel**

assassin *n agt.* **aj kamsinel**

assault *n.* **elq'ak sa' josq'il**
  n. **toch'ok**
  v. **toch'ok**

assemble *v.* **k'uub'ank**
  v. **xaqab'ank**

assess *n.* **yalok ix**

assignment *n.* **taqlil**
  n. **tzolomil**

assist *v.* **k'uluk**
  v. **sumenk**

assistance *n.* **kamab'k**
  n. **tenq'aal**
  n. **xtenq'ankil**

assistant *n agt.* **aj tenq'anel**

associate *n.* **komon**

association *n.* **molam**

asterisk *n.* **chahim'eetalil**
  n. **reetalilk'utb'ch'ool ejil**

asteroid *n.* **puukchahim**

asthma *n.* **x'am ja'aj**

astonished *adj.* **sachaamil xch'ool**

astonishment *n.* **sachb'ach'oolej**

astronaut *n agt.* **aj b'e choxa**
  n agt. **aj b'eenel sa' po**
  n agt. **aj ch'e'ol b'oq'ch'iich' iq'**

astronomer *n agt.* **aj ilol chahim**
  n agt. **aj nawchahim**

astronomy *n.* **nawchahim**

asymmetry *n.* **jech'-uhil**

at *prep.* **sa'**

at an angle *adj.* **an'o**

at dawn *adv phr.* **naq ta saqewq**

at dusk *adv phr.* **naq ta ewuuq**

at last *adv phr.* **toj reetal**

at midnight *adv phr.* **naq tk'e tuktu q'oqyin**

at night *adv phr.* **chi ru q'oqyin**

at noon *adv phr.* **naq tk'e waleb'**

at symbol (@) *n.* **aroow**

atheism   *n.* **maak'a' xyos**

atheist   *n agt.* **aj ateey**

athlete   *n agt.* **aj aanilanel**
           n agt. **aj b'atz'unel**

athleticism   *n.* **k'ilab'atz'unk**

Atlantic Ocean   *n.* **eetaj palaw**

atmosphere   *n.* **ru choxa**
              n. **xb'een tasal iq'**

atmospheric pressure
              n. **metz'ewil iq'**

atrium   *n.* **neb'aal**

attack   *n.* **k'uluk**
          v. **tikok**

attentive   *adj.* **q'un xch'ool**

attic   *n.* **xb'een che'**

attitude   *n.* **xaqalch'ool**

attorney   *n agt.* **aj na'onel chaq'rab'**

attraction   *n.* **ajok**

audacious   *adj.* **seeb'**

audience   *n.* **ab'inel**

auditory nerve   *n.* **xjis'ich'mul xikej**

August   *n.* **akoost**
          n. **xwaqxaqpo**

aunt   *n.* **ikan na'**
        n. **na' eechej**

aureola   *n.* **ru'uj tu'**

author   *n agt.* **aj e re**
          n agt. **aj tz'iib'ahom**
          n. **yoob'k'a'aq**

authority   *n agt.* **aj jolominel**

autonomic nervous system
          n. **xk'ub'lal ich'mulej xtaq rib'**
          n. **xk'ub'lal ich'mul yal jo'**

autumn   *n.* **otoony**
          n. **xraqik hab'alq'e**

avenue   *n.* **ruq'b'e**

aviary   *n.* **rochoch tz'ik**

aviation   *n.* **nawso'solch'iich'**

aviator   *n agt.* **aj ch'e'ol so'sol ch'iich'**

avocado   *n.* **o**

avoid   *v.* **kolok**

award   *n.* **raltoj**

awl   *n.* **jotzleb'**
       n. **k'ob'leb'**
       n. **pormon**

axe   *n.* **maal**

axis   *n.* **xch'oolil**

axle   *n.* **xb'aalil**

axon   *n.* **b'olsutaal'eek'**

B - b

baby   *n.* **b'ab'ay**
        n. **kach'in**

baby bib   *n.* **t'ikr re maqab'**

baby bottle *n.* **paach**
    n. **tu'unil**

baby goat *n.* **ral chib'aat**
    n. **ral yuk**

baby rattle *n.* **tzojtzoj**

baby room *n.* **xna'aj k'ula'al**

baby walker *n.* **xb'eeresib'aal k'ula'al**

babysitter *n agt.* **aj ilol k'ula'al**

back *n.* **ix**
    n. **ixkej**
    n. **xaal it**
    n. **xxaali it**

back of the hand *n.* **rix uq'm**

back yard *n.* **xneb'a' rix kab'l**

backache *n.* **rahil xalaa'it**

backbone *n.* **juruch'**

backpack *n.* **iiqaal**
    n. **kaxsoq'**
    n. **letzool**
    n. **mochiil**

backup copy *n.* **eeqajil**

backwards *adv.* **chi rix**
    adv phr. **q'ajel ix**
    adv phr. **sa' xsal**

bacteria *n.* **xxulel yajel**

bad *adj.* **ink'a us**
    adj. **lab'**
    adj. **maa'us**
    adj. **yib' ru**

bad advice *n.* **takchi'**

bad guy *n.* **yib' aj poyanam**

bad luck *n.* **awas**

bad odor *n.* **k'isk'is**

bad omen *n.* **ch'i'**

bad words *n.* **lolob' aatin**

badly *adv phr.* **moko chaab'il ta**

bag *n.* **b'ools**

bail *n.* **tojleb' re maak**

bait *n.* **xwah kar**

bake *v.* **jorank**
    v. **jorank**

baked *adj.* **jorinb'il**

baked potatoes *n.* **pomb'il paaps**

baker *n agt.* **aj kaxlanwahinel**

bakery *n.* **kaxlan wahib'aal**
    n. **k'ayib'aal kaxlan wa**

balance *n.* **tuqtuukil**
    v. **tuqub'ank**

balcony *n.* **kuukch'iich'**
    n. **ramleb'ch'iich'**
    n. **xramleb' ilob'aal**

bald *adj.* **t'ojoch**
    adj. **t'ojt'o**
    adj. **t'uru' xjolom**

ball *n.* **b'olotz**

ballerina *n agt.* **aj xajonel**

balloon *n.* **pam'iq'**

ballot *n.* **b'ootib'k**

ballplayer *n agt.* **aj b'olotz**

bamboo *n.* **simb'**

banana   *n.* **tul**

banana tree   *n.* **tul**

band   *n agt.* **aj wajb'**

bandage   *n.* **b'ir**
　　　　n. **b'ot'leb'**
　　　　n. **re lanok tiq'il**
　　　　n. **xiitleb' b'an**

bandaged   *adj.* **b'irb'o**

Band-Aid   *n.* **kuriit**
　　　　n. **xiitleb' b'an**

bank   *n.* **k'uuleb'aaltumin**
　　　　n. **rochochil tumin**

bank account   *n.* **ajlilk'uultumin**
　　　　n. **k'uul tumin**

bank teller   *n agt.* **aj xokol tumin**

banker   *n agt.* **aj eechal k'uuleb'aal tumin**

banknotes   *n.* **huhiltumin**

baptism   *n.* **kub'iha'**

baptismal certificate
　　　　n. **huhilkub'ha'**

bar (metal)   *n.* **koral ch'iich'**

bar soap   *n.* **b'arxab'on**

barbed wire   *n.* **k'ix k'ahamch'iich'**

barbeque stall   *n.* **sisib'aaltib'**

barbershop   *n.* **b'esleb'aal**

bargain   *n.* **kotzko xtz'aq**
　　　　n. **kub'enaq xtz'aq**
　　　　v phr. **xwech'b'al xtz'aq**

bark   *n.* **rix**
　　　　n. **rix che**
　　　　v. **wohok**

barley   *n.* **seb'aad**

barman   *n agt.* **aj tenq'**

barometer   *n.* **b'isleb'hab'**

barracks   *n.* **rochochil aj puub'**

barrel   *n.* **kumb'**
　　　　n. **tamleb'aalha'**

barren woman   *n.* **xma'al ixq**

barrier   *n.* **lit'leb'aal**

barter   *v.* **jalok**

basement   *n.* **rub'el kab'l**

base-ten   *adj.* **lajetqil**

base-twenty   *n.* **junqmayil**
　　　　n. **k'aalil**

basil   *n.* **alb'aak**

basin   *n.* **joom**
　　　　n. **roqtaq'a**

basket   *n.* **almul**
　　　　n. **chakach**

basketball   *n.* **b'olotz-uq'**
　　　　n. **b'olotz chakach**

basketball player   *n agt.* **aj b'olotz chakach**

bass drum   *n.* **nimla tun**

bat   *n.* **aj tz'uum xik'**
　　　　n. **cho'k'oj**
　　　　n. **sotz'**

batch   *n.* **teep**

bath salts   *n.* **k'aj atz'am b'an**

bathe   *v.* **atink**

bathing suit   *n.* **aq' re atink**
         n. **atiyach'**

bathroom   *n.* **atib'aal**

bathtub   *n.* **xna'aj ha' re atink**

battery   *n.* **b'ateriiy**
         n. **kaxmetz'ew**
         n. **tamleb'aal metz'ew**

battle   *n.* **pleet**
         n. **raaxiik'**
         n. **yalok**

battle-axe   *n.* **maal**

battleship   *n.* **jukub' re pleetik**

bay   *n.* **rokeb' palaw**

bayleaf   *n.* **xaxaq lawrel**

be   *v.* **wank**

be alive   *v.* **yo'yook**

be born   *v.* **siyaak**
         v. **yo'laak**

be careful   *phr.* **chaab'aanu went**

be disgusted   *v.* **yib'ok**

be familiar with   *v.* **na'ok**

be hungry   *v.* **ch'ume'k**
         v. **tz'okaak**

be indoctrinated   *v.* **tije'k**

be late   *v.* **najto'k**

be rich   *v.* **b'ihomink**

be sorry   *v phr.* **ch'inank ch'ool**
         v. **kiib'ch'oolink**
         v phr. **yot'ok ch'ool**

be syphilitic   *v.* **b'uxo'k**

be thirsty   *v.* **chaqi'eel**

beach   *n.* **re ha'**

bead   *n.* **q'ol**

beak   *n.* **ruuch e**

beam   *n.* **oqech**
         n. **tz'amb'a**

bean   *n.* **kenq'**

bear   *n.* **oos**
         n. **wonxul**

beard   *n.* **mach**

beast of burden   *n.* **xul iiqanel**

beat   *v.* **b'ujuk**
         v. **juylek**
         v. **ketok**
         v. **potz'ok**
         v. **sak'ok**
         v. **tenok**
         v. **wojok**

beat up   *v phr.* **tenok chi che'**

beater   *n.* **yuuleb'**

beautiful   *adj.* **ch'ina us**
         adj. **chaq'al ru**

beauty   *n.* **xchaq'al u**

beauty salon   *n.* **b'it'b'it'leb'aal**
         n. **t'ujleb'aal**

beaver   *n.* **kaxxul**

because   *conj.* **xb'aan naq**
         conj. **xmaak naq**

become   *v.* **hulak**
         v. **uxk**

become anemic   *v.* **puchirk**

become hard   *v.* **pekark**

become literate   *v.* **tzoltz'iib'ak**

bed   *n.* **ch'aat**
         n. **warib'**
bed crank *n.* **ruq' ch'aat**
bedbug   *n.* **k'ulim**
bedding *n.* **aq ru ch'aat**
         n. **ru ch'aat**
bedpan   *n.* **q'otq'ookil sek'**
         n. **xsek'ul tz'aj**
bedrail *n.* **ramleb'**
bedroom *n.* **warib'aal**
bedspread *n.* **ru warib'aal**
bee   *n.* **chawinik**
         n. **seer**
         n. **xulkab'**
beef   *n.* **xtib'el wakax**
beefsteak *n.* **kilinb'il tib'**
beehive *n.* **rochoch kab'**
         n. **xche'el kab'**
         n. **xna'aj kab'**
beeper   *n.* **k'ul'esilal**
         n. **tz'uy tz'iib'esil**
beer   *n.* **serwees**
         n. **tzo'xul ha'**
beeswax *n.* **tz'aak**
beet   *n.* **kik'xe'**
         n. **remolaach**
beetle   *n.* **b'itonk'ot**
         n. **pachi'**
         n. **pumpuri'**
before   *prep.* **chi rub'elaj**
         adv. **junxil**
         adv. **rub'elaj**
beg   *v.* **patz'ok**

beget   *v.* **k'ajolink**
beggar   *n agt.* **aj limoox**
         n. **kok' neb'a'**
         n. **neb'a'**
begin   *v.* **naqk**
         v. **ok**
         v. **tikib'ank**
         v. **tiklaak**
         v. **yoob'ank**
beginning *n.* **k'ojlajik**
         n. **tiklajik**
         n. **xtiklajik**
behind   *prep.* **chi rix**
believe *v.* **paab'ank**
believer *n agt.* **aj paab'anel**
believing *adj.* **aj paab'anel**
bell   *n.* **kampaan**
         n. **talanch'iich'**
         n. **tilin**
         n. **tzilinch'iich'**
bell tower *n.* **xna'aj kampaan**
         n. **xna'aj punitch'iich'**
bellboy *n agt.* **aj k'amol iiq**
belly   *n.* **puj**
         n. **sa'**
belly button *n.* **ch'up**
beloved *adj.* **rahro**
below   *adv.* **taq'a**
belt   *n.* **jit'leb'wex**
         n. **nimla siinch**
         n. **xb'ak'b'al wex**
         n. **xk'aamal**
         n. **xtaab'il**
         n. **xyi aq'**

bench   *n.* **ch'ina chunleb'**
        n. **chunleb'aal**
        n. **hilaal**
        n. **kelkookil tem**
        n. **tem**

bend   *v.* **hutzuk**
        v. **k'onok**
        v. **k'unuk**
        v. **liq'ok**
        v. **lokok**

benefit   *n.* **rusilal**

beret   *n.* **soq'keep**
        n. **soq'punit**

beside   *prep.* **sa' xk'atq**

bet   *v phr.* **yalok hu**

betray   *v.* **b'alaq'ink**

better   *adv phr.* **jwal us**

between   *prep.* **chi sa'**
        prep. **sa' xyanq**

bible   *n.* **loq'tasalhu**
        n. **santil hu**

bibliography   *n.* **esilalil**

bicycle   *n.* **b'aqlaq ch'iich'**
        n. **b'isikleet**

bid farewell   *v.* **chaq'rab'ink**

big   *adj.* **nim**

bigger than   *adv phr.* **nim chi ru**

bile   *n.* **k'a**
        n sd. **k'a'ej**

bilingual   *n agt.* **aj ka'aatin**
        adj. **ka'aatin**

bilingual education   *n.* **tijok sa' ka'aatinob'aal**

bill   *n.* **kweent**
        n. **sachom**

bill (legislative)   *n.* **xk'ub'ankil ru chaq'rab'**

billboard   *n.* **xna'aj esil**

bills   *n.* **huhiltumin**

billy club   *n.* **xuq'l**

binary system   *n.* **sum ajlil**

binder   *n.* **tahu**
        n. **xna'aj hu**
        n. **xokleb' hu**

binomial   *n.* **ka'eetalb'irok**

biography   *n.* **resil yu'amej**

biologist   *n agt.* **aj nawyu'amilal**

biology   *n.* **nawom chi rix yu'am**
        n. **nawyu'am**

biotope   *n.* **siyab'aal**

bird   *n.* **kok' xul**
        n. **tz'ik**

bird guano   *n.* **mayta'**

birdhouse   *n.* **rochochil tz'ik**

birth   *n.* **yo'lajik**

birth certificate   *n.* **hab'ilhu**
        n. **papelseya**
        n. **pereera**
        n. **reetalil xyo'lajik**
        n. **yo'lhu**

birth registry   *n.* **xtz'iib'ankil li yo'lajik**

birthday   *n.* **xkutankil yo'lajik**

bishop   *n.* **ob'iisp**

bison   *n.* **kaxwakax**

bite	*v.* **hach'lenk**
	v. **hach'ok**
	v. **jach'ok**
	v phr. **k'apok chi e**
	v. **k'atzok**
	v. **qachok**
	v. **ti'ok**
	n. **tiwb'il**
	v. **tiwok**
bitter	*adj.* **k'a**
bitterness	*n.* **q'etq'etil**
black	*adj.* **q'eq**
black crow	*n.* **q'eq'i ch'ejej**
black hole	*n.* **xhoplalil**
blackberry	*n.* **tokan**
blackboard	*n.* **tz'iib'leb'aal che'**
	n. **tz'iib'leb'che'**
blackmail	*n.* **takchi'**
blackmailer	*n agt.* **aj takchi'**
blacksmith	*n agt.* **aj tenol ch'iich'**
bladder	*n.* **xna'aj chu**
blanket	*n.* **isb'**
	n. **ru ch'aat**
bleach	*n.* **b'anha'**
bleachers	*n.* **tusb'il chunleb'al**
bleeding	*n.* **tz'eqok kik'**
blemish	*n.* **xox**
blend	*v.* **yuulink**
blender	*n.* **kaxka'**
	n. **puq'leb'**
	n. **uq'unleb'aal**

bless	*v.* **osob'tesink**
blessed	*adj.* **osob'tesinb'il**
blimp	*n.* **pamb'eeresinb'il**
blind	*adj.* **mutz'**
	n. **ramleb' saqen**
	adj. **xo't'**
blink	*v phr.* **eek'asink rix u**
	v. **mutz'mutz'ink**
	v. **rik'ok**
	v. **yuqyuqink**
blister	*n.* **porha'**
	n. **poxe'k**
	n. **puchha'**
bloating	*n.* **q'an yaj**
block	*v.* **ramok**
blood	*n.* **kik'**
	n. **kik'el**
	n. **kik'elej**
blood loss	*n.* **tz'eqok kik'**
blood pressure	*n.* **nat'ich'mul**
blood pressure meter	*n.* **ich'leb'ch'iich'**
blood sausage	*n.* **moronk**
blood test	*n.* **reetalil kik'**
bloody	*adj.* **kik' ru**
blouse	*n.* **kamiis ixq**
	n. **kaxpo'ot**
blouse (typical Mayan)	*n.* **po'ot**
blow	*v.* **apuunk**
	n. **temb'il**
	v. **waalunk**
blow out	*v.* **chupuk**
blow up	*v.* **apusink**

blowgun   *n.* **puub' che'**

blowtorch   *n.* **puub'xaml**

blue   *adj.* **raxtz'o'in**
      adj. **rax ju'in**
      adj. **rax q'u'in**

blue galaxy   *n.* **raxmoyinil tzoqchahim**

blue jeans   *n.* **loonil wex**
      n. **wex re loon**

bluish   *adj.* **raxmo'in**

blunt   *adj.* **room**

blush   *v.* **kaq'ok**

boar   *n.* **chakow**

board   *n.* **tz'alamche'**

board of directors   *n.* **jolomilal**
      n. **k'amolb'e**

boarding house   *n.* **warb'etaal**

boarding pass   *n.* **xhuhil purik**

boardwalk   *n.* **b'eeche'**

boast   *v phr.* **k'anasink rix**
      v phr. **nimob'eresink ib'**
      v. **wenb'enk ib'**

boastful   *adj.* **aj yoob'anel aatin**

boat   *n.* **b'aark**
      n. **jukub'**

bobbin   *n.* **xche'el noq'**

body   *n.* **tz'ejwalej**

body hair   *n.* **q'ol is**

body part   *n.* **cha'al**

body parts   *n.* **oq uq'**
      n. **xcha'alil li tib'elej**

body text   *n.* **esil tz'iib'anb'il sa' li hu**

body work   *n.* **kuukb'eleb'ch'iich'**

boil   *v.* **loqlotk**
      v. **woqxink**

boiling point   *n.* **woqxeel**

bolt of lightning   *n.* **lemskaaq**
      n. **xrepom kaaq**

bomb   *n.* **b'oom**

bond paper   *n.* **kaaxtinb'il hu**

bone   *n.* **b'aq**

bone tissue   *n.* **ch'utb'aq cha'al**

boneless   *adj.* **xjunes tz'ej**

bonus   *n.* **raltoj**

book   *n.* **hu**
      n. **liib'r**
      n. **tasalhu**

book bag   *n.* **sukhu**

bookcase   *n.* **rochochil tasal hu**
      n. **xna'ajtasalhu**
      n. **xna'aj hu**

bookstore   *n.* **k'ayib'aalhu**
      n. **k'ayib'aal tasal hu**

boot   *n.* **b'oot**
      n. **jurxaab'**
      n. **tzelek xaab'**

boots   *n.* **b'ootaxaab'**

border   *n.* **nub'aal**

bore   *v.* **hopok**
            v. **k'ob'ok**
            v. **titz'k**

bored   *adj.* **titz'jenaq**

borrow   *v.* **to'nink**

borrowed word   *n.* **to'aatin**
            n. **to'chi'**

bossy   *adj.* **aj taqlanel**

botany   *n.* **nawk'iche'**

both   *pron.* **wotz**

bother   *v.* **ch'i'ch'i'ink**

bottle   *n.* **meet**

bottle cap   *n.* **nat'b'iltz'ap**

bottle opener   *n.* **teeleb' meet**

bottlerocket   *n.* **jutzutzu**

bottom   *n.* **chi ixkej**
            n. **sa'**

boundary   *n.* **nub'aal**

bouquet   *n.* **junq'aal uutz'u'uj**

bow   *n.* **tzimaj**
            n. **xna' sijb'**

bowels   *n.* **sa'ej**

bowl   *n.* **sek'**

box   *n.* **ka'suut**
            n. **kaax**

box office   *n.* **tojleb'aal**

box truck   *n.* **motzo'ch'iich'**
            n. **nimla iiqob'aal ch'iich'**

boxing   *n.* **potz'b'aqib'k**

boy   *n.* **ch'ajom**
            n. **ch'ina al**

n. **ch'ina teelom**
n. **saaj al**

boyfriend   *n.* **suunal**
            n. **suunuhom**
            n. **xsum aam**
            n. **xsum ch'ool**

bra   *n.* **lamb'a tu'**
            n. **lantu'**

bracelet   *n.* **pulseer**
            n. **q'ol'uq'**

braces   *n.* **lit'ob'l uuch e**

brackets   *n.* **k'ontz'uq**
            n. **nimaljuch'**

brackish   *adj.* **remrem**

brag   *v.* **wenb'enk ib'**

braid   *v.* **kemok**
            n. **tz'uluk**

brain   *n.* **ulul**

brake   *v.* **aq'ab'ank**

brake fluid   *n.* **olb'lit'b'e**
            n. **olb'xaqleb'**
            n. **ruk'a'il lit'olb'**

brakes   *n.* **lit'b'e**
            n. **xaqleb'**

branch   *n.* **ruq'**
            n. **ruq'il**
            n. **ruq' che'**

brassiere   *n.* **lamb'a tu'**
            n. **lantu'**

brave   *adj.* **kaw rib'**
            adj. **wankil**

bravery   *n.* **winqilal**

bread   *n.* **kaxlan wa**

bread pan   *n.* **xk'ilul kaxlan wa**

break   *n.* **hilaal**
  v. **jorok**
  v. **much'uk**
  v. **q'etok**
  v. **toqok**

break down   *v.* **murink**
  v. **po'ok**

break one's word   *v.* **q'etok aatin**

breaker switch   *n.* **chuplech**

breakfast   *n.* **wa re eq'la**

breast   *n.* **re ch'ool**
  n. **tu'**
  n sd. **tu'ej**

breast milk   *n.* **xya'al tu'**

breastbone   *n.* **cholok'**

breastfeed   *v.* **tu'uk**

breath deeply   *v phr.* **jiq'ok ch'ool**

breathe   *v.* **musiq'ak**
  v. **musiq'ank**

breathe rapidly   *v phr.* **jiq'ok iq'**

briber   *n agt.* **aj b'alaq'**

bribery   *n.* **b'alaq'ik**

brick   *n.* **xan**

bricklayer   *n agt.* **aj tz'ak**

bridge   *n.* **q'a**

brief   *adj.* **jumpaat**
  adj. **ko'xib'**
  n. **xyach'winq**
  n. **yach'**

briefcase   *n.* **ch'inajelool**
  n. **kanhub'aal**
  n. **kaxchampa**
  n. **k'amleb'aal**

briefs   *n.* **ch'otwex**

bright   *adj.* **lemtz'**

bright red   *adj.* **kaqjorin**

brilliant   *adj.* **q'anq'an**

bring   *v.* **k'amok**
  v. **k'amok chaq**

broadcaster   *n.* **aj pukaatin**

broad-minded   *adj.* **nakuyuk**

broccoli   *n.* **b'rookl**
  n. **raxwak'**

broil   *v.* **pomok**

broken   *adj.* **jorol**
  adj. **much'ul**
  adj. **paq'al**
  adj. **toqolal**

broken leg   *n.* **toqol a'**

broken tooth   *n.* **xulum**

bronchitis   *n.* **xyajelpospo'oy**

bronze   *n.* **q'an ch'iich'**

brook   *n.* **roq ha'**

broom   *n.* **mesleb'**

broth   *n.* **kaalt**
  n. **xya'al ik**

brother (generic)   *n sd.* **asb'ej**

brother (older)   *n.* **as**

brother-in-law   *n.* **b'alk winq**

brown   *adj.* **kaqyojin**
  adj. **q'eqmoyin**

bruise   *n.* **raxtint**

brush   *n.* **b'onleb'**
            n. **ji'b'al e**
            n. **kok' pim**
            n. **k'atk'al**
            n. **machb'onleb'**
            n. **mesche'**
            n. **sepiiy**

bubble   *n.* **woqx**

bucket   *n.* **b'oot**
            n. **kub'eet**
            n. **kumb'i'uk'al**

buckle   *n.* **jit'aal**
            n. **xch'ina ch'iich'ul**

bud   *n.* **xtorol ru uutz'u'uj**

budget   *n.* **sachom**

buffalo   *n.* **kaxwakax**

bug   *n.* **k'ajxul**

bug spray   *n.* **xb'anol suq**

build   *v.* **kab'lank**
            v. **yiib'ank**

building   *n.* **nimla kab'l**
            n. **nimla ochoch**
            n. **ninqi'ochoch**

buildings   *n.* **nimqi kab'l**

bulb   *n.* **xe'**

bull   *n.* **k'olwakax**
            n. **toor**
            n. **xmama' wakax**

bull calf   *n.* **ral wakax**

bullet   *n.* **xnaq'puub'**

bullet casing   *n.* **rixnaq'puub'**

bullet shell   *n.* **rixxnaq'puub'**

bulletin   *n.* **yehol'esilal**

bumblebee   *n.* **honon**

bump   *n.* **b'uqux**

bumper   *n.* **kolten**

bun   *n.* **b'uq'**

bunch   *n.* **jun cheet**
            n. **kuut**

bureaucracy   *n.* **xb'ehil ru k'anjel**

burglar   *n agt.* **aj elq'**

burglary   *n.* **elq'**

burial notice   *n.* **xhuhil resil kamk**

burn   *v.* **choqlenk**
            v. **humuk**
            n. **k'atal**
            v. **k'atink**
            v. **k'atk**
            v. **k'atok**
            n. **k'atom**

burp   *n.* **qixb'**
            v. **qixb'ak**

bury   *v.* **muquk**

bus   *n.* **b'eleb'aalch'iich'**
            n. **b'eleb'poyanam**
            n. **kamyoneet**
            n. **poy ch'iich'**

bus station   *n.* **hilob'eleb'aal ch'iich'**
            n. **xna'aj b'eleb'aal ch'iich'**

bus stop   *n.* **xaqleb'aal ch'iich'**

bush   *n.* **chik che'**
          n. **kok' pim**
          n. **pim**

bust   *n.* **re ch'ool**
          n. **tu'**
          n sd. **tu'ej**
          n. **xtehelal xkux**

busy   *adj.* **laatz' ru**

but   *conj.* **a' ut**
          conj. **ab'an**

butcher   *n agt.* **aj k'ay tib'**

butcher shop   *n.* **k'ayib'aal tib'**

butt   *n.* **xko rit**

butter   *n.* **k'uub'anb'il olb'**
          n. **manteek**

butterfly *n.* **peepem**

buttock   *n.* **it**

buttocks *n.* **xko rit**

button   *n.* **b'otonx**
          n. **chapleb't'ikr**
          n. **kotchapleb'**

buy   *v.* **loq'ok**

buy one get one free   *phr.* **loq' jun ut yal siib'il li xkab'**

buzzer   *n.* **jultikleb'**
          n. **tz'iraych'iich'**

by   *prep.* **sa'**

by fraction   *adv.* **chi jachal**

by tens   *adv phr.* **chi lajetqil**

by the hundred   *adj.* **chi ok'aalil**

bye   *phr.* **inwan b'i'**

C - c

cabbage *n.* **repooy**
         n. **torol'ichaj**

cabin   *n.* **po'lem kab'l**

cabinet (presidential)
         n. **xjolomil awab'ejilal**

cable   *n.* **roopilch'iich'**

cable television   *n.* **xk'aamal kaxmu**

cactus   *n.* **peetaq**

cafe   *n.* **k'ayib'aal kape**
         n. **uk'leb'aal kape**

cafeteria *n.* **k'ayib'aal kape**
           n. **uk'leb'aal kape**

cage   *n.* **koral ch'iich'**
         n. **tz'alam**

cake   *n.* **kaxlank'uluj**
         n. **uutz'u'jinb'ilkaxlan wa**
         n. **xoyk'uluj**

calcium *n.* **kawb'aqel**

calculator   *n.* **ajleb'aal**
             n. **aj b'ironel**
             n. **b'irleb'aal**

calendar   *n.* **ajleb'aal kutan**
　　　　　n. **ch'olq'e**
　　　　　n. **xq'ehil kutan**

calf (of a cow)   *n.* **ch'ina wakax**
　　　　　n. **ral wakax**

calf (of the leg)   *n.* **xk'ot oq'**
　　　　　n. **xsu oq**
　　　　　n. **xt'oy oq'**

call   *v.* **b'oqok**

call (a name)   *v.* **k'ab'a'ink**

call button   *n.* **jultikleb'**
　　　　　n. **tz'iraych'iich'**

call center   *n.* **rochochil b'oqleb'**

calligraphy   *n.* **chaq'aliltz'iib'**
　　　　　n. **chaab'iltz'iib'**

calm   *adj.* **aj kuyunel**
　　　　　adj. **ch'anaak**

calm down   *phr.* **k'ojob' aach'ool**

calorie   *n.* **xtiqwal**

camel   *n.* **b'uq'ultzimitz**
　　　　　n. **kameey**

camera   *n.* **isihob'aal jalam'uuch**
　　　　　n. **jalam'uuchib'aal**
　　　　　n. **jalam'uuleb'**

camera (television)   *n.* **k'utleb' mu**

cameraman   *n agt.* **aj chapol'esil**

camisole   *n.* **b'atz'unk b'aatal**

camp   *n.* **kampameent**

campaign   *v.* **q'unb'esink**
　　　　　n. **yehokb'aanunk**

can   *n.* **laat**

can opener   *n.* **teeleb' laat**

canal   *n.* **numleb'ha'**

canary   *n.* **kok' q'an tz'ik**

cancelled   *adj.* **xraqman ru**

cancer   *n.* **kanser**
　　　　　n. **q'aayajel**
　　　　　n. **sob'yajel**

candidate   *n agt.* **aj okenel chi awab'ejink**

candle   *n.* **kanteel**
　　　　　n. **uutz'u'uj**

candlestick   *n.* **xna'aj kanteel**

candy   *n.* **kab'**
　　　　　n. **saa'us**

candy store   *n.* **k'ayib'aal k'areru**

canister   *n.* **laat**

cannon   *n.* **ru'uj puub'**
　　　　　n. **xb'oolpuub'**

canoe   *n.* **jukub'**

canton   *n.* **teep**
　　　　　n. **xteepal tenamit**

canvas   *n.* **loon**

canyon   *n.* **xyanq tzuul**

cap   *n.* **punit**
　　　　　n. **soq'keep**
　　　　　n. **tz'apb'al re**
　　　　　n. **tz'apil**
　　　　　n. **xta jolom**

capability   *n.* **seeb'alil**

cape   *n.* **kopmokooch**

capital   *n.* **xjolomiltenamit**

capital letter *n.* **astz'iib'**

caplet   *n.* **b'otb'an**
              n. **b'otb'il b'an**

capsule   *n.* **b'otb'an**
              n. **b'otb'il b'an**

captain   *n agt.* **aj jolominel**
              b'eeleb'

captive   *n agt.* **aj tz'alam**
              n. **preex**

captivity   *n.* **preexil**

car   *n.* **ch'ina b'eleb'aal**
              ch'iich'
              n. **ch'iich'**

car accident *n.* **xtoch'ol**
              b'eleeb'aal ch'iich'

car parts   *n.* **xcha'aleb'**
              b'eleb'aal ch'iich'

caramel   *n.* **kab'**

carbohydrates *n.* **sib'ha'**
              n. **xtz'aqob'l ajsiil**

carbon   *n.* **sib'eel**

carbon paper   *n.* **ab'aqhu**

carbonated drink *n.* **kaxlanha'**

carburetor   *n.* **yuuk'isib'aal**

carcass   *n.* **kamenaq**

card   *n.* **perhu**

cardboard   *n.* **karton**
              n. **pimilhu**
              n. **teb'tookil hu**

cardholder   *n.* **perhub'aal**

cardinal directions *n.* **xtz'uq**
              junajroqil

cardinal number *n.* **t'or'ajl**

cardiologist *n agt.* **aj**
              nawch'oolej

cardiology   *n.* **nawch'oolej**

career   *n.* **xb'ehil k'anjel**

caring   *n.* **xik aak'a'uxl**

carnation   *n.* **kalawx**

carpenter   *n agt.* **aj pech'ol che'**
              n agt. **aj peech'**

carpentry   *n.* **peech'ab'k**

carpet   *n.* **alfoombr**
              n. **ruhiltz'ak**
              n. **xsok oq**

Carribean sea *n.* **palaw kariiw**

carrier   *n agt.* **aj kelonel**

carrot   *n.* **q'anxe'**
              n. **sanahoor**

carry   *v.* **iiqank**
              v. **paqonk**

carry (in hand) *v.* **ch'ilonk**
              v. **hech'hotk**
              v. **jech'exink**
              v. **rininink**
              v. **telnak**

carry (on head) *v.* **b'itonk**

carry (on shoulder) *v.* **jelonk**
              v. **telonk**

carry (under the arm) *v.* **q'alnak**

cart   *n.* **iiqaal**
              n. **kareton**

n. **kareet**
n. **toltol**

cartridge   *n.* **xnaq' puub'**

carve   *v.* **let'ok**
v. **pech'ok**

case   *n.* **rix**
n. **rixch'iich'**

cask   *n.* **kumb'**
n. **tamleb'aalha'**

cassava   *n.* **tz'in**

cassette   *n.* **choqtin**
n. **xokleb'**

cast   *n.* **chunt'ikr**
v phr. **xb'otb'al chi chunt'ikr**

Castilian   *lang.* **kastiiy**
lang. **kaxlanchi'**
lang. **kaxlan aatin**

castrated   *adj.* **kapun**

cat   *n.* **mes**

catalysis   *n.* **xjalalik ru**

catalytic   *adj.* **metz'ewanb'il**

catalytic converter
n. **k'atolch'iich'**

catch   *v.* **ramok**
v. **saapunk**

catchment area   *n.* **roqtaq'a**

caterpillar   *n.* **kuluk**

cathedral   *n.* **nimla tijob'aal**

Catholic   *n.* **katoolk**

cattle   *n.* **wakax**

cattleman   *n agt.* **aj ilol wakax**

catwalk   *n.* **q'axleb'aal**

cauliflower   *n.* **koliplor**
n. **saqmot**
n. **saqwak'**

cause   *n.* **b'aan**

cause to hear   *v.* **ab'iresink**

cave   *n.* **julpek**
n. **ochoch pek**
n. **saqoonak**
n. **siwan**

caveman   *n.* **ch'olwinq**

cavity   *n.* **xul e**

CD   *n.* **sur chapleb'aal**

CD-ROM   *n.* **sur chapleb'aal**

cease   *v.* **ach'ab'ank**
v. **ch'anab'ank**
v. **raqe'k**
v. **ruujik**

cedar   *n.* **chakalte'**
n. **muy che'**
n. **sutz'uj**

cede way   *v phr.* **k'ehok numik**

Ceiba   *n.* **inup**

ceiling   *n.* **ru tz'amb'a**

ceiling fan   *n.* **xwalub'aal kab'l**

ceiling light   *n.* **saqenk'im**

celery   *n.* **aapy**
n. **kax'isk'i'ij**

celery salt   *n.* **atz'am aapy**

cell (biological)   *n.* **xna'yu'am**

cell (jail)   *n.* **ch'ilb'oqleb'**
n. **xraqlil xsa' tz'alam**

cell (phone) *n.* **b'oqleb'**
        n. **ch'ilb'oqleb'**

cell membrane *n.* **xtzuumal xna'yu'am**

cell nucleus *n.* **xyich'ool xna'yu'am**

cell phone *n.* **b'oqleb'**
        n. **ch'ilb'oqleb'**

cell phone signal *n.* **xkutum b'oqleb'**

cellar *n.* **xna'aj k'uleb'aal**

cellphone *n.* **ch'ilb'oqleb'**

cells *n.* **na'yu'am**

cellular (phone) *n.* **b'oqleb'**
        n. **ch'ilb'oqleb'**

cement *n.* **poq re tz'akab'ak**

cemetery *n.* **muqleb'aal**

Cenozoic era *n.* **ro' q'ekutan**

census *n.* **tz'ilpoyanam**

census taker *n agt.* **aj tz'ilpoyanam**

center *n.* **xyi**

centimeter *n.* **miin**

centipede *n.* **kojoj**
        n. **mutzuy**
        n. **pataal**

Central America *n.* **xyi ab'yayala**
        n. **yiib'ejilch'och'**

central nervous system
        n. **xtuslal'ich**
        n. **xyihil xk'ub'lal ich'mulej**

central processing unit
        n. **ch'olk'anjelob'aal**

century *n.* **ok'aal hab'**

certain *adj.* **ch'olch'o**

certainly *adv phr.* **ch'olch'o b'i'an**

cerulean *adj.* **raxpotz'in**
        adj. **saqirax**

cetaceans *n.* **ha'il ajtu'xul**

chain *n.* **b'aqb'il k'aham ch'iich'**
        n. **kareen**
        n. **q'ol**

chainsaw *n.* **jachleb'aal che'**

chair *n.* **chunleb'aal**
        n. **k'ojarib'**
        n. **tem**

Chalchitek *lang.* **chalchitan**

chalk *n.* **chuntz'iib'l**

chalkboard *n.* **tz'iib'leb'aal che'**
        n. **tz'iib'leb'che'**

challenge *n.* **tikb'il**
        v. **tikok**

challenger *n.* **tikonel**

chamber pot *n.* **xsek'ul tz'aj**

chameleon *n.* **pere'maal**
        n. **xyuwa'il paqmaal**

champagne *n.* **champan**

change *v.* **jalok**
        n. **jaltesink**

change of clothes *n.* **sumal'aq'**

channel *n.* **xb'e ha'**

chapel   *n.* **kapiiy**
          n. **tijob'aal**

chapter   *n.* **ch'ol**

charcoal *n.* **ru xaml**
          n. **ruuxam**
          n. **sib'j**

chard   *n.* **aselk**
          n. **jur'ichaj**

charge   *v phr.* **xk'ulb'al xtz'aq**

charger
          n. **metz'ewib'aalb'oql
          eb'**

charity   *n.* **uxtanank**

charming *adj.* **tk'ul ach'ool**

chassis   *n.* **tz'amb'ahilch'iich'**

chat   *v.* **aatinak**
          n. **seeraq'**

chauffeur *n agt.* **aj
          b'eresinelch'iich'**
          n agt. **aj ch'e'ol
          ch'iich'**

cheap   *adj.* **kotzko**
          adj. **kub'enaq xtz'aq**

check   *v.* **ilok**
          n. **tojleb'hu**
          n. **xhuhiltumin**

checkbook *n.* **xtasal xhuhil
          tumin**

check-up *n.* **rilom aj b'anonel**

cheek   *n.* **ko**

cheekbones *n.* **xko uhej**

cheeky   *adj.* **naxkuj rib'**

cheese   *n.* **kees**
          n. **q'emtu'**
          n. **q'emya'altu'**

chef   *n agt.* **aj k'uub'anel
          tzakahemq**

chemist   *n agt.* **aj k'ayinel b'an**
          n. **k'ayib'aal b'an**

cherry   *n.* **ab'aal**
          n. **serees**

chest   *n.* **maqab'**
          n. **re ch'ool**
          n. **re maqab'**

chest of drawers *n.* **xna'aj aq'**

chew   *v.* **hab'ok**
          v. **hot'ok**
          v. **k'oylenk**
          v. **k'uxuk**

chick   *n.* **ch'ina kaxlan**
          n. **kok' kaxlan**
          n. **ral kaxlan**

chick peas *n.* **karwans**

chicken   *n.* **kaxlan**
          n. **xtib'el kaxlan**

chicken breast *n.* **xsaqal
          kaxlan**

chicken wire *n.* **soq'ch'iich'**

chickenpox *n.* **atz'umxox**
            n. **ninqixox**

chieftain *n.* **awab'ej**
           n. **jolomil**

chigger   *n.* **xulk'aq**

child   *n.* **al**
          n. **k'ajol**

childhood *n.* **kok'alil**

children   *n.* **alaleb'**
            n. **kok'al**

chili pepper   *n.* **ik**
               n. **ki'il ik**

chill   *v.* **keresink**
            n. **wosol**
            n. **xsik ke**

chilly   *adj.* **ke**

chimney   *n.* **releb'aal sib'**
            n. **releb'sib'**
            n. **xb'ehil sib'**

chin   *n.* **ru'uj xkaalam e**
            n. **rub'el e**
            n. **xxuk e**

chinchilla   *n.* **k'axkuk**

Chinese   *n.* **aj mitz-u**

chisel   *n.* **jotzleb'**
            n. **pikleb'**
            n. **pormon**

chlorine   *n.* **b'anha'**

choice   *n.* **sik'ok-u**

choir   *n.* **komon b'ichank**
            n. **xch'uut aj b'ichk**

choke   *v.* **b'iq'e'k**
            v. **jiq'e'k**

choking   *n.* **paq'ek**

cholera   *n.* **nume'sa'xa'aw**

choose   *v.* **molok**
            v phr. **sik'ok u**
            v phr. **tihok u**

chop   *v.* **jesok**
            v. **qapok**
            v. **raqink**

            v phr. **setok chi kok'**
            v. **yok'ok**

chop wood   *v phr.* **yok'ok si'**

chore   *n.* **kok'anjel**
            n. **kub'siil**
            n. **tenq'**

chorizo   **b'utb'iltib'**
            n. **b'utb'iltib'aaq**

Chorti   *lang.* **ch'orti'**

Christian   *n.* **kristyaan**

Christian faith   *n.* **kristyaanil paab'aal**

chromosome   *n.* **iyajib'aal**

chronometer   *n.* **b'isleb'hoonal**

Chuj   *lang.* **chuj**

church   *n.* **iklees**
            n. **tijob'aal**

church services   *n.* **kuult**

churro   *n.* **k'ilimb'il saa'us**

chute   *n.* **jolool**

cicada   *n.* **chikiriin**

cider   *n.* **xya'al mansaan**

cigar   *n.* **may**
            n. **sik'l**

cigarette   *n.* **may**
            n. **sik'l**
            n. **xaqmay**

cilantro   *n.* **kok' samat**

cinder block   *n.* **pak'b'il tzak**

cinema   *n.* **eetalmu**
            n. **ileb'aalmu**
            n. **rochochil ilob'aal mu**

cinnamon   *n.* **kaneel**

circle   *n.* **kotko**
 n. **siril**
 n. **sirso**

circuit board   *n.* **jekb'ametz'ew**

circuit breaker
 n. **nimlaraqalmetz'ew**

circular   *adj.* **q'otq'o**
 adj. **sursu**

circulatory system
 n. **k'uub'suutaalkik'**

circus   *n.* **ch'uch'ib'leb'aal**
 n. **xna'aj payas**

circus tent   *n.* **kaxmuheb'aal
 ch'uch'ib'leb'aal**

citation particle, plural
 part. **chankeb'**
 part. **len**

citation particle, singular
 part. **chan**

citizen   *n.* **aj tenamit**

citrus fruit   *n.* **lamuunx**

city   *n.* **mama' tenamit**
 n. **nimla tenamit**

city hall   *n.* **poopol kab'l**

city improvement tax
 n. **hutojxoyiil**

civic   *adj.* **loq'altenamit**

civic leadership committee
 n. **jolomilk'aleb'aal**

civil marriage   *n.* **sumlaak chi
 ru chaq'rab'**

civil registry   *n.* **xna'ajil
 tz'iib'ahom k'ab'a'ej**

civil rights   *n.* **xk'ulub'poyanam**

civil servant   *n agt.* **aj k'anjel sa'
 chaq'rab'**

civilization   *n.* **tawloq'aal**

clamorous   *adj.* **t'ont'on xyaab'**

clamp   *n.* **yutleb'ch'iich'**

clan   *n.* **amaq'**
 n. **triiw**

class   *n.* **paay**
 n. **paayil**
 n. **ru tzoleb'aal**

classmate   *n.* **komon sa'
 tzoleb'aal**

classroom   *n.* **xsa' tzoleb'aal**

classrooms   *n.* **xtasalil xsa'
 tzoleb'aal**

claw   *n.* **ixi'ij**
 n. **nimqi ixi'ij**
 n. **yax**

clay   *n.* **seb'**
 n. **wa**

clay brick   *n.* **pak'b'il tzak**

clay frying pan   *n.* **konxik'**

clay pot   *n.* **ch'och' uk'al**

clean   *adj.* **ch'aj**
 adj. **ch'ajmich'aj**
 adj. **saq ru**

clean laundry   *n.* **saqi aq'**

clean up   *v.* **sab'esink**

clear   *adj.* **kutan**
 adj. **saqen**

adj. **tz'aqal re ru**
adj. **yamyo ruhil kutan**

clearance sale *n.* **rosojik k'ay**

cleavage *n.* **xtehelal xkux**

cleaver *n.* **ch'ina maal**
n. **ch'iich' re setok**

clever *adj.* **kaw rib'**
adj. **wankil**

client *n.* **nuumel ula'**

cliff *n.* **uul**
n. **uul ch'och'**
n. **uul pek**

climate *n.* **xch'och'il**

climb *v.* **lochte'ek**
v. **taqe'k**

clinic *n.* **b'anleb'aal**

clip *n.* **ch'ina yax ch'iich'**

clitoris *n.* **b'irk**

cloak *n.* **nimla t'ikr**
n. **raq' qaawa'**

clock *n.* **ilb'ahoonal**
n. **reloj**

close *v.* **tz'apok**

close friend *n.* **ech-aatin**

closed *adj.* **tz'aptz'o**

closed syllable *n.* **tz'ap yehiil**

cloth *n.* **kem**
n. **t'ikr**

clothes *n.* **tiqb'al**

clothes rack *n.* **lukleb'aal**

clothesline *n.* **heleb' puch'um**
n. **helleb'aal**

clothing *n.* **aq'ej**
n. **b'aatal**
n. **tiqb'al**
n. **t'ikr**

clothing designer *n agt.* **aj yib'anel eetalil aq'**

cloud *n.* **choq**

cloudless *adj.* **yamyo ruhil kutan**

cloudy *adj.* **muqb'il**
adj. **nub'un**

clove spice *n.* **kalawx q'een**

clown *n agt.* **aj ch'uch'**
n. **se'eel winq**

club *n.* **patb'**
n. **xuq'l**

clumsy *adj.* **jip**

coach *n agt.* **aj jolominel b'atz'unk**

coagulation (blood) *n.* **patkik'**

coals *n.* **ruuxam**

coast *n.* **re palaw**

coat *n.* **b'atb'a ib'**
n. **mama' pimil t'ikr**

cobbler *n agt.* **aj yiib'om xaab'**

cobblery *n.* **rochochil li yiib'leb'aal xaab'**

cobblestone *n.* **ruhib'e**

cobblestone street *n.* **xxanil b'e**

cobra *n.* **ch'ina perk'anti'**

Coca Cola *n.* **kokakool**

cochlea *n.* **xq'ootil xik**

cock *n.* **tzo'xul**
    n. **tzo' kaxlan**

cockroach *n.* **paachach**

cocktail *n.* **yuki'q'een**

cocoa *n.* **kakaw**

cocoa bean *n.* **xnaq' kakaw**

coconut *n.* **kook**

coefficient *n.* **aj k'ihanel ajl**

coffee *n.* **kape**

coffee cup *n.* **sek' re kape**

coffee maker *n.* **xna'aj kape**

coffee pot *n.* **xna'aj kape**
    n. **xxaaril kape**

coil *n.* **q'ochb'il noq' ch'iich'**

coin *n.* **ch'iich'tumin**
    n. **kok' tumin**

coitus *n.* **tz'ikib'**

Coke *n.* **kokakool**

colander *n.* **tz'ileb'**

cold *n.* **jolomb'ej**
    n. **ke**
    adj. **ke**

cold climate *n.* **kehilch'och'**

cold cuts *n.* **b'utb'iltib'**
    n. **pihamb'r**

cold tablets *n.* **re raxkehob'**

cold water *n.* **kehil ha'**

colic *n.* **xtib'l sa'ej**

collar *n.* **xkux aq'**

collect *v.* **molob'ank**

collection (of donations)
    n. **ch'uttenq'**

collection of country houses
    n. **kok'k'aleb'aal**

college professor *n agt.* **aj k'utunel re xnimal tzoleb'aal**

colloquial *adj.* **tiikil'aatin**

colon *n.* **ka'tz'uq**
    n. **luttz'uq**

color *n.* **b'on**
    n. **b'onol**

color tone *n.* **xchamal xb'onol**

colorless *adj.* **saqmoy**

colt *n.* **ral kawaay**

column *n.* **oqech**

comb *n.* **xiyab'**

combat *n.* **pleetik**

combed *adj.* **jot'b'il**
    adj. **t'e'b'il**

come *v.* **chalk**
    v. **k'ulunk**

come back *v.* **q'ajk**
    v. **suq'iik**

come in (plural) *phr.* **okanqex**

come in (singular) *phr.* **okan**

come on *phr.* **yo'o**

come on! *phr.* **yo'ooo**

comet *n.* **b'utzchahim**
    n. **muluq'utchahim**

comfortable *adj.* **sa**

comforter *n.* **ru warib'aal**

comma *n.* **k'onk'okiltz'uq**
n. **k'ontz'uq**

command *n.* **taqlahom**
v. **taqlank**

commandment *n.* **chaq'rab'**
n. **taqlahom**

comment *n.* **k'a'uxlal**

commentator *n agt.* **aj jultikahonel**
n agt. **aj yehonel'uxk**

commercial *n.* **yeechi'ink**

commission *v.* **ab'enank**
n. **taqlil**

commit adultery *v phr.* **k'atok oq**

commitment *n.* **laatz'al**

common noun *n.* **k'ab'a'ej k'a'aqru**

communicate *v.* **yehok**

communication *n.* **xyeb'al**

communications *n.* **aatinab'aal**

communications satellite
n. **chahimch'iich' re puktesink esil**

community *n.* **komonil**

community beautification tax
n. **hutojxoyiil**

community projects
n. **tusk'anjel komonil**

compact disk *n.* **sur chapleb'aal**

compact galaxy *n.* **junaj tzoqchahim**

companion *n.* **ochb'een**

compass *n.* **junajroqil**
n. **k'ixkoot**

compassion *n.* **rilb'al xtoq'ob'al**
n. **toq'ob'al u**

competence *n.* **seeb'alil**

complement *n.* **tz'aqob'**
v. **tz'aqob'resink**
n. **xtz'aqob'l**

complementary *adj.* **xtz'aqalil**

complete *adj.* **tz'aqal**

composite noun *n.* **ka' paay ru k'ab'a'ej**

compound *n.* **ka' paay ru**

comprehend *v.* **na'leb'ak**

compressor *n.* **xna'aj iq'**

computer *n.* **ulul ch'iich'**

computer disk *n.* **ululil xokleb'**
n. **xna'aj xokleb'**

computer programmer *n agt.* **aj yiib'om ulul ch'iich'**

computer science *n.* **tzolom chi rix ululch'iich'**

computer screen
n. **kaxmu'eetalil**

conceive *v phr.* **kanaak sa' yu'am**

concentrated
adj. **xokxoxch'ool**

concentration *n.* **xokch'oolej**

concentric *adj.* **xyirib'**

Concepción *nick.* **Konsep**

concert *n.* **wajb'ak**

concertina *n.* **b'aswajb'**

condemn *v phr.* **raqok aatin chi rix**
v. **tz'aqtaanank**

condiment *n.* **xb'anol tzakahemq**

conditional particle *part.* **raj**

condor *n.* **xmama' t'iw**

conductor *n.* **numsinel**

cone *n.* **jutz'ju**
n. **juutz'**
n. **ru chaj**

conference *n.* **xyeeb'al**

confess *v.* **xotonk**
v. **xootonink**

confession *n.* **xyehok maak**

confessional *n.* **xootonib'aal maak**

confetti *n.* **xk'aj hu**

confidant *n.* **paab'ajel**

confirmed bachelor *n.* **tiixil ch'ajom**

confuse *v.* **sachk**

confused *adj.* **sachenaq ru**

congratulations! *phr.* **sahil ch'oolejil choq' aawe**

congress
n. **k'uub'leb'chaq'rab'**
n. **rochochil aj k'uub'anel chaq'rab'**

congruent triangle *n.* **tawrib' oxxukuut**

conjoined twins *n.* **latzlut**

conjugate *v.* **b'atz'unenk**

conjugated *adj.* **b'atz'unenb'il**

conjunction *n.* **najunajin aatin**

conjunctivitis *n.* **rahil u**

connection *n.* **k'ultiq**

consequence *n.* **k'ulb'ilal**

consider *v phr.* **teeb'il xk'a'uxl**

considerate *adj.* **teeto xk'a'uxl**

consonant *n.* **xyaab'tz'iib'**

constellation *n.* **ch'uut chahim**
n. **tzoqtzokilchahim**
n. **xch'uutulal chahim**

constipation *n.* **yot'e'k sa'ej**

constitution *n.* **xchaq'rab' li tenamit**

construct *v.* **yiib'ank**

construction *n.* **yiib'ank xaqab'ank**

construction site *n.* **kab'lak**
n. **xna'aj yiib'ank xaqab'ank**

construction worker *n.* **aj yiib'ank xaqab'ank**

constructivism *n.* **kab'lanb'il na'leb'**

consult *v.* **aatinank**

consumer finance *n.* **tijok chi rix loq'ok**

contact lenses *n.* **ch'ik ileb'**

container *n.* **meet**

contemplate *v.* **ka'yank**
    v. **k'ulub'ank**

contempt *n.* **tz'eqtanank**

content *adj.* **k'ojk'o xch'ool**
    adj. **sa xch'ool**
    adj. **tuqtu xch'ool**

contentment *n.* **sahil ch'oolejil**

contents *adj.* **xsa'**

continent *n.* **pak'alilch'och'**

continuation *n.* **tiqam**

contract *n.* **xaqab'ank aatin**
    n. **xaq-aatin**

control *v phr.* **k'ehok eetal**

control tower *n.* **k'aak'aleb'aal**

controller *n.* **tuqb'ametz'ew**

controversial *adj.* **xik' naxye**

convent *n.* **konb'eent**

conventioneer *n agt.* **aj q'unob'tesinel**

convert *n.* **jaltesink**

convex *adj.* **b'uq'**
    adj. **b'uq'b'u**

convict *n.* **pereex**
    v phr. **raqok aatin chi rix**
    v phr. **teneb'ankil sa' xb'een**

cook *n agt.* **aj k'uub'anel tzakahemq**
    v. **chiqok**

cooked *adj.* **chiqb'il**
    adj. **k'ub'k'u**
    adj. **k'uub'aak**

cookhouse *n.* **chi re xam**
    n. **k'uub'leb'aal**
    n. **xna'aj xam**

cookie *n.* **xujsaa'us**

cooking oil *n.* **kax'olb'**
    n. **kaxlanq'ib'**

cool *adj.* **luulu**

cooperation *n.* **komontenq'**
    n. **tenq'aal**

cooperative *n.* **komonilk'anjel**

coordinate *n.* **xb'arxukil**

coordinate origin *n.* **xtiklajik xb'arxukil**

copier *n.* **jalam'uuchleb'**
    n. **jalam'uuchleb'aal ch'iich'**
    n. **puktasib'aalhu**

copper *adj.* **q'anch'ik'**
    n. **q'an ch'iich'**

copy *v.* **etalink**

copy machine
    n. **jalam'uuchleb'**
    n. **jalam'uuchleb'aal ch'iich'**
    n. **puktasib'aalhu**

cord *n.* **jusk'aam**

cordless phone *n.* **mak'aam b'oqleb'**

coriander *n.* **kulantr**

corkscrew *n.* **isib'aal tapon**
    n. **teeleb' meet**

corn *n.* **ixim**

corn (cutaneous) *n.* **pat**

corn (prepared for grinding)
 n. **b'uch**

cornea *n.* **xlemtz'iil u**

corner *n.* **jech'xuk**
 n. **loot'**
 n. **xuk**
 n. **xxuk b'e**

cornfield *n.* **k'al**
 n. **waj**

cornmeal *n.* **q'em**

cornmeal drink *n.* **q'em ha'**

cornstalk *n.* **roq waj**

coroner *n agt.* **aj ilol kamenaq**

corpse *n.* **kamenaq**

corral *n.* **xna'aj ketomq**
 n. **xoralwakax**

correcting fluid *n.* **tuqleb'**

corrections *n.* **xk'ub'laal tojb'a maak**
 n. **xk'uub'laltojb'ama ak**

cosmetics *n.* **sunob'resiil**

cosmology *n.* **suutalnawom**

cosmos *n.* **choxach'och'**

costume *n.* **eetz'aal**
 n. **k'utb'aatal**
 n. **uutz'u'ujinb'il eetz'unk**

cot *n.* **ch'ina ch'aat**

cotton *n.* **noq'**

cotton candy *n.* **ki'tuux**

cotton candy vendor *n agt.* **aj k'ay ki'tuux**

cotton swab *n.* **tuxil noq'**

cotton tree *n.* **xche'el noq'**

couch *n.* **potztem**
 n. **soq'il chunleb'**

cough *n.* **katzkatz kux**
 n. **kuxb'ej**
 n. **ojb'**
 v. **ojb'ak**

cough drops *n.* **b'an re ojb'**

cough please *phr.* **ojob'an b'aanu usilal**

cough syrup *n.* **uk'b'il b'an**

counselor *n agt.* **aj chi'resilnel**
 n agt. **aj k'ehol na'leb'**

count *v.* **ajlank**

country *n.* **nimla tenamit**

countryside *n.* **k'aleb'aal**

courageous *adj.* **kaw rib'**
 adj. **naxyoob' rib'**

course *n.* **ru tzolom**
 n. **tzolomil**

court *n.* **neb'aal**
 n. **poopol**
 n. **raqleb'aatin**

court case *n.* **ch'a'jkilal**

cousin *n.* **as e**

cousin (younger) *n.* **iitz'in'e**

covenant *n.* **sumwank**

cover *v.* **lepok**
 n. **ruhil**

n. **tz'apleb'**
v. **tz'apok**

cover page   *n.* **ruhil**
n. **xoy**

covet   *v.* **tzemok**

cow   *n.* **b'aak**
n. **na'wakax**
n. **wakax**
n. **xa'n wakax**

cowardly   *adj.* **aj xiw**
adj. **aj yop**

cowboy   *n agt.* **aj ilol wakax**

coyote   *n.* **tz'i' pim**
n. **tz'i' tzuul**
n. **xojb'**

CPU   *n.* **ch'olk'anjelob'aal**

crab   *n.* **tap**
n. **xtap palaw**

cracker   *n.* **kaxk'oyem**

cradle   *n.* **tz'alamch'aat**
n. **xkoral k'ula'al**
n. **xwaresib'aal k'ula'al**

craftsman   *n agt.* **aj k'anjel re k'a' re ru**

cramp   *n.* **muchkej**

cranium   *n.* **xb'aqel jolom**

crate   *n.* **kaxon**

crawl   *v.* **jukunk**
v. **k'achiik**

crayfish   *n.* **tap re nima'**

crayon   *n.* **b'onleb'**

cream   *n.* **uq'unil b'an**

crease   *n.* **xb'asb'al sa' xyi**

credential   *n.* **huraqb'atzolok**

creek   *n.* **ch'ina nima'**

creeper vine   *n.* **k'aamal pim**

crescent wrench
n. **q'otleb'ch'iich'**

crevice   *n.* **xtz'iral ch'och'**

crib   *n.* **tz'alamch'aat**
n. **xkoral k'ula'al**

cricket   *n.* **chili'**
n. **sij**
n. **tz'iray**

crime   *n.* **maak**

crippled   *adj.* **yeq**

crockery   *n.* **k'ila sek'**

crocodile   *n.* **mama' ayin**
n. **xyuwa'il ayin**

crooked   *adj.* **b'ach'b'o**
adj. **b'ech'**
adj. **jech'**
adj. **k'onk'o**
adj. **liq'lo**
adj. **rok'ox**
adj. **siq'il**
adj. **yokos**

cross   *n.* **krus**
v. **nume'k**
v. **q'axok**
v. **raqok**
n. **xukup**

crossroads   *n.* **xxaal b'e**

crosswalk   *n.* **xb'eleb'aal poyanam**
n. **xnumik poyanam**

crouch   *v.* **chok'laak**
  v. **chok'ob'ank**
  v. **k'ukub'ank**

crow   *n.* **ch'ejej**
  n. **qoch**

crowbar   *n.* **b'oq'leb'ch'iich'**

crowd   *n.* **aj ab'ine'leb'**
  n. **amaq' tenamit**
  n. **k'ehal**
  n. **k'ila poyanam**
  n. **naab'alil**

crown   *n.* **ajawilxoy**

crown (dental)
  n. **ruutz'u'ujinkil**

crucifix   *n.* **ch'ina xukup**

crude   *adj.* **chaq re ru**

cruelty   *n.* **numlab'al**

crush   *v.* **sob'ok**
  v. **tenok**
  v. **yab'ok**

crutch   *n.* **kuutiil**

cry   *n.* **yaab'**
  v. **yaab'ak**

cry out (in pain)   *v.* **aylok**

cubby   *n.* **xna'aj k'a re ru**

cube   *v.* **oxwahink**
  n. **waqxukuut**

cubit   *n.* **chumay**

cucumber   *n.* **pepiin**

cuff   *n.* **ruq'm aq'**
  n. **sa' ruq' aq'**

cultivate   *v.* **k'anjelank**

cultural identity   *n.* **oxloq' ilob'**

cultural values   *n.* **loq'alil na'leb'**

culture   *n.* **ch'och'el sululel**
  n. **oxloq'il na'leb'**

cup   *n.* **sek'**
  n. **taas**
  n. **uk'leb'lem**
  n. **wa'leb' sek'**

cupcake   *n.* **xelexkaxlanwa**

cure   *v.* **b'anok**
  v. **k'irtesink**

curious   *adj.* **aj kayanel**
  adj. **nakayan**

curriculum   *n.* **nimk'uub'tzolok**
  n. **xk'ub'laltzolok**

curriculum vitae   *n.* **esilnawom**

cursive   *n.* **q'inixtz'iib'**

cursor   *n.* **eetal**
  n. **numch'o**

curtain   *n.* **nimla ramleb'aal t'ikr**
  n. **ramleb'**
  n. **ramleb' saqen**

curve   *n.* **q'oot**

curved   *adj.* **q'otq'o**
  adj. **q'oot**

curved line   *n.* **k'onoljuch'**

cushion   *n.* **sok jolom**

custody   *n.* **kolok**

custom   *n.* **na'leb' xe'toon**

customs   *n.* **yu'aminb'il**

cut   *v.* **kuruk**
  v. **setok**

v. **yok'ok**
n. **yok'ol**

cut down   *v.* **jachok**

cut in strips   *v.* **jisok**

cutlery   *n.* **kok' ch'iich' re wa'ak**

cutting board   *n.* **tz'alamche' re setok**

CV   *n.* **esilnawom**

cyclist   *n agt.* **aj ch'e'ol b'aqlaq ch'iich'**

cylinder   *n.* **b'aral**
n. **b'olb'o**

cylindrical   *adj.* **b'olb'o**

cypress   *n.* **k'isis**
n. **sipres**

cyst   *n.* **saqijoj**

cytoplasm   *n.* **xya'alna'yu'am**

D - d

daisy   *n.* **markariit**

damn it   *phr.* **ay xkux na'**

damp   *adj.* **t'aqt'aq**

dance   *n.* **xajleb'**
v. **xajok**

dancer   *n agt.* **aj xajonel**

dandruff   *n.* **salb'a**

danger   *n.* **xiwxiw**

dangerous   *adj.* **xiw xiw**

dark   *adj.* **aak'ab'**
adj. **moymo**
adj. **q'ojyin**
adj. **tuh**

dark green   *adj.* **rax moyin**

darkness   *n.* **aak'ab'**

darn   *v.* **xiitink**

dash   *n.* **ch'inaaljuch'**
n. **ch'inq'ejuch**

dashboard   *n.* **xna'aj eetalil**

date   *n.* **xb'e li po**

date of birth   *n.* **xkutankil yo'lajik**

daughter   *n.* **ko'**
n. **rab'in**

daughter-in-law (of a man or woman)   *n.* **alib'**

dawn   *n.* **priim**

day   *n.* **kutan**

day after tomorrow   *n.* **kab'ej**

day before yesterday
n. **kab'ejer**

day of rest   *n.* **hilob'aal kutan**

dead   *adj.* **kamenaq**

deaf   *adj.* **tz'apxik**
adj. **tz'apyaab'il**

death penalty   *n.* **kamk tojb'a maak**
n. **teneb'anb'ilkamk**

debone   *v phr.* **isink b'aq**

debt   *n.* **b'ayom**
            n. **k'as**
decade   *n.* **lajeeb' hab'**
deceit   *n.* **b'alaq'**
December   *n.* **tisyemr**
            n. **xkab'aljuhilpo**
decipher   *v.* **nawyaalalink**
decipherment   *n.* **nawyaalal**
decongestant   *n.* **aj tuqub'anel sa'**
decorate   *v.* **uutz'u'ujink**
decoration *n.* **ruutz'u'ujil aq'**
            n. **xoy**
decorator   *n agt.* **aj uutz'u'ujinel**
decree   *n.* **ruq'b'chaq'rab'**
deductive   *adj.* **nimajel**
deep   *adj.* **cham**
deer   *n.* **kej**
defeat   *n.* **t'ane'k**
            n. **tz'eqok**
defecate   *v.* **k'otak**
            v phr. **tz'eqok ib'**
defend   *v.* **kolok**
defendant   *n.* **jitb'il**
            n. **q'ab'anb'il**
definitely *adv phr.* **jo'kan b'i'an**
defrost   *v phr.* **isink xkehil**
degrees   *n.* **b'isketiiq**
            n. **xteram**
degrees Fahrenheit
            n. **parenheitil b'iis**
dejected   *adj.* **ch'ina xch'ool**

dejection   *n.* **kamenaq xch'ool**
delay   *n.* **b'ayjik**
            v. **b'ayok**
delayed   *adj.* **xb'ay chaq**
delegate   *n.* **ruuchilawab'ej**
delicious   *adj.* **sa**
delight   *n.* **sahilank**
delighted   *adj.* **twulaq chi ru**
delinquent *n agt.* **aj maak chi ru chaq'rab'**
delivery truck   *n.* **xraqilal xsa'**
democracy   *n.* **junajch'oolej**
            n. **sahilwank**
demon   *n.* **anum**
            n. **maa'us**
            n. **tza**
demonstrate *v.* **k'utb'esink**
demonstration   *n.* **xk'utb'al**
dendrite   *n.* **xchaqijik**
denim   *n.* **t'ikr loon**
denominator *n.* **jarjek'il**
dent   *v.* **sob'ok**
            n. **sob'olal**
dental assistant   *n agt.* **aj tenq'anel risihom uuch e**
dental chair   *n.* **chunleb'aal**
dental clinic   *n.* **uuch eleb'aal**
dental floss   *n.* **noq' re uuch e**
dental instrument
            n. **k'anjeleb'aal ruuch e**

dentist   *n agt.* **aj ilol'uuch-e**
          n agt. **aj isihom ruuch e**

dentist office   *n.* **uuch eleb'aal**

denture   *n.* **pak'b'il ruuch e**

deny   *v phr.* **ink'a' xsumenkil**
       v. **jalmuqank**

deodorant   *n.* **xsununkil sa' tel**

departing flights information
          n. **esilal re elk**

department store   *n.* **mama' rochochil aq'ej**
          n. **nimla k'ayib'aal**

departmental government
          n. **rochoch ruuchilawab'ej**

departure   *n.* **elk**

departures   *n.* **na'elk**

dependent pronoun
          n. **chapchookil ruuchil k'ab'a'ej**

deposit receipt   *n.* **xhuhil li k'uulank**

depressed   *adj.* **kamenaq xch'ool**

depression   *n.* **lub'k ch'oolej**

depth   *n.* **chamal**

descendants   *n.* **ralal xk'ajol**

describe   *v.* **wech'ok**

description   *n.* **wech'ok**

desert   *n.* **chaqi ch'och'**

desire   *n.* **ajok**

desk   *n.* **chunleb'aal**
       n. **tz'iib'leb'meex**

desk mat   *n.* **ru meex**

despair   *n.* **sapsapink ib'**

dessert   *n.* **xtz'aqob' wa'**

destroy   *v.* **juk'uk**
          v. **po'ok**
          v. **sachok**

detain   *v.* **xaq'ab'ank**

detective   *n agt.* **aj tz'ilonel**

detergent   *n.* **poqxab'on**

develop photos
          v. **kutanob'resink**

development   *n.* **usaak wakliik**

devil   *n agt.* **maa'us aj winq**
        n. **tza**

dew   *n.* **chu' ke**
      n. **chu'ke**
      n. **k'ajob'**

dextrine   *n.* **latztz'in**

diadem   *n.* **nat'leb'ismal**

diagnose   *v.* **nawrub'elalink**

diagonal   *adj.* **salam**

diagram   *n.* **raqaxinkil**

dialect   *n.* **jalb'esiil'aatin**
          n. **ralab'aatinob'aal**
          n. **xjalanil ru aatin**

dialectal variety   *n.* **xcha'alil aatinob'aal**

dialectology
          n. **nawralab'aatinob'aal**

diameter   *n.* **xsa'kotko**

diamond *n.* **lemtz'pek**
    n. **salsookil kaaxukuut**
    n. **xaqamkaaxuk**

diamond-shaped *adj.* **b'arxuk**

diaper *n.* **panyal**

diarrhea *n.* **nume' sa'**
    n. **sa'ej**

diastolic blood pressure
    n. **metz'ew ich'mulej okik'**

dice *n.* **q'aqt**
    v phr. **setok chi kaaxukut**

dicotyledonous seed *n.* **lut-al iyaj**

dictate *v.* **yaab'asink**

dictator *n agt.* **aj taqlanel**

dictionary *n.* **molob'aal aatin**
    n. **sik'leb' aatin**
    n. **xtusulal aatin**

die *v.* **kamk**

dieresis *n.* **luttz'uqyaab'**

diesel *n.* **qishumha'**
    n. **ruk'a ch'iich'**
    n. **xya'al b'eleb'aal**
    n. **xya'al ch'iich'**

difficult *adj.* **ch'a'aj**
    adj. **raasa**

difficulty *n.* **ch'a'ajkil**
    n. **rahilal**

dig *v.* **aq'ink**
    v. **b'ekok**
    v. **pikok**

digestive system *n.* **sooto'y**

digging stick *n.* **awleb'**

digital camera *n.* **ch'eb'il jalam'uuchil**

dignitary *n.* **loq'al**

dignity *n.* **loq'alil**

diligence *n.* **sak'ahil**

diligent *adj.* **sak'a**

dilute *v.* **yuulink**

dime *n.* **lajeb' senta**

dimension *n.* **xnimal**

diner *n.* **wa'leb'aal**

dining room *n.* **wa'leb'aal**

dinosaur *n.* **ayin kaaq**

Dionisio *nick.* **Nich**

diphthong *n.* **kajunajink xna'tz'iib'**

diploma *n.* **eetalhu**
    n. **huraqb'atzolok**
    n. **reetalil tzolom**

dipstick *n.* **xche'el kaxolb' ch'iich'**

direct *v.* **jolomink**

direction *n.* **jayal**
    n. **tiikal**

director *n agt.* **aj k'amolb'e**
    n agt. **aj k'utunel b'e**
    n. **xb'eenil tijonel**

dirigible *n.* **pamb'eeresinb'il**

dirt *n.* **tz'ajn**

dirt path *n.* **ch'och'il b'e**

dirt road *n.* **pekilnimb'e**

dirty   *adj.* **b'alak'**
            adj. **b'ulux**
            adj. **pes**
            adj. **tz'aj ru**
            adj. **yib'ob'aal ru**

dirty words   *n.* **xik' aj aatin**

disappear   *v.* **muqunk**
            v. **sachk**

disappointed   *adj.* **kosa xch'ool**

disappointment   *n.* **rahob'k**

disaster prevention   *n.* **kawalil chi ru raaxiik'**

disco   *n.* **xajleb'aal**

discover   *n.* **na'ok**
            n. **ta'ok**
            n. **tehok ru**

discovery   *n.* **na'lenk**

discus throw   *n.* **kutuk suriil**

disdain   *n.* **xik' ilok**

disease   *n.* **yajel**
            n. **yajelil**

disease onset   *n.* **xtiklajik li yajel**

disguise   *n.* **eetz'aal**
           n. **k'utb'aatal**
           n. **uutz'u'ujinb'il eetz'unk**

disgust   *n.* **xik' ilok**

disgusting   *adj.* **xa'wil ru**

dish   *n.* **pulaat**
           n. **sek'**

dishonest   *adj.* **ink'a' us xna'leb'**

dishwasher   *n.* **ch'ajleb'aal sek'**
             n. **ch'ajleb' sek'**

disillusioned   *adj.* **kosa xch'ool**

disinfectant   *n.* **re chajok tiqil**
               n. **saqleb'**

disk   *n.* **surchoch**
           n. **sur chapleb'aal**

diskette   *n.* **chochtz'iib'**

dismay   *n.* **yot'ek ch'oolej**

disobey   *v.* **q'etok aatin**

disorganized   *adj.* **hirook**
               adj. **tzukinb'il ru**

display   *n.* **kaxmu'eetalil**

display case   *n.* **xlemul k'ayib'aal**

display shelves   *n.* **xna'aj k'ay**

displease   *v phr.* **po'ok ch'ool**

disposable   *adj.* **tz'eeqel**

disrespectful   *adj.* **ink'a' na'oxloq'in**

dissolve   *v.* **ha'ob'resink**

distance   *n.* **najtil**

distance education   *n.* **tijb'ajunesal**

distance or motion particle   *part.* **chaq**

distract   *v phr.* **jahok u**

distress   *n.* **ok k'a'uxl**

distribute   *v.* **jek'ok**

distributive number   *n.* **jek'b'il ajl**

distributor   *n.* **jek'inel**

district   *n.* **teep**
           n. **xteepal tenamit**
ditch   *n.* **cho'ok jul**
           n. **jul**
           n. **pahok jul**
           n. **roq ha'**
dive   *v.* **muqa'lik**
diverse   *adj.* **k'ilpoyanimil**
diversion *n.* **ajsink-u**
diversity *n.* **k'iilayehom
           b'aanuhom**
divide   *v.* **jachok**
           v. **jek'ink**
divided by *adj.* **jachinb'il chi**
diving board *n.* **pisk'leb'aal**
division   *n.* **tas**
           n. **xjek'inkil**
           n. **xtasalal**
division symbol (/)
           n. **reetaljek'ajl**
           n. **reetal jach'ajl**
divisor   *n.* **jeb'ib'aal**
divorce   *n.* **jachkab'al**
           n. **jachok-ib'**
dizziness *n.* **lub'ik**
dizzy   *adj.* **moymo ru**
do   *v.* **b'aanunk**
do you know each other?
           phr. **ma ak nakenaw
           eeru**
do you speak English? *phr.* **ma
           nakat-aatinak sa'
           inkles**

do you speak Q'eqchi'? *phr.* **ma
           nakat-aatinak sa'
           q'eqchi'**
dock   *n.* **xaqleb'jukub'**
           n. **xxaqleb'aal jukub'**
doctor   *n agt.* **aj b'anonel**
           n. **loktor**
doctrine   *n.* **tij**
           n. **tzoleb'**
document   *n.* **taqlhu**
           n. **tz'iib'anb'ilhu**
dodge   *v.* **kolok**
dog   *n.* **tz'i'**
doll   *n.* **pak'b'il k'uula'al**
           n. **poy'al**
dolphin   *n.* **q'olxulkar**
domestic departures *n.* **elk yal
           sa' xteep tenamit**
dominant   *adj.* **nataqlan**
Domingo   *nick.* **Ku'**
don't forget *phr.* **misach sa'
           laach'ool**
don't mention it
           phr. **matk'a'uxlak**
don't worry about it
           phr. **matk'a'uxlak**
donkey   *n.* **b'uur**
           n. **xul iiqanel**
door   *n.* **okeb'aal**
           n. **pweert**
           n. **re kab'**
door lock *n.* **rokeb' xlaawil
           kab'l**

doorbell   *n.* **b'oqleb'aal**

door-bolt   *n.* **k'aan**
             n. **nat'leb'**

doorpost   *n.* **champa**

dormitory   *n.* **warib'aal**

dormouse   *n.* **k'iche' ch'o**

dose   *n.* **xb'iisul b'an**

double bed   *n.* **nimla ch'aat**

doubt   *n.* **kiib'ank ch'ool**

doubt particle   *part.* **ta**

dough   *n.* **q'em**

dove   *n.* **mukuy**

down   *adj.* **chi rub'el**
        prep. **taq'a**

downpour   *n.* **kawil hab'**

downtown   *n.* **xyi tenamit**

dozen   *n.* **jun toseen**

dragonfly   *n.* **tuulux**

drain   *n.* **ha'ha'**
         n. **releb'tz'ajha'**
         n. **roq ha'il tzaj**

drape   *n.* **ramleb' saqen**

draw   *v.* **jalam'uuchink**

draw water   *v.* **lekok**

drawer   *n.* **k'uulchob'**
          n. **ralmeex**

drawers   *n.* **kaax**

drawstring (for a skirt)
          n. **xk'aamal uuq**

dread   *n.* **xiw**

dream   *n.* **matk'**
         v. **matk'ek**
         v. **na'uuchik**

dress   *n.* **b'estiiy**
         n. **jut-aq'**
         n. **tiqb'al**

dresser   *n.* **xna'aj aq'**

dribble   *v.* **leeleb'ak**
           n. **xya'al e**

drill   *n.* **hopleb'**
         n. **hopleb'che'**
         n. **hopleb'tz'ak**
         v. **hopok**
         n. **k'ob'leb'**

drink   *n.* **uk'a'**
         v. **uk'ak**

drinking fountain   *n.* **uk'leb'aal**

drinking glass   *n.* **b'aas**
                  n. **uk'leb'lem**

drip   *v.* **okesink**
        v. **rachrotk**
        v. **tz'iltz'otk**
        v. **tz'uqluk**

drive   *v.* **b'eeresink**

drive belt   *n.* **xk'aamal**

driver   *n agt.* **aj b'eresinelch'iich'**
          n agt. **aj ch'e'ol ch'iich'**

driver's license   *n.* **liseens**

driveway   *n.* **rokeb'aal b'eleb'aal ch'iich'**

drizzle   *n.* **kok' ruhil hab'**

drool   *n.* **xya'al e**

drop   *v.* **b'alq'usink**
      v. **koq'ok**

dropcloth   *n.* **mokooch**

drought   *n.* **saq'ehil**

drown   *v.* **jaq'e'k**
      v phr. **ok chi ha'**
      v. **paq'e'k**
      v. **xolk'ok**

drowning   *n.* **paq'e'k**

drug   *n.* **kaanilb'an**

drug dealer   *n agt.* **aj k'ay yib' aj b'an**

drug trafficker   *n agt.* **aj naark**

drug trafficking   *n.* **b'eeresink yib' aj k'ay**

drugstore   *n.* **k'ayib'aal b'an**
      n. **loq'leb'aal b'an**

drum   *n.* **job'wajb'**
      n. **moor**
      n. **nimla tun**
      n. **tamb'or**
      n. **tuntun**

drumstick   *n.* **ruq'wajb'**

drunk   *adj.* **kalajenaq**

dry   *adj.* **chaqi**
      v. **chaqob'resink**
      adj. **xujxuj**

dry cough   *n.* **katzkatz aj ja'aj**

dry skin   *n.* **chaqi ix**

dry spell   *n.* **saq'ehil**

duck   *n.* **patux**

dull   *adj.* **chupchu**

dust   *n.* **poqs**

duty   *n.* **kok'anjel**

duty free shop   *n.* **tiikil k'ayib'aal**

dwarf   *adj.* **met**

dye   *v.* **b'onok**

dysentery   *n.* **kik'sa'**

E - e

eagle   *n.* **t'iw**

ear   *n.* **xik**

ear of corn   *n.* **k'ux**

earache   *n.* **rahil sa' xik**

eardrum   *n.* **xulel xikej**

earlier   *adv.* **toj eq'la**

early   *adj.* **eq'la**

early morning   *n.* **hik'o**
      n. **ik'ek'**
      n. **priim**

earn   *v.* **echanink**
      v phr. **sik'ok ib'**
      v. **tzakink**

earn a living   *v phr.* **numsink kutan**

earphones   *n.* **ab'ib'aal**
      n. **xikelyaab'**

earring   *n.* **ka'xik**

Earth   *n.* **ruuchich'och'**

earthen   *adj.* **pak'b'il**

earthenware   *n.* **ch'och' uk'al**

earthquake   *n.* **hiik**

earthworm   *n.* **lukum**

earwax   *n.* **xk'ot xik**

easel   *n.* **xna'aj xhu b'ich**

east   *n.* **releb' saq'e**

Easter   *n.* **rahil kutan**

easy   *adj.* **ink'a' ch'a'aj**
         adj. **moko ch'a'aj ta**

easy chair   *n.* **nimla tem**

easy-going   *adj.* **tuqtu ru**

eat   *v.* **tiwok**
       v. **tzakank**
       v. **wa'ak**
       v. **wa'ok**

ebony tree   *n.* **q'eqi che'**

ebullience   *n.* **woqxeel**

echo   *n.* **chaq'om**
        n. **sumyaab'**

eclipse   *n.* **moyk ru li saq'e**
           n. **muqlaak kutan**
           n. **naxtiw rib' li saq'e ut li po**
           n. **tiwok posaq'e**
           n. **xyalojikeb' li saq'e ut li po**

ecological preserve   *n.* **kolb'il che'k'aam**

ecological values   *n.* **loq'alil sutam**

ecology   *n.* **nawyu'amilsutaal**
           n. **wanjik**

economics   *n.* **sachomj**

ecosystem   *n.* **k'uub'wank**

edge   *n.* **e**
        n. **tzelam**
        n. **xmar**

edgy   *adj.* **yo xsik**

edit   *v phr.* **na'leb'ank tz'iib'**
        v. **puktasink**

edition   *n.* **xpuktasinkil**

editorial   *n.* **k'a'uxlal**

educate   *v.* **tijok**

educated   *adj.* **tijb'il**

education   *n.* **xtijb'al**

educational aims   *n.* **xjayalihom tijok**

educational process   *n.* **ch'olk'anjel tijok**

educators   *n.* **xmolamil aj k'utunel**

eel   *n.* **k'anti' kar**

effervescent salts   *n.* **k'aj atz'am b'an**

effort   *n.* **yalok q'e**

egg   *n.* **mol**

eggplant   *n.* **tzaksu**

egocentrism   *n.* **pixilk'a'uxl**

eight   *num.* **(8.) waqxaqib'**

eighteen   *num.* **(18.) waqxaqlaju**

eighteenth *num.* **(18th.) xwajxaqlajuil**

eighteen-wheeler *n.* **motzo'ch'iich'**

eighth *n.* **jun xwaqxaqil** *num.* **(8th.) xwajxaq**

eightieth *num.* **(80th.) xkaak'aalil**

eighty *num.* **(80.) kaak'aal**

eighty-eight *num.* **(88.) waqxaqib' ro'k'aal**

eighty-five *num.* **(85.) oob' ro'k'aal**

eighty-four *num.* **(84.) kaahib' ro'k'aal**

eighty-nine *num.* **(89.) b'eleb' ro'k'aal**

eighty-one *num.* **(81.) jun ro'k'aal**

eighty-seven *num.* **(87.) wuqub' ro'k'aal**

eighty-six *num.* **(86.) waqib' ro'k'aal**

eighty-three *num.* **(83.) oxib' ro'k'aal**

eighty-two *num.* **(82.) wiib' ro'k'aal**

ejaculate *n.* **b'ub'** *v phr.* **isink xya'al tz'ejwal** *n.* **lal**

elastic *adj.* **q'ochq'och** *adj.* **rinrin**

elastic band *n.* **rinrin**

elation *n.* **anchal xmetzew**

elbow *n.* **ch'uukum** *n.* **rit telb'** *n.* **rit uq'b'**

elder *n.* **tiix**

elder (male) *n.* **cheekel winq** *n.* **mama'**

elect *v.* **xaqab'ank**

election *n.* **b'oot** *n.* **sik'ok-u**

electric bill *n.* **xhuhil li saqen**

electric current *n.* **metz'ewilxaml** *n.* **roqkaxlan xam**

electric energy *n.* **metz'ew kaxlan xaml**

electric light *n.* **kaxsaqenk**

electric meter *n.* **b'isb'ametz'ew**

electric saw *n.* **sirk'arch'iich'** *n.* **surjachleb'che'**

electric switch *n.* **raqb'ametz'ew**

electric tower *n.* **roqechil k'at**

electrical resistance *n.* **kawsik kaxaml** *n.* **k'uyum k'at**

electrician *n agt.* **aj yiib'om saqen**

electricity *n.* **elektrisidad** *n.* **metz'ewilxaml** *n.* **raqmetz'ew** *n.* **xaml**

electrocuted *adj.* **xrepomkaaq**

electrode *n.* **latzleb'ch'iich'**

electron *n.* **tiikil kaxlanxaml**

elementary school *n.* **tzoleb'aal xb'een na'aj**

elements *n.* **xcha'al**

Elena *nick.* **Len**

elephant *n.* **ch'em samxul**
n. **elepaant**
n. **samxul**

eleven *num.* **(11.) junlaju**

eleventh *num.* **(11th.) xjunlajuil**

elf *n.* **kok' xul**
n. **ranumal q'ojyin**
n. **xilik'**

ellipsis *n.* **oxtz'uq**
n. **tz'uqux**

elliptical galaxy *n.* **k'on tzoqchahim**

email *n.* **muhiltaql**

email address *n.* **reetalil tz'iib'aal**

embarrassed *adj.* **xutaanal**
adj. **xutaanaq**

embarrassment *n.* **xutaan**

embassy *n.* **rochochil ab'lil tenamit**

embers *n.* **ruuxam**

embrace *v.* **mek'onk**
v. **q'alunk**

embryo *n.* **ralyu'amej**

emergency exit *n.* **elkleb'aal sa' junpaat**

emergency preparedness *n.* **kawalil chi ru raaxiik'**

emotion *n.* **numsach'ool**
n. **sachb'ach'ool**

emotional *adj.* **numsaxch'ool**

emphasis particle *part.* **a'**

emphasize *v.* **ka'jultikank**

empty *adj.* **job'**
adj. **maak'a' xsa'**
v. **yamresink**
adj. **yamyo**

empty set *n.* **yamch'uut**
n. **yamyookil ch'uut**

enchilada *n.* **k'orkik'xe'**

encounter *n.* **ch'utamil**

encyclopedia
n. **ch'olob'aalna'leb'**
n. **na'leb'aal tasal hu**

end *v.* **choyok**
v. **oso'k**
v. **raqok**

end (spatial) *n.* **xmar**

end (temporal) *n.* **ch'otonik**
n. **oso'jik**
n. **raqik**

end piece *n.* **roq**

ending *n.* **raqtz'aqob'l**

endocrine gland *n.* **jek'cha'alil chi sa'**

endoplasmic reticulum
n. **k'ub'lb'eeleb'aal na' yu'am**

endorsement *n.* **k'ehok juch'**

enemy   *n.* **rajtziil**
          n. **xik'onel**

energetic   *adj.* **kaw rib'**

energy   *n.* **metz'ew**

engineer   *n agt.* **aj seeb'alk'anjel**

engineering   *n.* **nawk'anjel**

English   *lang.* **inkles**

enjoy   *v phr.* **ajsink u**

enjoyment   *n.* **sahilank**

enough   *pron.* **naab'al**
          adj. **tz'aqal**
          adj. **yo'oon ru**

enter   *v.* **ok**

entertain   *v phr.* **ajsink u**
          v phr. **jahok u**

entertaining   *adj.* **sa' xse'enkil**

entertainment   *n.* **ajsink-u**

enthusiasm   *n.* **anchal ch'oolej**

entrance   *n.* **okeb'aal**

entrust   *v.* **ab'enank**
          v. **payok**

entry   *n.* **okeb'aal**

entry platform   *n.* **ne'b'aal**

envelope   *n.* **rix esilhu**
          n. **rix taqlhu**

envious   *adj.* **aj kaqal**

environment   *n.* **sutam**

envy   *n.* **kaqal**
          n. **kaqi atawank**

enzyme   *n.* **xpaayil kawub'l**

eon   *n.* **q'e**
        n. **q'ekutan**

epidemic   *n.* **yajel nab'onok**
          n. **yajel naxb'on rib'**

epidemiologist   *n agt.* **aj nawkomonyajel**

epidemiology   *n.* **nawkomonyajel**

equality   *n.* **juntaq'eetil**

equation   *n.* **juntaq'eetin k'anjel'ajl**
          n. **sumch'a'ajkilal**

equator   *n.* **q'eq'ookil eetalil**

equilibrium   *n.* **tuqtuukil**

equinox   *n.* **xtuqlajik q'e**

equity   *n.* **juntaq'eetil**

equivocal particle   *part.* **na**

era   *n.* **q'e**
        n. **q'ekutan**

erase   *v.* **b'orok**
          v. **sachok**

erased   *adj.* **b'orb'il**

eraser   *n.* **b'orleb'**
          n. **masleb'**
          n. **sachleb'**

erection   *n.* **roq tz'ik**

erode   *v.* **ju'e'k**
          v. **uq'e'k**

erosion   *n.* **uq'e'k**
          n. **xch'ajom**

errand   *n.* **taqlil**

error   *n.* **paaltil**
           n. **sachalkil**
           n. **sachk**

eruption   *n.* **xa'awilk'u**

escalator   *n.* **metz'ewil'eeb'**
           n. **raqmetz'eweb'**
           n. **raq'metz'ewanb'il eeb'**

etc.   *adv.* **utwchx**

etcetera   *adv.* **utwchx**

eternity   *n.* **chalen q'e kutan**

ethics   *n.* **tiikalil**
           n. **tiikil loq'alil**

ethnic group   *n.* **poyanamilal**
           n. **xpaayil tenamitil**

ethnicity   *n.* **ralch'och'il**
           n. **xch'uutulal ilob'**

ethnolinguistics
           n. **nawpoyaatinob'aal**

etymology   *n.* **xxe'ilal**

eukaryote   *n.* **tz'aqalna'yu'am**

Europe   *n.* **junpak'alpalaw**

Eustachian tube   *n.* **numleb' yaab'ej**

evening   *n.* **chi q'eq**
           n. **q'ojyin**

ever   *adv phr.* **sa' jun sut**

every week   *adv phr.* **rajlal xamaan**

everything   *adj.* **chi junil**

everywhere   *prep.* **yalaq chi b'ar**

evidence   *n.* **eetalil maak**

evolutionary psychology
           n. **nawk'iijikch'ool**

ewe   *n.* **karneer**

exactly   *adv phr.* **jo'kan tz'aqal**

exam   *n.* **tz'ilb'a'ix**
           n. **tz'ilool'ix**
           n. **yalb'a'ix**

examination   *n.* **tz'ilb'a'ix**
           n. **tz'ilool'ix**
           n. **yalb'a'ix**

examine   *v.* **ilok**
           v. **tz'ilok-ix**

example   *n.* **reetalil**
           n. **xk'utb'al**

exchage (gifts)   *v.* **sumsihink**

exchage (words)   *v.* **sumchi'ib'k**

excited   *adj.* **rataw chi us**

excitement   *n.* **anchal ch'oolej**

exclamation point (!)
           n. **reetalsachb'ach'oolej**

excuse me   *phr.* **chinaakuy**

execution   *n.* **xb'aanunkil**

executive power   *n.* **xwankilal b'aanunel**

exercise   *v phr.* **ajsink u li tib'elej**
           v. **kawresink**

exhaust pipe   *n.* **releb'aalsib'**

exhort   *v phr.* **patz'ok b'aanunk**

exist   *v.* **yo'laak**

exit   *n.* **elkleb'aal**

exocrine gland *n.* **jek'cha'alil chi rix**

exosphere *n.* **raq xtasalil'iq'**

expand *v.* **yu'uk ru**

expense *n.* **sachom**

expensive *adj.* **terto xtz'aq**

explain *v.* **ch'olob'ank**

export *v.* **ab'lilk'ayink**
     n. **taqlilk'ay**

exportation *n.* **taqlilk'ay**

extension *n.* **ruq'il**

extension cord *n.* **xk'aamal saqen**

extensive *adj.* **b'ayk**
     adj. **makach'in**

exterior *adj.* **chi rix**

extinguish *v.* **chupuk**

extortionist *n agt.* **aj b'alaq'**

extracter *n.* **tz'ob'leb'**

extraterrestrial
     n. **maaruuchich'och'**
     n. **maawa' re ruchich'och'**

extrovert *adj.* **nache'ch'ot**

eye *n.* **sa' u**
     n. **xnaq' u**
     n. **xnaq' uhej**

eye drops *n.* **b'an re naq' u**
     n. **tz'uqb'il b'an re sa' u**

eye inflammation *n.* **xkuntz'i'**

eyebrow *n.* **maatzab' u**

eyedropper *n.* **tz'uqleb' b'an**

eyelash *n.* **rismal u**

eyelid *n.* **rix u**

eyewear shop *n.* **sa' uleb'aal**

F - f

fable *n.* **eek'anb'iltz'iib'**

face *n.* **u**
     n. **uhej**
     n. **xnaq' u**

facing *prep.* **chi ru**

facing up *prep.* **pak'po**

factor *n.* **roqel**

faculty *n.* **xmolamil aj k'utunel**

fail *v.* **tz'eqok**

faint *v.* **saqb'yino'k**

fainting spell *n.* **lub'k**
     n. **saqb'yino'k**

fair *n.* **nimq'e**

fairy *n.* **kok' xul**
     n. **ranumal q'ojyin**
     n. **xilik'**

faith *n.* **paab'aal**

faithful *adj.* **aj paab'anel**
     adj. **tiik xch'ool**

fake   *v phr.* **b'aanunk ib'**

fall   *v.* **sob'e'k**
            v. **tob'b'ak**
            n. **t'ane'k**
            v. **t'ane'k**

fall (season)   *n.* **otoony**
            n. **xraqik hab'alq'e**

fall in love   *v.* **payok**

fall sick   *v.* **t'anliik**

fallopian tube   *n.* **xnumleb'
            iyajiil**

false ceiling   *n.* **kaxlankaq'**

falsehood   *n.* **tik'ti'**

fame   *n.* **ka'xaqab'aal**

familiar   *adj.* **na'no ru**

family   *n.* **junkab'al**

family chores   *n.* **teneb'anb'il
            sa' junkab'lal**

family services   *n.* **xkolb'al rix
            junkab'al**

family tree   *n.* **reetalil iyajil**

famine   *n.* **we'ej**

fan   *n.* **apusinel na'ajej**
            n. **apuul**
            n. **kaxwaal**
            n. **waal**
            v. **waalesink**

fan belt   *n.* **xtaab'il xsa'**

far   *adj.* **najt**

far from   *adv phr.* **najt xk'atq**

fare   *n.* **pasaaj**

farewell   *n.* **chaq'rab'ink**

farm   *n.* **loq'b'ilch'och'**
            n. **rochoch ketomq**

farm animals   *n.* **ketomq**

farmer   *n agt.* **aj awinel**
            n agt. **aj ilol xna'aj
            ketomq**
            n agt. **aj k'aleb'aal**
            n agt. **aj k'alom**

farming   *n.* **xk'anjelankil li
            ch'och'**

fart   *n.* **kis**
            v. **kisik**

fashion designer   *n agt.* **aj
            yib'anel eetalil aq'**

fast   *v phr.* **ayuunink rix**
            v phr. **kuyuk sa'**
            n. **kuyuk sa'**
            adj. **paynum**

fastener   *n.* **jit'leb'**
            n. **kotoxch'iich'**

fat   *n.* **manteek**
            adj. **nim xtib'el**
            n. **olb'**
            adj. **t'inis**
            adj. **t'onos**
            n. **yolq'em**

fat tissue   *n.* **ch'utq'ooq cha'al**

father   *n.* **taat**
            n sd. **yuwa'b'ej**

father's sister   *n.* **ranab' xyuwa'**

father-in-law (of a man)
            n. **xyuwa' ixaqil**

father-in-law (of a woman)
            n. **xyuwa' b'eelom**

fathom   *n.* **moqoj**
    n. **q'aal**

fatty meat *n.* **k'ook'**

faucet   *n.* **teeleb'ha'**
    n. **xlaawil ha'**
    n. **xteeb'al ha'**
    n. **yaaw**

fault   *n.* **maak**

fault (geologic) *n.* **uq'e'k**

fauna   *n.* **ch'uuxul**
    n. **puukalxul**

favor   *n.* **usilal**

fax   *n.* **anum ch'iich'**
    n. **muhil'esil**
    n. **num'esil**

fax machine *n.* **anum ch'iich'**

fear   *n.* **xiw**

feather   *n.* **k'uuk'um**
    n. **rismal xul**
    n. **rismal xxik'**
    n. **xik'**

February *n.* **pewreer**
    n. **xkab'ilpo**

Federico *nick.* **Liik**

feed   *v.* **tzakank**

feed tray *n.* **b'ateey**

feel   *v.* **ch'e'ok**

feeling   *n.* **eek'ahom**
    n. **eek'aal**
    n. **eek'ob'aal**

feet   *n sd.* **oq'ej**

felines   *n.* **aj ixi'jeb'**

female   *adj.* **ixq**

females   *n.* **ixqilal**

femininity *n.* **ixqilal**

femur   *n.* **b'aq'el'a'**

fence   *n.* **koral**

fence gate *n.* **re b'e**

ferment   *v.* **ch'amok'**

fermented drink *n.* **b'oj**

fermented mush drink
    n. **ch'amb'ul**

fern   *n.* **ch'ut**
    n. **xxaq pim**

ferocity   *n.* **k'utuk josq'il**

Ferris wheel *n.* **kotkookil b'atz'uul**

ferry   *n.* **aj iiqom**
    n. **jukub'iiq**

fertilizer *n.* **q'eem**
    n. **raxonb'an**
    n. **xq'emal ru li ch'och'**
    n. **xq'emulch'och'**
    n. **xtzakahemq ch'och'**

fetus   *n.* **alk'uula'al**

fever   *n.* **kaqi yajel**
    n. **k'ehok tiq**
    n. **tiq**

few   *pron.* **ink'a' k'i**
    adj. **kach'in**

field   *n.* **awib'aal**
    n. **awleb'aal**
    n. **k'al**
    n. **k'aleb'aal**

n. **neb'aal**
n. **xoral**

fieldworker *n agt.* **aj k'aleb'aal**

fifteen *num.* **(15.) o'laju**

fifteenth *num.* **(15th.) ro'lajuil**

fifth *num.* **(5th.) ro'**

fifth grade *n.* **ro' na'aj**

fiftieth *num.* **(50th.) xlajee roxk'aalil**

fifty *num.* **(50.) lajeeb' roxk'aal**

fifty cents *n.* **jun tuxtun**

fifty-eight *num.* **(58.) waqxaqlaju roxk'aal**

fifty-five *num.* **(55.) o'laju roxk'aal**

fifty-four *num.* **(54.) kaalaju roxk'aal**

fifty-nine *num.* **(59.) b'elelaju roxk'aal**

fifty-one *num.* **(51.) junlaju roxk'aal**

fifty-seven *num.* **(57.) wuqlaju roxk'aal**

fifty-six *num.* **(56.) waqlaju roxk'aal**

fifty-three *num.* **(53.) oxlaju roxk'aal**

fifty-two *num.* **(52.) kab'laju roxk'aal**

fig *n.* **iko**

fight *v.* **ch'e'ok**
v. **yalok**

fighter *n agt.* **aj pleet**

figure *n.* **eetalil**

figures *n.* **eetalilatq**

filament (flower) *n.* **roq xwinkil atz'um**

file *n.* **ji'leb'**
n. **ji'leb'ch'iich'**
v. **ji'ok**
n. **k'uulhu**
n. **xokleb'**
v. **xokok**

fill *v.* **b'utuk**
v. **nujab'resink**

filling (dental) *n.* **b'utb'il uuch e**

film *n.* **eek'mu**
n. **jalam'uuch**
n. **q'och-eetalil**

filth *n.* **tz'ajn**

fin *n.* **xik'**

final *adj.* **ch'otonel**

finally *adv.* **retal**
adv phr. **toj reetal**

find *v.* **tawok**

fine *n.* **muult**
adj. **q'unq'un ru**
n. **tojl**
n. **tojmaak**

finger *n.* **ru'uj uq'**

fingernail *n.* **ixi'ij**

fingerprint *n.* **ru'uj uq'b'**

finish *v.* **choyok**
v. **raqok**

fire *n.* **xam**

fire brigade   *n agt.* **aj ch'upul xaml**

fire extinguisher   *n.* **chupleb'xaml**

fire truck   *n.* **pujha'nel ch'iich'** *n.* **tz'ub'pajha'**

firearm   *n.* **puub'**

firefly   *n.* **mams** *n.* **xamxul**

fireman   *n agt.* **aj chupulxam** *n agt.* **aj tenq' sa' li raxiik'**

fireplace   *n.* **k'ub'** *n.* **xna'aj xam**

firewood   *n.* **kaqcha** *n.* **si'**

fireworks   *n.* **jutzutzu**

first   *num.* **(1st.) xb'een**

first aid   *n.* **ramb'al ru yajel**

first aid kit   *n.* **xna'aj b'an**

first grade   *n.* **xb'een na'aj**

first of all   *adv phr.* **xb'een wa**

first-born   *n.* **xb'een alal**

fish   *v phr.* **chapok kar** *n.* **kar** *v.* **karib'k** *n.* **karil** *v.* **karink**

fish for shrimp   *v.* **k'oxib'k**

fish net   *n.* **ch'antun** *n.* **soq' re karab'k** *n.* **xsokilkar** *n.* **yooy**

fish scale   *n.* **pati kar**

fish tank   *n.* **nimla xna'ajkar**

fish trap   *n.* **ra'l kar** *n.* **traamp**

fishbowl   *n.* **xna'ajkar**

fisherman   *n agt.* **aj kar**

fishhook   *n.* **chapleb' kar** *n.* **kuux re karab'k** *n.* **ra'leb'kar**

fishing line   *n.* **kordel** *n.* **k'aam**

fishing net   *n.* **yooy**

fishmonger   *n agt.* **aj k'ay kar**

fist   *n.* **moch'**

five   *num.* **(5.) oob'**

five cents   *n.* **oob' senta**

five hundred   *n.* **o'k'aal xkab' roq'ob'**

five quetzals   *n.* **oob' ketzal**

fix   *v.* **k'uub'ank** *v.* **yiib'ank**

flag   *n.* **lakaam** *n.* **q'uq'il t'ikr**

flagpole   *n.* **roqechal q'uq'il t'ikr**

flame   *n.* **raq'xam**

flamingo   *n.* **kaxjukin** *n.* **kaxsaq eknil**

flannel   *n.* **q'unil t'ikr**

flash   *n.* **repsaqenk**

flashlight   *n.* **kaxchaj**

flat   *adj.* **perpo**
        adj. **ruutaq'a**
        adj. **tach'to**

flat figures   *n.* **helhookil eetalilatq**

flattering compliment
        n. **xulil'aatin**

flatulence   *n.* **kis**

flavor   *n.* **sahil**

flea   *n.* **k'aq**
        n. **uk'**

flee   *v.* **eelelik**

flesh   *n.* **tib'**
        n. **tib'elej**
        n. **tz'ej**

flight attendant   *n agt.* **aj k'anjel sa' so'sol ch'iich'**

flint   *n.* **tok'**

flip   *v.* **suurisink**

flipchart   *n.* **b'alq'hu**

flirtatious remark   *n.* **xulil'aatin**

float   *v.* **pamamnak**

flood   *n.* **b'ut**

floor   *n.* **ch'och'**
        n. **ru ch'och'**
        n. **ru tz'ak**

floppy disk   *n.* **chochtz'iib'**
        n. **ululil xokleb'**
        n. **xna'aj xokleb'**

flora   *n.* **puukalche'k'aam**

florist   *n.* **k'ayib'aal uutz'u'uj**

floss   *n.* **noq' re uuch e**

flour   *n.* **k'aj**
        n. **k'ajil kaxlanwa**
        n. **xpoqsil kaxlanwa**

flour (wheat)   *n.* **xk'aj ariin**

flow   *v phr.* **yo i roq**

flower   *n.* **atz'um**
        v. **atz'umak**
        n. **uutz'u'uj**

flower bed   *n.* **ruutz'uujil kab'l**

flower bouquet   *n.* **junq'aal uutz'u'uj**

flower carpet   *n.* **ruutz'u'ujil ru b'e**

flower garden   *n.* **xna'aj uutz'u'uj**

flower petal   *n.* **xcha'al uutz'u'uj**
        n. **xxaq xcha'al uutzu'uj**

flower shop   *n.* **k'ayib'aal uutz'u'uj**

flower vase   *n.* **na'aj uutz'u'uj**

flowerbed   *n.* **xna'aj uutz'u'uj**

flowerpot   *n.* **xna'aj uutz'u'uj**

flu   *n.* **jolomb'ej**
        n. **ojb'**

fluorescent marker
        n. **lemtz'juch'leb'aal**

flute   *n.* **xolb'**

fly   *v.* **purik**
        v. **rupik**
        v. **waalunk**

fly (insect)   *n.* **b'ujl**
        n. **saqxul**

n. **suq**
n. **utz'**

fly (of pants)   *n.* **re xch'ool wex**

flyer   *n.* **esilhu**

flying serpent   *n.* **raxk'aj**

flying squirrel   *n.* **rupkuk**

foal   *n.* **ral kawaay**

foam   *n.* **woqx**

fog   *n.* **sujew**
n. **tuntunkil choq**

foggy   *adj.* **choq ru**

fold   *v.* **b'asok**
v. **mochok**
v. **q'etok**
n. **xb'asb'al**

folder   *n.* **tahu**
n. **xna'aj hu**
n. **xokleb' hu**

follow   *v.* **taaqenk**

fondness   *n.* **q'unal**

food   *n.* **tib'el wa**
n. **tzakahem**
n. **wa'al**

foolish   *adj.* **jip**

foolishness   *n.* **eetil**

foosball table   *n.* **b'olotz meex**

foot   *n sd.* **oq'ej**

footballer   *n agt.* **aj b'atz'unel b'olotz oq**
n agt. **aj b'olotz**

footboard   *n.* **roq ch'aat**

footbridge   *n.* **q'axleb'aal**

footprint   *n.* **nums**
n. **oqej**
n. **oqil**

for   *prep.* **cho'q re**
adv. **re**

for a long time   *adj.* **naab'al honal**

for what?   *interr.* **k'a'ru aj e**

force   *n.* **metz'ew**

forearm   *n.* **xnaq' telb'**
n. **xtoon telb'**

forehead   *n.* **peekem**
n. **u**

foreign   *adj.* **mu'us**

foreign language   *n.* **ab'lil aatinob'aal**
lang. **kaxlanchi'**
lang. **kaxlan aatin**

foreign particle   *part.* **kax**

foreigner   *n.* **ab'lil poyanam**
n. **aj mu's**
n. **kaxlan winq**

forest   *n.* **k'iche'**
n. **ninqi che'**

forge   *v phr.* **jalok ru yaal**

forger   *n agt.* **aj jalonel**

forgery   *n.* **jalok ru yaal**

forget   *v phr.* **sachk sa' ch'ool**

forgetful   *adj.* **nasach sa' xch'ool**

forgive   *v phr.* **kuyuk maak**

forgive me *phr.* **chaakuy inmaak**

fork *n.* **chikleb'**
  n. **orkeet**
  n. **pikleb'**
  n. **rastriiy**
  n. **xokleb'**

forked branch *n.* **ra' che'**
  n. **xaal che'**

form *n.* **chankatq ru**
  n. **jultikaal**
  v. **pak'ok**
  n. **rilb'al**

former times *n.* **najter q'e kutan**

formula *n.* **b'ehul**
  n. **k'ucha'alk'anjel**

formulation *n.* **xjultikankil**

fornicate *v.* **yumb'eetak**

fornicator *n agt.* **aj yumb'eet**

fortieth *num.* **(40th.) xka'k'aalil**

fortune teller *n agt.* **aj q'e**

forty *num.* **(40.) ka'k'aal**

forty-eight *num.* **(48.) waqxaq'ib' roxk'aal**

forty-five *num.* **(45.) oob' roxk'aal**

forty-four *num.* **(44.) kaahib' roxk'aal**

forty-nine *num.* **(49.) b'eleb' roxk'aal**

forty-one *num.* **(41.) jun roxk'aal**

forty-seven *num.* **(47.) wukub' roxk'aal**

forty-six *num.* **(46.) waq'ib' roxk'aal**

forty-three *num.* **(43.) oxib' roxk'aal**

forty-two *num.* **(42.) wiib' roxk'aal**

fountain *n.* **pak'yu'amha'**
  n. **releb'aal ha'**
  n. **yo'leb'aal ha'**
  n. **yo'lejeb'ha'**

four *num.* **(4.) kaahib'**

four days ago *n.* **kaajer**

four hundred *n.* **jun oq'ob'**

four thousand *n.* **lajeeb' oq'ob'**

fourteen *num.* **(14.) kaalaju**

fourteenth *num.* **(14th.) xkaalajuil**

fourth *num.* **(4th.) xka**

fourth grade *n.* **xka na'aj**

fowl *n.* **ketomq**
  n. **tz'ik**

fox *n.* **aj ow**
  n. **yak**

fraction *n.* **jachb'il'ajl**

fractional *n.* **jachlil'ajl**

fractionally *adv.* **chi jachal**

fracture *n.* **toqol**

fragment *v.* **murink**

fragrant *adj.* **k'ajo' sununkil**
  adj. **sununk**

fraud   *n.* **b'alaq'**

freckle   *n.* **k'inich**

free   *v.* **ach'ab'ank**

free agency *n.* **xch'ool**
             nataqlank re
             n. **xtaql xch'ool**

free will   *n.* **xch'ool nataqlank**
             re
             n. **xtaql xch'ool**

freeze   *v.* **keho'k**

freezer   *n.* **kehob'resib'aal**
             n. **saqb'achleb'aal**
             n. **xna'aj elaat**

French bread
             n. **atz'aminb'ilkaxlan**
             wa
             n. **siip kaxlan wa**

french fries *n.* **kilinb'il paaps**

French toast *n.* **tz'aab'il kaxlan**
             wa

frequency   *n.* **kok'ajil xsa'**
             n. **xjartawahil**

frequently   *adv phr.* **junes yo**
             adv phr. **rajlal rajlal**

fricative   *n.* **jilb'il yaab'**
             n. **nut'b'il yaab'**

Friday   *n.* **b'yers**

fridge   *n.* **kehob'resilb'aal**
             n. **keeleb'aal**
             n. **reepri**

fried   *adj.* **kilinb'il**

fried chicken *n.* **kilinb'il kaxlan**

friend   *n.* **amiiw**
             n. **lo'y**

friendly   *adj.* **sa na'aatinak**

friendship   *n.* **lo'yil**

fright   *n.* **xib'esink**
             n. **xiw**

frog   *n.* **amoch**
             n. **kaq ra'**
             n. **pelpel**

from   *part.* **aj**
             prep. **chalen**
             prep. **re**

from now on *adv.* **chalen**
             anaqwan

front yard   *n.* **neb'aal kab'l**

frost   *n.* **sujen**

fruit   *n.* **ki'il q'een**
             n. **ru**
             n. **ru che'**
             n. **saa'us**
             n. **u**

fruit of the cactus *n.* **ru peetaq**

fruit shop   *n.* **k'ayib'aal saa'us**

fruit slices *n.* **tz'aab'il ki'ik**
             q'een

frustration *n.* **ch'inaak ch'ool**

fry   *v.* **k'ilink**
             v. **pomok**
             v. **sisank**

frying pan   *n.* **k'ileb'aal**
             n. **k'ilolb'**
             n. **xartin**

fuel   *n.* **ruk'a ch'iich'**
             n. **xya'al b'eleb'aal**
             n. **xya'al ch'iich'**

full   *adj.* **b'ut'**
           adj. **b'uuy**
           adj. **nujenaq**
           adj. **tz'ajtz'otk**

full moon *n.* **tiixil po**
           n. **xoronikpo**

fumigation pump *n.* **xkukil li puutzink**

fumigator *n.* **xkukil li puutzink**

fun   *n.* **ajsib'aal'u**
           n. **hoonalhilaal**
           n. **xhoonal asjsink-u**

function   *n.* **xk'anjel**

fundamental *n.* **k'ub'el**

funnel   *n.* **b'ut'leb'**

funny   *adj.* **sa' xse'enkil**

fur   *n.* **ta**

fur coat   *n.* **tz'uumil chakeet**

furious   *adj.* **yo xjosq'il**

furrow   *n.* **ch'ol**
           n. **cho'ok jul**
           n. **pahok jul**
           n. **qeer**
           n. **suurk**
           n. **suut**
           n. **tzol**

fury   *n.* **josq'il**

fussy   *adj.* **wech' re**

future   *n.* **chaalel**
           n. **moqon**

future tense *n.* **moqonil'uxk**

G - g

galaxy   *n.* **saqonaqilchahim**
           n. **tzoqchahim**

gallery   *n.* **chinamiit**

gallon   *n.* **ch'inapuum**
           n. **ho'meet**
           n. **kalon**
           n. **yook**

gambling   *n.* **b'uulik**

game   *n.* **b'atz'uul**
           n. **xul k'iche'**

gangway   *n.* **q'axleb'aal**

garage   *n.* **xna'aj b'eleb'aal ch'iich'**

garbage   *n.* **mul**
           n. **mulel**

garbage can *n.* **xchakachil mul**
           n. **xna'aj mul**

garbage collector *n agt.* **aj xokol mul**

garbanzo beans *n.* **karwans**

garden   *n.* **kok'awinq**
           n. **xna'aj kok'awinq**

garden shed *n.* **na'aj re muhenk**

gardener   *n agt.* **aj ilol uutz'u'uj**

garden-house *n.* **tz'alam**

garlic *n.* **anx**
    n. **jolom q'een**

Garífuna *lang.* **karifuna**

gas *n.* **humb'ookilha'**
    n. **jumha'elch'iich'**
    n. **ruk'a ch'iich'**
    n. **xya'al b'eleb'aal**
    n. **xya'al ch'iich'**

gas dispenser *n.* **ralpuub'**

gas pump *n.* **xkumb'il ruk'a' poych'iich'**

gas station
    n. **k'ayib'aalhumb'ookilha'**
    n. **rochochil ruk'a' poych'iich'**

gaseous *adj.* **b'ookil**

gases *n.* **b'ookatq**

gasoline *n.* **humb'ookilha'**
    n. **jumha'elch'iich'**
    n. **ruk'a ch'iich'**
    n. **xya'al b'eleb'aal**
    n. **xya'al ch'iich'**

gate *n.* **okeb'aal**
    n. **pweert**
    n. **re kab'**

gather *v.* **molob'ank**
    v. **molok**
    n. **xyuch'inkil xsa'**

gauze *n.* **kok' t'ikr**
    n. **k'aj sut**
    n. **k'aj t'ikr**

gearshift *n.* **k'ub'**

gender *n.* **chankilal**

gender equality *n.* **xjuntaq'eetil xwinqul**

generalize *v.* **junajink**

generation *n.* **puukalil**

generosity *adj.* **usilalch'ool**

genitals *n.* **cha'alil**

genitals (female) *n.* **b'o**
    n. **b'uuy**
    n. **k'oopopo'**

genitals (male) *n.* **tz'ejwal**

genius *n.* **numseeb'**

genre *n.* **chankilal**

gentilic particle *part.* **aj**

gentle *adj.* **q'un xch'ool**

geography
    n. **k'utleb'ruuchich'och'**
    n. **xcha'alil ruuchich'och'**

geometric figure *n.* **b'isb'il eetalil**

geometric shape *n.* **b'isb'il eetalil**

get *v.* **k'uluk**
    v. **tawok**

get better *v.* **usaak**

get dressed *v phr.* **k'ehok aq'**

get drunk *v.* **kaltesink**

get lost *v.* **sachk**

get ready *v.* **kawresink**

get sad *v phr.* **raho'k xch'ool**

get sick *v.* **yajerk**

get tired   *v.* **lub'k**

get undressed   *v phr.* **isink aq'**

get up   *v.* **wakliik**

ghost   *n.* **anumal**

giant   *adj.* **nimnim**
       adj. **tutz'tu**
       adj. **yak'ach**

gift   *n.* **maatan**
     n. **si**

gill   *n.* **xoob'**

gills   *n.* **pospo'ykar**

ginger   *n.* **xanxiiwr**

giraffe   *n.* **yak'achkej**

girl   *n.* **ch'ina ixqa'al**
     n. **saaj ixqa'al**

girlfriend   *n.* **suunal**
           n. **suunuhom**
           n. **xsum aam**
           n. **xsum ch'ool**

give   *v.* **k'ehok**
     v. **q'axtesink**

give alms   *v phr.* **k'ehok limoox**

give back   *v.* **q'ajsink**

give birth   *v.* **alank**
         v. **yo'laak**

give it a shot   *v phr.* **yalok ch'ool**

give one's opinion   *v phr.* **aatinak chi rix**

give up   *v phr.* **q'axtesink ib'**

give way   *v phr.* **k'ehok numik**

glacial erosion   *n.* **xch'ajom saqb'ach**

glacial zone   *n.* **keehil siraal**

glacier   *n.* **pekilha' ch'och'**

glad   *adj.* **sa xch'ool**

gladiola   *n.* **karayool**
       n. **xb'aar li qaawa'**

gland   *n.* **xtz'aqob'cha'al**

glass   *n.* **b'otb'okilsek'**
      n. **lem**
      n. **meet**
      n. **saqenlem**
      n. **uk'leb'lem**

glass cabinet   *n.* **xlemul k'ayib'aal**

glasses   *n.* **anyooj**
        n. **lem'u**

globalize   *v.* **junajink**

globe   *n.* **reetalil ru chi ch'och'**
      n. **xt'oram ruuchich'och'**

gloom   *n.* **rahil ch'oolejil**

gloomy   *adj.* **ra xch'ool**

glossary   *n.* **ch'olob'aal'aatin**
        n. **tusleb' aatin**

glottal   *n.* **nat'yaab'**

glottalization   *n.* **nat'yaab'**

glove   *n.* **b'atb'a uq'**
      n. **xta uq'**

glue   *n.* **letzleb'**
     v. **letzok**

glyph   *n.* **eetaltz'iib'**
      n. **mayertz'iib'**

gnat   *n.* **k'uxuk**
        n. **suq**

gnaw   *v.* **hot'ok**

go   *v.* **xik**

go astray   *v.* **sachk**

go broke   *v.* **neb'a'o'k**

go down   *v.* **kub'eek**

go home   *v.* **q'ajk**

go horseback riding   *v phr.* **taqe'k chi rix kawaay**

go hungry   *v.* **we'ejink**

go out   *v.* **elk**

go up   *v.* **taqe'k**

goal   *n.* **ahom**
        n. **jayalihom**
        n. **k'as**

goalie   *n agt.* **aj ramonel b'olotz**

goalkeeper   *n agt.* **aj ramonel b'olotz**

goalposts   *n.* **okeb'aal b'olotz**

goat   *n.* **chib'aat**
        n. **yuk**

god   *n.* **qaawa'**
       n. **tyox**

god's will   *n.* **xtaql xch'ool li tyox**

goddaughter   *n.* **waltatyox ixq**

goddess   *n.* **qaana'**

godfather   *n.* **yuwa'chinb'ej**

godmother   *n.* **na'chinb'ej**

godson   *n.* **waltatyox winq**

goiter   *n.* **b'uq' ja'aj**

gold   *n.* **ka'xik**
        n. **q'anich'iich'**
        n. **q'an pwaq**

golden   *adj.* **nalemtz'un**
          adj. **q'anjorin**

gonorrhea   *n.* **pojkun**

good   *adj.* **chaab'il**
        adj. **q'axal us**
        adj. **us**

good luck   *n.* **rax muhel**

good luck!   *phr.* **us chat-elq**

good night (plural)   *phr.* **chexwarq**

good value   *n.* **chaab'il xtz'aq**

goodbye   *v.* **chaq'rab'ink**
           phr. **inwan b'i'**

goods   *n.* **k'alomal**

goose   *n.* **ch'onpatz**
         n. **kaans**
         n. **t'int'ookil patux**

gopher   *n.* **b'a**

gored   *adj.* **xeq'el**

gorge   *n.* **xyanq tzuul**

gorilla   *n.* **mama' max**

gossip   *n.* **yoob'ank aatin**

gourd   *n.* **joom**
         n. **k'um**
         n. **seel**

govern   *v.* **awab'ejink**
          v. **poopirk**
          v. **taqlank**

government *n.* **awab'ej**
    n. **awab'ejilal**

government identification
    n. **huxaqalil**
    n. **hu chi ru chaq'rab'**
    n. **xaaqalhu**
    n. **xhuhul tenamit**

governor *n.* **ruuchilawab'ej**

grade *n.* **rajlil ketom**
    n. **xtz'aq**

graft *n.* **raxtul**

grain *n.* **t'orol**

gram *n.* **xna'b'iisaalob'**

grammar
    n. **xtuqlal'aatinob'aal**

granary *n.* **rochochil hal**
    n. **xna'aj hal**

grandchild *n sd.* **iib'ej**

grandchildren *n.* **wiheb'**

granddaughter *n.* **ixqi i**
    n sd. **iib'ej**

grandfather *n.* **mama'**
    n. **mel**
    n. **yuwa'chin**

grandmother *n.* **ixa'an**
    n. **na'chin**

grandparents *n.* **mel**
    n. **yuwa'chinb'ejeb'**

grandson *n sd.* **iib'ej**
    n. **teelom i**

grape *n.* **kaxlant'usub'**
    n. **t'usub'**
    n. **uuw**

grapefruit *n.* **toronj**

graph paper
    n. **kaxukuutinb'ilhu**

grasp *v.* **chapok**

grass *n.* **aq**
    n. **ichaj**
    n. **pach'aya'**

grasshopper *n.* **aj pitz'**
    n. **chili'**
    n. **raxq'een**
    n. **saak'**

grate *v.* **jichok**

grater *n.* **jisleb'**

grave *n.* **julel kamenaq**

gravel *n.* **k'ajpek**
    n. **k'uhilpek**

gravestone *n.* **eetalkamenaq**

gravity *n.* **xmetz'ew raalal**
    n. **xmetz'ew xyi li ruchich'och'**

gravy *n.* **xya'al tib'**

gray *adj.* **chaacha**

gray hairs *n.* **saqi ismal**

grease *n.* **manteek**
    n. **olb'**
    n. **yolq'em**

greasy *adj.* **b'ik'b'ik'**

great grandchild *n sd.* **iimamb'ej**
    n. **mam**

great grandfather *n.* **mel**

great! *phr.* **chaaab'il**

great-grandchild *n.* **xikin i**

great-grandfather *n.* **xikin mama'**
  n. **xna'chin inyuwa'**

great-grandmother *n.* **xikin xa'an**
  n. **xna'chin inna'**

greatness *n.* **nimal**

greedy *adj.* **aj atawanel**

green *adj.* **rax**

green bean *n.* **k'aam keenq'**
  n. **q'ap**

greengrocer *n.* **k'ayib'aal xaq ut xe' pim**

greenish *adj.* **raxmo'in**

greet *v phr.* **k'ehok sahil ch'ool**
  v phr. **sahil ch'oolib'k**

greeting *n.* **sahil ch'oolej**

grid *n.* **kaxukutinb'il**

grief *n.* **k'a'uxl**
  n. **rahil ch'oolej**

grill *n.* **pomleb'**
  v. **pomok**

grilled *adj.* **pomb'il**

grilled meat *n.* **sisanb'iltib'**

grime *n.* **tz'ajn**

grind *v.* **ke'ek**
  v. **ke'ok**
  v. **sob'ok**
  v. **tenok**
  v. **yab'ok**

grinding stone *n.* **ka'**

grip *n.* **roq**

groan *v.* **tz'uyink**

grocer *n agt.* **aj k'ay xxe' pim**

grocery store *n.* **nimla k'ayib'aal**

ground floor *n.* **xb'een tasal kab'l**

ground meat *n.* **ke'b'il tib'**
  n. **setinb'il tib'**

group *n.* **ch'uut**

group of three *n.* **oxichal**

grove *n.* **ch'ina k'iche'**

grow *v.* **k'iik**
  v. **nimank**
  v. **ninqank**

growl *v.* **q'urq'utk**
  v. **tz'uytz'utk**

growth *n.* **k'i**

grumpy *adj.* **ch'ich'i re**

grunt *v.* **q'urq'utk**
  v. **tz'uytz'utk**

guard *n.* **taaqinel**

guayaba *n.* **pata**

guess *v.* **eek'ank**
  v. **q'ehink**

guest *n.* **ula'**
  n. **waril**

guicoy *n.* **ik'oy**

guide *n agt.* **aj k'amolb'e**
  n agt. **aj k'utunel b'e**

guideline *n.* **esilal**

guilt *n.* **maak**

guilty   *adj.* **aj b'aanun re**
           adj. **maakonel**

guinea hen   *n.* **kokech**

guinea pig   *n.* **q'an tu'lay aj
             imul**

guisquil   *n.* **ch'ima**

guitar   *n.* **kitaar**
           n. **suwajb'**
           n. **tzintzin**

gulf   *n.* **nimla rokeb'
           palaw**

gullible   *adj.* **jun chi aatin**

gully   *n.* **uul**
           n. **xiik'**

gum   *n.* **k'oy**
           n. **toq'**

gum seller   *n agt.* **aj k'ay
             kok'toq'**

gum tissue   *n.* **xtib'el xtoon
             ruuch e**

gums   *n.* **sa' e**
           n. **xtib'el xtoon
           ruuch e**

gun   *n.* **puub'**

gunpowder   *n.* **poqsxaml**

guts   *n.* **k'amk'otej**
           n. **sooyom**

gym   *n.* **q'ochleb'aal**

gymnasium   *n.* **q'ochleb'aal**

gynecologist   *n agt.* **aj
               nawcha'al'ixq**

gynecology   *n.* **nawcha'al'ixq**

H - h

habitation   *n.* **ochochil**

hacksaw   *n.* **ch'ina k'arch'iich'**

haggle   *v phr.* **xwech'b'al
         xtz'aq**

hail   *n.* **saqb'ach**

hair   *n.* **ismal**
         n. **rismal jolom**

hair band   *n.* **yutleb'**

hair part   *n.* **b'e jolom**

hair pin   *n.* **chapleb'ismal**
           n. **yut'ismal**

hair tie   *n.* **yutleb'**

hairband   *n.* **nat'leb'ismal**

hairbrush   *n.* **xiyab'**

hairdresser   *n agt.* **aj b'esonel**

hairnet   *n.* **mochleb' ismal**

hairy   *adj.* **tun is**

half   *n.* **jun jachal**
          n. **yi**
          n. **yijach**
          n. **yijachal**

half dollar   *n.* **jun tuxtun**

half dozen   *n.* **waqib'**

hall   *n.* **jaleb'aal**

hallucination *n.* **wax'ilom**

hallway *n.* **xmu kab'l**

halve *v.* **jachok**

ham *n.* **jamon**
      n. **xorb'il tib'**

hamburger *n.* **kaxlan xut'**

hamlet *n.* **kok'k'aleb'aal**

hammer *n.* **ruq'wajb'**
      n. **tenleb'**
      n. **t'ojleb'**
      v. **t'ojok**

hammock *n.* **ab'**
      n. **t'uuyleb'**

hand *n.* **uq'm**

hand towel *n.* **t'ikr re chaqob'resink uq**

handbroom *n.* **mesche'**

handcuffs *n.* **xkux uq'b' ch'iich'**

handful *n.* **jun mooch'**

handgun *n.* **kach'in puub'**

handicapped *n.* **yo'rahil**

handkerchief *n.* **kok' sut**
      n. **sut**

handle *v.* **b'iqok**
      v. **jilok**
      n. **k'ub'**
      n. **roq**
      n. **xxik**

handsaw *n.* **ch'ina k'arch'iich'**

hang *v.* **lukub'ank**

hang on a second
      phr. **chinaawoyb'en b'ayaq**

hang out (clothing) *v.* **heleb'ank**
      v. **helok**

hang up *v.* **t'uyub'ank**

hangar *n.* **xna'aj so'sol ch'iich'**

hanger *n.* **xlokochil t'ikr**

happen *v.* **uxk**
      v. **yook**

happiness *n.* **sahil ch'oolejil**

happy *adj.* **k'ojk'o xch'ool**
      adj. **maausilanb'il**
      adj. **sahil ch'ool**
      adj. **sa xch'ool**
      adj. **usilanb'il**

happy birthday *phr.* **sahil ch'oolejil choq' aawe sa' laakutan**

happy to hear it *phr.* **sa inch'ool chi rab'inkil**

hard *adj.* **ch'a'aj**
      adj. **kaw**
      adj. **yotyot**

hard disk *n.* **rululil**

harden *v.* **pekark**

hardware store *n.* **k'ayib'aal k'anjelob'aal**

hard-working *adj.* **aj k'anjel**

hare *n.* **k'iche' imul**
      n. **xa'an imul**

harm *n.* **toch'ok**

harmony (musical)
  n. **sahilyaab'**

harmony (social) *n.* **sahil wank**

harp   *n.* **rinwajb'**

harvest   *n.* **ch'oqom**
          v. **q'olok**
          n. **q'olom**
          n. **xokok**

hat   *n.* **punit**

hate   *v.* **jatz'uuchink**
          v. **xik'uchink**
          n. **xik' ilok**

hatred   *n.* **xik' ilok**

hauler   *n agt.* **aj kelonel**

have   *v phr.* **wank e**

have a nice day
          phr. **chaanumsi chi
          us li kutan**

have a nice week
          phr. **chaanumsi chi
          us li xamaan**

have a seat *phr.* **chunlan**

have difficulty breathing at night
          v. **aakanak**

have nightmares *v.* **aakanak**

have sexual relations
          v. **aatinank**

have you got a minute? *phr.* **ma
          wan b'ayaq
          aahoonal**

hawk   *n.* **k'uch**
          n. **liklik**

hay   *n.* **aq**
          n. **k'im**
          n. **tam**

he   *pron.* **a'an**

he who knows *n.* **na'ol**
          n. **na'onel**

head   *n.* **jolom**

head pad *n.* **b'itool**
          n. **xsok b'itom**

head strap *n.* **taab'**

headache *n.* **jolomb'ej**
          n. **rahil jolom**
          n. **xtib' jolom**

headband *n.* **t'upuy**

headboard *n.* **jolom ch'aat**

headdress *n.* **t'upuy**

headphones *n.* **ab'ib'aal**
          n. **xikelyaab'**

headstone *n.* **eetalkamenaq**

heal   *v.* **b'anok**

health   *n.* **kawilal**

health center *n.* **b'anleb'aal**

health education *n.* **tijok chi rix
          kawilal**

health problems *n.* **yajel
          qatib'el**

healthy   *adj.* **kawal**

heap   *n.* **jun tuub'**

hear   *v.* **ab'ink**

hearing   *n.* **ab'ib'aal**
          n. **ab'ink**

heart   *n.* **ch'ool**
             n. **ch'oolej**

heart attack *n.* **xlub'ik li ch'ool**
             n. **xxaqliik aamej**

heat   *n.* **q'ixnal**
             v. **tiqwasink**

heater   *n.* **luhasib'aal**

heaven   *n.* **choxa**

heavy   *adj.* **aal**

heavyset person *n.* **t'inis**

heel   *n.* **rit oq**

heel (of a shoe) *n.* **rit xaab'**

height   *n.* **nim xteram**
             n. **xmajolil**

heir   *n agt.* **aj maatan**

helicopter   *n.* **tulux ch'iich'**

hell   *n.* **tojleb'aal maak**
             n. **xb'alb'a**

hello   *phr.* **chan xaawil**

helmet   *n.* **kolb'ajolom**
             n. **uk'alpunit**

help   *phr.* **chineetenq'aaaq**
             v. **kamab'k**
             v. **tenq'ank**
             n. **tenq'aal**
             n. **xtenq'ankil**

help yourself *phr.* **chap aawe**

hemmorhage   *n.* **pujkik'**

hemoglobin   *n.* **b'onkik'**
             n. **kaqkik'**

hemp   *n.* **kawil k'aam**

hen   *n.* **tux kaxlan**
             n. **xa'an kaxlan**

hendecagon   *n.* **junlajuxuk**

hepatitis   *n.* **q'anil**
             n. **q'anyajel**

heptagon   *n.* **wuqxuk**

her   *pron.* **a'an**

herbicide   *n.* **b'anpim**

herbs   *n.* **sununkil pim**

herd of cattle *n.* **k'ila wakax**

herder   *n agt.* **aj ilol wakax**
             n agt. **aj k'aak'alehom ketomq**

herdsman   *n agt.* **aj ilol wakax**
             n agt. **aj k'aak'alehom ketomq**

here   *adv.* **arin**
             adv. **ayi'**
             adv. **sa'in**

here it is   *phr.* **wahi'**

hero   *n agt.* **aj kolom**
             n. **xnimal winq**

heron   *n.* **jotz**
             n. **patux ha'**
             n. **saqikil**

hexagon   *n.* **waqxuk**

hi   *phr.* **chan xaawil**

hiccough   *n.* **chuq'ub'**
             v. **chuq'ub'ak**
             v phr. **k'ehok chuq'ub'**

hiccup   *n.* **chuq'ub'**
             v. **chuq'ub'ak**
             v phr. **k'ehok chuq'ub'**

hide   *v.* **jalmuqank**
             v. **muquk**

n. **rix xul**
n. **tz'uumal**

hide one's shame *v phr.* **moyok xutaan**

hieroglyphic *n.* **mayertz'iib'**

high   *adj.* **najt xteram**
adj. **nim xteram**
adj. **yak'ach**

high school *n.* **xkab' na'aj tzoleb'aal**

highlight *v.* **ka'jultikank**

hill   *n.* **tzuul**

hills   *n.* **kelkookil tzuul**
n. **tzoltzookiltzuul**

him   *pron.* **a'an**

hip   *n.* **k'onx a'**
n. **xko it**

hippopotamus *n.* **aaqha'**
n. **kax aaq**

hire   *v phr.* **k'ehok k'anjel**

historian *n agt.* **aj yehomb'aanuhem**

history   *n.* **jultik uxk**
n. **resilal b'aanuhom**
n. **resilal wank**
n. **uxb'il b'aanunb'il**
n. **yehom'uxb'il**

hit   *v.* **b'ujuk**
v. **ketok**
v. **potz'ok**
v. **sak'ok**
v. **tenok**
v. **wojok**

hit the road *v phr.* **chapok b'e**

hoarse   *adj.* **nim sa' xkux**

hoe   *n.* **asaron**
n. **jookleb'**

hog   *n.* **aaq**

hold   *v.* **chapok**
v. **q'unuk**

hold up   *v.* **b'ayok**

hole   *n.* **hopolal**
n. **jul**
n. **k'ob'b'il**
n. **xk'ob'lal**

hole punch *n.* **hopleb'**
n. **hopleb'che'**
n. **hopleb'hu**

hollow   *adj.* **hopo**

hollow out *v.* **job'enk**

holster   *n.* **xna'aj puub'**

holy   *adj.* **osob'tesinb'il**
adj. **wankil**

holy image *n.* **jalam'uuch**

holy spirit *n.* **santil musiq'ej**

holy week *n.* **rahil kutan**

home economics *n.* **sachomj junkab'lal**
n. **tzolomilk'uub'**

homeostasis
n. **hilhookilna'yu'am**

homework *n.* **k'anjel**

homicide *n.* **kamij winq**

homonym *n.* **juneetilk'ab'a'**

honest *adj.* **maak'a' naxch'e'**

honesty *n.* **tiikilal**

honey   *n.* **xya'al kab'**

hood   *n.* **lep ch'iich'**

hood support   *n.* **xche'el lep ch'iich'**

hoof   *n.* **ixi'ij**

hook   *n.* **lokoch**

hope   *n.* **ch'ool re**
           v. **yo'nink**

horizontal   *adj.* **q'e'q'o**

horizontal line   *n.* **q'eq'ookil juch'**

horn   *n.* **jayaab'wajb'**
           n. **kaxxuxb'**
           n. **q'anch'iich'**
           n. **trompeet**
           n. **xukub'**

hornet   *n.* **ch'ub'**

horse   *n.* **kawaay**
           n. **tzimitz**

hortensia   *n.* **orteens**

hose   *n.* **hoyal**
           n. **simb'tz'uum**
           n. **xb'eleb'aal ha'**

hospital   *n.* **nimlab'anleb'aal**
           n. **rochochil yaj**

hospital bed   *n.* **kaxch'aat**

hospital gown   *n.* **raq' aj b'anonel**

hospital robe   *n.* **raq' yaj**

hostage   *n.* **chapb'il**

hot   *adj.* **q'ix**
           adj. **tiq**
           adj. **tiqwal saq'e**

hot chocolate   *n.* **tiqwal kakaw**

hot climate   *n.* **tiqwalch'och'**

hot dog   *n.* **salchiich**

hot sauce   *n.* **putz'b'il pix ik**

hot water   *n.* **q'ix ha'**
            n. **tiqwal ha'**

hotel   *n.* **ochochnaal**

hot-water bottle   *n.* **xb'ooxil tiqwal ha'**

hour   *n.* **hoonal**
           n. **oor**

house   *n.* **kab'l**
           n. **ochoch**

housepainter   *n agt.* **aj b'ononel kab'l**

housewife   *n agt.* **aj k'anjel sa' kab'l**

how are you?   *phr.* **chan ru wankat**
               phr. **ma sa laach'ool**

how do you pronounce [   ]?   *phr.* **chan ru nakaayaab'asi [   ]**

how do you say [   ]?   *phr.* **chan ru nayehman [   ]**

how far?   *interr.* **jo' najtil**

how long ago?   *interr.* **jarmayer**

how many times?   *interr.* **jarsut**
                  interr. **jarwa**

how many?   *interr.* **jarub'**

how much each time?   *interr.* **jarjartk**

how much for each?   *interr.* **jarjar**

how much? *interr.* **jar**
    interr. **jo' k'ihal**
    interr. **jo' nimal**

how old are you? *phr.* **jarub' chihab' wan aawe**

how's the weather? *phr.* **chan ru li kutan**

how? *interr.* **chan ru**

however *conj.* **a' chik ut**
    conj. **ab'anan**
    conj. **yalaq chan ru**

howl *v.* **oq'lok**
    v. **tz'uyte'ek**
    v. **wote'ek**

hug *v.* **mek'onk**
    v. **q'alunk**

hug each other *v phr.* **q'alunk ib'**

human *n.* **poyanam**

human biology *n.* **poyanimil nawyu'am**

human rights *n.* **xk'ulub'poyanam**

human skeleton *n.* **yolojilb'aq**

humanity *n.* **poyanimil**

humble *adj.* **q'un**
    adj. **tuulan**

humid *adj.* **lan lan**
    adj. **t'aqt'aq**

humidity *n.* **xlanlanil**

humiliated *adj.* **tz'eqtananb'il**

humiliation *n.* **maajewank**

humility *n.* **xtuulanil**

hummingbird *n.* **tz'unun**

hundred *n.* **ok'aalil**

hundredth *num.* **(100th.) ro'k'aalil**

hunger *n.* **ch'um**
    n. **we'ej**

hungry *adj.* **tz'okaaq**

hunt *v.* **tzakib'k**
    v. **yohob'k**

hunter *n agt.* **aj yo**

hurricane *n.* **kaqsut-iq'**

hurry *v.* **seeb'ank**

hurt *v.* **raho'k**
    n. **toch'ok**
    adj. **toch'ool**

husband *n.* **b'eelom**

husk *n.* **rix**

husk (grain) *n.* **sol**

hut *n.* **paapa'x**
    n. **po'lem kab'l**

hydrogen *n.* **ha'il**

hydrology *n.* **nawha'il**

hydrosphere *n.* **ruuchiha'**

hymen *n.* **ranq'**

hymnal *n.* **b'ichleb'**

hypertension *n.* **numt'ikt'ot-aam**

hyphen *n.* **ch'inaaljuch'**
    n. **ch'inq'ejuch**

hypocritical *adj.* **ka'pak'al u**

hypotension *n.* **yalaalt'ikt'ot-aam**

hypothermia *n.* **keho'ktib'elej**

hypothesis *n.* **k'a'uxlanb'il**

hypothetical *adj.* **k'a'uxlanb'il**

I - i

I *pron.* **laa'in**

I am lost *phr.* **sachsookin**

I disagree *phr.* **ink'a' naxk'ul inch'ool**

I don't feel very well *phr.* **ink'a' jwal sa naweek'a**

I don't know *phr.* **ink'a' ninnaw**

I don't like [ ] *phr.* **ink'a' nahulak chi wu [ ]**

I don't mind *phr.* **maak'a' ink'as chi rix**

I don't speak English *phr.* **ink'a' nin'aatinak sa' inkles**

I don't speak Q'eqchi' *phr.* **ink'a' nin'aatinak sa' q'eqchi'**

I feel sick *phr.* **yo inyajel**

I hope so *phr.* **maare jo'kan**

I know *phr.* **ninnaw**

I like [ ] *phr.* **nahulak chi wu [ ]**

I miss you *phr.* **nakatinjultika**

I only speak a little Q'eqchi' *phr.* **yal b'ayaq nin'aatinak sa' q'eqchi'**

I only speak a little Spanish *phr.* **yal b'ayaq nin'aatinak sa' kastiiy**

I understand *phr.* **xintaw ru**

I'd love to *phr.* **us raj**

I'm at home *phr.* **wankin sa' wochoch**

I'm bored *phr.* **xintitz'**

I'm exhausted *phr.* **lub'luukin**

I'm fine thanks *phr.* **us wankin b'antyox**

I'm full *phr.* **nujenakin**

I'm going out *phr.* **ok we chi elk**

I'm in a bad mood *phr.* **ch'ich'i' we** *phr.* **yo wix**

I'm in a hurry *phr.* **twaj ru**

I'm looking forward to it *phr.* **yo inch'ool chi royb'eninkil**

I'm not sure *phr.* **ink'a' ch'olch'o**

I'm sorry *phr.* **chaakuy inmaak**

I'm thirsty *phr.* **chaqiq we**

I'm tired *phr.* **tawajenaqin**

I'm worried *phr.* **yo ink'a'uxl**

I've been busy *phr.* **jwal laatz' wu**

I've got to go *phr.* **tento tinxik**

ice   *n.* **ke**
             n. **pekb'ach**
             n. **pek ha'**
             n. **saqb'ach**

ice bag   *n.* **xb'ooxil saqb'ach**

ice cream   *n.* **ki'b'ach**
             n. **ki'ilsaqb'ach**
             n. **ki'il saqb'ach saa'us**

ice cream cart *n.* **xtoltolil ki'il saqb'ach saa'us**

ice cream vendor *n agt.* **aj k'ay ki'ilsaqb'ach**

icepack   *n.* **xb'ooxil saqb'ach**

icon   *n.* **eetaltaql**

iconography *n.* **ch'utub'eetalil**
             n. **sik'ok-eetalil**

ICU   *n.* **xna'aj nimqal yaj**

ID   *n.* **huxaqalil**
             n. **hu chi ru chaq'rab'**
             n. **xaaqalhu**
             n. **xhuhul tenamit**

idea   *n.* **k'a'uxl**
             n. **na'leb'**

ideal   *n.* **sik'mank'a'uxl**

identity   *n.* **loq'al wankilal**
             n. **loq'-ilok**

ideograph   *n.* **tz'iib'uuchil**

ideological imposition
             n. **minb'ilna'leb'**

idiolect   *n.* **raatinul**

idiomatic   *adj.* **aatinob'aalil**

idiot   *n.* **yajti'ox**

idol   *n.* **jalam'uuch**

if   *conj.* **wi**

iguana   *n.* **iwaan**

ill   *adj.* **yaj**

illness   *n.* **yajel**
             n. **yajelil**

ill-tempered *adj.* **yo rix**

illustration *n.* **xsahob'resinkil**

imagination
             n. **k'a'uxlanb'ilna'leb'**

imitate   *v phr.* **ech ajaatink**

immediately *adv.* **aka'**
             adv phr. **anaqwan tz'aqal**
             adv. **koko**
             adv phr. **sa' jumpaat**
             adv. **tikto**

immoral   *adj.* **tz'i'ej**

immoral practices *n.* **tz'i'ej na'leb'**

impatient   *adj.* **ch'ich'i re**
             adj. **ch'iq' rik'in k'a re ru**

important   *adj.* **aajel**

impressed   *adj.* **nasach xch'ool**

imprint   *n.* **puktasib'aalhu**

imprison   *v phr.* **k'ehok sa' tzalam**

improve   *v.* **usaak**

improvization *n.* **yoob'kink**

impulsive *adj.* **yal naxkuti rib'**

in *prep.* **sa'**

in a moment *adv phr.* **ake' hoon**

in accordance with *adv phr.* **jo' chan ru**

in four days *n.* **ko'ej**
    adv. **wej**

in front *prep.* **u**

in front of *prep.* **chi ru**
    prep. **sa' xka'yab'aal**

in love *adj.* **xikenaq xch'ool**

in order to *prep.* **cho'q re**

in peace *adv.* **kalkab'**

in seven days *adv.* **wuqub'ix**

in the afternoon *adv phr.* **chi ru li ewu**

in the early morning *adv phr.* **chi ru li saqewk**

in the evening *adv phr.* **chi ru q'oqyin**

in the first place *adv phr.* **xb'een wa**

in the morning *adv phr.* **chi ru li eq'la**

in thirds *adj.* **oxjach**

in three days *adv.* **oxej**

in three parts *adj.* **oxjach**

in-box *n.* **k'uulb'ahu**

incense *n.* **kaxlan pom**
    n. **pom**
    n. **sununkil k'ol**

incense burner *n.* **k'atleb'aal pom**

inclining *adj.* **an'o**

incomplete *adj.* **ink'a' tz'aqal**

incubator *n.* **kaxsuk**

indefinite or future particle
    part. **aq**

independence *n.* **junesalil**

independent *adj.* **junesalil**

independent pronoun *n.* **junesal ruuchil k'ab'a'ej**

index *n.* **tusna'leb'**

index finger *n.* **k'utunel ru'uj uq'**

indicate *v.* **k'utuk**

indictment *n.* **jitom**

indifferent *adj.* **maak'a' naraj wi'**

indigenous *n.* **ralch'och'**
    n. **tzaqal winq**
    n. **yaal winq**

individual *n.* **junaqlil**

individually *adv.* **chi junaqlil**

indoctrinate *v.* **tijok**

induce *v.* **aalenk**

inductive *adj.* **taqb'eetil**

inductively *adv.* **sa' taqb'eet**

industrial *adj.* **k'uub'k'ay**

industrial arts *n.* **tzolyiib'ahom**

inexpensive *adj.* **kub'enaq xtz'aq**

infarct *n.* **xlub'ik li ch'ool**

infatuation *n.* **jipo'k**

infection *n.* **q'aak**

inference *n.* **jo'kanil**

infinite
    adj. **maachoyb'ach'u ut**

infinite set *n.* **maalajkch'uut**

infix *n.* **sa'iltz'aqob'l**

inflamed *n.* **kaqpech'in**

inflammation *n.* **sipook**
    n. **siipilal**

inflate *v.* **apusink**

inform *v.* **ch'olob'ank**

information *n.* **esilal**

information office *n.* **xna'aj aj k'ehol esil**

information technology *n.* **esilal nawk'anjelahom**

infrared light *n.* **xche' kaqixaml**

inhabitant *n.* **echkab'al**

inhaler *n.* **jiq'leb'aal b'an**

initial side (of an angle) *n.* **xk'atq xtiklajik**

inject *v.* **kutuk**

injection *n.* **b'akuun**
    n. **kutb'il b'an**
    n. **yeksyon**

injure *v.* **jot'ok**
    v. **tawasink**

injured party *n.* **toch'ol**

injury *n.* **yok'olal**

ink *n.* **xya'al puktasiilhu**

ink pad *n.* **xb'onilkaaxt**

inner cell components
    n. **kok'cha'al**

inner ear *n.* **numleb'yaab' xik**

inner tube *n.* **homtol'iq'**
    n. **iq'ob'aal**

innocent *adj.* **maak'a' xmaak**

inquire *v.* **patz'ok**

insect *n.* **inseekt**
    n. **kok' xul**
    n. **k'ajxul**

insect bite *n.* **xtiwom xul**

insecticide *n.* **b'antz'ipxul**
    n. **lajtesib'aalxul**
    n. **xb'anil xxulil awimq**
    n. **xb'anol suq**

insecure *adj.* **yal yalok re**

insecurity *n.* **ink'a' tuqtu xch'ool**
    n. **xiwxiwil**

insensitive *adj.* **maak'a' naraj wi'**

inside *prep.* **chi sa'**
    prep. **sa'**

insistence particle *part.* **pe'**

insole *n.* **xsa' xaab'**

insolent *adj.* **maak'a' xxutaan**

insomnia *n.* **maak'a'il wara**

instep *n.* **ru oq**

instrument *n.* **k'anjelob'aal**

insult *n.* **hob'ok**

intelligence *n.* **na'leb'**

intelligent *adj.* **ch'ukch'u xk'a'uxl**
adj. **wan xna'leb'**

intensive care unit *n.* **xna'aj nimqal yaj**

intention *n.* **rajb'al**

intercultural *adj.* **sa' k'ilawank**

interculturality *n.* **wotzb'aanuhem**

interest *n.* **raltumin**

interference *n.* **ch'ik-ib'**

interjection *n.* **xyikutb'il aatin**

intermediate point *n.* **yanqil**

international *adj.* **ab'liltenamit**

international check-in *n.* **na'ilman xhuhil re najtil tenamit**

international departures *n.* **elk sa' najtil tenamit**

internationalize *v.* **sutruuchich'och'ink**

internationally *adv.* **sutruuchich'och'**

internet *n.* **muhilsik'leb'**

interpretation *n.* **jalok-aatin**

interrogate *v.* **patz'ok**

interrogative *n.* **patz'leb' aatin**

interrogative particle *part.* **ma**

interrupt *v.* **jot'ok**

interruptor *n.* **raqb'ametz'ew**

interval *n.* **yanq**

interview *n.* **titz'ok**

interviewer *n.* **aj pech'onel**

intestinal gas *n.* **q'an yaj**

intestines *n.* **k'amk'otej**
n. **sooyom**

intonation *n.* **xyaab'kuxil**

intone *n.* **yaab'kuxink**

intransitive (verb) *n.* **junesal'uxk**

intravenous line *n.* **kawub'l kik'**

intravenous solution *n.* **sweer**

introduction *n.* **xch'olob'ankil**

introverted *adj.* **ink'a' na'eek'an**

invent *v.* **yoob'ank**

invented *adj.* **yoob'anb'il**

invention *n.* **yoob'**

inventor *n.* **yoob'k'a'aq**

investigate *v.* **tz'ilok-ix**

investigator *n agt.* **aj tzilol'ix**
n agt. **aj tzilonel**

invite *v.* **b'eenink**
v. **b'oqok**

invoice *n.* **huhil-loq'om**
n. **xhuhilk'uluk**
n. **xhuhil loq'om**

involuntary reflex *n.* **seeb'al rib'**

iodine *n.* **mertyolaat**

ionosphere *n.* **xamlt'or**

IOU *n.* **hu xaqb'anb'il xwankil**
n. **xhuhiltoj**

iris (eye)   *n.* **xlem u**

iron   *n.* **ch'iich'**
            n. **ji'leb'aal**
            n. **ji'leb't'ikr**

iron (clothing)   *n.* **ji'leb' t'ikr**
            v. **ji'ok**

iron bars   *n.* **tz'alam**

ironing board   *n.* **ji'leb'aal**
            n. **tz'alam re ji'ok aq'**

ironmonger   *n agt.* **aj k'ay**
            ch'iich'

irrealism   *n.* **k'a'uxlanb'ilal**

irresponsibility   *n.* **ninqilwank**

irresponsible   *adj.* **maak'a' xk'as**
            chi rix
            adj. **ninqiwank**

irresponsibly   *adv.* **ninqilwankil**

irrigate   *v.* **hoyok**
            v. **t'aqresink**

irritation   *n.* **josq'ok**

is anything wrong?   *phr.* **ma ra**
            xk'ul

island   *n.* **ch'ina ochoch**
            n. **ch'och'ilha'**
            n. **ch'och' sutsu chi**
            ha'
            n. **muhul**

            n. **neb'a ha'**
            n. **xch'och palaw**
            n. **xyampi ha'**

isolation   *n.* **junesal**

it   *pron.* **a'an**

it doesn't matter   *phr.* **maak'a'**
            naxye
            phr. **moko wan ta**
            xloq'al

it is not   *phr.* **maawa'**

it will be that (him, her, it)
            pron. **a'anaq**

it will be this   *pron.* **a'aq**

it's not important   *phr.* **moko**
            wan ta xloq'al

it's not worth it   *phr.* **maak'e**
            xloq'al

it's OK   *phr.* **us maak'a naxye**
            phr. **us naq nawil**

it's up to you   *phr.* **a' yaal aawe**

itch   *n.* **katz**
            n. **katzkatz**
            n. **wotz'ok**
            n. **wotz'okil**

Itza   *lang.* **itza'**

IV   *n.* **kawub'l kik'**
            n. **sweer**

J - j

jack   *n.* **taqsiil**

jacket   *n.* **chakeet**
            n. **q'ixleb'aq'**
            n. **q'ixt'ikr**

jaguar   *n.* **b'alam**
           n. **hix**

jail   *n.* **tz'alam**

jail cell *n.* **xraqlil xsa' tz'alam**

Jakaltek [aka Popti]
           lang. **jakalteka**

janitor   *n agt.* **aj ilol okeb'aal**

January   *n.* **eneer**
           n. **xb'eenilpo**

jasmine   *n.* **jasmin**

javelin throw   *n.* **kutuk q'e'che'**

jaw   *n.* **rub'el e**
           n. **xkaalam e**

jealous   *adj.* **sowen**

jealousy   *n.* **kaqal**
           n. **sowenal**
           n. **sowenk**

jeans   *n.* **loonil wex**
           n. **wex re loon**

Jeep   *n.* **k'aleb'aal poy ch'iich'**

jersey   *n.* **b'atz-aq'**

Jew   *n.* **juliis**

jewel   *n.* **q'ol**

jeweller   *n agt.* **aj tenol ch'iich'**
           n agt. **aj yiib'om q'ol**

jewelry   *n.* **kok' tenb'il ch'iich'**

jewelry store   *n.* **k'ayib'aal kok' tenb'il ch'iich'**

Jewish   *adj.* **aj juliis**

job   *n.* **kub'siil**
           n. **k'anjel**
           n. **tenq'**

job orientation   *n.* **xna'leb'ankil k'anjel**

join   *v.* **ch'utub'ank**
           v. **laq'ab'ank**

joint (bones)   *n.* **k'ulb'ab'aq**

joke   *v.* **ch'uch'ib'k**

journalist   *n agt.* **aj k'ehol esil**
           n agt. **aj molol'esil**

Juan   *nick.* **Xiwan**

judge   *n agt.* **aj raqol'aatin**
           n agt. **aj raqol chaq'rab'**
           v phr. **raqok aatin**

judgment   *n.* **raqb'a' aatin**

judicial power   *n.* **xwankilal raqonel**

judicial system
           n. **xk'uub'lalraqleb'a atin**

jug   *n.* **puk'xaar**
           n. **xaar**

juice   *n.* **xya'al**

juice press   *n.* **pitz'leb'**
           n. **yatz'leb'**

juicer   *n.* **yatz'leb'**

July   *n.* **juul**

jump   *v.* **pisk'ok**
           v. **pitzok**

June   *n.* **juun**

jungle   *n.* **k'iche'b'aal**

Jupiter   *n.* **ro' ralsaq'e**

jury   *n.* **raqonel chaq'rab'**

just   *adj.* **tiik xch'ool**

just joking *phr.* **yal ch'uch'ib'k we**

just kidding *phr.* **yal ch'uch'ib'k we**

just now *conj.* **toja'**

justice *n.* **chaq'rab'**
n. **raqok aatin**
n. **tiikilwank**
n. **tz'ilok maak**

K - k

K'iche *lang.* **k'iche'**

kangaroo *n.* **k'unuch imul**

Kaqchikel *lang.* **kaqchikel**

keep *v.* **k'aak'alenk**
v. **xokok**

keeper *n agt.* **aj k'aak'anel**

kerosene *n.* **b'ookhumha'**
n. **humb'ookilha'**

ketchup *n.* **keb'il pix**

kettle *n.* **ak'ach**

key *n.* **alpek'iich'**
n. **jaqleb'**
n. **laaw**
n. **teeleb'**

key (of keyboard) *n.* **ru tz'iib'leb'**

keyboard *n.* **ru ululch'iich'**
n. **tz'iib'leb'**
n. **xche'e'b'al**

keychain *n.* **chapteeleb'**

kick *v.* **lapok**
v phr. **lapok chi oq**
v. **t'i'ok**
v. **xaab'ank**
v. **yeq'ok**

kid *n.* **ral chib'aat**
n. **ral yuk**

kidnapper *n agt.* **aj elq'**

kidnapping *n.* **muquk poyanam**

kidney *n.* **kenq'**

kill *v.* **kamsink**

kilo *n.* **kiil**

kilometer *n.* **hiil**

kind *adj.* **chab'il xch'ool**

kinesiology *n.* **naw'q'och**

kinetic energy *n.* **xmetz'ew tiik**

king *n.* **ajaw**

kingdom *n.* **wankilal**

kiosk *n.* **ja'leb'aal**
n. **wakax kab'l**

kiss *v phr.* **tz'ub'uk u**
v phr. **utz'uk u**

kitchen *n.* **chi re xam**
n. **k'uub'leb'aal**

kite *n.* **rupelhu**

Kleenex *n.* **huhil sut**

knead   *v.* **q'emrasink**
         v. **yoq'ok**
knee   *n.* **xb'een aq**
knee guard   *n.* **b'atb'een'aq**
knee pad   *n.* **b'atb'een'aq**
         n. **b'een'aqej**
         n. **sok xb'een'aq**
         n. **xlanb'al xb'een'aq**
knee patch   *n.* **b'een'aqej**
         n. **sok xb'een'aq**
         n. **xlanb'al xb'een'aq**
knee-high stocking   *n.* **xta a'**
kneel   *v.* **wiq'laak**

knife   *n.* **b'itzilch'iich'**
         n. **ch'ina ch'iich'**
         n. **sekch'iich'**
knit   *v.* **kemok**
knot   *n.* **t'oklal**
         n. **t'ok'**
         n. **xtok'**
know   *v.* **na'ok**
         v. **nawink**
know how to act   *v phr.* **eek'aj ib'**
knowledge   *n.* **nawom**
Kool-Aid   *n.* **b'onb'ilha'**

L - l

lab   *n.* **tz'ileb'aal**
         n. **tz'ileb' rix yajel**
laboratory   *n.* **tz'ileb'aal**
         n. **tz'ileb' rix yajel**
laborer   *n agt.* **aj k'anjel**
lace   *n.* **re t'ikr**
ladder   *n.* **eskaleer**
         n. **eeb'**
         n. **taqleb'aal**
Ladino   *n.* **aj mu's**
         n. **kaxlan winq**
ladle   *n.* **lekleb'**
         n. **nimla lek**
lady   *n.* **qana'**
ladybug   *n.* **kokxul**

lagoon   *n.* **kaq'naab'**
         n. **pumpuukil ha'**
lake   *n.* **kaq'naab'**
         n. **nimla kaqnab'**
         n. **palaw**
         n. **pumpuukil ha'**
lamb   *n.* **b'oreeg**
         n. **chib'aat**
         n. **kordeer**
         n. **ob'eja**
lame   *adj.* **sik**
         adj. **yeq**
lamp   *n.* **kanxam**
         n. **lampr**
         n. **saqenb'aal**
         n. **xam**

land   *n.* **ch'och'**
            v. **k'ochlaak**

landing strip *n.* **k'ochleb'aal**
            ch'iich'

landslide *n.* **uq'ul**
            n. **uul**

language *n.* **aatinob'aal**
            n. **yehom**

language policy *n.* **xna'leb'il**
            nawaatinob'aal

lantern   *n.* **kanxam**
            n. **lampr**
            n. **xam**

lard   *n.* **k'ook'**
            n. **olb'**
            n. **yolq'em**

large bag *n.* **iiq**

large hummingbird *n.* **pap**
            tz'unun

lasso   *n.* **laas**

last   *v.* **b'ayk**
            adj. **ch'otonel**
            adj. **marilb'ej**
            adj. **raqik**
            adj. **roso'jik**
            adj. **rosob'**

last month *n.* **li po ak xnume'**

last name *n.* **xsum k'ab'a'ej**

last night *n.* **ewer chi q'eq**

last son   *n.* **ch'i'p**

last week *adv phr.* **chi ru li**
            xamaan xnume'

last year *adv phr.* **chi ru li hab'**
            xnume'

latch   *n.* **k'aan**
            n. **nat'leb'**

latchkey *n.* **ralteeleb'**

late   *adj.* **ewu**
            adj. **najt kutan**

later   *adv.* **jo' wanaq**
            adv. **moqon**

latex   *n.* **kik'che'**

latitude   *n.* **xhelam**
            n. **xk'atqil**

latrine   *n.* **k'otleb'aal**

laugh   *v.* **se'ek**

launch   *n.* **much' jukub'**

laundress *n agt.* **aj puch'unel**

laundromat *n.* **xpuchleb'aal**
            tenamit

laundry   *n.* **aq' re puch'e'k**

laundry basket *n.* **xchakachil**
            aq'

laundry room *n.* **cha'jleb'aal**

lava   *n.* **woqxkum**
            n. **xa'awku**

law   *n.* **chaq'rab'**

lawn   *n.* **pach'aya'**

lawnmower *n.* **setleb'**
            pach'aya'

lawyer   *n agt.* **aj na'onel**
            chaq'rab'

laziness   *n.* **q'emkunal**

lazy   *adj.* **aj q'em**
            adj. **jip**
            adj. **jok**
            adj. **q'emkun**

lead   *v.* **jolomink**
            v phr. **k'amok b'e**
            v phr. **k'utuk b'e**

lead (metal) *n.* **rax ch'iich'**

leaf   *n.* **q'een**
            n. **xaq**

lean   *v.* **kuutunk**

leaning   *adj.* **an'o**

leap   *v.* **pisk'ok**
            v. **pitzok**

learn   *v.* **tzolok**

learning   *n.* **xtzolb'al**

leather   *n.* **tz'uumal**

leave   *v phr.* **chapok b'e**
            v. **elk**

leave me alone
            phr. **minaach'ich'i**

leave one behind *v.* **q'axok**

leaves   *n.* **xxaq**
            n. **xxaqeb'**

left   *adj.* **sa' tz'e**
            adj. **tz'e**

leg   *n.* **a'**

leg pain   *n.* **rahil ruuch a'**

legal adult *n.* **tz'aqalil hab'**

legend   *n.* **seeraq'**

legibility *n.* **xch'olch'ookilal**

legislation *n.* **nawchaq'rab'ik**

legislative power *n.* **xwankilal chaq'rab'inel**

legislative system
            n. **xk'ub'leb'aalchaq'r ab'**

legislator *n.* **aj k'uub'anelchaq'rab'**

lemon   *n.* **lamuunx**

lemon tea   *n.* **k'isk'im**

lemonade   *n.* **xya'al lamunx**

lend   *v.* **jalb'eetink**
            v. **jalok**
            v. **to'nink**

length   *n.* **nimroq**
            n. **xnimal roq**

leopard   *n.* **cho'hix**
            n. **hix**

leper   *n.* **saqleb'**

leprotic   *adj.* **saqleb' rix**

lesson   *n.* **tzolom k'anjel**

let go   *v.* **ach'ab'ank**
            v. **tob'ok**

let me know *phr.* **chaayehaq we**

let through *v phr.* **k'ehok numik**

let's go   *phr.* **yo'o**

letter   *n.* **esilhu**
            n. **tz'iib'**

letter body *n.* **nayeeman sa' li esilhu**

letter carrier *n agt.* **aj kanab'om esilhu**

letterhead *n.* **k'uut**

lettuce   *n.* **lechuuk**
            n. **woch ichaj**

leukemia *n.* **xyajel kik'**

level *n.* **tas**
n. **tuqb'iis**
n. **tuqleb'**

lever *n.* **k'ub'**

lexicographer *n agt.* **aj nawtus'aatin**

lexicography *n.* **nawtus'aatin**

lexicon *n.* **molob'aal aatin**
n. **sik'leb' aatin**
n. **xtusulal aatin**

liar *n agt.* **aj tik'ti'**

liberalism *n.* **ach'ab'ilal**

liberate *v.* **ach'ab'ank**

librarian *n agt.* **aj ilol k'ila tasal hu**

library *n.* **rochochil tasal hu**
n. **xna'aj tasal hu**

license *n.* **ach'ab'alhu**

license plate
n. **rajlilb'eleb'ch'iich'**
n. **reetalil b'eleb'aal ch'iich'**
n. **xaqch'iich'**

lick *v.* **req'ok**

lid *n.* **tz'apleb'**

lie *n.* **tik'ti'**

lie (tell falsehoods) *v.* **b'alaq'ik**
v phr. **pak'ok aatin**
v. **tik'ti'ink**
v. **yik'ti'ink**

lie down *v.* **sotlaak**
v. **yoklaak**
v. **yokob'ank**

life *n.* **yu'am**
n. **yu'amej**

life expectancy *n.* **yu'amil**

life sentence *n.* **tzapliik junelik**

lift *v.* **paqonk**
v. **waklesink**

light *v phr.* **k'ehok xam**
v. **lochok**
adj. **saqen**
n. **saqen**
v. **tz'ab'ok**

light (in weight) *adj.* **poy**
adj. **seeb'**

light (not dark) *adj.* **raxk'urin**
adj. **saqen**

light airplane *n.* **ch'ina so'sol ch'iich'**

light bulb *n.* **b'omb'iiy**
n. **sulem**
n. **xnaq' saqen**

light refraction *n.* **jalb'ehil saqen**

light switch *n.* **chupleb' saqen**
n. **raqleb' saqen**

lighter *n.* **lechleb'**

light-hearted *adj.* **se'se' ru**

lightning *n.* **raq'kaaq**
n. **repom**

lightning bolt *n.* **lemskaaq**
n. **xrepom kaaq**

lightning bug *n.* **mams**

like *adj.* **chanchan**
adj. **jo'**
adj. **xchaq'**

like that   *adv phr.* **chi kama'an**
             adv. **kama'an**

like this   *adv phr.* **chi kama'in**
             adv. **kama'in**

likeness   *n.* **taq'eetil**

liking   *n.* **sahil**

lily   *n.* **asuseen**

limbs   *n.* **roq ruq'm**

lime (stone)   *n.* **chun**

limp   *v.* **yeqo'k**

line   *n.* **juch'**
            n. **jusk'aam**
            n. **tzol**
            n. **tzolil**

linear function   *n.* **junaj k'anjel**

lined up   *adj.* **tzoltzo**

linguistic borrowing   *n.* **to'chi'**

linguistic community
            n. **xmolamil aatinob'aal**

linguistic development
            n. **waklesink naw'aatinob'aal**

linguistic norms   *n.* **xtz'iib'ul aatinob'aal**

linguistics   *n.* **naw'aatinob'aal**
              n. **nawchi'**

link (in a chain)   *n.* **tiqilal**

linkage of syllables
            n. **k'ulb'atz'iib'**

lion   *n.* **xyuwa'il xul**

lips   *n.* **tz'uumal e**

lipstick   *n.* **laasp re xtz'uumal e**

liquify   *v.* **putz'ink**
            v. **uq'unink**

liquor   *n.* **traaw**

listen   *v.* **ab'ink**

listless   *adj.* **maak'a' naraj wi'**

liter   *n.* **liitr**
            n. **meetilsu**

literacy   *n.* **nawtzoltz'iib'**
            n. **tzoltz'iib'ank**

litter   *n.* **mul**

little   *adv.* **ch'in**

little bell   *n.* **ral punitch'iich'**

little by little   *adv.* **ch'inqal**
                   adv phr. **chi ch'inqil**

live   *v.* **na'ajink**
            v. **wank**

liver   *n.* **ch'och'**
            n. **saaseb'**

livestock   *n.* **ketomq**

living room   *n.* **hilaal**

lizard   *n.* **tolokok**

loan   *n.* **k'asib'k**
            n. **to'**
            v. **to'nink**

location   *n.* **na'ajej**

lock   *n.* **kantaaw**
            n. **nat'leb' okeb'aal**
            n. **pek'iich'**
            n. **tz'apleb'**

lock up   *v.* **tz'apok**

locker   *n.* **xna'aj k'a re ru**

logic   *n.* **tuqtuukil k'a'uxl**
               n. **tusnaw**

Lola   *nick.* **Lool**

loneliness   *n.* **juntaalil**

lonely   *adj.* **junesal**

long   *adj.* **jukuch**
               adj. **lujuch**
               adj. **najt roq**
               adj. **nim roq**
               adj. **nim xkelam**

long jump   *n.* **najtil pisk'ok**

long vowel   *n.* **sum na'tz'iib'**

longaniza   *n.* **b'utb'il paayil tib'**
               aaq

longing   *n.* **atawank**

longitude   *n.* **kelam**
               n. **xnajtil roq**

look   *v.* **ka'yank**

look for   *v.* **sik'ok**

look out   *phr.* **k'e reetal li**
               taab'aanu

look!   *phr.* **iliii**

loom   *n.* **kemleb'**
               n. **k'uub'ch'iich'kem**

loop   *n.* **xxik aq'**

loose   *adj.* **yotzotznak**
               adj. **yootzan**

loosen   *v.* **kotzok**

loot   *v.* **min'isink**
               v. **minyamtesink**

lord   *n.* **ajaw**
               n. **qaawa'**

loroco (edible herb)
               n. **tz'aktz'um**

lose   *v.* **sachok**

lose (a game) *v.* **tz'eqok**

lose (a possession)   *v.*
               phr. **tz'eqok ib'**

lose your train of thought   *v.*
               phr. **b'orok na'leb'**

loss of blood   *n.* **tz'eqok kik'**

lot   *n.* **waqlajuk'aam**

lotion   *n.* **sununkil b'ook**

lottery   *n.* **b'uuleb'**
               n. **b'uuleb'aal**
               n. **b'uulik**
               n. **b'uuluk**
               n. **pumb'uul**
               n. **yalok hu**

loud   *adj.* **kaw**
               adj. **kaw xyaab'**
               adj. **yaab'il**

loudspeaker   *n.* **chajb'a'e**
               n. **puktasib'aal aatin**

louse   *n.* **uk'**

love   *v.* **oxloq'ink**
               n. **rahok**
               v. **rahok**
               n. **rahom**

low   *adj.* **kach'in xteram**

low neck   *n.* **xtehelal xkux**

lower case letter   *n.* **iitz'intz'iib'**

lubricant   *n.* **kax'olb'**

Lucas   *nick.* **Kax**

luggage   *n.* **iiq**

luggage tram *n.* **b'elahom iiq**

lukewarm *adj.* **luulu**

lullaby *n.* **b'ich k'uula'al**

lunar capsule *n.* **k'achleb'aal sa' po**

lunar eclipse *n.* **muqlaak po**
n. **muqpo**

lunar module *n.* **k'achleb'aal sa' po**

lunch *n.* **wa re wa'leb'**

lung *n.* **pos**
n. **pospo'oy**

Luz *nick.* **Lus**

lynx *n.* **yak**

lyre *n.* **tusch'iich'wajb'**

Lázaro *nick.* **Las**

M - m

macaw *n.* **mo'**

machete *n.* **tz'alamch'iich'**

machine *n.* **k'uub'ch'iich'**
n. **maak**

machine gun *n.* **k'ilapotz' puub'**
n. **paraq'aq'a**

macro competencies *n.* **ninqi seeb'alil**

mad *adj.* **kaan ru**
adj. **look**
adj. **wax ru**

made of clay *adj.* **pak'b'il**

magazine *n.* **ch'ina tashu'esil**
n. **xnaq' puub'**

magic *n.* **nawalil**
n. **tuul**

magical *adj.* **sachb'ach'oolej**

magician *n agt.* **aj eek'**
n agt. **aj nawal**

magician's hat *n.* **xpunit aj eek'**

magnet *n.* **tz'ub'ch'iich'**

magnetic resonance imaging *n.* **tz'ub'ch'iich'b'il eek'ch'iich'**

magnetism *n.* **metz'kelob'**

magnolia *n.* **k'onop**

mahogany *n.* **sutz'ujl**

maid *n.* **aj k'anjel sa' kab'l**

mail *n.* **taql**

mailbag *n.* **xchampa aj kanab'om esilhu**
n. **xkoxtalil li esilhu**

mailbox *n.* **xkaxonil esilhu**
n. **xna'aj esilhu**
n. **xna'aj taql**

mailman *n agt.* **aj kanab'om esilhu**

mainland *n.* **kontineent**

maize   *n.* **ixim**

make   *v.* **b'aanunk**
           n. **paak'ilal**
           v. **yiib'ank**

make an offering *v.* **mayejak**

make clear *v phr.* **xtawb'il li manawb'il**

make the sign of the cross *v phr.* **k'utuk eetalil**

make tortillas *v.* **xorok**

make war *v.* **katunink**

malaria   *n.* **raxkihob'**

male (of animals) *adj.* **k'ol**

male (of birds) *adj.* **tzo'**

male (of humans) *adj.* **teelom**

males   *n.* **winqilal**

mall entrance *n.* **xmu mama' k'ayib'aal**

mallet   *n.* **tenleb'**

Mam   *lang.* **mam**

mamey   *n.* **saltul**

mammal *n.* **tu'unel**

mammalian *n.* **tu'unel**

man   *n.* **teelom**
           n. **winq**

mandate *n.* **taqlankil**

mango   *n.* **mank**
           n. **q'unixholob'oob'**

manhood *n.* **winqilal**

manioc *n.* **tz'in**

manioc bread *n.* **tz'in**

manner *n.* **naraj**

manservant *n agt.* **aj tenq'**

manuscript *n.* **uq'miltz'iib'**

many   *adj.* **k'ihal**
           pron. **k'ila**
           adj. **mayalok**

map   *n.* **reetalil ch'och'**

maracas *n.* **jook'**
           n. **tzujtzuj**

marble   *n.* **saqi pek**

marbles *n.* **mitz' b'olotz**
           n. **mitzt'orotz**
           n. **t'orlemtz'**

Marcelina *nick.* **Liin**

Marcelino *nick.* **Liin**

March   *n.* **maars**
           n. **roxilpo**

marchant *n agt.* **aj yakonel**

Marcos *nick.* **Kux**

mare   *n.* **xna' kawaay**

margarine *n.* **xxeeb'ul pim**

marimba *n.* **tusb'ilche'wajb'**
           n. **tusb'il che' son**
           n. **tusche'wajb'**

marines *n.* **rampalaw**

marionette *n.* **poyb'atz'uul**

mark   *v.* **eetalink**
           v. **jalam'uuchib'k**

marker *n.* **b'onleb'**

market *n.* **k'ayiil**

marmot *n.* **kaxmis**

married man *n.* **sumsuukil**

married woman *n.* **sumsuukil**

marrow *n.* **sulutz**
    n. **xsulutzil b'aq**

marry *v.* **sumlaak**

marsh *n.* **saab' ha'**

María *nick.* **Mar**

masculine particle *part.* **aj**

masculinity *n.* **winqilal**

mashed potatoes *n.* **puq'b'il paaps**

mask *n.* **k'oj**

mason *n agt.* **aj tz'ak**

masonry *n.* **tz'akkab'l**

mass *n.* **miix**

masterly *adj.* **xaaqilalk'utuk**

mat *n.* **aj**
    n. **poop**

match *n.* **kaxtok'**
    n. **lochleb' xaml**
    n. **poos**
    n. **tokxaml**

maternity ward *n.* **alab'tesib'aal**

math *n.* **naw'ajl**
    n. **nawom chi rix ajl**

mathematically *adv.* **chi'ajlil**

mathematician *n agt.* **aj naw'ajl**

mathematics *n.* **naw'ajl**
    n. **nawom chi rix ajl**

Matilde *nick.* **Mat**

mattress *n.* **ru ch'aat**
    n. **xsokel ru ch'aat**

mature *adj.* **aj cheek**

mauve *adj.* **kaq moyin**

May *n.* **maay**
    n. **ro'ilpo**

Maya *n.* **aj mayab'**
    adj. **mayab'**
    adj. **maay**
    adj. **maayil**
    n. **ralch'och'**
    n. **tzaqal winq**
    n. **yaal winq**

Maya calendar *n.* **ch'olq'e maayab'**

Maya culture *n.* **maayil na'leb'**

Maya priest *n agt.* **aj k'atol mayej**

Maya pyramid *n.* **ox'ukab'l mayab'**

Maya spiritualist *n.* **aj mayej**

Maya tradition *n.* **maayil na'leb'**

Mayan *adj.* **maayil**

Mayan glyph *n.* **mayertz'iib' maay**

Mayan languages
    n. **aatinob'aal maay**

Mayan numbers *n.* **eetalil ajl mayab'**

maybe *adv.* **maare**
    adv. **tana**

mayo *n.* **mayonees**
    n. **t'oqtzak**

mayonnaise *n.* **mayonees**
    n. **t'oqtzak**

mayor   *n.* **aj jolominel k'aleb'aal**
        n. **xb'eenil poopol**

me too   *phr.* **laa'in ajwi'**

meadow   *n.* **potreer**

meal   *n.* **tib'el wa**
        n. **tzakahem**
        n. **wa**

mean   *adj.* **kaq ru xch'ool**

meaning   *n.* **xyaalalil**

means of communication
        n. **aatinab'aal**
        n. **puktasib'aal esil**

measles   *n.* **kaqlamj**
        n. **sarampyon**

measure   *v.* **b'isok**
        v. **ch'ikok**

measure (by one hundred)
        n. **ok'aalil b'isleb'**

measuring cup   *n.* **b'isleb' sek'**

measuring tape   *n.* **b'isleb'**
        n. **eetaal**

meat   *n.* **tib'**

meat grinder   *n.* **ke'leb'aal tib'**

meatballs   *n.* **t'ort'ookil tib'**

mechanic   *n agt.* **aj k'uub'anel poych'iich'**
        n agt. **aj xiitinelch'iich'**
        n agt. **aj yiib'om ch'iich'**

media   *n.* **aatinab'aal**
        n. **puktasib'aal esil**

medical examiner   *n agt.* **aj ilol kamenaq**

medical professional   *n agt.* **aj nawk'anjel yajel**

medical record   *n.* **resilal yajel**

medicine   *n.* **b'an**
        n. **k'iila b'an**
        n. **nawb'anok**

medicine cabinet   *n.* **xna'aj b'an**

medicine cart   *n.* **xtoltolil b'an**

Mediterranean Sea
        n. **q'otch'och'ilpalaw**

medlar   *n.* **nispr**

meek   *adj.* **q'axal q'un**
        adj. **tuulan**

meet   *v phr.* **k'uluk ib'**
        v phr. **tawok u**

meeting   *n.* **ch'utamil**

meeting hall   *n.* **ch'uutleb'aal**
        n. **ch'uutleb'aalkab'l**

meeting place   *n.* **ch'uutleb'aal**
        n. **ch'uutleb'aalkab'l**

meiosis   *n.* **jek'muriil**
        n. **jek'pojk'ok**

melody   *n.* **kuxil**
        n. **yaab'ich**

melon   *n.* **melon**

melt   *v.* **ha'ob'resink**

member   *n.* **komonil**

memorize   *v.* **k'uulank**
        v. **tuub'ank**

mend   *v.* **xiitink**

meninges   *n.* **kolb'a'ich'mulej**

menses   *n.* **kaqlak**

menstruate *v.* **puch'uk**

menstruation *n.* **kaqlak**

menudo *n.* **xkok' xch'al xul**

merchant *n agt.* **aj k'ay**
　　　　　n agt. **aj k'ayinel**
　　　　　n agt. **aj loq'onel**
　　　　　n. **yakonel**

Mercury *n.* **xb'een ralsaq'e**

meridian *n.* **numlentz' saqen**

Merry Christmas *phr.* **sahil ch'oolejil choq' aawe sa' ralankil**

Mesoamerica *n.* **xyi ab'yayala**
　　　　　n. **yiib'ejilch'och'**

mesosphere *n.* **rox tasal'iq'**

Mesozoic era *n.* **xka q'ekutan**

message *n.* **seeraq'**

message (written) *n.* **esil nayehman sa' li hu**

messenger *n agt.* **aj b'eetaql**

metal *n.* **ch'iich'**
　　　n. **pu'ak**

metal bars *n.* **koral ch'iich'**

metal beam *n.* **oqechch'iich'**

metal carriage insert *n.* **kuukb'eleb'ch'iich'**

metal door *n.* **tz'apokeb'ch'iich'**

metal pipe *n.* **b'olb'okiil ch'iich'**

metal tube *n.* **b'olb'okiil ch'iich'**
　　　　　n. **homch'iich'**

metaphysics *n.* **xe'k'a'uxl**

metasphere *n.* **xkab't'or**

meteor *n.* **chahimpek**
　　　n. **k'ajchahim**

meteorite *n.* **xk'otchahim**

meteorology *n.* **nawq'ehil**

methane *n.* **b'ookha'**

method *n.* **b'ehil**
　　　n. **xb'ehul**

methodological steps *n.* **tusb'ehul**

methodology *n.* **nawb'ehil**

meticulous *adj.* **natz'ilok chi us**

Mexico *n.* **meej**

microorganism *n.* **mitz'k'icha'al**

microphone *n.* **aatik'uul**
　　　　　n. **aatinob'aal**
　　　　　n. **pukyaab'**

microscope *n.* **ileb'aalmitz'**

microscopic *adj.* **mitz'cha'al**

microwave oven *n.* **mikro oont**
　　　　　n. **pomleb'aal tzakahemq**

midday *n.* **jun wa'leb'**

middle *n.* **sa' xyi**
　　　n. **yi**
　　　n. **yiib'ej**

middle finger *n.* **xyihil ru'uj uq'**

midge *n.* **k'uxuk**
　　　n. **suq**

midnight *n.* **tuqtu q'ojyin**

midwife *n agt.* **aj xokol'al ixq**

migraine   *n.* **rahil jolom**

migrant   *n agt.* **aj b'e**

Miguel   *nick.* **Mek**

mild   *adj.* **luulu**
    adj. **q'axal q'un**
    adj. **tuulan**

milk   *n.* **leech**
    n. **xya'al tu'**
    v. **yatz'ok**

milkshake   *n.* **puq'b'il**

Milky Way   *n.* **saqb'e**
    n. **xtzoq saq'e**

mill (grain)   *n.* **keleb'aal**
    n. **k'uub'poch'leb'**
    n. **poch'leb'**

miller   *n agt.* **aj poch'onel**

millet   *n.* **kok' ixim**

millimeter   *n.* **mitz'jisb'ilis**

million   *n.* **oob' chuy xwaq k'alab'**

mime   *n.* **sa' memil**

mimeograph   *n.* **pukleb'hu**

mince   *v phr.* **setok tib'**

mind   *n.* **k'a'ux**

mini tamale   *n.* **kok' poch ob'en**

minimal pair   *n.* **xsumalil**

miniskirt   *n.* **ch'ot b'estiiy**

minivan   *n.* **saajil poy ch'iich'**

mint   *n.* **isk'i'ij**

minus sign (-)   *n.* **reetaljeb'ok-ajl**

minute   *n.* **k'asal**

miracle   *n.* **sachb'ach'oolej**

miraculous
    adj. **sachb'ach'oolej**

mirror   *n.* **lem**

miscarriage   *n.* **numsink-al**
    n. **tz'eqok k'ula'al**

mischievous   *adj.* **xulil**
    adj. **xul aj al**

misdemeanor   *n.* **kok' maak**

mission   *n.* **rajom**
    n. **taqlankil**

mist   *n.* **musmus hab'**
    n. **sujew**

mistake   *n.* **sachjik**

mitochondria   *n.* **alab'metz'ew**

mitosis   *n.* **pojk'ok**
    n. **xmurinkil rib'**

mix   *v.* **junajink**
    n. **yuul**

mixed number   *n.* **jachlil'ajl**

mixer   *n.* **b'ukleb'aal**
    n. **kaxkojl**
    n. **puq'leb'**
    n. **yuuleb'**

model   *n.* **paak'ilal**

modern warfare   *n.* **ak'il raaxiik'**

modify   *v.* **tz'aqob'resink**

module   *n.* **xch'uutulal**
    n. **xtasalil**

mojarra   *n.* **chakti'**

molar   *n.* **ka'**
    n. **ka' e**

mold   v. **pak'ok**

mole   n. **chut**

moment   n. **hoonal**
              n. **junpaatil**

Monday   n. **luuns**
              n. **xb'een kutan**

money   n. **loq'leb'**
              n. **pu'ak**
              n. **tumin**

money box   n. **k'ohaal**

monitor   n. **kaxmu'eetalil**

monja blanca   n. **saqihix**

monkey   n. **b'atz'**
              n. **max**

monocotyledonous seed
              n. **jun'al iyaj**

monologue   n. **aatinak-ib'**

monomial   n. **junajeetalb'irok**

month   n. **po**
              n. **pohol**

monthly pay   n. **po**

monument   n. **eetalil jalam u**
              n. **eetalil patz'e'k**

moods   n. **ru ch'oolej**

moody   adj. **yo rix**

moon   n. **po**

moon landing   n. **k'ochlaak sa'**
              li po

mop   n. **masleb'tz'ak**

Mopan   lang. **mopan**

moral (to a story)   n. **xcha'al**
              seeraq'

moral principle   n. **chaq'rab'**

morality   n. **oxloq'ilal**

more   adv. **chik**
              adv. **q'axal**
              adj. **toj**

more and more   adv phr. **rajlal**
              naab'al

morgue   n. **kamna'aj**
              n. **xna'aj kamenaq**

Mormon   adj. **aj mormon**

morning   n. **eq'la**

morning star   n. **kaqchahim**
              n. **kutan chahim**

morpheme   n. **k'ajyaab'aatin**

morphology
              n. **nawk'ajyaab'aatin**

mortgage
              n. **xchapliikroqruq'b'**

mosquito   n. **ch'een**
              n. **kok' utz'**
              n. **suq**
              n. **utz'**

moth   n. **max**

mother   n sd. **na'b'ej**

mother tongue   n. **xb'een**
              aatinob'aal

mother's brother   n. **ikan**

mother's milk   n. **xya'al tu'**

mother's sister   n. **xchaq'na' na'**

mother-in-law   n. **xna'**
              wechb'een

mother-in-law (of a man)   n. **xna'**
              ixaqil

mother-in-law (of a woman)
 n. **xna' b'eelom**

mother-of-pearl *n.* **jutz'un pemech**

motivate *v.* **k'utb'esink**

motivating
 adj. **waklesinelch'ool**

motor *n.* **ch'oolmetz'ew**
 n. **eek'metz'ew**
 n. **motor**
 n. **xch'ool ch'iich'**

motor oil *n.* **kax'olb' poych'iich'**
 n. **xkax'olb' poych'iich'**

motorboat *n.* **kaxjukub'**

motorcycle *n.* **kawaaya ch'iich'**
 n. **moot**
 n. **paattzim**

motorist *n.* **aj kawaayach'iich'**

motorized
 adj. **kawaayach'iich'i nb'il**

motto *n.* **k'a'uxlil**

mount *v.* **taqe'k**

mount a horse *v phr.* **taqe'k chi rix kawaay**

mountain *n.* **k'iche'**
 n. **tzuul**

mountain lion *n.* **kaqkoj**

mountain range *n.* **kelkookil tzuul**
 n. **tzoltzookiltzuul**

mountain ridge *n.* **kelkookil tzuul**
 n. **tzoltzookiltzuul**

mountain spirit *n.* **tzuultaq'a**

mouse *n.* **uch ch'o**
 n. **xa'nch'o**

mouse pad *n.* **ch'ohib'aal**

mousetrap *n.* **xra'al ch'o**

mouth *n.* **e**

mouthful *n.* **jun nub'uk**

move *v.* **eek'asink**

movie *n.* **eek'mu**
 n. **eek' jalam'uuch**
 n. **jalam'uuch**

movie screen *n agt.* **xlemul kaxmuhel**

movie theater *n.* **eetalmu**
 n. **ileb'aalmu**
 n. **rochochil ilob'aal mu**

moving picture *n.* **eek' jalam'uuch**

mow *v.* **setok**

MRI machine
 n. **tz'ub'ch'iich'b'il eek'ch'iich'**

much *adj.* **jwal**
 pron. **naab'al**
 pron. **xiikil**

muck *n.* **tz'ajn**

mud *n.* **sulul**

mug *n.* **xaar**

mugger *n agt.* **aj maq'onel**

mugging *n.* **maq'ok**

mulberry *n.* **tokan**

mule   *n.* **muul**

multicellular *adj.* **k'ilana'yu'am**

multicultural *adj.* **k'ilana'leb'**

multiculturality *n.* **k'iilayehom b'aanuhom**

multiethnic *adj.* **k'ilpoyanimil**

multilingual
         adj. **k'ila'aatinob'aal**

multiple *n.* **puktaal**

multiplication *n.* **puktahil'ajl** *n.* **puktasiil**

multiplication sign (x)
         n. **eetalpuk-ajl** *n.* **reetal puktasiil**

multiplication symbol (x)
         n. **eetalpuk-ajl** *n.* **reetal puktasiil**

multiplied *adj.* **puktasinb'il**

multiplied by *phr.* **puktasink chi**

multiplier *n.* **puktasinel**

multiply *v.* **puktasink** *v.* **puktasink ajl**

mumble *v.* **hasb'ak**

mummy *n.* **b'atxaqam**

mumps *n.* **b'uq' kux** *n.* **papeer**

municipality *n.* **teepalpoopol**

murder *v.* **kamsink** *n.* **kamsiik**

murderer *n agt.* **aj kamsinel**

murmurs *n.* **sak'ok aatin**

muscle tear *n.* **yu'uk ichmul**

muscles *n.* **tib'elej**

mush   *n.* **matz'** *n.* **saqjuy** *n.* **uq'un**

mushroom *n.* **okox**

music   *n.* **son** *n.* **wajb'ak**

music education *n.* **tijb'ab'ich**

music stand *n.* **xna'aj xhu b'ich**

musical group *n agt.* **ch'uut aj wajb'**

musical instrument *n.* **wajb'**

musical note *n.* **xyaab' b'ich**

musician *n agt.* **aj wajb'**

Muslim *n.* **musulman**

mustache *n.* **xmach u**

mute   *adj.* **mem**

mutual help *n.* **kamab'k**

my   *adj.* **in**

mysterious *adj.* **muqmuukil**

mysteriously
         adv. **muqb'aanunb'il**

mystery *n.* **muqmuukilal**

myth   *n.* **yoob'k'a'uxl**

N - n

nail   *n.* **chapleb'**
     n. **ixi'ij**
     n. **klaawx**
     n. **sub'inch'iich'**
     n. **t'ojom**

nail clippers *n.* **setleb' ixi'ij**

nail polish *n.* **yulb'ilb'on**

naive   *adj.* **maak'a' xna'leb' naxk'ut rib'**

naked   *adj.* **mich'mo**
     adj. **moq'mo**
     adj. **t'urt'u**
     adj. **t'ust'u**
     adj. **yach'yo**

nakedness *n.* **t'usam**

name   *n.* **k'ab'a'**
     n sd. **k'ab'a'ej**
     v. **k'ab'a'ink**
     v. **xaqab'ank**

name of recipient *n.* **xk'ab'a' li taak'ulu'q re**

name of sender *n.* **xk'ab'a' li nataqlan re**

nameplate *n.* **eetalil**

namesake *n.* **eeqaj**
     n. **tz'ob'ay**

nametag *n.* **ch'ina eetalil**

nape of the neck *n.* **rix ja'aj**
     n. **rix kux**

napkin   *n.* **lanb'alwa**
     n. **lanleb'**
     n. **xt'ikrul wa**

narcotic *n.* **kaanilb'an**

narrate *v.* **seeraq'ik**

narrate (and divulge something) *v.* **ab'iresink**

narration *n.* **yehom**

narrator *n agt.* **aj yehonel**

narrow *adj.* **kach'in ru**
     adj. **kok' ru**
     adj. **laatz'**

nasal   *n.* **ujinb'ilyaab'**

nasal mucus *n.* **sam**

nasalization *n.* **ujinb'ilyaab'**

national identity *n.* **xtenamitil ilob'**

national palace *n.* **rochochil awa'b'ejink**

nationality *n.* **xtenamitil**

native country *n.* **ch'och'el**

Natividad *nick.* **Nat**

natural resources *n.* **eechej ch'och'**
     n. **eechej che'k'aam**
     n. **rawimal ch'och'**

natural sciences *n.* **tzolomilchoxach'och'**

naturally *adv.* **jo'kan**
　　　　　adv. **jo' chanru**

nature *n.* **choxach'och'**

naughty *adj.* **xulil**
　　　　　adj. **xul aj al**

navel *n.* **ch'up**

navigator *n agt.* **aj b'ehenel**

navy blue *adj.* **rax moyin**

near *adj.* **nach'**
　　　adv phr. **nach' xk'atq**
　　　adj. **rik'in**

nearly *adv phr.* **kach'in chik (ma)**

nebulizer *n.* **puutz'leb'aal**

nebulous galaxy *n.* **choqlil tzoqchahim**

necessity *n.* **rajb'al ru**

neck *n.* **ja'aj**
　　　n. **kux**

necklace *n.* **q'ol**

necktie *n.* **b'eq**
　　　　n. **yutkux**

need *n.* **rajb'al ru**

needle *n.* **kuux**

needle (hypodermic)
　　　　n. **jutz'kutleb'**

needle (of a tree) *n.* **xaqchaj**

needle (sewing) *n.* **b'ekleb' k'ix**
　　　　n. **jutz'b'ojleb'**

negate *v.* **q'etok**

negation particle *part.* **ma**

negative *adj.* **q'etq'etil**
　　　　　adj. **yiib'na'leb'**

negative electric charge
　　　　n. **xsak'om tiikil kaxlanxaml**

neighbor *n.* **as itz'in**
　　　　　n. **echkab'al**

neighborhood *n.* **teep**
　　　　　　n. **xteepal tenamit**

neither *conj.* **chi moko**

neologism *n.* **ak'aatin**
　　　　　n. **yoob'aal aatin**

nephew *n.* **ral chaq'na'**
　　　　n. **ral we**

Neptune *n.* **xwaqxaq ralsaq'e**

nerve *n.* **ich'mej**

nerve tissue *n.* **ch'ut-eek' cha'al**

nervous system *n.* **ch'uut ich'mul**

nest *v.* **sokink**
　　　n. **sok xul**
　　　n. **suk**

net *n.* **champa**
　　n. **kelkookil soq'**
　　n. **keelsoq'**

net bag *n.* **soq'**

nettle *n.* **la**
　　　　n. **panchool**

neuron *n.* **xyihil xk'ub'lal ich'mulej**

neutron star *n.* **kehil chahim**

never   *adv phr.* **ma jun wa**
           adv. **maajaruj**
           adv. **maajoq'e**

nevertheless   *conj.* **ab'anan**

new   *adj.* **ak'il**
           adj. **ak'**

new moon   *n.* **al po**

news   *n.* **yehol'esilal**

newspaper *n.* **b'anb'alil esil**
           n. **esilhu**
           n. **nawil hu**
           n. **periood**
           n. **tz'iib'anb'il esil**
           n. **xhuhul esil**

newspaper boy   *n agt.* **aj jek'ol preens**

newsprint *n.* **nut'leb'hu**

next   *adj.* **sa' jun chik**

next month   *n.* **li po chalk re**

next to   *prep.* **chi xk'atq**
           prep. **nach' rik'in**

next week   *adv phr.* **chi ru li xamaan chalk re**

next year   *n.* **li hab' chalk re**

nice to meet you   *phr.* **nasaho inch'ool xnawb'al aawu**

nickel   *n.* **oob' senta**

nickname   *n.* **yoob'k'ab'a'**

niece   *n.* **ralal ikan**
           n. **ral chaq'na'**
           n. **xrab'in we**

niece (from a younger sibling)
           n. **xrabin iitz'in**

niece (from an older sibling)
           n. **xrab'in as**

night   *n.* **chi q'eq**
           n. **q'ojyin**

night stand   *n.* **ch'ina meex warib'aal**

night table   *n.* **ch'ina meex**
           n. **ch'ina meex warib'aal**

nightclub   *n.* **xajleb'aal**

nightgown   *n.* **jur aq'**

nine   *num.* **(9.) b'eleeb'**

nineteen   *num.* **(19.) b'eleelaju**

nineteenth   *num.* **(19th.) xb'ele'lajuil**

ninetieth   *num.* **(90th.) xlajee ro'k'aalil**

ninety   *num.* **(90.) lajeb' ro'k'aal**

ninety-eight   *num.* **(98.) waqxaqlaju ro'k'aal**

ninety-five   *num.* **(95.) o'laju ro'k'aal**

ninety-four   *num.* **(94.) kaalaju ro'k'aal**

ninety-nine   *num.* **(99.) b'elelaju ro'k'aal**

ninety-one   *num.* **(91.) junlaju ro'k'aal**

ninety-seven   *num.* **(97.) wuqlaju ro'k'aal**

ninety-six   *num.* **(96.) waqlaju ro'k'aal**

ninety-three *num.* **(93.) oxlaju ro'k'aal**

ninety-two *num.* **(92.) kab'laju ro'k'aal**

ninth *num.* **(9th.) xb'elee**

nipple *n.* **ru'uj tu'**

nit *n.* **k'ot uk'**

nitrate *n.* **ratz'amilq'olch'iich'**

nitroglycerine *n.* **ha'ilyol**

no *adv.* **i'**
   adv. **ink'a'**
   adv phr. **moko [ ] ta**

no entry *phr.* **maak'a' nume'k**

no one *pron.* **maa'ani**

noble *adj.* **chaab'il xch'ool**

nod off *v.* **xiiqank**

noise *n.* **eek'ank**
   n. **xkuxb'il**
   n. **yaab'**

noisy *adj.* **xik' naxye**

nominate *v.* **xaqab'ank**

nonagon *n.* **b'eleexuk**

nonperishable *n.* **yo'yookilal**

noodles *n.* **tayarin**

noon *n.* **tuqtu waleb'**

norm *n.* **xtz'iib'ul**

north *n.* **releb' iq'**

North America *n.* **xjolom ab'yayala**
   n. **xye ab'yayala**

north pole *n.* **xtaqe'qil ruuchich'och'**

nose *n.* **u'uj**
   n. **u'ujej**

nostril *n.* **sa' u'uj**

nosy *adj.* **nakujkut**

not *adv.* **ink'a'**
   adv phr. **moko [ ] ta**

not at all *phr.* **maak'a'**

not bad *phr.* **wan b'ayaq rusilal**

not even *adv phr.* **ma chan naxye**

not guilty *adj.* **maak'a' xmaak**

not so well *phr.* **ink'a' jwal us**

not yet *adv.* **maaji'**

notch *v phr.* **isink sa' re che'**

note *n.* **esilhu**
   n. **xyaab' b'ich**

notebook *n.* **tz'iib'leb'aalhu**

nothing *pron.* **maajun**
   pron. **maak'a'**
   pron. **maalay**
   pron. **yal ta k'a'**

nothing at all *adv phr.* **maak'a' chi junwaakaj**

nothing more *phr.* **ka'aj wi a'an**

nothing of the kind *adv phr.* **moko a'an ta**

notice *n.* **esilal**
   v phr. **k'ehok eetal**

noun *n.* **k'ab'a'atq**
   n. **k'ab'a'ej**

nova   *n.* **ak'chahim**

November   *n.* **nowyemr**
           n. **xjunlajuhilpo**

now   *adv.* **anaqwan**

nowadays   *n.* **anaqwan q'e kutan**

nowhere   *adv.* **maab'ar**

nucleus   *n.* **xch'ool**
           n. **xyich'ool xna'yu'am**

number   *n.* **ajl**
           n. **rajlil**

numeracy   *n.* **nawajlil**

numeral   *n.* **ajl**

numeration *n.* **ajlil**

numerator *n.* **jek'iil**

nun   *n.* **mayr**
           n. **rixkil paab'aal**

nurse   *n agt.* **aj ilolyaj**
           n agt. **aj tenq' re b'anok**
           v. **tu'resink**
           n agt. **xtenq' aj b'anonel**

nursing home   *n.* **xna'ajeb' cheek**

nut   *n.* **nwes**

nut (fastener) *n.* **jit'leb'**
           n. **kotoxch'iich'**

nylon   *n.* **nayl**

O - o

oak   *n.* **arkute'**
           n. **ji**

oar   *n.* **kanaleet**
           n. **paleet**

oasis   *n.* **hilob'aal k'iche'**

oath   *n.* **somenkil**
           n. **sumenk aatin**

obedient   *adj.* **napaab'an**

obey   *v.* **ab'ink**
           v. **paab'ank**

object of a suitor's affection
           n. **payom**

objective *n.* **ahom**

obligation *n.* **teneb'aal**

obscenity *n.* **tz'i'ej aatin**

obscure   *adj.* **ink'a' ch'olch'o**

observe   *v.* **ka'yank**
           v phr. **k'ehok eetal**

obsidian   *n.* **xmar choxa**
           n. **xmaal kaaq**

obstetrician   *n agt.* **aj xokonel**

obstetrics *n.* **nawxokok**

obstinate *adj.* **jip**

occlusive *n.* **tz'apyaab'**

occupation *n.* **laatz'al**

ocean   *n.* **palaw**
           n. **xnimalpalaw**

octagon *n.* **waqxaqxuk**

octahedron *n.* **waqxaqxuk-u**

October *n.* **oktuuwr**
  n. **xlajehilpo**

octopus *n.* **moch'kar**

odd numbers *n.* **maasumal'ajl**

of *prep.* **re**

of course *phr.* **usaq b'i'**

of course not *phr.* **ink'a' b'i'**

offended *adj.* **hob'il**

offense *n.* **nimlamaak**

offensive words *n.* **sak'ok aatin**

offer *v.* **yeechi'ink**

office *n.* **rochochilmolam**
  n. **tz'iib'leb'aal**

often *adv phr.* **kok'atq xsa'**
  adv. **kok'sa'**

oil *n.* **aseet**
  n. **olb'**
  n. **olb'il b'an**
  n. **q'olch'och'**
  n. **xkax'olb' poych'iich'**
  n. **yolq'em**

oil filter *n.* **tz'ilb'akax'olb'**
  n. **tz'ileb' olb'**

ointment *n.* **b'anol u**
  n. **b'iqb'ilb'an**
  n. **olb'il b'an**
  n. **pomaat**
  n. **sununkil b'an**
  n. **t'oq't'ookil b'an**
  n. **uq'unil b'an**

old *adj.* **junxil**
  adj. **mama'**
  adj. **najter**
  adj. **qeel**
  adj. **q'eel**
  adj. **tiix**

old man *n.* **tiix**

old woman *n.* **tiix**

olden days *n.* **najter q'e kutan**

older sibling *n sd.* **anab'ej**
  n sd. **asb'ej**
  n sd. **chaq'na'b'ej**

older sister *n.* **chaq'na'**

olive *n.* **asetuun**

omen *n.* **xq'ehinkil**

on parole *adj.* **wank sa' ilb'il**

on probation *adj.* **wank sa' ilb'il**

on top *prep.* **sa' xb'een**

on trial *adj.* **wank sa' raqb'a aatin**

once *adv.* **junsut**
  adv. **junwa**

once more *adv phr.* **jun sut chik**

oncilla *n.* **k'amb'olay**

one *num.* **(1.) jun**

one cent *n.* **jun senta**

one fourth *n.* **jun xka**

one hundred *n.* **(100.) o'k'aal**

one hundred quetzals *n.* **o'k'aal ketzal**

one million *n.* **kiib' oq'ob' xkab' xchuy**

one more   *adv.* **jun chik**

one time   *adv.* **junwa**

onion   *n.* **seb'ooy**
     n. **tuxim**

only   *adj.* **ka' aj wi'**
    adj. **yal**

only child *n.* **junaatal alalb'ej**

only one *adj.* **jun aj wi'**

onomatopoeia *n.* **yaab'k'ab'a'il**

onwards *adv.* **chi ru**

open   *v.* **jaqok**
    adj. **pahpo**
    v. **tehok**
    adj. **tehto**

open syllable *n.* **jap yahiil**

opener *n.* **jaqleb'**
    n. **teeleb'**

opening *n.* **pahal**
    n. **xhopolal**

operating system *n.* **xk'ub'lal xsa'**

operating table *n.* **xmesul cho'ok**

operation *n.* **cho'ok**

opine *v phr.* **aatinak chi rix**

opossum *n.* **aj b'oox uch**
    n. **aj uch**
    n. **b'aqlaq xul**

opportunity *n.* **okenk**

opposite *prep.* **xjunpak'alil (li...)**

optic nerve *n.* **eek'al uhej**

optimism *n.* **kawil ch'ool**

or   *conj.* **malaj**
    conj. **malaj ut**

oral rehydration solution
    n. **ich'mulb'an**
    n. **k'uub'anb'il b'an**
    n. **uk'metz'ewilb'an**

orange *adj.* **chiin**
    n. **chiin**
    adj. **kaqiq'an**
    adj. **q'an kaqin**

orange juice *n.* **xya'al chiin**

orange tree *n.* **chiin**

orbit *n.* **suutilal**
    n. **xb'e'chahim**
    n. **xb'e ruuchich'och'**

orchard *n.* **kok'awinq**
    n. **xna'aj kok'awinq**

order *v.* **ch'olob'ank**
    n. **ruq'b'chaq'rab'**
    n. **taqlahom**
    v. **taqlank**
    v. **tusub'ank**
    v. **tusuk**

ordinal number *n.* **ch'ol ajl**
    n. **tusb'a'ajl**

ordinary *adj.* **chaq re ru**

oregano *n.* **oreek**

organ *n.* **cha'al**
    n. **tz'uywajb'**

organelle *n.* **kok'cha'al**

organized *adj.* **ch'olch'o nak'anjelak**
    adj. **tustu ru**
    adj. **tusul**

organizer *n agt.* **aj b'uub'anel**

organs   *n.* **cha'alil**

orientation   *n.* **ch'olna'leb'**

origin   *n.* **roqel**
    n. **xtiklajik**

orphan   *n.* **neb'a'**

ORS   *n.* **ich'mulb'an**
    n. **k'uub'anb'il b'an**
    n. **uk'metz'ewilb'an**

orthodontist   *n agt.* **aj tiikob'resinel'uuch-e**

orthography   *n.* **nawtz'iib'ak**
    n. **tuqlaaltz'iib'**
    n. **tuqtutz'iib'**

ostrich   *n.* **najtil t'uru' ak'ach**

other   *adj.* **jalan**

other people's   *adj.* **ab'l**

otoscope   *n.* **kaxkukay**
    n. **kaxlan xam**

ounce   *n.* **ons**

our abandoned house   *phr.* **qapo'lem**

our ruins   *phr.* **qapo'lem**

our rustic abode   *phr.* **qapo'lem**

out of order   *phr.* **moko us ta**

outcome   *n.* **xraqik**

outlet   *n.* **chapleb'metz'ew**
    n. **nub'leb'aal**
    n. **ruq'il**

outlet (electrical)   *n.* **chapleb' saqen**

outrigger   *n.* **jukub'**

outside   *prep.* **chi rix**

outskirts   *n.* **re tenamit**

outstanding   *adj.* **us'elk**

oval   *adj.* **b'aq'**
    n. **b'aq'al**
    adj. **b'aq'b'o**

ovary   *n.* **xn'aj alaal**

oven   *n.* **joor**
    n. **pomleb'aal**

oven vent   *n.* **rokeb'l sib'**

over   *prep.* **sa' xb'een**

over there   *adv phr.* **sa' a'an**
    adv phr. **toj le'**

overcast   *adj.* **muqb'il**

overcoat   *n.* **jut aq'**
    n. **jut t'ikr**

overhead projector
    n. **kutleb'mu**
    n. **repolmu**
    n. **repom**

overtake   *v.* **q'axok**

owe   *v.* **k'asok**

owl   *n.* **joob'aq**
    n. **warom**

own   *v.* **eechanink**

owned   *adj.* **wan aj eechal re**

ox   *n.* **b'ooyx**
    n. **kapuninb'il wakax**
    n. **kapunwakax**
    n. **pakun wakax**

oxidation   *n.* **mo'**

oxidize   *v.* **mo'onk**

oxygen *n.* **b'ook-iq'**
  n. **b'ookol**
  n. **xb'ook iq**

oxygen tank *n.* **xna'aj iq'**

oxygenation *n.* **xb'ookil-iq'**

ozone *n.* **jal'iq'**

P - p

Pablo *nick.* **Lo**

Pacific Ocean *n.* **tuulan palaw**

pacifist *n agt.* **aj tuqtuukilnel**

pack *v.* **b'atok**

package *n.* **ab'en**

packet *n.* **k'amom**

paddle *n.* **kojl**
  n. **paleet**

paddock *n.* **potreer**

padlock *n.* **nat'leb' okeb'aal**

page number *n.* **rajlil**

pail *n.* **b'oot**
  n. **ch'inkumb'**

pain *n.* **q'oq**
  n. **rahil**
  n. **rahilal**

painful *adj.* **ra**

painkiller *n.* **re xkotzb'al xrahil**
  n. **re xkub'sinkil xrahil**

paint *n.* **b'on**
  v. **b'onok**

paintbrush *n.* **b'onleb'**

painted face *n.* **b'onb'il u**

painted house *n.* **b'onb'il ochoch**

painter *n agt.* **aj b'ononel**

paintgun *n.* **puub'b'on**

painting *n.* **b'omb'il eetalil**
  n. **kaaxukuut**

pair *n.* **alab'**
  n. **jun suumal**
  n. **sumal**

palace *n.* **rochochil'awab'ej**

palatal *n.* **xb'een'e yaab'**

palate *n.* **xb'een'e**

pale *adj.* **saqb'etin**
  adj. **saqkirin**

Paleozoic era *n.* **rox q'ekutan**

pall *n.* **paqleb'**

palladium *n.* **saqmuch'iich'**

pallbearer *n agt.* **aj iiqanel**

pallor *n.* **saqb'et**

palm (of the hand) *n.* **sa' uq'**
  n. **xsa' uq'b'**

palm tree *n.* **b'ob'**
  n. **kala'**
  n. **xeek'**

pamphlet *n.* **b'asb'il tasalhu**

pan   *n.* **k'ileb'aal**
         n. **xartin**

pancreas *n.* **maal**

pans   *n.* **chiqleb'**

pant cuff *n.* **xb'asalal**

pant leg *n.* **roq wex**

panther *n.* **aj b'oob'**
         n. **hix**

panties *n.* **kok' aq' re ixq**

pantry   *n.* **xna'aj tzakahemq**

pants   *n.* **wex**

panty   *n.* **yach'**

papaya   *n.* **putul**

paper   *n.* **hu**
         n. **huhil**

paper bag *n.* **ch'ina huhiljelool**

paper clip *n.* **chapleb'hu**
           n. **nat'leb'hu**

paper collator *n.* **tusleb'hu**

paper punch *n.* **hopleb'hu**

paper roll *n.* **b'otb'il hu**

paper towel dispenser
         n. **xche'el li b'otb'il hu**

papyrus *n.* **xche'elhu**

parable *n.* **jaljookil ru aatin**

parabola *n.* **q'ot-eetalil**

parade   *v phr.* **b'eek chi tustu**
         n. **tusilb'eek**

paradigm *n.* **chaab'ilob'resink**

paradise *n.* **choxahil wank**

paragraph *n.* **ch'ol'aatin**
          n. **raqalk'a'uxl**

parakeet *n.* **puyuch'**

parallel line *n.* **laq'juch'**
              n. **laq'lookil juch'**

paralytic *n.* **sik**

paralyzed *adj.* **sik**

paramedic *n agt.* **aj ilom yaj**

paraphrase *v.* **ch'ool'aatin**
           n. **yu'yuukil k'a'uxl**

parasol *n.* **mu**

parasympathetic autonomic
    nervous system
         n. **xk'ub'lal ich'mul ak re**

parcel   *n.* **ab'en**
         n. **k'amb'il esilhu**

pardon me *phr.* **chinaakuy**

parentheses *n.* **k'ontz'uq**
            n. **nimaljuch'**
            n. **nimaljuch'**

parents *n.* **yuwa'b'ejeb'**

parents (my) *n.* **inna' inyuwa'**

parents-in-law *n.* **hi'om e**
               n. **xyuwa' b'eelomej**
               n. **xyuwa' ixaqilb'ej**

park   *n.* **ajsib'aal u**
         n. **ja'leb'aal'u**
         n. **ja'leb'ch'ool**

parking lot
         n. **hiltasib'aalch'iich'**

parking meter *n.* **xhilob'aal b'eleb'aalch'iich'**

parrot   *n.* **chocho'**
          n. **loor**

parsley   *n.* **perejil**

part   *n.* **ch'ol**
          n. **raqal**
          n. **teep**
          n. **xjachalal**

particle *n.* **k'aj'aatin**
          n. **k'ajtz'iib'**

particle physics *n.* **k'aj nawcha'al**

partner   *n.* **echaalal**
          n. **komon**

partridge *n.* **kormaach**

parts of speech *n.* **xraqilal li aatinob'aal**

party   *n.* **nimq'e**
          v. **nimq'ehink**

pass   *v.* **nume'k**
          v. **q'axok**

pass gas *v.* **kisik**

passage   *n.* **numleb'aal**

passenger *n agt.* **aj b'eenel**

passer-by *n agt.* **aj b'e**

passion   *n.* **anchal xch'ool**

passive   *adj.* **ink'a' na'oken**

passive voice *n.* **nume'k'uluk**

passport *n.* **numilhu**

past tense *n.* **numenaqil'uxk**

pasta   *n.* **paast**

pastor   *n.* **pastor**

pastor (animals) *n.* **aj ilolketomq**

pastor (religious) *n agt.* **aj k'ehol kuult**

pasture   *n.* **koral wakax**
          n. **potreer**
          n. **rax ch'och'**
          n. **wa'lem**

patch   *n.* **letzb'il b'an**

path   *n.* **ch'ina b'e**
          n. **jalb'e**
          n. **numleb'aal**
          n. **ruqb'e**

pathological *adj.* **xyajelil**

pathology *n.* **nawyajel**

patient   *n.* **yaj**

patient chart *n.* **eetalil yaj**

patio   *n.* **neb'a**

patriotic *adj.* **aj raholtenamit**

patriotic symbols *n.* **reetaltenamit**

patrol   *n.* **b'eetak'aak'alenel**
          v. **b'eetak'aak'alenk**

patronym *n.* **xsum k'ab'a'ej**

pattern   *n.* **reetalil**

pattern (clothing) *n.* **ru aq'**

pavement *n.* **tz'akalb'e**

paw   *n.* **roq**

pay   *v.* **tojok**

payment plan *n.* **xhuhil tojok**

payphone *n.* **tojb'il b'oqleb'**

payroll   *n.* **xhuhil tojok**

PC   *n.* **ulul ch'iich'**

pea   *n.* **arb'eej**
            n. **kaxche'kenq'**

peace   *n.* **sahil ch'oolej**
            n. **tuqtuukilal**

peaceful   *adj.* **q'un xch'ool**
            adj. **tuulan**

peach   *n.* **turans**
            adj. **turans**

peach fuzz *n.* **q'ol is**

peacock   *n.* **tzo' pu'**

peak   *n.* **ru'uj tzuul**
            n. **xb'een tzuul**

peanut   *n.* **maniiy**

pear   *n.* **peer**
            n. **raxki'**

pearl   *n.* **q'ol**

peas   *n.* **arb'eej**
            n. **kaxche'kenq'**

peasant   *n agt.* **aj se' k'al**

pedagogue   *n agt.* **aj nawtijok**

pedagogy   *n.* **nawtijok**

pedal   *v phr.* **ek'asink chi oq**
            n. **leplepb'aal**
            v. **perperink**
            n. **tiikisib'aal**

pedestrian *n agt.* **aj b'eenel**
            n agt. **aj numelb'e**

Pedro   *nick.* **Lu'**

pee   *v.* **chu'uk**

peel   *v.* **b'ich'ok**
            v. **jotzok**
            v phr. **mich'ok ix**

peeler   *n.* **jotzleb'**

peep   *v.* **yaab'ak**

peg   *n.* **kapoteer**
            n. **lokoch**
            n. **lukub'al**

pegboard   *n.* **lukleb'**

pen   *n.* **ha'il tz'iib'leb'**
            n. **kik' tz'iib'**
            n. **k'uk'umtz'iib'**
            n. **tz'iib'leb'**
            n. **tz'iib'leb'on**

penal code *n.* **raschaq'rab' chi
            rix tojb'amaak**

penalty   *n.* **tojleb'aal maak**

pencil   *n.* **tz'iib'leb' che'**

pencil sharpener *n.* **jotzleb'
            tz'iib'leb' che'**

penguin   *n.* **kaxpatz xul**

penicillin *n.* **chunilb'an**

peninsula   *n.* **ru'uj ch'och'**
            n. **ruq'b'ich'och'**

penis   *n.* **b'irich**
            n. **kun**
            n. **kunutz'**
            n. **pirich**
            n. **pur**
            n. **tz'ejwal**
            n. **tz'ik**
            n. **xche'el ab'aj**

penitentiary system
            n. **xk'uub'laltojb'ama
            ak**

penny   *n.* **jun senta**

pentagon   *n.* **o'xukuut**

penultimate   *adj.* **rub'elal xraqik**

people   *n.* **kristian**
    n. **poyanam**
    n. **tenamitil**

pepper   *n.* **kaxlan q'een**
    n. **pens**

pepper shaker   *n.* **xna'aj k'aj pens**

peppercorn   *n.* **t'orol pens**

per capita income   *n.* **junq eechej**

perform   *v.* **k'utb'esink**

perform rituals   *v.* **wa'tesink**

perfume   *n.* **jaq'b'ab'**
    n. **sunob'l**
    n. **sununkil b'ook**

perhaps   *adv.* **maare**
    adv. **tana**

period   *n.* **raqleltz'uq**
    n. **raqtz'uq**
    n. **tiiqeltz'uq**
    n. **tz'uq**

permanently open   *adj.* **jaqam**

permit   *v.* **k'ehok**

perpendicular line   *n.* **raqro juch'**

person   *n.* **kristian**
    n. **poyanam**

personal values   *n.* **rehil loq'alil**

perspire   *v.* **tiqob'ak**

perymenium tuerkheimii   *n.* **tza'aj**

pessimism   *n.* **k'ahil ch'oolej**

pessimistic   *adj.* **aj sik'onel xyib'al ru**

pestle   *n.* **ruq' ka'**

petroleum   *n.* **petrool**
    n. **q'olch'och'**

Petrona   *nick.* **Pet**

petticoat   *n.* **xta-uuq**

petty   *adj.* **aj pix**

pew   *n.* **hilaal**

pharmacist   *n agt.* **aj k'ayinel b'an**

pharmacologist   *n agt.* **aj nawb'an**

pharmacy   *n.* **k'ayib'aal b'an**
    n. **loq'leb'aal b'an**

pheasant   *n.* **chakmut**

philosopher   *n agt.* **aj tz'ilom k'a'uxl**

philosophically   *adv.* **xe'nawomil**

philosophy   *n.* **xe'nawom**

phone   *n.* **aatinob'aal ch'iich'**
    n. **b'oqleb'**
    n. **b'oqleb'aal**
    n. **b'oqleb'aal ch'iich'**
    n. **teleef**

phone card   *n.* **tarjeet re b'oqleb'**

phone charger   *n.* **metz'ewib'aalb'oqleb'**

phone line   *n.* **xk'aamal b'oqleb'aal**

phone number *n.* **rajlil b'oqleb'**

phoneme *n.* **ch'oolyaab'**

phonetics *n.* **yaab'aatin**
    n. **yaab' kux**

photo *n.* **jalam'uuch**

photo album
    n. **k'uuleb'jalam'uuch**

photocopier *n.* **jalam'uuchleb'**
    n. **jalam'uuchleb'aal ch'iich'**
    n. **puktasib'aalhu**

photocopy *v.* **jalam'uuchink**
    n. **jalam'uuchu**

photographer *n agt.* **aj isihom jalam'uuch**

photosynthesis *n.* **xrajikraxil**

phrase *n.* **kok'raq aatin**
    n. **raqal'aatin**

physical education
    n. **q'ochleb'tzolom**
    n. **tijb'a'ajsiil**

physician *n agt.* **aj b'anonel**
    n. **loktor**

physics *n.* **nawcha'al**

piano *n.* **meexwajb'**

picante sauce *n.* **putz'b'il pix ik**

pick up *v.* **xokok**

pickaxe *n.* **pikleb'**

pickpocket *n agt.* **aj elq' karteer**

pickup truck *n.* **ch'ina iiqob'aal ch'iich'**

picture *n.* **jalam u**

piece *n.* **ch'iil**
    n. **ch'otolal**
    n. **ch'uyul**
    n. **jachal**
    n. **tolche'**
    n. **wechelal**

pig *n.* **aaq**
    n. **kuy**

pigeon *n.* **mukuy**

piggy bank *n.* **k'ohaal**

pigpen *n.* **rochoch aaq**

pile up *v.* **b'uyuxink**

pilgrim *n agt.* **aj b'e**

pill *n.* **ch'ina b'an**
    n. **nuq'b'ilb'an**
    n. **pastiiy**

pillar *n.* **roqechal xmukab'l**

pillow *n.* **sok jolom**

pillowcase *n.* **rix sok jolom**

pilot *n agt.* **aj b'eresinelch'iich'**
    n agt. **aj ch'e'ol ch'iich'**

pimple *n.* **tzelek**

pin *n.* **kok' kuux**
    n. **xukub'k'ix**

pin cushion *n.* **xna'aj kuux**

pincer *n.* **k'uxch'iich'**
    n. **yax**

pinch *v.* **ch'epok**
    v. **ch'uyuk**
    v. **jochok**
    v. **xeb'ok**

pine *n.* **chaj**

pineapple   *n.* **ch'op**

pineapple juice   *n.* **xya'al ch'op**

pink   *adj.* **kaq saqin**
    adj. **saqikaq**

pinkie finger   *n.* **xch'i'pul uq'mej**

pinwheel   *n.* **ch'ina ral simaj**

pipe   *n.* **kachiimp**

pipe (metal)   *n.* **simb'ch'iich'**

pipe (plastic)   *n.* **simb'plaast**

piss   *v.* **chu'uk**

pistol   *n.* **kok' puub'**

pit   *n.* **jul**

pitcher   *n.* **puk'xaar**
    n. **xaar**

pitchfork   *n.* **orkeet**
    n. **rastriiy**

pituitary gland   *n.* **k'uub'aal sam**

pity   *n.* **toq'ob'al u**

pizza   *n.* **piitza**

piñata   *n.* **puk'um**
    n. **uutz'u'ujinb'il saa'us**

place   *v.* **kanab'ank**
    v. **k'ehok**
    n. **na'aj**
    n. **na'ajej**

place name   *n.* **k'ab'a'na'jej**

placenta   *n.* **riiqk'uula'al**

plain   *n.* **helo**
    n. **roq taq'a**
    n. **taq'a**

plaintiff   *n.* **jitonel**

plait   *v.* **kemok**
    n. **tz'uluk**

plan   *n.* **tusk'anjel**
    v. **tusk'anjelank**

plane   *n.* **ji'leb'che'**
    v. **ji'ok**

plane figures   *n.* **helhookil eetalilatq**

plane ticket   *n.* **xhuhil purik**

planet   *n.* **nimlachahim**
    n. **ralsaq'e**
    n. **xtumb'choxa**

plant   *n.* **awinq**
    v. **awok**

plantain   *n.* **ch'ol tul**
    n. **saqi tul**
    n. **sayi'**

plantain chip   *n.* **k'orechtul**

plantation   *n.* **loq'b'ilch'och'**

planted   *adj.* **awo**

plants   *n.* **kok' che'**

plaque   *n.* **sol**

plaster   *n.* **yees**

plastic   *n.* **plastiik**

plastic arts   *n.* **tzoljalam'uuch'ink**

plastic bag   *n.* **kaxtzuychampa**

plastic tube   *n.* **hompaq'**

plate   *n.* **ch'och' sek'**
    n. **helhokil sek'**
    n. **wa'leb' sek'**

platform *n.* **taqleb'**
    n. **taqleb'aal**

play (instruments) *v.* **toch'ok**

play bill *n.* **eetalil hu**

play instruments *v.* **wajb'ak**

play sports *v phr.* **ajsink u li tib'elej**

play the flute *v.* **xolb'ak**
    v. **xolib'k**

playful *adj.* **aj b'atz'unel**

playground *n.* **neb'aal**

playing field *n.* **b'atz'ub'aal**
    n. **jomal**

plaza *n.* **xnimal neb'aal**

plead *v.* **patz'ok**

plead guilty *v phr.* **yehok maak**

please *phr.* **b'aanu usilal**
    v phr. **sahob'resink ch'ool**

please say that again *phr.* **b'aanu ye jun sutaq chik**

please speak slowly *phr.* **b'aanu usilal aatinan chi timil**

please write it down *phr.* **b'aanu usilal tz'iib'a**

pleased *adj.* **k'ojla xch'ool**

pleasing *adj.* **sa**

pleasure *n.* **sahilank**

pleat *n.* **xtusb'al xsa'**

pledge of allegiance *n.* **xtij tenamit**

pliers *n.* **k'atzleb'**
    n. **k'uxch'iich'**
    n. **yaxch'iich'**

plot *n.* **waqlajuk'aam**
    n. **xoral**

plowed land *n.* **cho'leb' ch'och'**

plug *n.* **chapleb'metz'ew**
    n. **chapleb' saqen**
    n. **nub'leb'aal**

plum *n.* **ab'aal**
    n. **sirweel**

plumb *n.* **alalch'iich'**
    n. **tiikalxaqab'aal**

plumb line *n.* **jiileb'**

plumber *n agt.* **aj letzolsimb'ha'**
    n agt. **aj yiib'om ha'**

plunder *v.* **min'isink**
    v. **minyamtesink**

plural *adj.* **k'ihalatq**

pluralization particle *part.* **eb'**

pluricellular *adj.* **k'ilana'yu'am**

plus sign (+) *n.* **reetaltamok-ajl**
    n. **reetal molam ajl**

plush toy *n.* **kaxtzukxul**

Pluto *n.* **xb'ele' ralsaq'e**

PO Box *n.* **xkaxonil esilhu**

pocket *n.* **b'oox**

poem *n.* **uutz'u'jinb'il aatin**

poet *n agt.* **aj uutz'u'ujinel aatin**

poetry *n.* **uutz'u'jinb'iltz'iib'**

poetry collection *n.* **xhuhul uutz'u'jinb'il aatin**

point   *v.* **jayalink**
            n. **tz'uq**

pointed   *adj.* **jutz'**
            adj. **jutz' ru'uj**
            adj. **q'es**

poison   *v phr.* **kamsink chi uk'b'il**
            n. **may**

pole   *n.* **oqech**

police   *n agt.* **aj chaponel**
            n agt. **aj iloltenamit**
            n agt. **aj k'aak'alenel**

police car *n.* **k'aak'aleb'aal ch'iich'**

police officer *n agt.* **aj chaponel**
            n agt. **aj iloltenamit**
            n agt. **aj k'aak'alenel**

police station *n.* **xna'aj aj ilol tenamit**

policeman   *n agt.* **aj chaponel**
            n agt. **aj iloltenamit**
            n agt. **aj k'aak'alenel**

policeman's belt *n.* **xk'aamal sa' aj puub'**

policy   *n.* **xna'leb'il**

polio   *n.* **luqaak**

polish   *v.* **mesok**

political party *n.* **ch'uut awab'ejilal**

politician *n agt.* **aj yalol u chi awab'ejink**

pollen   *n.* **poqsiyaal**

pollination *n.* **poqsiyajink**

polyglot   *n agt.* **aj ka'aatin**
            n agt. **aj k'ila'aatin**

polygon   *n.* **k'ila'u**

polynomial *n.* **k'ila eetalb'irok**

polysyllable *n.* **k'ilayehiil**

pomade   *n.* **yulb'ilb'an**

pomegranate *n.* **kranaa**

poncho   *n.* **isb'**

pond   *n.* **pumpuukil ha'**

ponder   *v.* **na'leb'ak**

pony   *n.* **ch'ina kawaay**

pool   *n.* **atib'aal**
            n. **numxib'aal**

poor   *adj.* **kaqcha**
            adj. **neb'a'**
            adj. **toq'ob' ru**

poorly   *adv phr.* **moko chaab'il ta**

popcorn   *n.* **moqx**

pope   *n.* **paap**

poppy   *n.* **amapool**

Popti [aka Jakaltek] *lang.* **popti**

Poqomam   *lang.* **poqomam**

Poqomchi   *lang.* **poqomchi'**

porcelain   *n.* **porselaan**

porcupine   *n.* **k'ix uch**

pork   *n.* **xtib'el aaq**

pork rind   *n.* **chiron**

pork rinds *n.* **xujanb'iltib'**

pork sausage *n.* **choriis**

porridge *n.* **matz'**
    n. **saqjuy**
    n. **uq'un**
port *n.* **hilob'jukub'**
    n. **xaqleb'jukub'**
porter *n agt.* **aj k'amol iiq**
positive *adj.* **tz'aqal ru**
    adj. **us li naraj**
positive electric charge
    n. **xsak'om tiqkaxlanxaml**
possess *v.* **eechanink**
possessions *n.* **eechej**
possessive *n.* **eechaninb'il**
post *n.* **oqech**
    n. **taql**
post office *n.* **nums'esilb'aal**
    n. **rochochil esilhu**
post office box *n.* **xkaxonil esilhu**
postage *n.* **eetaltoj**
    n. **tiimbr**
    n. **xtojb'al relik**
postage stamp *n.* **eetal**
postcard *n.* **jalam'uuchil taql**
    n. **tarjeet postal**
poster *n.* **esilhu**
    n. **k'utleb'hu**
    n. **ninqiperhu**
posture *n.* **xaqal**
    n. **xaaqalil**
pot *n.* **joomuk'al**
    n. **uk'al**

potato *n.* **kaxlan is**
    n. **paaps**
potential energy *n.* **xmetz'ew k'a'aq ru**
potter *n agt.* **aj pak'ol**
    n agt. **aj pak'onel**
pottery *n.* **pak'b'il**
pound *n.* **b'iis'aal**
    n. **liiwr**
    v. **t'i'ok**
pour *v.* **hoyok**
    v. **pajink**
    v. **xulub'ank**
pouteria sapota *n.* **saltul**
poverty *n.* **neb'a'il**
powder *n.* **poqsxaml**
power *n.* **ruhan**
    n. **wankil**
power switch *n.* **chupleb' saqen**
    n. **raqleb' saqen**
powerstrip *n.* **jekb'ametz'ew**
practice *v.* **b'aanunk**
    n. **xb'aanunkil**
pragmatism *n.* **oksinb'il na'leb'**
prairie *n.* **roq taq'a**
    n. **taq'a**
praise *n.* **nimank u**
    n. **terq'usink k'ab'a'**
prawns *n.* **jit**
    n. **k'ox**
pray *v.* **tijok**
prayer *n.* **tij**

prayer book *n.* **oxloq'il hu**

praying mantis *n.* **tz'upq'een**

preach *v.* **k'eelenk**

Precambrian era *n.* **xb'een q'ekutan**

precious metal *n.* **chaab'il ch'iich'**

precipice *n.* **chamal jul**
   n. **uul**

precipitation *n.* **rachhab'**

predicate *n.* **ch'olob'ihom**

predict *v.* **q'ehink**

prediction *n.* **xq'ehinkil**

prefix *n.* **tiktz'aqob'l**

pregnancy *n.* **yu'amil**

pregnant *adj.* **sa' yu'am**
   adj. **yaj aj ixq**

preoccupation *n.* **xtib' jolom**

prepaid phone card *n.* **tojhuil b'oqleb'**

prepare *v.* **kawresink**

preposition *n.* **q'inolaatin**
   n. **xtiqb'al aatin**

preschool *n.* **k'aytesiil**

prescription *n.* **reetalil b'an**
   n. **xhuhul b'an**

present *v.* **k'utb'esink**
   v. **q'axtesink**
   adj. **wan**

present tense
   n. **anaqwankil'uxk**

presentation *n.* **xch'olob'ankil**

presenter *n agt.* **aj xaqab'anel**

preserve *v.* **kolb'eetank**

president *n.* **awab'ej**
   n. **xb'eenil awab'ej**

press *n.* **nat'leb'**
   v. **nat'ok**
   v. **pitz'ok**

pressing machine *n.* **nat'leb'**

pressure cooker *n.* **nat'b'il uk'al**
   n. **tz'aptz'ookil uk'al**

pretty *adj.* **ch'ina us**
   adj. **chaq'al ru**

prevent *v.* **ramok**
   v. **romok**

prey *n.* **tzak**

price *n.* **xloq'al**
   n. **xtz'aq**

pride *n.* **wankil**

priest *n agt.* **aj k'ehol miix**
   n. **chimam**
   n. **payr**
   n. **xb'eenil aj tij**

primate *n.* **aj maxxul**

prince *n.* **xch'ajom ajwal**

princess *n.* **rab'in ajwal**

principal *n.* **xb'eenil tzoleb'aal**
   n. **xjolomil tzoleb'aal**

principal's office *n.* **jolomilal tzoleb'aal**
   n. **jolomnib'aal**
   n. **xna'aj xb'eenil**

print house *n.* **pukhub'aal**

printer   *n.* **pukleb'hu**
           n. **puktasib'aalhu**
           n. **puktasiil**

printer cartridge   *n.* **na'aj b'onhu**

printer ink   *n.* **xya'al puktasiilhu**

printer's   *n.* **pukhub'aal**

prison   *n.* **tz'alam**

prison system   *n.* **xk'ub'laal tojb'a maak**
           n. **xk'uub'laltojb'amaak**

prisoner   *n agt.* **aj tz'alam**
           n. **preex**

private   *adj.* **wan aj eere**

prize   *n.* **maatan**

probably   *adv.* **maare**

problem   *n.* **ch'a'ajkil**

process   *n.* **ch'olk'anjel**

processor   *n.* **ch'olk'anjelob'aal**

prodigy   *n.* **numseeb' xch'ool**

product   *n.* **na'el**
           n. **x'el**

productivity   *n.* **ruuch**

profession   *n.* **k'anjel**

professional   *n agt.* **aj nawk'anjel**
           n. **nimru'ajk'anjel**
           n. **tz'aqal'ajk'anjel**

professionalism   *n.* **nawk'anjelil**

prognosticate   *v.* **q'ehink chi ru**

program (TV)   *n.* **k'uub'anb'il k'anjel**
           n. **k'uub'ank**

progress   *n.* **wakliik**
           v. **wakliik**
           v. **yu'k**

progressive particle   *part.* **yo**

progressivity   *n.* **wakliikil**

projector   *n.* **kutleb'mu**
           n. **repolmu**
           n. **repom**

prokaryotic cell   *n.* **ch'emna'yu'am**

promise   *v phr.* **sumenk ru aatin**

promissory note   *n.* **hu xaqb'anb'il xwankil**
           n. **xhuhiltoj**

prompter   *n agt.* **aj jultikahonel**

pronoun   *n.* **ruuchil k'ab'a'ej**

pronounce   *v.* **yaab'asink**

pronunciation   *n.* **xyaab'asinkil**

proof   *n.* **k'utb'esil**

propaganda   *n.* **pukta'esil**

propane   *n.* **b'ookilxaml**
           n. **iq'xaml**

propeller   *n.* **sururu**

proper noun   *n.* **xk'ab'a'il**

property line   *n.* **nub'aal**

prophase   *n.* **xb'een pojk'ok**

propose   *v.* **xaqab'ank**

prostitute *n.* **kaan ru ixq**
    n. **k'ayihom rib'**
    n. **puut**

prostitution *n.* **puutink**

protagonist *n agt.* **aj b'aanunel**

protect *v.* **kolok**
    v. **tenq'ank**

protection *n.* **kole'k**

protein *n.* **ajsiil**
    n. **kawub'l**

Protestant *n.* **kapiiy**

proton *n.* **tiqkaxlan xaml**

protractor *n.* **b'isxuk**

proud *adj.* **kaw xch'ool**
    adj. **numtaak**
    adj. **q'etq'et**

proverb *n.* **jaljookil'aatin**
    n. **tawilna'leb'**

pruning shears *n.* **setleb' uutz'u'uj**

psychologically
    adv. **nawtuqch'oolil**

psychologist *n agt.* **aj nawtuqch'ool**

psychology *n.* **nawtuqch'ool**

psychotherapist *n agt.* **aj aatinanel rik'in yaj**

psychotherapy *n.* **aatinak rik'in yaj**

pubis *n.* **peekem kun**

public *adj.* **re tenamit**

public services *n.* **k'a'aq re ru li tenamit**

public telephone
    n. **raatik'aamch'iich' tenamit**

publication *n.* **xpuktasinkil**

publish *v phr.* **puktasink esil**

published *adj.* **puktasinb'il**

publisher *n.* **pukhub'aal**

pull *v.* **jukunk**
    phr. **kelo**
    v. **kelonk**

pumice *n.* **maqs**

pumpkin *n.* **k'um**

pumpkin seed *n.* **sakil k'um**

punctuation mark *n.* **reetalil tz'aqob'tz'iib'**

punish *v.* **k'ajtesink**

punishment *n.* **tojb'a maak**
    n. **tojleb'aal maak**

pupil *n.* **tijom**
    n. **tzolom**

pupil (eye) *n.* **xtehelem'u**

puppet *n.* **poyb'atz'uul**

purchase *v.* **loq'ok**
    n. **loq'om**

purple *adj.* **q'eqmoyin**

purse *n.* **b'ools**
    n. **xna'aj tumin**

pursue *v.* **taaqenk**

pus *n.* **pojel**
    n. **pojk**

push *v.* **minok**
    v. **miikisink**

	v. **tiikink**
	phr. **tiikis**
put	*v.* **kanab'ank**
	v. **k'ehok**
put off	*v.* **b'ayok**
put on	*v phr.* **tiqok ib'**
puzzled	*adj.* **sachenaq ru**
PVC	*n.* **simb'plaast**
pyjamas	*n.* **aq' re wark**
	n. **warib'aq**
	n. **warib'aal aq**

pyramid	*n.* **jutz'-eetalil**
	n. **ox'u**
pyramid (four-sided)	*n.* **jutz' kaaxukuut**
pyramid (monument)	*n.* **jutz'il na'aj**
	n. **jutz'ochochilpek**
	n. **ox'ukab'l**
pyramid (three-sided)	*n.* **jutz' oxxukuut**

Q - q

Q'eqchi'	*lang.* **q'eqchi'**
Qanjobal	*lang.* **q'anjob'al**
quail	*n.* **tonq'**
	n. **turunhut tz'ik**
quantity	*n.* **nimal**
quarrel	*n.* **raaxiik'**
quarter	*n.* **jun kaajachal**
	n. **jun xka**
	n. **o'laju xk'ak'aal senta**
queen	*n.* **ixajaw**
	n. **xoq'jaw**
question	*n.* **patz'om**
question mark (?)	*n.* **reetalil patz'omq**
questionnaire	*n.* **raqalyalb'a'ix**

quetzal	*n.* **jun ketzal**
	n. **q'uq'**
quickly	*adv phr.* **sa' jumpaat**
quiet	*adj.* **ink'a' na'aatinak**
	adj. **kulku**
	adj. **k'irnak**
	adj. **tuulan**
quince	*n.* **mem'riiy**
quite	*adv.* **chi xjunil**
	adv. **us**
quiz	*n.* **yalok ix**
quotation marks	
	n. **ka'muluq'utiltz'uq**
quotes	*n.* **ka'muluq'utiltz'uq**
quotient	*n.* **xjek'iil**

R - r

rabbit   *n.* **imul**
            n. **xa'an imul**

rabies   *n.* **wax ru**

raccoon   *n.* **ow**

radiation   *n.* **xnumsinkil**

radiator   *n.* **tuqtiq**
            n. **wosleb'**

radio   *n.* **ray**

radio (receiver)   *n.* **ab'ib'aalson**
            n. **ab'ib'aal aatin**

radio (transmitter)
            n. **puktasib'aal**

radio antenna   *n.* **xmisik'**
            puktasib'aal

radio studio   *n.* **xtoonal li**
            ab'ib'aal aatin

radio tower   *n.* **puktasib'aal**
            kab'l najt xteram

radio transmitter   *n.* **numsib'aal**
            esil

radioactivity   *n.* **numsiilk'anjel**

radish   *n.* **kaqxe'**

Rafael   *nick.* **Rap**

raffle   *n.* **b'uuleb'**
            n. **b'uulik**
            v. **b'uulink**
            n. **pumb'uul**

raffle a prize   *v phr.* **b'uulink**
            maatan

raffle money   *v phr.* **b'uulink**
            tumin

raft   *n.* **poyte'**
            v. **poyte'ib'k**

rafter   *n.* **b'aqsotz'**
            n. **xb'e ch'o**

rag   *n.* **sut**
            n. **xputz't'ikr**

railing   *n.* **ramleb'**

rain   *n.* **hab'**
            n. **hab'al**

rain with hail   *n.* **b'achal hab'**

rainbow   *n.* **kaqlaaq'**
            n. **xokaq'ab'**

rainfall meter   *n.* **b'isleb'hab'**

rainy   *adj.* **kutankil hab'**
            adj. **yo hab'**

raise   *v.* **paqonk**
            v. **taqsink**
            v. **waklesink**
            v. **xaqab'ank**

raise to the fifth power
            v. **ro'wahink**

rake   *n.* **jochleb'**
            n. **jochleb'mul**
            n. **rastriiy**

ram   *n.* **karneer**

rancid   *adj.* **ch'am**

range	*n.* **kelkookil tzuul**
	n. **tzoltzookiltzuul**
ransom	*n.* **tumin re uuchil**
rape	*n.* **muxuk**
	v. **muxuk**
	n. **xminb'al ru**
rapids	*n.* **xkawil roq ha'**
rapist	*n agt.* **aj muxunel**
rare	*adj.* **toj rax**
rash	*n.* **porha'**
	adj. **yal naxkuti rib'**
rasp	*n.* **ji'leb'**
	n. **ji'leb'ch'iich'**
rat	*n.* **ch'o**
	n. **uch ch'o**
rate	*n.* **aj b'isonel na'leb'**
rather	*adv.* **chi xjunil**
	adv. **us**
ratio	*n.* **aj b'isonel na'leb'**
rattle	*n.* **luk'luk' che'**
raven	*n.* **tuntz'oq**
ravine	*n.* **uul**
	n. **xiik'**
raw	*adj.* **rax**
raw materials	*n.* **usil k'a'aq re ru**
ray	*n.* **perkar**
razor	*n.* **johob'a mach**
	n. **jooleb'**
	n. **jooleb'mach**
	n. **nawaaj**
razor blade	*n.* **xileet**
read	*v phr.* **ilok ru hu**

ready	*adj.* **k'ub'k'u**
realistic	*adj.* **sa' yaal na'aatinak**
reality	*n.* **xyaalalil**
realize	*v phr.* **k'ehok eetal**
really	*adv phr.* **elik chi yaal**
really?	*phr.* **ma yaal**
rear-view mirror	*n.* **ilb'a'ixlem**
	n. **ka'yab'aal ixkej**
	n. **lemaal'ix**
reason	*v.* **na'leb'ank**
rebar	*n.* **b'aqch'iich'**
rebellious	*adj.* **ink'a' na'ab'in**
rebirth	*n.* **rajikab'aal**
reborn	*v.* **rajikru**
	v phr. **yo'laak xka'wa**
receipt	*n.* **huhil-loq'om**
	n. **xhuhilk'uluk**
	n. **xhuhil loq'om**
receive	*v.* **k'uluk**
receive rites	*v.* **wa'tesiik**
receive visitors	*v.* **ula'anink**
receiver	*n agt.* **aj k'ulul re**
	n. **k'ulul**
	n. **k'ulunel**
recent	*adj.* **toje'**
reception	*n.* **k'uleb'aal**
receptionist	*n agt.* **aj k'ulul ula'**
recess	*n.* **ajsib'aal'u**
	n. **hoonalhilaal**
	n. **xhoonal asjsink-u**
recipe	*n.* **reetalil k'uub'ank**

recipe book *n.* **xhuhuil'esil**

recipient *n agt.* **aj k'ulul re**
  n. **xk'ab'a' li taak'ulu'q re**

reciprocal *adj.* **sumenk-ib'**

recital *n.* **kawyehink**

recitation *n.* **kawyehink**

recite *v.* **yaab'asink**

recline *v.* **salab'ank**

reclined *adj.* **salso**

recognize *v.* **na'link**

recompense *n.* **k'ajk'amunkil**

record *v phr.* **chapok aatin**
  n. **surb'ich**

record a video *v.* **chapokmu**

record player
  n. **surb'ichleb'aal**

recording studio *n.* **xna'aj aj aatinanel**

recreation *n.* **ajsib'aal'u**
  n. **hilaal**
  n. **hoonalhilaal**
  n. **xhoonal asjsink-u**

recreation center *n.* **xna'aj ajsink u**

rectangle
  n. **kelkookilkaaxukuut**

rectangular *adj.* **kelkookil kaaxukuut**

rectum *n.* **mam**

recyclable *adj.* **ak'oresiil**

recycle *v.* **ka'oksink**

recycling *n.* **xka'oksinkil**

red *adj.* **kaq**

red blood cells *n.* **kaqkil mitz'kotkik'**
  n. **xxulel kik'el**

red face *n.* **kaqxot'ink**

red wine *n.* **q'eqil b'iin**

redact *v phr.* **na'leb'ank tz'iib'**

reddish-gray *adj.* **tz'ib'**

reduce *v.* **k'osok**

reed *n.* **aj**

reef *n.* **pekil ha'**

referee *n agt.* **aj tuqub'anel**

refine *v.* **hesok**

refinement *n.* **xhesb'al**

reflect *v.* **k'oxlank**

reflection (light) *n.* **xk'utum xaml**

reflection (thought)
  n. **xk'a'uxlankil**

reflexive particle *part.* **ib'**

reforest *v.* **ka'awk**

reforestation *n.* **ka'awb'il**

reforested *adj.* **xka'awb'il**

reform *v.* **tuqub'ank**
  n. **xtuqub'ankil**

refraction *n.* **jalb'ehil saqen**

refrain *n.* **jaljookil'aatin**
  n. **tawilna'leb'**

refreshment *n.* **kolb'ach'ool**

refrigerator *n.* **kehob'resilb'aal**
 n. **keeleb'aal**
 n. **reepri**

refuse *v phr.* **ink'a'**
 xq'ulub'ank

register *v.* **poqlenk**

regret *v phr.* **ch'inank ch'ool**
 v. **kiib'ch'oolink**
 v phr. **yot'ok ch'ool**

regulator *n.* **tuqb'ametz'ew**

rehearse *v.* **yalb'ek**
 v. **yalok**

rehydration *n.* **xka'ha'resinkil**

reign *v.* **poopirk**

reject *v.* **tz'eqtaanank**

rejected *adj.* **tz'eqtananb'il**

rejection *n.* **tz'eqtanaank**

relative *n.* **cha'al**
 n. **komon**
 n. **ruk'**

relatives *n.* **amaq'il tenamit**

relaxed vowel *n.* **jayaab'**
 na'tz'iib'

release *v phr.* **k'ehok sa'**
 sahilal

religion *n.* **paab'aal**

reluctantly *adv phr.* **kab' rix**
 ch'ool

remain *v.* **kanaak**

remainder *n.* **jeb'ok**

remains *n.* **ela'**
 n. **rela'**

n. **xb'een**
n. **xeel**

remedy *n.* **b'an**

remember *v.* **jultikank**
 v phr. **naqk sa' ch'ool**

remove *v.* **isink**
 v. **sote'k**

rename *v.* **ka'k'a'b'aink**

rendition *n.* **t'ane'k**

renew *v.* **ak'o'k**
 v. **ak'ob'resink**

renewable *adj.* **ak'ob'resink**

renown *n.* **ka'xaqab'aal**

repatriate *n.* **sutq'isinb'il**
 v. **sutq'iik**

repeat that *phr.* **ye wi'chik**

repent *v phr.* **ch'inank ch'ool**
 v. **yot'o'k**

repentance *n.* **ek'ank ib'**

repetition *n.* **ka'sutink**
 n. **ka'wahink**

reply *v.* **chaq'ok**
 v. **sumenk**

report *n.* **esilk'anjel**

reporter *n agt.* **aj k'ehol esil**
 n agt. **aj molol'esil**
 n agt. **aj tz'iib'anel esil**

represent *v.* **eeqajink**
 v. **uuchilink**

representative *n.* **aj**
 k'uub'anelchaq'rab'
 n. **uuchilej**

representativity *n.* **uuchininkil**

reprimand *v.* **q'usuk**

reproduce *v.* **alab'tesink**
      v. **ka'sutink**

reptile *n.* **ahin jukxul**
      n. **jukxul**

request *n.* **ajb'il**
      n. **patz'b'il**
      v. **tz'aamank**

rescue *v.* **kolok**

rescue unit *n.* **xmolam aj kolonel**

research *v.* **tz'ilok-ix**

researcher *n agt.* **aj tzilol'ix**
      n agt. **aj tzilonel**

reseed *v.* **ka'awk**

reside *v.* **wank**

resonant *adj.* **yaab'il**

resource *n.* **eechej**

resource conservation
      n. **xkolb'al rix li loq'laj che'k'aam**

respect *n.* **oxloq'il**
      v. **oxloq'ink**

respected *adj.* **oxloq'inb'il**

respectful *adj.* **na'oxloq'in**

respiration *n.* **musiq'**

respiratory system
      n. **musiq'ab'aal**

respire *v.* **musiq'ak**

respond *v.* **chaq'ok**
      v. **sumenk**

responsibility
      n. **k'amch'oolanink**

responsible *adj.* **aj ch'oolanel**

rest *v.* **hilank**
      n. **hiil**
      n. **rela'**

restaurant *n.* **nimlawa'leb'aal**
      n. **nimla k'ayib'aal tzakahemq**
      n. **wa'leb'aal**

restless *adj.* **yal k'a' naxb'aanu**

result *n.* **na'el**
      n. **x'el**

resumé *n.* **esilnawom**

resurrection *n.* **kab'yo'lajik**

retina *n.* **jayiltz'uumal'u**
      n. **xyi**

retreat *v.* **eelelik**

retribution *n.* **eeqaj**

return *v.* **q'ajk**
      v. **q'axtesink**
      v. **sutq'iik**

reuse *v.* **ka'oksink**
      n. **xka'oksinkil**

reversed *adj.* **xsal**

reversible *adj.* **junpak'alil**
      adj. **xsutq'isinkil chi rix**

revert *v.* **sutq'iik**

revolting *adj.* **yib' yib'**

revolution *n.* **sutrix**

revolver *n.* **kok' puub'**

revolving drum *n.* **pumb'uul**

reward *v.* **k'ajk'amunk**
n. **k'ajk'amunkil**

rewrite *v.* **ka'tz'iib'ank**

rhinoceros *n.* **kaxchixl**

rhodium *n.* **q'anmuch'iich'**

rhomboid *adj.* **b'arxuk**

rhombus *n.* **salsookil kaaxukuut**
n. **xaqamkaaxuk**

rhubarb *n.* **rub'aarb'**

rhyme *n.* **uutz'u'jinb'ilraq**

rhythm *n.* **roqil**

rib *n.* **poolok'il**
n. **xb'aqel xukuy**
n. **xchakachil b'aq**
n. **xukuy**

ribbon *n.* **jisil t'ikr**
n. **tz'uleb'**

ribosome *n.* **mitz'k'amk'ot**

ribs *n.* **kostiiy**

Ricardo *nick.* **Rik**

rice *n.* **aros**

rice paddy *n.* **xna'aj aros**

rich *adj.* **b'ihom**
adj. **sa**

riches *n.* **b'ihomal**

rickets *n.* **chaqi'oqil**
n. **numay**

riddle *n.* **jorb'ana'leb'**

ride *v phr.* **taqe'k chi rix kawaay**

ride (a horse) *v.* **kawaayink**

ridgepole *n.* **tz'amb'a**

rifle *n.* **puub'**

right (correct) *adj.* **q'axal chaab'il**

right (spatial) *adj.* **sa' nim**

right away *adv phr.* **ak anaqwan**

right here *adv phr.* **arin tz'aqal**

right there *adv phr.* **aran tz'aqal**

righteous *adj.* **tiik xch'ool**

righteousness *n.* **xyaalal**

rights *n.* **k'ulub'**
n. **k'ulub'em**
n. **xk'ulub'poyanam**

ring *n.* **b'ot**
n. **ch'ina sursukil ch'iich'**
n. **matq'ab'**
v. **tzinb'ak**

ring (phone) *n.* **yaab'aal**

rinse *v.* **nub'resink**

ripe *adj.* **chaq'**
adj. **q'an**
adj. **yuq'uq'nak**

rise *v.* **taqsink**
v. **wakliik**
v. **xaqliik**

river *n.* **nima'**
n. **roq ha'**

river rock *n.* **pekil nima'**

rivet *n.* **ka't'oj**

roach *n.* **paachach**

road *n.* **b'e**
n. **nimb'e**

n. **nimla b'e**
n. **numleb'aal**

roadrunner *n.* **rak'ach tzuul**

roar   *v phr.* **chajok e**

roast   *v.* **pomok**
          v. **sisank**

roast beef *n.* **pomb'il tib'**

roasted   *adj.* **pomb'il**

roasting pan *n.* **pomleb'**

Roberto *nick.* **Rob'**

robot   *n.* **yolojch'iich**
          n. **yu'am ch'iich**

robust   *adj.* **kaw rib'**

rock   *n.* **pek**
          n. **pekal**

rodents   *n.* **aj k'oyoneleb'**
          n. **aj setoneleb'**

roll   *v.* **b'arb'arink**
          n. **q'ooch**

roll out *v.* **helok**

roll paper dispenser *n.* **xche'el li b'otb'il hu**

rolling pin *n.* **b'ola**
          n. **kok'poli'n**

rolls   *n.* **kok' kaxlan wa**
          n. **potzkaxlanwa**

roof   *n.* **xb'een kab'l**

rooftop terrace *n.* **xb'een ochoch**

room   *n.* **kwaart**
          n. **sa' kab'l**

rooster   *n.* **tzo'xul**
          n. **tzo' kaxlan**

root   *n.* **xe'**

roots   *n.* **xxe'il**

rope net *n.* **soq'**

rosary   *n.* **rajleb' tij**

rose   *n.* **k'ix'atz'um**
          n. **roos**

rose bush *n.* **roos**

rosemary *n.* **romeer**

rotation *n.* **sutrib'**

rotten   *adj.* **q'aaneq**

rough   *adj.* **b'urux**
          adj. **chaq re ru**
          adj. **k'urux**
          adj. **purux**
          adj. **q'es ru**
          adj. **turux**

round   *adj.* **kotko**
          adj. **q'otq'o**
          adj. **sursu**
          adj. **t'ort'o**

roundabout *n.* **k'ulb'aq'qax'ib'**

route   *n.* **numleb'aal**

row   *v phr.* **b'eeresink jukub'**
          v. **juyuk**
          v. **kojlenk**
          n. **tzol**
          n. **tzolil**

rower   *n agt.* **aj b'eresinel jukub'**

rub   *v.* **b'iqok**
          v. **jilok**

rubber   *n.* **kik'che'**
          n. **rin**

rudder	*n.* **xik'jukub'**		ruling	*n.* **ruq'b'chaq'rab'**
rude	*adj.* **maak'a' xxutaan**		rum	*n.* **ron**
rug	*n.* **alfoombr**		rumor	*n.* **yoob'ank aatin**
	n. **ruhiltz'ak**		run	*v.* **aanilak**
	n. **xta ru ch'och'**			*v.* **chak'chotk**
ruins	*n.* **po'lem**		run out	*v.* **oso'k**
	n. **xtz'akeb' xe'toon**		runner	*n agt.* **aj aanilanel**
rule	*v.* **awab'ejink**		runway	*n.* **k'ochleb'aal**
	v. **poopirk**			**ch'iich'**
	v. **taqlank**		Ruperto	*nick.* **Rup**
	n. **xtz'iib'ul**		rust	*n.* **mo'**
ruler	*n.* **juch'leb'**			*v.* **mo'onk**
	n. **ruuchilawab'ej**		ruthless	*adj.* **maak'a' xkuyum**
	n. **tikil che'**		Rómulo	*nick.* **Room**
	n. **tiikal juch'leb'**			
rules	*n.* **xchaq'rab'il**			

S - s

sack	*n.* **koxtal**		safety	*n.* **wank sa' xyaalal**
	v. **min'isink**		safety pin	*n.* **xukub'k'ix**
	v. **minyamtesink**		saffron	*n.* **asapran**
sacred	*adj.* **oxloq'**		sail	*v phr.* **b'eek chi ru ha'**
sacrifice	*n.* **mayej**			*n.* **b'eel**
sacristan	*n agt.* **aj ilol tijob'aal**		sailor	*n agt.* **aj b'eresinel**
	n. **pixcal**			**jukub'**
sad	*adj.* **k'uul ru**		saint	*n agt.* **aj santil**
	adj. **rahil ch'ool**			**paab'anel**
	adj. **ra xch'ool**			*n agt.* **aj tiikilal**
sadden	*v phr.* **raho'k xch'ool**			*n.* **saant**
sadness	*n.* **q'oq**		salad	*n.* **ichaj tzakahemq**
	n. **rahil ch'oolejil**		salad bowl	*n.* **xna'aj murinb'il**
safe	*n.* **pak'b'il tz'ak**			**sa us**

salamander *n.* **paqmaal**
　　　　　n. **xna' k'anti'**

sale 　*n.* **kotzko xtz'aq**
　　　　n. **kub'enaq xtz'aq**

sales clerk *n agt.* **aj k'ay**

salesman *n agt.* **aj k'ay**
　　　　n agt. **aj k'ayinel**

saliva 　*n.* **chuub'**

salsa 　*n.* **putz'b'il pix ik**
　　　　n. **xya'al pix**

salt 　*n.* **atz'am**

salt shaker *n.* **xna'aj atz'am**

salty 　*adj.* **k'ipitz'in**
　　　　adj. **pitz'pitz'**

same 　*adj.* **junaj**
　　　　adj. **juneet**
　　　　adj. **juntaq'eet**
　　　　adj. **na'ajil**

same as usual *phr.* **jo' junelik**

same to you *phr.* **jo'kan ajwi'
　　　　tinye aawe**

sand 　*v.* **ji'ok**
　　　　n. **samahi'**

sandal 　*n.* **perxaab'**

sandfly 　*n.* **k'uxuk**
　　　　n. **suq**

sandpaper *n.* **ji'leb'**
　　　　n. **k'arhu**
　　　　n. **q'unleb'**

sap 　*n.* **q'ol**
　　　　n. **ya'al**

sardines *n.* **saqi kar**

sash 　*n.* **k'aamal sa'**

satellite *n.* **aj b'e chahim**
　　　　n. **b'eenelchahim**
　　　　n. **chahimch'iich'**

satellite dish *n.* **esilsek'
　　　　chahimch'iich'**

satisfied *adj.* **k'ojkookilch'ool**
　　　　adj. **saasa xch'ool**

Saturday *n.* **saaw**
　　　　n. **xwaqkutan**

Saturn 　*n.* **satuurn**
　　　　n. **xwaq ralsaq'e**

sauce 　*n.* **putz'b'il**

saucepan *n.* **mansek'**
　　　　n. **per'uk'al**

saucer 　*n.* **platiiy**

sausage *n.* **b'utb'iltib'**
　　　　n. **salchiich**

savannah *n.* **sabaan**

save 　*v.* **kolok**
　　　　v. **k'uulank**
　　　　v. **xokok**

savings *n.* **k'o'al**

savings account *n.* **ch'uut
　　　　tumin**

savings passbook *n.* **xtasal
　　　　xhuhil tumin**

savor 　*v.* **yalok**

saw 　*n.* **jachleb'**
　　　　n. **kelk'arch'iich'**
　　　　n. **k'ixsetleb'**
　　　　n. **seruch**
　　　　v. **setok**
　　　　n. **xeer**

sawdust *n.* **k'ajche'**

saxophone *n.* **ch'ere'wajb'**

say   *v.* **yehok**

say again *phr.* **ye wi'chik**

saying   *n.* **jaljookil'aatin**
           n. **tawilna'leb'**

scabbard *n.* **rixch'iich'**

scabies   *n.* **tuxl**

scaffolding *n.* **k'ochkaq'l**
           n. **lochte'b'aal**
           n. **taqleb'**
           n. **taqleb'aal**

scale   *n.* **b'isleb'**
           n. **b'isleb'aal**
           n. **peex**
           n. **rep'ix**
           n. **solel**
           n. **tuqb'isleb'**
           n. **xsol rix**

scale (reptilian) *n.* **pat**

scan   *v.* **k'atok-eetalil**

scanned *adj.* **k'atb'il-eetalil**

scanner *n.* **k'atleb'-eetalil**
           n. **numjalam'uuch**

scar   *n.* **eetalil yok'ol**
           n. **reetalil tiq'ilal**
           n. **xna'aj tiiq'**
           n. **yotolal**
           n. **yotom**

scarce *adj.* **majel**
           adj. **we'ej**

scarcity *n.* **we'ejil**

scarecrow *n.* **xxib'enkil k'al**

scared *adj.* **xiwajenaq**
           adj. **yo xiw**

scarf   *n.* **lanb'aja'aj**
           n. **xb'aatal ja'aj**

scarlet *adj.* **kaq kaq**

scene   *n.* **raqalilk'utb'esink**

schedule *n.* **hoonalil**
           n. **q'eqhilk'anjel**
           n. **xhoonalil**

scholarship *n.* **tenq'**

school   *n.* **tzoleb'aal**

school bag *n.* **sukhu**

science   *n.* **nawom chi rix k'a
           re ru**
           n. **nawsutam**

scientist *n agt.* **aj
           chamalnawom**

scissors *n.* **ka'lach'**
           n. **setleb'**
           n. **tixeer**

scold   *v.* **ch'iilank**
           v. **q'usuk**

scoop   *v.* **jokok**

scooter   *n.* **nuchkawaay
           ch'iich'**

score   *n.* **rajlil ketom**
           n. **tusb'ich**

scorpion *n.* **xook'**

scrambled eggs *n.* **yulenb'il
           molb'**

scrap of cloth *n.* **rela' t'ikr**

scrape   *v.* **jichok**
           v. **jochok**
           n. **jochol**
           v. **jokok**
           v. **jot'ok**

v. **qirok**
v. **q'oyok**

scraper   *n.* **jotzleb'**

scratch   *v.* **ch'uyuk**
v. **jochlenk**
v. **jochok**
n. **jochol**
v. **parok**
v. **q'oyok**
n. **q'oyol**

screen (dividing)   *n.* **tasl**

screen (TV)   *n.* **ileb'**
n. **lemaal**
n. **xlemul kaxmuhel**

screw   *n.* **b'alent'ojiil**
n. **b'arch'iich'**
n. **jit'iil**
v phr. **jit'ok kotox ch'iich'**
n. **torniiy**

screwdriver   *n.* **b'otz'leb'**
n. **hitb'arch'iich'**
n. **hitleb' kotox ch'iich'**
n. **k'ixleb'**

scribe   *n agt.* **aj tz'iib'**

scrotum   *n.* **ab'aj**
n. **ab'ajil**

scrub   *v.* **ji'lenk**
v. **kich'kich'ink**
n. **kok' pim**
n. **k'atk'al**

scuba dive   *v.* **muqa'lik**

sculptor   *n agt.* **aj pak'onel**
n agt. **aj pech'onel**

scythe   *n.* **k'onk'ookil ch'iich'**

sea   *n.* **palaw**
n. **xnimalpalaw**

sea shell   *n.* **xpemechil palaw**

sea snail   *n.* **soch**

seafood   *n.* **xxulel palaw**

seagull   *n.* **xtz'ik ha'**

seahorse   *n.* **xch'ina kawaay palaw**

seal   *n.* **kaxt**
v. **kaaxtink**
v. **latzok**
n. **tz'i'ha'**

seam   *n.* **b'ojom**

seamstress   *n agt.* **aj b'ojonel ixq**

search   *v.* **tziib'aak**

seashore   *n.* **re palaw**

season   *n.* **estasion**
v. **tiikob'resink**
n. **xq'ehil**

seasoning   *n.* **xb'anol**
n. **xsahob' tzakahemq**
n. **xyuutzakahemq**

sebaceous gland   *n.* **k'uub'aal xeeb'**

Sebastián   *nick.* **B'ex**

second   *num.* **(2nd.) xkab'**

second grade   *n.* **xkab' na'aj**

second language
n. **xkab'aatinob'aal**

second language acquisition
n. **xb'ehul k'utuk xkab'aatinob'aal**

second to last *adj.* **rub'elal xraqik**

secret *n.* **muqmukilna'leb'**
n. **muqmukil aatin**

secretary *n agt.* **aj k'ulul ula'**
n agt. **aj tz'iib'**

section *n.* **ch'uutal**

sector *n.* **teep**
n. **xteepal tenamit**

security *n.* **ch'oolch'oolkilal**

security camera
n. **chapleb'jalam'u**

security door *n.* **k'ulb'lem**
n. **tz'apokeb'ch'iich'**

security guard *n agt.* **aj k'aak'alom**
n agt. **aj puub'**

sedative *n.* **re kubsink rahil**

see *v.* **ilok**

see you later *phr.* **chi qilaq qib'**

see you soon *phr.* **jo' wan chik**

seed *n.* **iyaj**
n. **sakil**
n. **xnaq'**

seedbed *n.* **iyajiil**
n. **mu'**

seek *v.* **sik'ok**

segment *n.* **xch'uylal**

segregate *v.* **murink**

seismologist *n agt.* **aj nawhiik**

seismology *n.* **nawhiik**

seldom *adv phr.* **naj xyanq**

self-absorbed *adj.* **k'uul ru**

self-esteem *n.* **kawresil-ib'**

selfish *adj.* **kaq ru xch'ool**

self-test *n.* **tz'ilok ib'**
v phr. **tz'ilok ib'ink**

sell *v.* **k'ayink**

semen *n.* **b'ub'**
n. **lal**

semester *n.* **xwaq po**

semi truck *n.* **motzo'ch'iich'**

semicircle *n.* **jachsirso**
n. **yiisirso**

semicolon *n.* **raqyanq**
n. **xjolom muluq'util tz'uq**

semiconductor *n.* **numleb' kaxlanxaml**

send *v.* **taqlank**

sender *n agt.* **aj taql'esil**
n agt. **aj taqlanel re**
n. **xk'ab'a' li nataqlan re**

sensational *adj.* **xik' naxye**

sense of hearing *n.* **ab'ib'aal**

sense of humor *n.* **se'se'il ch'oolej**

sense of sight *n.* **ileb'aal**
n. **ilob'aal xsa'u**

sense of smell *n.* **utz'leb'aal**

sense of taste *n.* **yaleb'aal**

sense of touch *n.* **eek'ob'aal**
　　　　n. **ixkej**

sensitive *adj.* **yal maatoch'**

sentence *n.* **ch'ol'aatin**
　　　　n. **raqal'aatin**
　　　　n. **tojok maak**
　　　　n. **xhuhultojb'amaak**

sentiment *n.* **eek'ahom**
　　　　n. **eek'aal**

sepal *n.* **xxaq atz'um**

separate *adv.* **jach'bil**
　　　　v. **jachok**
　　　　v. **jilosink**
　　　　v. **murink**
　　　　v. **raqaxink**

separated *adv.* **jach'bil**

September *n.* **sektiyemr**
　　　　n. **xb'elehilpo**

serenade *n.* **ajsi'baalb'ich**
　　　　n. **aj si'b'ich**

serious *adj.* **tiik ru**

servant *n.* **moos**

serve *v.* **k'ehok**

serve a sentence *v phr.* **tojok maak**

service window *n.* **ch'ina k'uleb'aal**

servitude *n.* **moosil**

sesame seeds *n.* **jonjoli**

set *n.* **ch'uut**
　　　n. **sahob'k'utleb'aal**
　　　n. **xyik'utb'esink**

set up *v.* **k'uub'ank**

seven *num.* **(7.) wuqub'**

seventeen *num.* **(17.) wuqlaju**

seventeenth *num.* **(17th.) xwuqlajuil**

seventh *num.* **(7th.) xwuq**

seventieth *num.* **(70th.) xlajee xkaak'aalil**

seventy *num.* **(70.) lajeeb' xkaak'aal**

seventy-eight *num.* **(78.) waqxaqlaju xkaak'aal**

seventy-five *num.* **(75.) o'laju xkaak'aal**

seventy-four *num.* **(74.) kaalaju xkaak'aal**

seventy-nine *num.* **(79.) b'elelaju xkaak'aal**

seventy-one *num.* **(71.) junlaju xkaak'aal**

seventy-seven *num.* **(77.) wuqlaju xkaak'aal**

seventy-six *num.* **(76.) waqlaju xkaak'aal**

seventy-three *num.* **(73.) oxlaju xkaak'aal**

seventy-two *num.* **(72.) kab'laju xkaak'aal**

sew *v.* **b'ojok**
　　　v. **kuuxink**

sew buttonholes *v phr.* **yiib'ank sa' ru t'ikr**

sew eyelets *v phr.* **yiib'ank sa' ru t'ikr**

sew on buttons *v phr.* **k'ehok b'otonx**

sewing machine *n.* **b'ojleb'**
    n. **b'ojleb' ch'iich'**
    n. **k'uub'ch'iich'b'ojleb'**

sewing workshop *n.* **b'ojleb'aal**

sex (gender) *n.* **chankilal**

sexual assault *n.* **muxuk**

shackle *n.* **q'otol**

shade *n.* **mu**

shade (under trees) *n.* **xmu che'**

shadow *n.* **mu**

shadow (of animate being)
    n. **muhej**

shake *v.* **chiq'chiq'ink**
    v. **chiq'ok**
    v. **puxink**

shallow *adj.* **ink'a' cham**

shame *n.* **xutaan**

shampoo *n.* **sasalxab'on**
    n. **xampu**

shape *v.* **pak'ok**

share *v.* **jek'ok**
    v. **sihink**
    v. **wotzok**

shark *n.* **ayin kar**
    n. **mama' kar**
    n. **tiburon**

sharp *adj.* **q'es**

sharpen *v phr.* **jotzok ru'uj**
    v phr. **k'ehok q'esnal**

sharpen (a point) *v phr.* **xjotzb'al ru'uj**

sharpness *n.* **xq'esnal**

shave *v.* **johok**

shave (wood) *v.* **ji'ok**

shaved ice *n.* **saqb'ach ha'**

shaving *n.* **xhumalilche'**

shaving cream *n.* **woqx re joohok**

shawl *n.* **peeraj**

she *pron.* **a'an**

shears *n.* **ka'lach'**
    n. **setleb'**
    n. **tixeer**

sheath *n.* **rix**
    n. **rixch'iich'**

sheep *n.* **karneer**
    n. **tzukxul**

sheet *n.* **jayil'isb'**

sheet music *n.* **tusb'ich**

shelf *n.* **tasal**
    n. **t'anruche'**

shell *n.* **pemech**
    n. **rixnaq'puub'**
    n. **soch**

shelves *n.* **tusleb'aal k'ay**

shepherd *n.* **aj ilolketomq**

shield *n.* **lak'am**

shin *n.* **ru tzelek**
    n. **xmap oq**

shin guard *n.* **ramtzelek**

shine	v. **lemlotk**
	v. **mesok**
shiny	adj. **nalemtz'un**
ship	n. **b'aark**
	n. **mama' jukub'**
shirt	n. **ch'otlepon**
	n. **kamiis**
	n. **yaalt'ikr**
shirt (woman's)	n. **lepon**
shirt cuff	n. **xkux ruq' aq'**
shiver	v. **parpotk**
	v. **siksotk**
	n. **xsik ke**
shoe	n. **xaab'**
shoe brush	n. **mesleb' xaab'**
shoe mold	n. **reetalil xaab'**
shoe polish	n. **b'onxaab'**
	n. **xlemtz' xaab'**
shoe store	n. **k'ayib'aal xaab'**
shoe workshop	n. **rochochil li yiib'leb'aal xaab'**
shoelace	n. **xk'aamal xaab'**
shoemaker	n agt. **aj yiib'om xaab'**
shoemaker's	n. **rochochil li yiib'leb'aal xaab'**
shoeshiner	n agt. **aj b'onol xaab'**
	n agt. **aj mesol ru xaab'**
shoeshiner kit	n. **xkaxon aj b'onol xaab'**
shoetree	n. **reetalil xaab'**

shoot	v. **kutuk**
	v. **puub'ak**
	v. **puub'ank**
	n. **xtuxmel**
shooting star	n. **jus chahim**
shop	n. **k'ayib'aal**
	n. **loq'leb'aal**
shopkeeper	n agt. **aj yakonel**
shore	n. **chi re ha'**
short	adj. **ch'ot**
	adj. **ka'ch'in roq**
	adj. **ka'ch'in xteram**
	adj. **tupus roq**
short vowel	n. **junil na'tz'iib'**
shorten	v. **k'olok**
shorthand	n. **seeb'altz'iib'**
shortly	adv. **ake'**
shorts	n. **ch'otwex**
	n. **mut aq'**
	n. **wex ch'ot roq**
shot	n. **b'akuun**
	n. **kutb'il b'an**
	n. **traaw**
	n. **yeksyon**
shotgun	n. **toqb'ilpuub'**
shoulder	n. **xb'een tel**
shoulder blade	n. **b'aqel xb'een tel**
shout	v phr. **chajok e**
	v phr. **q'ichok e**
shovel	n. **lekleb'**
	n. **lekleb'ch'och'**
	n. **paal**
show	v. **k'utuk**

show off   *v.* **wenb'enk ib'**

shower   *n.* **atib'aal**
    n. **kawil hab'**

shriek   *v.* **yaab'ak**

shrimp   *n.* **jit**
    n. **k'ox**
    v. **k'oxib'k**

shrink   *v.* **k'osok**

shrub   *n.* **chik che'**
    n. **pim**

shudder   *n.* **xsik ke**

shut   *v.* **tz'apok**

shut up! (singular)
    phr. **matchoqin**

shutters   *n.* **ramch'iich'**

shy   *adj.* **aj xiw**

Siamese twins   *n.* **latzlut**

sibling-in-law   *n.* **b'alk**
    n. **ech alalb'ej**

sibling's child   *n.* **ikaq'b'ej**

sick   *adj.* **yaj**

sicken   *v.* **yajerk**

sickle   *n.* **k'onk'ookil ch'iich'**

sickness   *n.* **yajel**
    n. **yajelil**

side   *n.* **k'atq**
    n. **pak'al**
    n. **ru**

sideboard   *n.* **xn'aj sek'**

sidewalk   *n.* **reb'e**

sieve   *n.* **tz'ileb'**
    v. **tz'ilok**

sight   *n.* **ileb'aal**
    n. **ilob'aal xsa'u**

sign   *n.* **eetal**
    n. **eetalil**
    n. **k'utleb'hu**

signal   *v.* **k'utb'esink**

signature   *n.* **juch'**

signature of sender   *n.* **xjuch' li nataqlan re**

silence   *n.* **ch'anaak**
    n. **ch'anch'o**

silent   *adj.* **kulku**

silhouette   *n.* **kootal**
    n. **muhelil**

silk   *n.* **lemtz'ti'kr**
    n. **seet**

silver   *n.* **plaat**
    n. **saqi ch'iich'**
    n. **saqi pwaq**
    adj. **saqpotz'in**

silver screen   *n agt.* **xlemul kaxmuhel**

silverware   *n.* **kok' ch'iich' re wa'ak**

similar   *adj.* **chanchan**
    adj. **chanchan aj wi' a'an**
    adj. **jo'**
    adj. **ru**

similar figures   *n.* **chanchanil eetalilatq**

simmer   *v phr.* **woqxink chi timil**

sin   *n.* **maak**
             v phr. **sik'ok maak**

since   *adv.* **chalen**
             adv. **tojaq**

since then   *adv.* **chalen chaq**

sinew   *n.* **ich'**
             n. **ich'mul**

sing   *v.* **b'ichank**

singer   *n agt.* **aj b'ichanel**

single bed   *n.* **ch'aat re junesal**

singular   *adj.* **junaatalil**

sink   *n.* **ch'ajleb'**
             n. **ch'ajleb'aal uq'b'**
             v. **muqunk**
             v. **nuq'unk**
             v. **sob'e'k**
             v. **sub'e'k**

sinner   *n agt.* **aj maak**

Sipakapa   *lang.* **sipakapense**

sir   *n.* **qawa'**

siren   *n.* **yaab'aal**

sister (older, of a female)
             n. **chaq'na'**

sister (older, of a male) *n.* **anab'**

sister (younger, of a male or
         female) *n.* **iitz'in ixq**

sister-in-law *n.* **b'alk ixq**

sit   *v.* **chunlaak**
             v. **woq'laak**

six   *num.* **(6.) waqib'**

six-pack   *n.* **waqib' ru**

sixteen   *num.* **(16.) waqlaju**

sixteenth   *num.* **(16th.)**
             xwaqlajuil

sixth   *num.* **(6th.) xwaq**

sixth grade *n.* **xwaq na'aj**

sixtieth   *num.* **(60th.) roxk'aalil**

sixty   *num.* **(60.) oxk'aal**

sixty-eight *num.* **(68.)**
             waqxaqib' xkaak'aal

sixty-five   *num.* **(65.) oob'**
             xkaak'aal

sixty-four   *num.* **(64.) kaahib'**
             xkaak'aal

sixty-nine   *num.* **(69.) b'eleb'**
             xkaak'aal

sixty-one   *num.* **(61.) jun**
             xkaak'aal

sixty-seven *num.* **(67.) wuqub'**
             xkaak'aal

sixty-six   *num.* **(66.) waqib'**
             xkaak'aal

sixty-three *num.* **(63.) oxib'**
             xkaak'aal

sixty-two   *num.* **(62.) wiib'**
             xkaak'aal

size   *n.* **nimal**
             n. **ninqal**
             n. **xnimal**

skeleton   *n.* **b'aqel**
             n. **yolojilb'aq**

sketch   *v.* **jalam'uuchink**

sketch artist *n agt.* **aj jalom**
             uuchinel

skin   *v.* **b'ich'ok**
      v. **mich'ok**
      n. **rix xul**
      n. **tz'uumalej**

skin cream   *n.* **b'an re ixkej**

skin infection   *n.* **joj**

skin rash   *n.* **chachib'**

skin spots (white)   *n.* **saqlep**

skirt   *n.* **b'otb'il aq'**
      n. **chet-aq'**
      n. **kaxlanuuq**

skirt (typical indigenous)   *n.* **uuq**

skull   *n.* **xb'aqel jolom**
      n. **xjolom kamenaq**

skunk   *n.* **aj paar**

sky   *n.* **choxa**

sky blue   *adj.* **raxjo'in**
      adj. **raxpotz'in**
      adj. **saqirax**

skylight   *n.* **rokeb'aal saqen**
      n. **saqenk'im**

slave   *n.* **moos**

slavery   *n.* **moosil**

sledgehammer   *n.* **jorleb'pek**

sleep   *v.* **wark**

sleep well   *phr.* **chexwarq**

sleep well (singular)
      phr. **chatwarq chi us**

sleepiness   *n.* **wara**

sleeping pills   *n.* **b'an re wark**

sleepy   *adj.* **yo xwara**

sleeve   *n.* **ruq'b'**

slice   *n.* **jun surul**
      v. **k'okok**

sliced bread   *n.* **setb'ilkaxlanwa**

slick   *adj.* **yolyol**

slide   *v.* **b'alok**
      v. **jole'k**
      n. **jolool**
      v. **yole'k**
      v. **yolk'ok**

sling   *n.* **jok'**
      v. **jok'ib'k**
      n. **oont**
      n. **rant'in**
      n. **sut**

slip   *n.* **aq' re sa' aq'ej**
      v. **b'alok**
      v. **jole'k**
      n. **xta-uuq**
      v. **yole'k**
      v. **yolk'ok**

slipper   *n.* **pere'xaab'**

slippery   *adj.* **yolyol**

slippery place   *n.* **jolool**

sloping   *adj.* **an'o**

slow   *adj.* **elajik**
      adj. **k'ooq**
      adj. **leb'eb'nak**
      adj. **riil**
      adj. **timil**

slowly   *adv.* **chi timil**

slowly go broke   *v.* **neb'a'irk**

slurs   *n.* **sak'ok aatin**

small   *adj.* **ch'ina**
      adj. **kach'in**

adj. **kok'**
adj. **mitz**

small boat   n. **ch'ina jukub'**

small intestine   n. **kok' k'amk'ot**

small village   n. **kok'k'aleb'aal**

smaller than   adv phr. **ka'ch'in chi ru**

smallpox   n. **ninqixox**

smart   adj. **wan xna'leb'**

smell   n. **utz'leb'aal**
n. **utz'leb'aal**
v. **utz'uk**
n. **utz'uk**

smelly   adj. **chu**

smile   n. **se'**
v. **se'ek**

smock   n. **ramb'atz'aj**

smoke   v. **mayib'k**
n. **sib'**
v. **sib'tehenk**
v. **sik'lik**

smooth   adj. **ji'ji'**
v. **ji'ok**
adj. **q'un**
adj. **tiik**
adj. **yolyol**

snack   n. **kolb'ach'ool**

snail   n. **pemech**
n. **pur**
n. **t'ot'**
n. **tziitzib'**

snake   n. **k'anti'**

sneakers   n. **kok' xaab'**

sneeze   v. **at'isb'ak**

sniff   v. **utz'uk**

snore   v. **jilq'ank**
v. **joq'ank**
v. **qoorank**
v. **q'uusank**

snout   n. **ru'uj**

snow   n. **xchu' ke**

snowcone   n. **saqb'ach ha'**

so   adv. **jo'kan**

soak   v. **tz'ahok**
v. **tz'uqresink**

soap   n. **xab'on**

soap dish   n. **xna'aj xab'on**

soccer   n. **b'olotz oq**

soccer ball   n. **b'olotz oq**

soccer player   n agt. **aj b'atz'unel b'olotz oq**
n agt. **aj b'olotz**

social equality   n. **juntaq'eetil amaq'il**

social security   n. **xch'olch'ookil amaq'il**

social studies   n. **amaq'il loq'alil**
n. **naw'amaq'il**
n. **tzolomilkomon**

social values   n. **amaq'il loq'alil**

social worker   n agt. **aj waklesihom ch'uut**

socialism   n. **komonilwank**

society   n. **amaq'il**

socio constructivism
  n. **amaq'kab'lk'a'uxl**

sociolinguistics
  n. **naw'amaq'ilchi'**

sociologist *n.* **aj nawkomonil**

sociology *n.* **naw'amaq'il**
  n. **nawkomonil**

sock *n.* **b'atb'al oq**
  n. **tz'apb'al oq**
  n. **xta oq**
  n. **xta xaab'**

socket *n.* **chapleb' saqen**

soda *n.* **kaxlanha'**

sofa *n.* **potztem**
  n. **soq'il chunleb'**

soft *adj.* **potzpotz**
  adj. **q'ochq'och**
  adj. **q'un**
  adj. **roq'roq'**
  adj. **yab'yab'**
  adj. **yuq'yuq'**

soft drink *n.* **kaxlanha'**
  n. **kaxuk'a'**

soft palate *n.* **xb'een'e**

soil *n.* **ch'och'**

solar eclipse *n.* **muqlaak saq'e**
  n. **muqsaq'e**

solar system *n.* **wankilal saq'e**
  n. **xtusulal ruuchich'och'**

soldering iron *n.* **xiitleb'ch'iich'**

soldier *n agt.* **aj kookox**
  n agt. **aj puub'**
  n. **soldaa**

sole *adj.* **jun aj wi'**
  n. **sa' oq**
  n. **xsa' oq**

sole (footwear) *n.* **sa' roq xaab'**

solid *adj.* **kaw ru**

solidarity *n.* **junajil**

solution (to a problem)
  n. **yiib'ank ch'a'ajkilal**

solve *v.* **ch'olob'ank**

solve equations *v phr.* **yiib'ank ch'a'ajkilal**

solvent *n.* **aj ha'resinel**

some *pron.* **b'ayaq**
  adj. **junaq**
  adj. **ka'b'ayaq**
  adj. **k'a'na**

somebody else's *adj.* **ab'l**
  adj. **jalan aj e**

sometimes *adv.* **ramro'**
  adv phr. **sa' junq sut**
  adv phr. **wan naq**

son *n.* **al**
  n. **alal**

son (of a mother) *n.* **yum**
  n. **yumej**

son (of god) *n.* **k'ajolb'ej**

song *n.* **b'ich**

songbook *n.* **b'ichleb'**

son-in-law (of a man or woman)
  n sd. **hi'b'ej**

soon *adv.* **ake'**
  adv phr. **chi seeb'**
  adv. **tikto**

sorcerer *n.* **awasinel**
          n. **tuulanel**

sore   *n.* **saan**
          n. **tiq'ilal**
          n. **yok'olal**

sorghum   *n.* **kok' ixim**

sorrow   *n.* **k'a'uxl**

sorry I'm late *phr.* **chinaakuy xinb'ayon chaq**

sorry to keep you waiting
          phr. **chinaakuy xatink'e chi oyb'enink**

soul   *n.* **aamej**
          n. **ch'oolej**

soul mate *n.* **xsum aam**

sound   *v.* **tzinb'ak**
          v. **tzinb'ank**
          n. **xkuxb'il**
          n. **yaab'**
          n. **yaab'kuxink**

sounds good *phr.* **sa naxye**

soup   *n.* **kaalt**
          n. **soop**
          n. **ya'al**

sour   *adj.* **ch'am**
          adj. **k'a**
          adj. **remrem**
          adj. **rub'rub'**

south   *n.* **rokeb' iq'**

South America *n.* **roq ab'yayala**

south pole *n.* **xtaq'ahil ruuchich'och'**

sow   *v.* **awok**
          v. **hirok**
          n. **ixqi aaq**
          n. **xa'an aaq**

sown   *adj.* **awo**

space   *n.* **yanq**

space capsule *n.* **b'oq'ch'iich' iq'**

space shuttle
          n. **choxahilb'eeleb'**
          n. **jukub' iq'**

space station *n.* **na'leb'aal ch'iich' iq'**

space suit *n.* **puraq'**
          n. **purik aq' aj b'eenel sa' po**
          n. **raq' aj b'eenel sa' po**

space travel *n.* **b'eek xb'aan choxach'och'**

spaceship *n.* **jukub' iq'**

spade   *n.* **paal**

Spanish   *lang.* **kastiiy**
          lang. **kaxlanchi'**
          lang. **kaxlan aatin**

sparrow   *n.* **tz'unun**
          n. **wilix**

speak   *v.* **aatinak**
          v. **aatinamank**
          v. **seeraq'ik**

speak slowly *phr.* **ye chi timil**

speaker   *n.* **meexwajb'**
          n. **pukyaab'**
          n. **yaab'aal**

spear   *n.* **jutz'che'**
         n. **jutz'leb'**
         n. **topleb'**

spearmint   *n.* **isk'i'ij**

species   *n.* **ch'uutulal**

spectacles   *n.* **anyooj**
         n. **lem'u**

spectator   *n agt.* **aj ilonel**

speech   *n.* **aatinom**

speech impairment   *n.* **tos e**

speed   *n.* **metz'ewil**
         n. **raanil**

spend   *v.* **sachok**

sphere   *n.* **t'ort'o**

spherical   *adj.* **t'ort'o**
         adj. **t'ort'ookil**

sphygmomanometer
         n. **ich'leb'ch'iich'**

spice   *n.* **k'ay**
         n. **xb'anol**
         n. **xsahob' tzakahemq**
         n. **xyuutzakahemq**

spider   *n.* **aj am**
         n. **x'am**

spider web   *n.* **xkem aj am**

spin   *v.* **k'aamak**
         v. **sutisink**

spinach   *n.* **espinaak**

spinal column   *n.* **juruch'**

spindle   *n.* **peteet**

spine   *n.* **juruch'**
         n. **k'ix**

spiral galaxy   *n.* **kototiil tzoqchahim**

spirit   *n.* **aamej**
         n. **ch'oolej**
         n. **mu**
         n. **muhel**
         n. **musiq'ej**

spirits   *n.* **kaxlan b'oj**

spiritual guide   *n agt.* **aj q'e**

spit   *n.* **chuub'**
         v. **chuub'ak**

spiteful   *adj.* **naxk'uula ra sa' xch'ool**

splash   *v.* **pach'lenk**
         v. **pach'ok**
         v. **rachok**
         v. **repok**

split   *v.* **jachok**
         v. **kiib'ank**
         v. **kuruk**
         v. **toqok**
         v. **xerok**

spoiled   *adj.* **q'aajenaq**

sponge   *n.* **sob'sob'k'uub'**

spool   *n.* **xche'el noq'**

spoon   *n.* **jokleb'**
         n. **kuchaar**
         n. **lekleb'**

spoonful   *n.* **jun kuchaar**

sport utility vehicle   *n.* **ch'ina poy ch'iich'**

sportsman   *n agt.* **aj b'atz'unel**

sportswear   *n.* **aq' re b'atz'unk**

spot   *n.* **xox**

spotless *adj.* **t'uj**

sprain *n.* **b'ach'al**

spray *n.* **puutz'leb'aal**
    v. **puutzink**

spread out *v.* **chirok**
    v. **helok**

spring *n.* **ch'ina ha'**
    n. **kumb'**
    n. **k'ak'naab'**
    n. **tuq**
    n. **uk'leb'aal**

spring (metal) *n.* **pitzk'**

spring (season) *n.* **primab'eer**
    n. **tikkehil kutan**

sprout *n.* **xtuxmel**

spy *v phr.* **lemaank sa' muqmu**

square *n.* **eswaayr**
    adj. **kaaxukuut**
    n. **kaaxukuut**
    n. **kaaxukuutleb'**
    v phr. **puktasink ib'**
    n. **xnimal neb'aal**

squash *n.* **k'um**
    n. **seel**

squeejee *n.* **mesol lem**

squeeze *v.* **pitz'ok**
    v. **yatz'ok**

squirrel *n.* **kuk**

stab *v phr.* **k'ob'ok chi ch'iich'**
    v. **xeq'ok**

stable *n.* **xna'aj wakax**

stadium *n.* **b'atz'unleb'aal**

stage *n.* **k'utb'esib'aal**
    n. **xyik'utb'esink**

staging *n.* **sahob'k'utleb'aal**

stain *v.* **b'onok**

stained glass *n.* **ramleb'aal lem**

staircase *n.* **eeb'**

stake *n.* **awleb'**

stalk *n.* **xche'el pim**

stall *n.* **xna'aj wakax**

stallion *n.* **kawaay**
    n. **kranyon**

stammer *v phr.* **lotz re**
    v phr. **tat re**

stamp *n.* **eetaltoj**
    n. **kaxt**
    v. **kaaxtink**
    n. **tiimbr**
    n. **xtojb'al relik**

stamp pad *n.* **xb'onilkaaxt**

stand *v.* **xaqliik**

standing *adj.* **xaqam**

stands *n.* **tusb'il chunleb'al**

stanza *n.* **raapal**

staple *v.* **chapokhu**

stapler *n.* **k'achleb'**
    n. **k'atz'leb'hu**
    n. **k'axleb'hu**

star *n.* **chahim**

start *n.* **xtiklajik**

starting today *adv.* **chalen anaqwan**

state capital *n.* **rochoch ruuchilawab'ej**

state house *n.* **rochoch ruuchilawab'ej**

statue *n.* **jalam'uuch**
n. **pak'b'il poyanam**
n. **poyanamb'iltz'ak**

steak *n.* **kilinb'il tib'**

steal *v.* **elq'ak**
v. **ixi'jink**
v. **jochok**
v. **uq'mink**

steam *n.* **b'ook**
n. **tiqwal**

steamer trunk *n.* **mama' kaax**

steel *n.* **kulb'ch'iich'**

steel nail *n.* **kulb't'ojom**

steering wheel *n.* **jayab'aalb'e**
n. **xch'e'b'al**
n. **xche'el tiikob'aal b'e**

stela *n.* **tz'ak-eetalil**

stem *n.* **roq'**
n. **xche'el pim**

stenography *n.* **seeb'altz'iib'**

step *n.* **eeb'**
n. **yok**

stepdaughter *n.* **ka' ralal**
n. **xkab' rab'in**
n. **xka' alalb'ej**

stepfather *n.* **ka'yuwa'**
n. **xkab' yuwa'**

stepmother *n.* **ka'na'**
n. **xkab' na'**

steps *n.* **taqleb'aal**

stepson *n.* **kab' alal**
n. **xkab' alal**

stereo *n.* **pumleb'yaab'**

sterile (man) *n.* **maa'alwinq**

sterile (woman) *n.* **maa'al'ixq**

sterilized water *n.* **b'an ha'**

stethoscope *n.* **ab'ib'leb'aal'ch'ool**
n. **ab'ib'leb'aal aam**
n. **ab'ib'leb'aal yajel**

stew *n.* **chiqb'il tib'**

sticker *n.* **eetalil**
n. **latz-eetal**
n. **letzelhu**

stiff *adj.* **chek'**

stigma (flower) *n.* **ru'uj atz'um**

still *conj.* **toj**

still life *n.* **xaqxo jalam'uuch**

stimulant *n.* **kawresinel ch'ool**

stimulate *v.* **kawresink ch'ool**

stimulus *n.* **kawresil**

stingray *n.* **perkar**

stingy *adj.* **aj pix**
adj. **pix**

stinking *adj.* **chu**

stir *v.* **junajink**
v. **yuuk'ink**

stitch *v phr.* **ranok chi noq'**

stocking *n.* **b'atb'al oq**
n. **tz'apb'al oq**

         n. **xta oq**
         n. **xta xaab'**

stomach *n.* **job'nil**
         n. **sa'**

stomach ache *n.* **rahil sa'ej**
         n. **sa'ej**

stomach acid *n.* **yib'onik sa' sa'ej**

stone   *n.* **pek**
         n. **pekal**

stop   *v.* **xaq'ab'ank**

stop it! *phr.* **xxaqlin**

stopper *n.* **tapon**

storage battery
         n. **k'uulmetz'ew**

store   *n.* **k'ayib'aal**
         n. **loq'leb'aal**

storm   *n.* **kaqsut-iq'**
         n. **kaaq**

story   *n.* **seeraq'**

stove   *n.* **chiqleb'**
         n. **estuuf**
         n. **kaxlan chiqleb'**
         n. **kaxxaml**
         n. **q'ixaml**

straight *adj.* **tiik**

straight line *n.* **tiikaljuch'**
         n. **tiikil juch'ul**

strain   *v.* **tz'ilok**

strainer *n.* **tz'ileb'**

strait   *n.* **laatz'**

strange *adj.* **xik' ru**

stranger *n.* **najtil poyanam**
         n. **najt xtenamit**

stratosphere *n.* **xkab' tasal iq'**

straw   *n.* **k'im**
         n. **tz'ub'leb'**

straw hut *n.* **k'imal kab'l**

strawberry *n.* **met' tokan**
         n. **pechtokan**
         n. **perees**

stream *n.* **nima'**
         n. **roq ha'**

streamer *n.* **milmich' hu**

street   *n.* **numleb'aal**
         n. **roqb'e**

street corner *n.* **xxuk b'e**

street sweeper *n agt.* **aj mesunel**

streetlight *n.* **ch'ina kaaxukuutil lem**

strength *n.* **metz'ew**

stress   *n.* **ch'ich'i'il**
         v. **kawyaab'ink**
         n. **yaab' aatin**

stress on last syllable *n.* **xmaril kawil yaab'**

stress on second to last syllable
         n. **xkab' kawil yaab'**

stress on third to last syllable
         n. **rox kawil yaab'**

stressed vowel *n.* **kawyaab' na'tz'iib'**

stretch *v.* **rinok**
         v. **yu'uk**

stretcher *n.* **ch'ina ch'aat**

strict *adj.* **tz'aqal re ru naraj**

strike *v.* **b'ujuk**
    v. **ketok**
    v. **potz'ok**
    v. **sak'ok**
    v. **tenok**
    v. **wojok**

string *n.* **k'aam**

string bean *n.* **q'ap**

strip *n.* **xk'aamal**
    n. **xtaab'il**

strong *adj.* **kaw**
    adj. **kaw xmetz'ew**

structural geology
    n. **nawk'uub'tzuul**

structure *n.* **rilb'al**

stubborn *adj.* **jip**
    adj. **numjip**

student *n.* **tijom**
    n. **tzolom**

student desk *n.* **meexil tz'iib'**

study *v phr.* **ilok chi us**
    v. **tzolok**
    n. **xna'aj tzolok**

study guide *n.* **xb'ehulk'utuk**

stuff *v.* **b'ut'uk**

stuffed animal *n.* **kaxtzukxul**

stump *n.* **toon**

stupid *adj.* **jip**
    adj. **jok**

stutter *v phr.* **lotz re**
    v phr. **tat re**

style (flower) *n.* **roq-atz'um**

sub ceiling *n.* **kaxlankaq'**

subconscious
    n. **rub'elal'aj'ookil**

subject *n agt.* **aj b'aanunel**
    n. **b'aanunel**
    n. **nak'ab'a'iik**
    n. **ru tzolom**

submarine *n.* **jukub' re rub'elha'**

substitute *n.* **eeqaj**

subtract *v.* **jeb'ok**

subtraction *n.* **jeb'ok**
    n. **jeb'ok-ajl**

succeed *v.* **elab'k**

success *n.* **elab'k**

suck *v.* **tz'ub'uk**

suddenly *adv.* **maare**

suffer *v.* **raho'k**

sufficient *adj.* **tz'aqal**

suffix *n.* **raqtz'aqob'l**

sugar *n.* **asuukr**
    n. **k'ajkab'**

sugar bowl *n.* **xna'aj k'aj kab'**

sugarcane *n.* **asuukr utz'ajl**
    n. **utz'ajl**
    n. **utz'aal**

suggest *v.* **sihokna'leb'**

suit *n.* **junxaqalil t'ikr**

suit case *n.* **iiq**

sullen *adj.* **moymo ru xtib'el**

sulphur *n.* **rarehilpoq**

sum   *n.* **ch'utub'ank**
         n. **molool**
         n. **tamok-ajl**
         n. **xmola**

summarize *v.* **k'osok**

summarized *adj.* **k'osb'il**

summary *n.* **xk'oslal**

summer *n.* **saq'ehil**

summit *n.* **ru'uj tzuul**
         n. **xb'een tzuul**

summon *v.* **b'oqok**

sun   *n.* **saq'e**

sun belt *n.* **tiqwal siraalch'och'**

sun dry *v phr.* **k'ehok chi ru saq'e**

sun god *n.* **b'alamq'e**

sunburn *n.* **k'atom saq'e**

sunburn lotion *n.* **b'an xk'atom saq'e**

Sunday *n.* **tomiin**

sunflower *n.* **k'onon**

sunglasses *n.* **moyileb'**

sunny *n.* **saq'ehil kutan**

sunrise *n.* **eq'laaho'k**

sunset *n.* **ewuuk**

sunshade *n.* **mu**

sunshine *n.* **roq saq'e**

sunstroke *n.* **lub'k chi ru saq'e**

supermarket *n.* **nimla k'ayib'aal**

supernova *n.* **pukchahim**

supersonic *adj.* **numkawyaab'**

supervisor *n agt.* **aj ilolk'anjel**
            n agt. **aj ilom aj k'anjel**

supper *n.* **wa re ewu**

suppository *n.* **b'aqil b'an**
             n. **ch'ikb'ilb'an**

supreme court
         n. **nimalraqb'leb'aatin**
         n. **xnimal raqb'a chaq'rab'**

sure   *phr.* **jo'kan tz'aqal**

surface *n.* **xb'een**

surface area *n.* **xsa' ruhil**

surgeon *n agt.* **aj cho'onel**

surgical instruments
         n. **xk'anjelob'aal aj b'anonel**

surgical scar *n.* **cho'b'ol**

surname *n.* **xsum k'ab'a'ej**

surprise *n.* **maatan**

surprised *adj.* **nasach xch'ool**
           adj. **sachaamil xch'ool**

surrender *v phr.* **q'axtesink ib'**
           v phr. **xe'xke rib'**

surround *v.* **sutuxink**

survey *n.* **ka'ch'olob'ank**
        v. **patz'ok**
        n. **raqalyalb'a'ix**

suspect *v.* **k'a'uxlak**
         n. **poyanam wan aatin chirix**

suspender *n.* **riiqankil**
    n. **xk'aamal**

suspension points *n.* **oxtz'uq**
    n. **tz'uqux**

sustainability *n.* **ilok ib'**

suture *n.* **b'ojok tiq'il**
    n. **xiitink tiq'il**

SUV *n.* **ch'ina poy ch'iich'**

swallow *v.* **nuq'uk**

swamp *n.* **k'anha'**
    n. **saab'**
    n. **saab' ha'**

swan *n.* **kaxkatras**
    n. **yenyookil patux**

swear (an oath) *v.* **ch'olob'ank**

sweat *n.* **tiqob'**

sweater *n.* **q'ixt'ikr**

sweatpants *n.* **potzwex**

sweats *n.* **potzwex**

sweep *v.* **mesunk**

sweet *adj.* **ki'**

sweet corn *n.* **al ixim**

sweet potato *n.* **is**
    n. **paaps**

sweet roll *n.* **kab'il kaxlan wa**

sweets *n.* **kab'**

swelling *n.* **sipook**
    n. **siipilal**
    n. **teb'elal**

swim *v.* **numxik**

swimmer *n agt.* **aj muqa'l**
    n agt. **aj numxinel**

swimming *n.* **numxik**

swimming pool *n.* **atib'aal**
    n. **numxib'aal**

swimsuit *n.* **aq' re atink**
    n. **atiyach'**

swindle *n.* **maq'ok sa' b'alaq'**

swindler *n agt.* **aj maq'onel**

swine *n.* **aaq**

swing *n.* **ab'**
    n. **t'uuyleb'**

switch *n.* **raqb'ametz'ew**

swollen *n.* **kaqpech'in**

sword *n.* **makaan**
    n. **nimla ch'iich'**

swordfish *n.* **jutz' kar**

syllabary *n.* **xhuhul raq**
    n. **yehiileb'**

syllable *n.* **yehiil**

symbol *n.* **eetal**

symbolism *n.* **eetalilul**

symmetric figure *n.* **juntaq'eetil
    eetalil**

symmetry *n.* **tiik-uhil**

symptoms *n.* **xtiklajik li yajel**

synaleph *n.* **k'ulb'atz'iib'**

synonym *n.* **juneetil'aatin**
    n. **juntaq'eetil'aatin**
    n. **juntaq'eetyaalalil**

syntax *n.* **nawtus'aatin**

synthesis *n.* **xb'ehul k'osok**

syphilis *n.* **b'ux**

syringe *n.* **jerink**
         n. **kutleb'**

syrup   *n.* **b'an uk'b'il**

systolic blood pressure
         n. **metz'ew ich'mulej elkik'**
         n. **xmetz'ew ich'mulej elkik'**

T - t

tab   *n.* **sachom**

table   *n.* **meex**

tablecloth   *n.* **ru meex**
             n. **xtameex**

tablet   *n.* **ch'ina b'an**
             n. **nuq'b'ilb'an**
             n. **pastiiy**

taboo   *n.* **awas**

tack   *n.* **ch'int'ojiil**
             n. **tachweel**

taco   *n.* **b'otwa**

tact   *n.* **eek'ob'aal**
             n. **ixkej**

tail   *n.* **ye**

tail wing   *n.* **xye so'sol ch'iich'**

tailor   *n agt.* **aj b'ojonel**

take   *v.* **chapok**

take (an amount of time)
             v. **b'aayk**

take communion *v.* **loq'oniik**

take note of *v phr.* **k'ehok eetal**

take notes   *v.* **tz'iib'ak**

take out   *v.* **isink**

take pictures *v.* **jalam'uuchib'k**

take possession of *v.* **eechank**

take your time *phr.* **b'aanu sa' xyaalal**

talc   *n.* **poqb'an**
             n. **poqilsunob'l**
             n. **putzputzb'an**

talcum powder *n.* **poqb'an**
             n. **poqilsunob'l**
             n. **putzputzb'an**

tale   *n.* **seeraq'**

talk   *v.* **aatinak**
             v. **aatinamank**
             v. **seeraq'ik**

talkative   *adj.* **aj num aatin**
             adj. **yal sa' re naxik**

tall   *adj.* **najt roq**
             adj. **najt xteram**
             adj. **nimnim**
             adj. **nim roq**
             adj. **nim xteram**
             adj. **tutz'tu**
             adj. **yak'ach**

talon   *n.* **nimqi ixi'ij**

tamale   *n.* **ob'en**

tamarind   *n.* **wach'iil**

tambourine   *n.* **kottzuj**
    n. **tzojtzojch'iich'**

tan   *v phr.* **chiqok tz'uum**

tangerine   *n.* **mandariin**

tangle   *v.* **pixlenk**
    v. **tzuklenk**

tap   *n.* **yaaw**

tape   *n.* **letzleb'**
    v. **letzok**

tape player   *n.* **chapleb'aal aatin**
    n. **chapleb'aatin**
    n. **taab'leb'aal b'ich**

tape recorder   *n.* **chapleb'aal aatin**
    n. **chapleb'aatin**
    n. **chapleb' aatin**

tapir   *n.* **tixl**

tar   *n.* **q'eqitz'aakalb'e**

tarantula   *n.* **q'eq aj am**

target shoot   *v phr.* **b'atz'unk puub'ak**

tarp   *n.* **mokooch**

task   *n.* **kub'siil**
    n. **tenq'**

taste   *v phr.* **hulak chi uhej**
    n. **yaleb'aal**
    v. **yalok**
    v phr. **yalok xsahil**

tasty   *adj.* **sa**
    adj. **saasa**

tattoo   *n.* **eetalil xtz'uumal**

tax   *n.* **toj**

tax identification number
    n. **ajlilkomontoj**
    n. **rajliltoj**

taxes   *n.* **toj chi ru awab'ej**

taxi   *n.* **taks**

taxi stand   *n.* **xna'aj taks**

TB   *n.* **xyajel pospo'oy**

tea   *n.* **te**

teach   *v.* **k'utuk**
    v. **tzolok**

teacher   *n agt.* **aj k'utunel**
    n. **aj tzolonel**
    n. **q'usunel**

teaching   *n.* **nawk'utuk**

teaching methods   *n.* **xb'ehul k'utuk**

teaching module   *n.* **xtasalil tzolok**

teaching staff   *n.* **xmolamil aj k'utunel**

team   *n.* **aj b'atz'uneleb'**
    n. **xmolamil b'atz'unk**

team jersey   *n.* **b'atz-aq'**

teapot   *n.* **xxaaril te**

tear   *v.* **pejok**
    v. **q'ichok**
    v. **q'irok**
    v. **re'ok**
    n. **xya'al u**

teat   *n.* **ru'uj tu'**
    n. **tu'**

technology   *n.* **nawk'anjelahom**

technology use *n.* **oksink nawk'anjelahom**

tectonic plates *n.* **tasal ruuchich'och'**

teeth *n.* **ruuch e**

Tektitek *lang.* **tektiteko**

telegram *n.* **junpaatil'esil**
   n. **k'aj'esil**

telegraph *n.* **pitz'leb'taql**

telegraph machine
   n. **numsib'aal k'aj' esil**

telegrapher *n agt.* **aj numsihom k'aj' esil**
   n. **nums'esilb'aal**

telephone *n.* **aatinob'aal ch'iich'**
   n. **b'oqleb'**
   n. **b'oqleb'aal**
   n. **b'oqleb'aal ch'iich'**
   n. **teleef**

telephone bill *n.* **xhuhil li aatik'aam ch'iich'**

telescope *n.* **ilob'aal chahim**
   n. **najt-ileb'**

television *n.* **kaxmu**
   n. **kaxmu helleb'**
   n. **lemaal'esil**
   n. **teleb'ision**

television antenna *n.* **xmisik' kaxmu**

tell stories *v.* **seeraq'ik**

teller *n agt.* **aj xokol tumin**

telophase *n.* **xka pojk'ok**

temperate zone *n.* **keekehil siraalch'och'**

temperature *n.* **tiqkehil**
   n. **xtiqwalil**

temple *n.* **ermiit**
   n. **kapiiy**
   n. **tijob'aal**

temples *n.* **k'atq jolom**
   n. **toon xik**

tempt *v.* **aalenk**

temptation *n.* **atawank**

ten *num.* **(10.) lajeeb'**

ten cents *n.* **lajeb' senta**

ten quetzals *n.* **lajeb' ketzal**

tender *adj.* **q'un**

tenderness *n.* **q'unil**

tendon *n.* **ich'**
   n. **ich'mul**

tennis shoes *n.* **aanilxaab'**
   n. **potzxaab'**

tent *n.* **kaxmuheb'aal**

tenth *num.* **(10th.) xlajee**

terminal *n.* **hilob'eleb'aal ch'iich'**

terminal side (of an angle)
   n. **xk'atq xraqik**

termites *n.* **k'ams**

terrace *n.* **tz'akal'ochoch**

terrain *n.* **waqlajuk'aam**
   n. **xoral**

terrified *adj.* **naxiwak**

test   *n.* **tz'ilb'a'ix**
          v. **tz'ilok-ix**
          n. **tz'ilool'ix**
          n. **yalb'a'ix**
          n. **yalok ix**

testicles *n.* **ab'aj**
          n. **ab'ajil**
          n. **molb'**
          n. **naq' it**
          n. **naq' kun**

testify   *v phr.* **yehok aatin sa'
          chaq'rab'**

testimony *n.* **yehom**

tetrasyllable *n.* **kaayehiil**

text message *n.* **esil sa' tz'iib'**

thank   *v.* **b'antyoxink**

thank you *phr.* **b'antyox**

thank you very much
          phr. **naab'alwa
          b'antyox**

thankful, grateful
          adj. **nab'anyoxin**

thanks   *phr.* **b'antyox**

thanks for your help
          phr. **ninb'anyoxi laa
          tenq'**

that   *pron.* **a'an**
          pron. **naq**
          pron. **wan le'**

that depends *phr.* **toja' yaal**

that one *pron.* **a'an a'an**
          pron. **a'wa'ran**
          pron. **wan le'**

that one (over there)
          pron. **a'wanle'**

that's all *phr.* **ka'aj wi a'an**

that's enough *phr.* **tz'aqal**

that's interesting *phr.* **us raj**

that's it *phr.* **ka'aj wi a'an**

that's life *phr.* **jo'kan li wank**

that's true *phr.* **yaal**

that's why *conj.* **a' ajb'an**
          conj. **jo'kan**
          conj. **jo'kan naq**

thatch   *n.* **k'imal kab'l**

the (plural) *art.* **eb' li**

the (singular) *art.* **li**

the day before *n.* **jun kutan
          rub'elaj**

the day before a party
          n. **mixpirik**

theater   *n.* **k'utb'esib'aal**

theatrical *adj.* **k'utb'il**

theatrical production
          n. **k'utb'ahom**

theft   *n.* **elq'**

them   *pron.* **eb' a'an**

thematic *adj.* **xna'leb'il**

theme   *n.* **na'leb'**
          n. **xna'leb'il**

then   *adv phr.* **jo'kan b'i'**

there   *adv.* **aran**
          adv. **le'**
          adv phr. **sa' a'an**

there is no more *phr.* **maak'a' chik**

there still are... *phr.* **toj ruch...** *phr.* **toj wan...**

thermometer *n.* **b'isleb'tiq** *n.* **re b'isok tiq**

thermos *n.* **kaxsu** *n.* **k'uuleb'aaltiq**

thermosphere *n.* **xka tasal'iq'**

thermostat *n.* **tuqb'ametz'ew**

thesaurus *n.* **xch'oolaatin juntaq'eetil**

these *pron.* **a'ineb'** *pron.* **eb' a'in**

they *pron.* **a'aneb'** *pron.* **eb' a'an**

thick *adj.* **b'urux b'urux** *adj.* **leb'lo** *adj.* **nim xsa'** *adj.* **pim** *adj.* **sas** *adj.* **teb'es** *adj.* **t'ikt'o**

thicken *v.* **sasob'resink**

thief *n agt.* **aj elq'** *n.* **jochonel** *n.* **piyok**

thigh *n.* **ru a'** *n.* **tib'elej** *n.* **tz'ej**

thimble *n.* **xkolb'al ru'uj uqb'**

thin *adj.* **b'aq xtib'el** *adj.* **b'arich'** *adj.* **jay**

thing *n.* **k'a'aq re ru** *n.* **k'a'atq ru**

thing to be weighed *n.* **aalom**

think *v.* **k'a'uxlak** *v.* **k'oxlak**

think nothing of it *phr.* **matk'a'uxlak**

thinker *n agt.* **aj k'a'uxl**

third *n.* **oxjachal** *num.* **(3rd.) rox**

third grade *n.* **rox na'aj**

third to last *adj.* **roxch'otonel**

thirst *n.* **chaqi'el**

thirsty *adj.* **chaqiq re**

thirteen *num.* **(13.) oxlaju**

thirteenth *num.* **(13th.) roxlajuil**

thirtieth *num.* **(30th.) xlajee xka'k'aalil**

thirty *num.* **(30.) lajeeb' xka'k'aal**

thirty-eight *num.* **(38.) waqxaqlaju xka'k'aal**

thirty-five *num.* **(35.) o'laju xka'k'aal**

thirty-four *num.* **(34.) kaalaju xka'k'aal**

thirty-nine *num.* **(39.) b'elelaju xka'k'aal**

thirty-one *num.* **(31.) junlaju xka'k'aal**

thirty-seven *num.* **(37.) wuqlaju xka'k'aal**

thirty-six *num.* **(36.) waqlaju xka'k'aal**

thirty-three *num.* **(33.) oxlaju xka'k'aal**

thirty-two *num.* **(32.) kab'laju xka'k'aal**

this *pron.* **a'in**

this evening *adv phr.* **chi ru li q'oqyin a'in**

this month *n.* **li po a'in**

this one *pron.* **a'an a'in**
    pron. **a'in**

this week *n.* **li xamaan a'in**

thorax *n.* **maqab'**
    n. **polook'**

thorn *n.* **k'ix**
    n. **xk'ix**

though *conj.* **us ta**

thought *n.* **k'a'uxl**

thoughtful *adj.* **tk'a'uxlaq**

thousand *n.* **lajeeb' syent**
    n. **lajeek'aal rox oq'oob'**

thread *n.* **k'aam**
    n. **noq'**

thread a needle *v phr.* **xnoq'inkil li akuux**

threat *n.* **k'ehok xiw**

threaten *v phr.* **k'ehok xiw**
    v. **seb'esink**
    v. **xib'enk**

three *num.* **(3.) oxib'**

three by three *adv.* **ox ox**

three days ago *adv.* **oxejer**

three hundred *n.* **o'lajuk'aal**

three thousand *n.* **lajeek'aal xwaqxaq roq'ob'**

three times *adv.* **oxsut**
    adv. **oxwa**

thresh *v.* **ch'epok**
    v. **iximaak**

throat *n.* **sa' kuxej**
    n. **xolol**
    n. **xsa' ja'aj**

throne *n.* **k'ojarib'aal**

through *prep.* **rik'in**
    prep. **sa'**
    prep. **sa' xk'ab'a'**
    prep. **sa' xmaak**
    prep. **xb'aan**

throw *v.* **kutuk**
    v. **pumuk**
    v. **puulesink**
    v. **rumuk**
    v. **tz'eqok**

thumb *n.* **na' uq'm**
    n. **xmama'il uq'mej**

thumbnail photo *n.* **mitz'jalam'u**

thumbtack *n.* **ch'int'ojiil**
    n. **tachweel**

thunder *n.* **kaaq**
    n. **xyaab' kaaq**

thunderstorm *n.* **repom kaaq**

Thursday *n.* **jweews**
    n. **xkakutan**

thus   *adv phr.* **chi kama'an**
          adv phr. **chi kama'in**

tiara   *n.* **nat'leb'ismal**

tick   *n.* **sip**

ticket   *n.* **tojl**

ticket office   *n.* **k'ayib'aal b'oleet**

ticket taker   *n agt.* **aj k'aak'anel**

ticket window   *n.* **tojleb'aal**

tickle   *n.* **katzkatz**
       n. **wotz'otz'**
       v. **wotz'otz'ink**

tie   *v.* **b'ak'ok**
     n. **b'eq**
     v. **jit'ok**
     n. **korb'aat**
     n. **yutkux**

tiger   *n.* **hix**

tiger cat   *n.* **k'amb'olay**
       n. **saq b'alam**

tighten   *v.* **nat'ok**

tightrope walker   *n agt.* **aj b'eenel chi ru b'aqb'il k'aam sa iq'**

tile   *n.* **ch'ejej**
     n. **lemtz'un xan**

tilled land   *n.* **cho'leb' ch'och'**

time   *n.* **kutan**
      n. **q'iil**
      n. **sut**
      n. **taqik**

time particle   *part.* **chaq**

times   *n.* **eetalpuk-ajl**
      n. **reetal puktasiil**

tin   *n.* **laat**

tin cup   *n.* **ch'iich' sek'**

tin plate   *n.* **ch'iich' sek'**

tin roofing sheet   *n.* **k'imalch'iich'**

tire   *v.* **lub'k**
     n. **roq poy ch'iich'**
     n. **tolb'ech'iich'**
     n. **tool**

tired   *adj.* **lub'lu**
      adj. **tawajenaq**

tissue   *n.* **tz'uumal**

tissues   *n.* **huhil sut**

tithing   *n.* **lajetqil**

title   *n.* **huraqb'atzolok**
     n. **jolomil na'leb'**
     n. **k'ajk'amontzolok**

to   *prep.* **chi**
   prep. **cho'q re**
   prep. **sa'**

to feel itchy   *v.* **amamnak**

to grow old   *v.* **tixk**

to the left   *adv phr.* **chi tz'e**

to the right   *adv phr.* **chi nim**

to your left   *adv phr.* **sa' laatz'e**

to your right   *adv phr.* **sa' laanim**

toad   *n.* **amoch**
     n. **k'oopopo'**

toast   *v.* **jorank**
     n. **k'orechkaxlanwa**

toasted   *adj.* **jorinb'il**

toaster   *n.* **jorinkleb'**
     n. **k'ileb'aal**

n. **k'orechib'aal**
n. **k'orleb'**

tobacco *n.* **may**

today *n.* **anaqwan**
adv. **hoon**

together *adv.* **ch'utch'u**
adv. **laq'lo**
adj. **ochb'eninb'il**
adj. **sa' komonil**

toilet *n.* **k'otleb'aal**
n. **tz'eqleb'aal**

toilet paper *n.* **hu re li k'otak**

tolerance *n.* **xk'uyb'al**

tolerate *v.* **kuyuk**

toll *v.* **tzinb'ank**

toll booth *n.* **rochoch aj titz'ol toj**

tomato *n.* **pix**

tomato juice *n.* **xya'al pix**

tomato sauce *n.* **ke'b'il pix**
n. **puq'b'il pix**

tomorrow *adv.* **hulaj**

tomorrow afternoon *adv phr.* **hulaj ewu**

tomorrow evening *adv phr.* **hulaj chi q'eq**

tomorrow morning *adv phr.* **hulaj chi eq'la**

Tomás *nick.* **Max**

ton *n.* **junmay kintal**
n. **xyuwa'ilb'iis**

tongs *n.* **q'esyaxch'iich'**
n. **yax**

tongue *n.* **aatinob'aal**
n. **ru'uj aq'**
n. **xtib'el ru'uj aq'**

tongue (of a shoe) *n.* **raq'xaab'**

tongue depresser *n.* **kub'sib'aal ru'uj aq'**

tongue twister *n.* **t'ilb'a'u'ji'aq**
n. **t'ilru'uj'aq**

tonight *n.* **hoon chi q'eq**

tonsillitis *n.* **xyajelxnaq'ja'aj**

too *adv phr.* **jo'kan aj wi'**

too bad (for you)! *phr.* **ink'a' us xat-elq**

too much *adv.* **numtajenaq**

tool *n.* **k'anjelob'aal**

toolbox *n.* **xkaxonil k'anjeleb'aal**

tooth *n.* **e**
n. **ruuch e**

toothache *n.* **rahil ruuch e**

toothbrush *n.* **ji'leb'-e**
n. **re chajok sa' e**
n. **xji'b'al ruuch e**

toothless *adj.* **lolom re**
adj. **t'omt'o re**

toothpaste *n.* **xq'emal ruuch e**
n. **xxab'onil ruuch e**

top *n.* **ru'uj**
n. **sururu**
n. **sururub'atz'uul**
n. **tz'apleb'**

toponym *n.* **k'ab'a'na'jej**

torch   *n.* **b'eexam**
           n. **kanxam**
           n. **lampr**
           n. **xam**

torso   *n.* **maqab'**
           n. **yiitoq**

tortilla   *n.* **wa**

tortoise   *n.* **kok**

tostada   *n.* **xujwahiltib'**

total   *n.* **tamok-ajl**

total eclipse *n.* **juntz'ap tiwok**

toucan   *n.* **raxpan**
           n. **seelapan**

touch   *v.* **ch'e'ok**
           n. **eek'ob'aal**
           n. **ixkej**

tourist   *n agt.* **aj ab'l tenamit**
           n agt. **aj b'e**

tow truck *n.* **xook'il ch'iich'**

toward   *prep.* **chi xk'atq**

towel   *n.* **chaqihob' t'ikr**
           n. **masleb'ix**
           n. **potzt'ikr**
           n. **tuntuukir t'ikr**
           n. **tuwaay**

tower   *n.* **kab'l najt xteram**
           n. **toor**

town   *n.* **tenamit**

town leader *n.* **aj jolominel k'aleb'aal**

toy   *n.* **b'atz'uul**

toy store *n.* **k'ayib'aal b'atz'uul**

trace   *v.* **jalam'uuchib'k**
           v. **juch'uk**

tractor   *n.* **b'ekol ch'och'**
           n. **hixch'iich'**

trade   *v.* **jalok**

tradition *n.* **najter na'leb'**

traditional
           adj. **najterilk'utb'esink**

traffic   *n.* **xk'ihal b'eleb'aalch'iich'**

traffic circle *n.* **k'ulb'aq'qax'ib'**

traffic light *n.* **kaxlan xamlel b'e**
           n. **k'utb'a numleb'**
           n. **k'utul numeb'aal**

traffic sign *n.* **reetalil b'e**

traffic signal *n.* **ilb'anumleb'**
           n. **k'ehol numleb'**

trailer truck *n.* **motzo'ch'iich'**

train   *v.* **jultikank**
           n. **k'anti'ch'iich'**
           n. **tren**

tramp   *n.* **neb'a'**

transform *n.* **jaltesink**

transformer *n.* **jalb'a'metz'ew**

transitive (verb) *n.* **ka'kab'iluxk**

translation *n.* **jalok-aatin**

transmit   *v.* **numsink**

transparent *adj.* **kutaniru**
           adj. **saqen ru**

transparent roof panel
           n. **saqenk'im**

transport *n.* **b'eleb'aal**

trap   *n.* **ch'imb'**
           n. **ch'imb'ul**
           v. **ch'imb'unk**
           n. **ra'al**
           v. **ra'alenk**

trapeze artist *n agt.* **aj t'uyanel**

trash   *n.* **mul**
           n. **mulel**

trash can *n.* **xchakachil mul**
           n. **xna'aj hu**
           n. **xna'aj mul**

travel   *v.* **b'eek**
           v. **b'eenink**

travel allowance
           n. **eeqajsachomj**

travel around *v.* **b'eenink**

travel through the forest
           v. **k'iche'b'aalik**

travel through the mountains
           v. **k'iche'b'aalik**

traveler   *n agt.* **aj b'e**

tray   *n.* **b'elaal tzakahemq**

treasure   *n.* **k'o'al**

treatment *n.* **b'ane'k**

tree   *n.* **che'**

tree trunk *n.* **roq**
           n. **toon**
           n. **xtoonal ruq'b'**

trees   *n.* **che'eb'**

tremble   *v.* **parpotk**

trial   *n.* **raqok aatin**

triangle   *n.* **b'alxuk**
           n. **oxxukuut**

tributary *n.* **ruq' nima'**

tribute   *n.* **toj**

trim   *v.* **k'osok**
           v. **setok**

trinomial *n.* **ox'eetalb'irok**

trip   *v.* **tichk'ok**

tripe   *n.* **k'aamk'ot**

triphthong *n.* **oxjunajink xna'tz'iib'**

tripod   *n.* **chak'oq**
           n. **oxxaala**

trisyllable *n.* **oxraqyehok**

troglodyte *n.* **ch'olwinq**

trophy
           n. **k'ajk'amonkmetzew**
           n. **maatanej**
           n. **xmaatanil li yaloku**

Tropic of Cancer *n.* **taqe'q q'eq'ookot eetalil**

Tropic of Capricorn *n.* **taq'a q'eq'ookot eetalil**

tropics   *n.* **tiqwal siraalch'och'**

troposphere *n.* **xb'een tasal iq'**

trough   *n.* **job'che'**

trousers   *n.* **wex**

trowel   *n.* **ji'leb'tz'ak**
           n. **tz'akleb'**
           n. **xlek aj tz'ak**

truck *n.* **kamyon**
    n. **teken ch'iich'**

true *adj.* **yaal**

trumpet *n.* **jayaab'wajb'**
    n. **kaxxuxb'**
    n. **q'anch'iich'**
    n. **trompeet**

trumpeter *n.* **aj wajb'a'apuul**

trunk *n.* **kaax**
    n. **xe'**
    n. **xna'aj iiq**

trunk (fruit bearing) *n.* **raqan**

truth *n.* **xyaalal**
    n. **yaal**

try *v.* **yalok**

t-shirt *n.* **ch'otlepon**

tuberculosis *n.* **kuxb'ej**
    n. **xyajel pospo'oy**

Tuesday *n.* **maarts**
    n. **xkab'kutan**

tumpline *n.* **taab'**

tune in *v.* **rab'inkil**

turkey *n.* **ak'ach**
    n. **xtib'el ak'ach**

turkey soup *n.* **kaq ik**

turn *v.* **b'alq'usink**
    v. **q'otok**

turn around *v.* **b'alq'usink**
    v. **q'otonk**

turn red *v.* **kaq'ok**

turn signal *n.* **ch'ina elajinel**
    n. **patz'num**
    n. **patz'numleb'**

turnip *n.* **naaw**
    n. **saqxe'**

turtle *n.* **kok**

turtle shell *n.* **rix kok**

tusk *n.* **tz'i' e**

TV *n.* **kaxmu**
    n. **lemaal'esil**

twelfth *num.* **(12th.)**
    xkab'lajuil

twelve *num.* **(12.) kab'laju**

twentieth *num.* **(20th.)**
    xjunmayil

twenty *num.* **(20.) jun may**

twenty-day period *n.* **k'aal**

twenty-eight *num.* **(28.)**
    waqxaq'ib' xka'k'aal

twenty-first *num.* **(21st.) xjun**
    xka'k'aalil

twenty-five *num.* **(25.) oob'**
    xka'k'aal

twenty-five cents *n.* **o'laju**
    xk'ak'aal senta

twenty-four *num.* **(24.) kaahib'**
    xka'k'aal

twenty-nine *num.* **(29.) b'eleb'**
    xka'k'aal

twenty-one *num.* **(21.) jun**
    xka'k'aal

twenty-second *num.* **(22nd.)**
    xkab' xka'k'aalil

twenty-seven *num.* **(27.) wukub'**
    xka'k'aal

twenty-six *num.* **(26.) waqib' xka'k'aal**

twenty-three *num.* **(23.) oxib' xka'k'aal**

twenty-two *num.* **(22.) wiib' xka'k'aal**

twice *adv.* **ka'wa** *adv.* **ka'ta**

twig *n.* **ch'ina ruq'**

twins *n.* **lut**

twist *v.* **k'onok** *v.* **siq'ok** *v.* **yokosink**

twisted *adj.* **q'otq'o** *adj.* **q'oot**

two *num.* **(2.) wiib'**

two days ago *n.* **kab'ejer**

two days later *n.* **kiib' kutan chi rix**

two hundred *n.* **lajeek'aal**

two thousand *n.* **oob' oq'ob'**

two times *adv.* **ka'wa** *adv.* **ka'ta**

tympanic membrane *n.* **xulel xikej**

type *n.* **chankatq ru** *n.* **paay** *n.* **paayil**

typewriter *n.* **k'uub'tz'iib'leb'** *n.* **tz'iib'leb' ch'iich'**

typhoid *n.* **kaqi yajel**

typical *adj.* **ok eechej**

Tz'utujil *lang.* **tz'utujil**

U - u

udder *n.* **xtu' wakax**

ugly *adj.* **jo'maajo'** *adj.* **xa'b'eetal** *adj.* **yib' ru**

ultraviolet light *n.* **xche' saq'e**

umbrella *n.* **muheel** *n.* **paraaw** *n.* **xik'sotz'**

uncle *n.* **ikan**

uncombed *adj.* **ink'a' t'e'b'il**

uncomfortable *adj.* **ch'a'aj treek'a** *adj.* **kosa**

unconscious *adj.* **ink'a' jultik re** *adj.* **junpaatilsachk**

unconverted (archaic) *n.* **ch'olwinq**

under *prep.* **chi rub'el** *prep.* **rub'el**

underpants *n.* **kok' aq' re winq**

undersea earthquake *n.* **palawhiik**

439

undershirt *n.* **ch'ot t'ikr**

underskirt *n.* **xta-uuq**

understand *v.* **na'leb'ak**
    v phr. **tawok u**
    v phr. **tawok xyaalal**

undertaker *n agt.* **aj ilom kamenaq**

underwear *n.* **kok' aq' re ixq**
    n. **kok' aq' re winq**
    n. **xta b'aatal**
    n. **xyach'winq**
    n. **yach'**

underworld *n.* **xb'alb'a**

undo *v.* **juk'uk**
    v. **po'ok**

undress *v phr.* **isink aq'**

unfortunate *adj.* **kaqcha**

unhappiness *n.* **maasahil wank**

unicellular *adj.* **junilna'yu'am**

uniform *n.* **aq'**

union *n.* **junajihom**
    n. **laq'ab'ank**

unique *adj.* **jun**
    adj. **junrib'**

unit *n.* **junqalil**
    n. **xraqalil**

unit of ten *n.* **lajetqil**

United Nations *n.* **xmolamil k'iila tenamital**

United States *n.* **ch'uutal tenamit**

unity *n.* **junajil**
    n. **junqalil**

universe *n.* **choxach'och'**

university *n.* **nimaltzoleb'aal**
    n. **xnimal ru tzoleb'aal**

university level *n.* **xkaatanal tzolok**

unknown *adj.* **aak'ab'**
    adj. **manawb'il**

unoccupied *adj.* **yamyo ru**

unpaved road *n.* **pekilnimb'e**

unpredictable *adj.* **ink'a' nanawman k'a tb'aanu**

unravel *v.* **hitok**

unreliable *adj.* **moko naxsume ta jo'yaal**

unripe *adj.* **al**
    adj. **rax**
    adj. **toj al**

unroll *v.* **b'orok**

unsatisfied *adj.* **ch'iqch'o xch'ool**

untangle *v.* **hirok**
    v. **hitok**

untie *v.* **b'orok**
    v. **hitok**
    v. **k'ixok**

until *conj.* **retal**
    conj. **tixto toj**
    conj. **toj**

until now *conj.* **toja'**

untrue *adj.* **moko yaal ta**

unuseful *adj.* **maak'a' rusil**

unwind *v.* **b'orok**

up *prep.* **taqe'q**

upper case *n.* **astz'iib'**

upset *adj.* **nach'a'ajko'**

Uranus *n.* **xwuq ralsaq'e**

urban center *n.* **tenamitil teepal**

urinary pain *n.* **ra chu'**

urinate *v.* **chu'uk**

urine *n.* **chu'**

Ursa Major *n.* **wuqchahim**

Ursa Minor *n.* **nach'ilchahim**

us *pron.* **laa'o**

use up *v.* **sachik**

used *adj.* **lil**
  adj. **qeel**

useful *adj.* **aajel**
  adj. **wan rusil**

usher *n agt.* **aj hiltesinel**

uterus *n.* **alob'aal**
  n. **kub'sa'**
  n. **sa' ixq**

utility room *n.* **xna'aj k'a'aq re ru**

utterance indicating a close call *interj.* **uy**

utterance indicating a minor failure *interj.* **t'**

utterance indicating danger *interj.* **uyaluy**

utterance indicating hope or a wish *part.* **taxaq**

utterance indicating lack of interest *interj.* **i'**

utterance of disapproval *interj.* **sht!**

utterance of disgust *interj.* **chix**

utterance of doubt or disagreement *interj.* **eh**

utterance of pain *interj.* **ay**

utterance of pain or pity *interj.* **aaa**

utterance of surprise *interj.* **eh!**

utterance of understanding *interj.* **ah** *interj.* **ih**

utterance seeking recognition *interj.* **sht**

V - v

vacation *n.* **xq'ehil hilaal**

vaccination *n.* **b'akuun**

vacuole *n.* **julel**
  n. **tz'ilol**

vacuum cleaner *n.* **jiq'leb'mul**

vagina *n.* **mi'**

vain *adj.* **namunta**

validation *n.* **ustaanankil**
             n. **xsumenkil**

valley   *n.* **ru taq'a**
          n. **taq'a**

valuable *adj.* **loq'al**

value   *n.* **xloq'al**
          n. **xtz'aq**

value-added tax *n.* **komontoj**

values   *n.* **loq'alil**
          n. **tiikalil**
          n. **tiikil loq'alil**

variable *n.* **xjalanil**

variant form *n.* **raatinxcha'alil**
              aatinib'aal
              n. **xjalob'aatinob'aal**

variety   *n.* **paay**
          n. **paayil**

varnish   *n.* **lemtz'b'on**
          v. **lemtz'b'onik**

vase   *n.* **xjaar uutz'u'uj**
          n. **xna'aj uutz'u'uj**

VAT   *n.* **komontoj**
          n. **toj**

vegetable *n.* **ruuch che'k'aam**
           n. **supq'een**
           n. **xe' ru che'**

vegetable seller *n agt.* **aj k'ay**
                  xe' ru che'

vegetables *n.* **ru ut xe' pim**

vegetation *n.* **che'k'aam**

veil   *n.* **b'eel**

vein   *n.* **ich'**
          n. **ich'mul**

velar   *n.* **xb'een'e yaab'**

velocity *n.* **metz'ewil**
          n. **raanil**

venison   *n.* **xtib'el kej**

Venus   *n.* **kaqchahim**
          n. **xulab'**

verb   *n.* **xch'oolaatin**

verbal   *adj.* **yeeb'il**

verse   *n.* **ch'ol'uutz'ujinb'il**
          aatin
          n. **raqaltz'iib'**
          n. **raapal**
          n. **xtz'iib'ul b'ich**

vertebrate *n.* **b'aqil xuleb'**

vertical *adj.* **xaqxo**

vertical line *n.* **xaqxookil juch'**

vertigo   *n.* **lub'ik**

very   *adv.* **jwal**

very bitter *adj.* **k'aak'a**

very clean *adj.* **ch'aj ch'aj**

very fermented
          adj. **ch'amch'am**

very fine *adj.* **musmus**

very good *adj.* **q'axal us**

very important *phr.* **jwal aajel**

very salty *adj.* **num atz'am**

very stiff *adj.* **chek'chek'**

very white *adj.* **saqpotz'in**
            adj. **saqpuk'in**

vest   *n.* **aq' ch'ot ruq'**

vestment *n.* **nimla t'ikr**
          n. **raq' qaawa'**

veterinarian   *n agt.* **aj ilom xul**

veterinary store   *n.* **k'ayib'aal b'an re ketomj**

vial   *n.* **mitz'meetil b'an**

vice president
   n. **xkab'awa'b'ejil**
   n. **xkab'il awab'ej**

vicious   *adj.* **maak'a' xkuyum**

Victor   *nick.* **B'it**

victory   *n.* **echanink**
   n. **ketok**

video   *n.* **ilob'aal mu**

video camera
   n. **chapleb'jalam'u**
   n. **xokleb' mu**

videocassette   *n.* **xna'aj lemal eetalil**

view   *n.* **ilob'aal**

vigorous   *adj.* **kaw rib'**

vile   *adj.* **tz'i'b'eetal**

village   *n.* **tenamit**

vindictive   *adj.* **naxk'e reeqaj naxk'ul**

vine   *n.* **aq'**
   n. **k'aam**

vine snake   *n.* **raxk'aj**

vinegar   *n.* **b'inaayr**
   n. **b'oj ha' tzakahemq**

violate   *v.* **muxuk**

violation   *n.* **muxuk**

violent   *adj.* **ch'impo'**
   adj. **josq'**

violet   *adj.* **raxtint**

violin   *n.* **jitz'jitz'**

violinist   *n agt.* **aj iitz'in**

viper   *n.* **k'anti' ra xmay re**
   n. **xna' k'anti'**

virgin   *n.* **tuq'ixq**

virtual education
   n. **muhilb'atijok**

virus   *n.* **xmaxel**

viscous   *adj.* **waa**

vise   *n.* **chapleb'**

vision   *n.* **ileb'aal**
   n. **ilob'aal xsa'u**

visit   *n.* **hulak**
   n. **ula'**
   v. **ula'ak**
   v. **ula'ank**

visitor   *n.* **ula'**

visitor log   *n.* **tasal hu re ula'**

visor   *n.* **ilob'aal**
   n. **lep-punit**

visual arts
   n. **tzoljalam'uuch'ink**

vitamin   *n.* **kawub'lb'an**

vitamin C   *n.* **b'itamin Se**

vocabulary   *n.* **tusleb'aal aatin**

vocalize   *v.* **yaab'ank**

voice   *n.* **ja'ajul**

volcanic   *adj.* **xk'uhil**

volcano   *n.* **k'u**
   n. **puub' tzuul**

volcanology   *n.* **nawk'uhil**

volleyball *n.* **b'olotz sum uq'ib'k**
n. **sak'lemb'ilb'olotz**

volunteer work *n.* **kamab'k**

vomit *n.* **xa'aw**
v. **xa'wak**
n. **xawak**

vote *v.* **juch'uk**
v. **xaqab'ank**

voter *n agt.* **aj juch'unel**

voucher *n.* **eeqajsachomj**

vowel *n.* **xna'tz'iib'**

vowels *n.* **xna'tz'iib'eb'**

vulcanologist *n agt.* **aj nawk'uhil**

vulgar *adj.* **lolob'**

vulnerability *n.* **rahob'tesink wank**

vulture *n.* **so'sol**

vulva *n.* **b'irk**
n. **choy**
n. **pirk'**

W - w

wages *n.* **po**

wagon *n.* **kareton**

waist *n.* **sa' yi**
n. **yi**
n. **yiib'ej**
n. **yiitoq**

waistband *n.* **xyi**

wait *v.* **oyb'enink**

wait a minute
phr. **chinaawoyb'en b'ayaq**

waiter *n agt.* **aj k'ehonel tzakahemq**

waiting room *n.* **na'aj re oyb'enink**
n. **oyb'eb'aal**

wake up *v.* **ajk**

walk *v.* **b'eek**

walkie talkie *n.* **numsib'aal esil**

walking stick *n.* **b'axton**
n. **xuq'**

walkway *n.* **ch'ina b'e**
n. **q'axleb'aal**

wall *n.* **kuuk**
n. **kuukil tz'ak**
n. **ru tz'ak**
n. **tz'ak**

wall clock *n.* **ilob'aal hoonal**

wallet *n.* **xna'aj huhil tumin**

walnut tree *n.* **nokal**

want *v.* **atawank**
v. **rahink**

war *n.* **kamsink-ib'**
n. **pleet**
n. **raaxiik'**
n. **yalok**

wardrobe *n.* **xna'aj aq'**

warehouse *n.* **k'uuleb'aal**

warm *adj.* **tiq**

warn *v.* **q'usuk**

warp *v.* **b'atok**

warrior *n agt.* **aj yalonel**

warship *n.* **jukub' re pleetik**

wary *adj.* **sa' xyaalal**

wash *v.* **ch'ajok**
　　　v. **puch'uk**

wash basin (clothing) *n.* **xna'aj puch'um**

wash with soap *v.* **xab'onink**

washbasin *n.* **kaxemel**
　　　n. **kaxjoom**
　　　n. **puch'leb'**
　　　n. **tamb'aha'**

washbowl *n.* **kaxemel**
　　　n. **kaxjoom**
　　　n. **puch'leb'**
　　　n. **tamb'aha'**

washing machine
　　　n. **metz'ewilpuch'leb'**
　　　n. **puch'leb'aal ch'iich'**

wasp *n.* **ch'ub'**

waste *v.* **tz'eqink**

waste time *v.* **b'ayok ib'**

wastebasket *n.* **xchakachil mul**
　　　n. **xna'aj mul**

wastepaper bin *n.* **xna'aj hu**

watch *n.* **uq'mil k'uthoonal**

watch out *phr.* **k'e reetal li taab'aanu**

watch over *v.* **ilok**
　　　v. **k'uulank**

watchmaker *n agt.* **aj yiib'om reloj**

water *n.* **ha'**
　　　v. **hoyok**

water bill *n.* **xhuhil li ha'**

water fountain *n.* **uk'leb'aal**

water jar *n.* **kukb'**

water jug *n.* **xaaril ha'**

water meter *n.* **ajleb'ilha'**

water pump *n.* **k'uub'kutha'**
　　　n. **tzub'pajha'**

water tank *n.* **pumleb'ha'**
　　　n. **xna'aj ha'**

water tap *n.* **teeleb'ha'**
　　　n. **xlaawil ha'**
　　　n. **xteeb'al ha'**

water well *n.* **uk'leb'aal ha'**

waterfall *n.* **pach'il ha'**
　　　n. **pajaj ha'**
　　　n. **rusos**
　　　n. **t'anleb'aalha'**
　　　n. **xpisk' ha'**
　　　n. **xulk'ukil nima'**

watering can *n.* **chaab'**
　　　n. **chirleb'**
　　　n. **kira'sleb'**

watering hole *n.* **xna'aj ha'**

watermelon *n.* **kaxq'ooq'**
　　　n. **sandiiy**

watershed *n.* **roqtaq'a**

wave   *n.* **b'oolha'**
            n. **xrepom palaw**

wax seal   *n.* **t'oqb'on**

we   *pron.* **laa'o**

weak   *adj.* **lub'lu**
            adj. **maak'a' xmetz'ew**
            adj. **q'un**

weak signal *n.* **jwal kach'in xkutum**

wealth   *n.* **b'ihomal**

wealthy   *adj.* **b'ihom**

weapons   *n.* **kamsib'aal**
            n. **kamsiil**

weary   *adj.* **tawajenaq**

weasel   *n.* **saqb'in**

weather   *n.* **kutan**

weather satellite
            n. **chahimch'iich' aj na'onel ru li ruchich'och'**

weather vane *n.* **eetalnum'iq**

weave   *v.* **kemok**

wedding   *n.* **sumlajik**

Wednesday   *n.* **miercools**

weeds   *n.* **chamal pim**
            n. **pim**

week   *n.* **wuq'ix**
            n. **xamaan**

weevil   *n.* **max**
            n. **maxel hal**

weigh   *v.* **aalank**
            v. **b'isok**

weight   *n.* **aalal**

welcome   *adj.* **usilk'ulunk**

welcome to all of you
            phr. **usilk'ulunk cho'q eere**

well   *conj.* **b'i'**
            adv. **chaab'il**
            adv. **us**

well (water) *n.* **ch'ina ha'**
            n. **kumb'**
            n. **k'ak'naab'**
            n. **tuq**

well done   *adj.* **chaq' chi us**
            adj. **rek'**

well done!   *phr.* **chaab'il xaab'anu**

west   *n.* **rokeb' saq'e**

wet   *adj.* **b'aqx**
            adj. **luub'**
            adj. **raap**
            v. **t'aqresink**
            adj. **t'aqt'aq**
            adj. **t'oqx**
            adj. **tz'uuq**

whale   *n.* **b'ayeen**
            n. **xna' kar**

what a pity *phr.* **k'a' xja'lenkil**

what a shame *phr.* **k'a' xja'lenkil**

what are you doing? (singular)
            phr. **k'a'ru yookat**

what did you say? *phr.* **k'a'ru xaaye**

what does [   ] mean?
    phr. **k'a'ru naraj naxye [   ]**

what happened? *phr.* **k'a'ru xk'ulman**

what is happening? *phr.* **k'a'ru yo**

what is that? *phr.* **k'a' ru a'an**

what is this? *phr.* **k'a' ru a'in**

what size? *interr.* **jo' ch'inal**

what's the matter? *phr.* **k'a'ru xk'ulman**

what's your email? *phr.* **chan ru la weetalil sa' internet**

what's your phone number? *phr.* **b'ar rajlil laab'oqleb'**

what? *interr.* **k'a'**
    interr. **k'a'ru**

whatever *conj.* **yalaq b'ar wan**
    conj. **yalaq k'a'ru**

wheat *n.* **riximul kaxlan wa**
    n. **triiw**

wheel *n.* **roq**
    n. **roq poy ch'iich'**
    n. **rueed**
    n. **sursu**
    n. **tolb'ech'iich'**
    n. **xb'eelil**

wheel chair *n.* **b'eleb'aal tem**
    n. **kaxlan tem**
    n. **toltem**

wheelbarrow *n.* **iiqaal**
    n. **karetiiy**
    n. **toltol**

wheelchair *n.* **b'eleb'aal tem**
    n. **xb'eeleb'aal yaj**

when *pron.* **naq**

when? *interr.* **joq'e**

whenever *conj.* **yalaq joq'e**

where are you from? *phr.* **aj b'arat**
    phr. **b'ar wan aatenamit**

where are you? *phr.* **b'ar wankat**

where do you come from?
    phr. **b'ar nakatchal**

where do you live? *phr.* **b'ar wan aawochoch**

where is the toilet? *phr.* **b'ar wan li tz'eqleb'aal**

where? *interr.* **b'ar**

wherever *conj.* **yalaq b'ar**

whetstone *n.* **hux**
    n. **ji'leb'**

which? *interr.* **b'ar wan re**
    interr. **k'a'ru**

which? (plural) *interr.* **b'ar wankeb'**

which? (singular) *interr.* **b'ar wank**

whichever *conj.* **yalaq**

whip *v.* **juylek**
    n. **tz'uum**

whirlpool *n.* **suut ha'**

whisk   *v.* **yulenk**

whiskey   *n.* **wiisk**

whisper   *v.* **hasb'ak**
           v phr. **jiq'jiq'ink ib'**

whisper sweetly *v.* **payok**

whistle   *v phr.* **b'oqok chi yaab'**
           v. **xuxb'ak**

whistle (object) *n.* **b'ololch'iich'**
           n. **kaxb'olol**

whistle (sound) *n.* **xuxb'**

white   *adj.* **saq**

white blood cells *n.* **saqkil mitz'kotkik'**

white gold *n.* **saqi pwaq**

white orchid *n.* **saqihix**

White Out *n.* **tuqleb'**

white wine *n.* **saqi b'iin**

white-nosed coati *n.* **sis**

whitish   *adj.* **saqjorin**

who?   *interr.* **ani**

whoever   *pron.* **yalaq ani**

whole   *adj.* **tzaqal jun**

whose? (plural) *interr.* **aniheb' aj e**

whose? (singular) *interr.* **ani aj e**

why not?   *phr.* **k'a'ut naq ink'a'**

why?   *interr.* **k'a'ut**

wide   *adj.* **nim ru**

wide open *adj.* **ch'a'ch'o**

widow   *n.* **malka'an**

widower   *n.* **te'elch'ool**

width   *n.* **xnimal ru**

wife   *n sd.* **ixaqilb'ej**

wig   *n.* **pak'b'il ismal**

wild bee   *n.* **aaq kab'**

wild boar *n.* **k'iche' aaq**

wild cardamom *n.* **tz'i' k'iche'**

wild cilantro *n.* **samat**

wild dove *n.* **uut**

wild grass *n.* **pim**

wild horse *n.* **t'initz**

win   *v phr.* **k'ehok k'as**
           v. **tzakib'k**

wind   *n.* **iq'**

wind erosion *n.* **xch'ajom iq'**

windmill   *n.* **ke'leb'aal**

window   *n.* **b'entaan**
           n. **ch'uukib'aal**
           n. **rokeb'aal saqen**

window pane *n.* **lem**

windshield *n.* **mesb'a lem**

windshield wiper *n.* **masleb'ha'**

windy   *adj.* **iq' xsa'**

wine   *n.* **b'iin**

wing   *n.* **xik'**

winter   *n.* **hab'al q'e**

wipe   *v.* **mesok**

wiper   *n.* **mesol lem**

wire   *n.* **k'ahamch'iich'**

wise	*adj.* **wan xna'leb'**
witch	*n.* **awasinel**
	n. **tuulanel**
with	*prep.* **rexb'een**
	prep. **rik'in**
with pleasure	*adv phr.* **chi sa xch'oolil**
with what?	*interr.* **k'a'ru aj ik'in**
with whom?	*interr.* **ani aj ik'in**
without	*prep.* **maawa' rik'in**
witness	*n agt.* **aj kuutunel**
	n. **testiig**
witness statement	*n.* **yehok aatin sa' chaq'rab'**
wolf	*n.* **aj xoj**
	n. **loob'**
	n. **tz'i' k'iche'**
woman	*n.* **ixq**
womb	*n.* **alob'aal**
	n. **kub'sa'**
	n. **sa' ixq**
wood	*n.* **che'**
wood drum	*n.* **ch'ina tun**
	n. **che'wajb'**
woodcarver	*n agt.* **aj pech'ol che'**
woodpecker	*n.* **pich'**
	n. **tzentzejer**
woods	*n.* **k'iche'**
woodshop	*n.* **peech'leb'aal**
wool	*n.* **laan**
word	*n.* **aatin**
work	*n.* **k'anjel**

work bench	*n.* **xmeexul li peech'ab'k**
work metal	*v.* **pu'akink**
work of art	*n.* **b'onb'il q'esnalna'leb'**
work out	*v phr.* **xtawb'il li manawb'il**
workbench	*n.* **meex re k'anjelak**
worker	*n agt.* **aj k'anjel**
workplaces	*n.* **xna'aj li k'anjel**
workshop	*n.* **k'uub'leb'aal**
	n. **rochochil k'anjel**
	n. **xna'aj k'anjeleb'aal**
	n. **yiib'leb'aal**
world	*n.* **ruuchich'och'**
world map	
	n. **reetalilruuchich'och'**
worm	*n.* **b'itzkiri'**
	n. **chajal**
	n. **chupil**
	n. **hay**
	n. **koton is**
	n. **kuluk**
	n. **k'ixix**
	n. **k'utub'**
	n. **lukum**
	n. **motzo'**
	n. **pirik'**
	n. **tin**
	n. **tzonok'**
worried	*adj.* **yo xk'a'uxl**
worry	*n.* **xtib' jolom**

worse   *adv phr.* **jwal ink'a us**

worsen   *v phr.* **nimank ru**

worship   *v.* **loq'onink**
             v phr. **xb'aanunkil mayejak**

worthiness   *n.* **loq'alil**

worthy   *n.* **loq'al**

would you like a drink?   *phr.* **ma tawaj uk'ak**

wound   *n.* **saan**
             n. **tiq'ilal**
             n. **yok'olal**

woven shoulder bag   *n.* **champa**

wrap   *v.* **lanok**
             v. **q'ochok**
             n. **xta**
             v. **xut'uk**
             v. **yutuk**

wrap-around *n.* **xta**

wrapped   *adj.* **b'irb'o**

wrath   *n.* **josq'il**

wrench   *n.* **q'otleb'ch'iich'**

wring   *v.* **b'alq'usink**
             v. **yatz'ok**

wrinkled   *adj.* **mochmo**
             adj. **mochox**

wrinkles   *n.* **yoch**

wrist   *n.* **xkux uq'b'**

wristwatch   *n.* **uq'mil k'uthoonal**

write   *v.* **tz'iib'ak**

write a check   *v phr.* **xk'eb'al xhuhul tojleb'**

write up   *v phr.* **na'leb'ank tz'iib'**

writer   *n agt.* **aj tz'iib'**

writing   *n.* **tz'iib'**

written request   *n.* **hupatz'om**
             n. **hutz'aam**

wrong   *adj.* **ink'a' us**
             adj. **moko yaal ta**

X - x

Xinca   *lang.* **xinka**

X-ray   *n.* **numsinb'il'eetalil**
             n. **xjalam'uuchil**

X-ray machine   *n.* **eek'ch'iich'**

X-ray plate *n.* **reetalil b'aq**

xylophone   *n.* **xolb'ch'iich'**

Y - y

yamstick *n.* **awleb'**

yard   *n.* **neb'aal**

yawn   *v phr.* **japink e**

year   *n.* **chihab'**
           n. **hab'**

yeast   *n.* **xsiiptz'ub'**
           kaxlan wa

yellow   *adj.* **q'an**

yellow gold *n.* **q'an pwaq**

yellow hornet *n.* **q'anch'ub'**

yellowish *adj.* **q'anb'uyin**
           adj. **q'anmalaw**
           adj. **q'antzoq'i**

yes   *adv.* **enhe'**
           adv. **heehe'**
           adv. **us**

yesterday *n.* **ewer**

yesterday evening *n.* **ewer**
           chi q'eq

yesterday morning *n.* **ewer**
           eq'la

yoke   *n.* **yunta**

yoke (of oxen) *n.* **b'ooyx**

yolk   *n.* **xq'anal mol**

you (plural) *pron.* **laa'ex**

you (singular) *pron.* **laa'at**

you're right *phr.* **yaal**
           laak'a'uxl

you're welcome *phr.* **maak'a'**
           naxye

you're wrong *phr.* **moko yaal**
           ta laak'a'uxl

young   *adj.* **al**
           adj. **ch'ajom**
           adj. **saaj**

young man *n.* **ch'ajom**

young men *n.* **xerek' winq**

young woman *n.* **ixqa'al**
           n. **tuq'ixq**

younger sibling (brother or
    sister) *n*
           sd. **iitz'inb'ej**

younger than *adv phr.* **ka'ch'in**
           chi ru

youth   *n.* **ch'ajomal**

Z - z

zeal   *n.* **sowenk**

zebra   *n.* **b'alaq xul**
            n. **jilix kawaay**

zeppelin   *n.* **pamb'eeresinb'il**

zero   *n.* **sero**
            n. **yam**
            num. **(0.) maajun**

zinc   *n.* **sink**

zip drive   *n.* **k'osleb'**

zipper   *n.* **k'erex**
            n. **tz'apleb'**

zoo   *n.* **rochoch xul**
            n. **xna'ajleb'aalxul**
            n. **xna'aj k'ila xul**

zoologist   *n agt.* **aj nawxul**

zoology   *n.* **nawxul**

APPENDICES

Xraqikeb' Ch'ol

APPENDICES

Xraqikeb' Ch'ol

NOTES ON Q'EQCHI' LINGUISTIC BORROWING

(Chirixeb' li to'chi' Q'eqchi')

Included in some of the entries in Section II of this reference work are notes on linguistic borrowing taken from the Q'eqchi' loanword database compiled by Søren Wichmann and Kerry Hull. The World Loanword Database (WOLD) is the result of a collaborative effort called the Loanword Typology Project (LWT) coordinated by Uri Tadmor and Martin Haspelmath between 2004 and 2008. As of 2015 the results of this project reside on the World Wide Web at: http://wold.livingsources. org/.

The list of 1,460 meanings on which the vocabularies represented in the WOLD project are based is called the Loanword Typology meaning list, which was in turn based on the list of the Intercontinental Dictionary Series. The Q'eqchi' database constitutes 1,995 Q'eqchi'/English word pairs which were analyzed by Wichman and Hull for evidence of borrowing from other languages (European and Mesoamerican). I have included their conclusions on borrowing and donor language as a note to these entries using the numbers of their classification scheme:

(1) Clearly borrowed
(2) Probably borrowed
(3) Perhaps borrowed
(4) Very little evidence for borrowing
(5) No evidence for borrowing

Many other entries in Section II contain notes on Spanish loanwords which are not a part of the World Loan Word Database—these notes are my own.

NOTES ON Q'EQCHI' PATRONYMS AND TOPONYMS

(Chirixeb' li xsum k'ab'a'ej ut k'ab'a'na'jej Q'eqchi')

In addition to the WOLD notations, I have adapted information on Q'eqchi' surnames from Burkitt's *Notes on the Keckchi' Language* and made notes on the likely or possible origin of Q'eqchi' surnames using the following scheme:

(B1) Clearly borrowed
(B3) Perhaps borrowed

Also, this edition contains a number of new entries for Q'eqchi' place names and their English translations. This is not yet a complete list, but the entries for Q'eqchi' place names were taken from *Toponimias Maya Q'eqchi.* Guatemala City, Guatemala, 2003. Published by Academia de Lenguas Mayas de Guatemala. The English translations of the Q'eqchi' place names based on their etymologies are my own; I hope to include a more complete listing in future editions of this dictionary.

Note: The modern Q'eqchi' alphabet does not use the letter "c". However, since many Q'eqchi' place names are registered officially in Guatemala using a Spanish rendering (which includes the letter "c"), in this dictionary I have included a section for these names which begin with the letter "c" in the official government registry.

LIST OF ABBREVIATIONS USED

(Xk'osb'al ru li aatin neke'oksiman chi sa')

Abbrev.		Term	Definition
adj	=	adjective	A word that modifies nouns and pronouns, primarily by describing a particular quality of the word they are modifying.
adv	=	adverb	A word that functions as a modifiers of verbs or clauses, and in some languages as a modifier of adjectives.
adv phr	=	adverbial phrase	A group of two or more words that function together as an adverb.
art	=	article	A member of a small class of words found in certain languages that are linked to nouns and that typically have a grammatical function identifying the noun as a noun rather than describing it.
conj	=	conjunction	A member of a small class of words distinguished in many languages by their function as connectors between words, phrases, clauses, or sentences.

interj	=	interjection	A part of speech signifying an emotion or mental state by means of a standardized instinctive utterance.
interr	=	interrogative	A word used in forming or constituting a question.
lang	=	language	The system of communication used by a particular community or geographic region.
n	=	noun	A word that can function as the main or only element of subjects of verbs, or of objects of verbs or prepositions.
n agt	=	agent noun	A noun that denotes an agent that performs the action denoted by the verb from which the noun is derived.
n comp	=	compound noun	A noun that is made with two or more words that acts as a single unit and can be modified by adjectives and other nouns.
n sd	=	suffix-dropping noun	A noun that drops its suffix when marked for possession by personal pronouns.
nick	=	nickname	A name substituted for the proper name of a person which connotes affection or familiarity.

num	=	numeral	A word, letter, symbol, or figure expressing a number; number.
part	=	particle	A small word of functional or relational use that is neither a verb nor a noun.
phr	=	phrase	A small string of words standing together as a single conceptual unit
prep	=	preposition	Words found in many languages that are used before nouns, pronouns, or other substantives to form phrases functioning as modifiers of verbs, nouns, or adjectives, and that typically express a spatial or temporal relationship.
pron	=	pronoun	Any member of a small class of words found in many languages that are used as replacements or substitutes for nouns and noun phrases, and that have very general reference.
sur	=	surname	A hereditary name given to all members of a family. In English and Q'eqchi' linguistic communities it usually follows the given or first name.

v	=	verb	Any member of a class of words that function as the main elements of predicates, that typically express action, state, or a relation between two things, and that may be inflected for tense, aspect, voice, mood, and to show agreement with their subject or object.
v phr	=	verb phrase	A group of words including a verb and its complements, objects, or other modifiers that functions syntactically as a verb.
Var	=	variant form	A way of writing or pronouncing a word which is used by some people as an alternative to the standard or generally accepted form.

BIBLIOGRPAHY

(Reetalil k'ila tasal hu oksinb'ileb')

Ager, Simon. 2014. Q'eqchi' pronunciation. On: Omniglot: The online encyclopedia of writing systems and alphabets website. (Available on the internet at http://www. Omniglot.com/writing/qeqchi.htm, Accessed on 2014-04-28.)

ALMG. 2003. Toponimias Maya Q'eqchi. Guatemala City, Guatemala. (Academia de Lenguas Mayas de Guatemala.)

ALMG. 2004. Xtusulal Aatin Sa' Q'eqchi: Vocabulario Q'eqchi'. Guatemala City. (Academia de Lenguas Mayas de Guatemala.)

ALMG. 2004. Xk'ub'lal Xyaab' Q'eqchi: Gramática Descriptiva Idioma Q'eqchi'. Coban, A.V., Guatemala: Academia de Lenguas Mayas de Guatemala.

ALMG. 2004(?). Eb' li Ak' Aatin sa' li Aatinob'aal Q'eqchi': Actualización Lexical Q'eqchi'. Guatemala City: Academia de Lenguas Mayas de Guatemala.

ALMG. 2005. Xk'utb'al Xtz'iib'ankil Q'eqchi: Gramática Normativa Q'eqchi'. Guatemala City, Guatemala: Academia de Lenguas Mayas de Guatemala.

ALMG. 2008. Molob'aal Aatin Q'eqchi. Coban (Kob'an xch'och'el tezulutlan) Guatemala: Academia de Lenguas Mayas de Guatemala.

Burkitt, Robert. 1902. Notes on the Kekchi' Language, American Anthropologist, pp 441 - 463.

465

Caal, Luz Maria and Chub Choc, Pedro. 2015. Q'eqchi' Mayan Words for Mammals. (Available on the internet at http://maya-archaeology.org/mayan-anthropology-ethnography-archaeology-art-history-iconography-epigraphy-ethnobotany/qeqchi-mayan-words-for-animals-mammals-alta-verapaz-guatemala.php, Accessed on 2015-05-28.)

Cahill, Nathan. 2014. Community Cloud Forest Conservation. (Available on the internet at http://www.cloudforest con-servation.org/ community/qeqchi.php, Accessed on 2014-08-10.)

Caz Cho, Sergio. 2007. Xtz'ilb'al rix li aatinak sa' Q'eqchi'. (Informe de Variacion Dialectal en Q'eqchi'.) Antigua, Guatemala. OKMA—Oxlajuuj Keej Maya' Ajtz'iib'. Guatemala, Guatemala : Cholsamaj.

CODISRA. 2010 Fuente Indicadores y Estadísticas por Pueblos y Comunidades Linguísticas de Guatemala, Comisión Presidencial contra la Discriminación y el Racismo contra los Pueblos Indígenas de Guatemala.

Cu Cab, Carlos Humberto. 1998. Q'eqchi' - Kaxlan aatin ut Kaxlan aatin - Q'eqchi'. Guatemala City: Instituto de Lingüística de la Universidad Rafael Landívar.

Haeserijn, Esteban. 1979. Q'eqchi' – Diccionario K'ekchi' Español. Editorial Piedra Santa.

Kaufman, Terrence with John Justeson. 2003. A Preliminary Mayan Etymological Dictionary. Foundation for the Advancement of Mesoamerican Studies. (Available online at http:// www.famsi.org/reports/01051/pmed. pdf, Accessed on 2015-05-28.)

Kockelman, Paul. 2003. The Meanings of Interjections in Q'eqchi' Maya. *Current Anthropolgy*, Vol 44, No 4, August-October.

K'u Kab', Kalich. 2012. Tusleb'aal Aatin Q'eqchi' – Inglés – Español. First ed. Chamelco, Alta Verapaz, Guatemala.

Lewis, M. Paul, Gary F. Simons, and Charles D. Fennig (eds.). 2014. *Ethnologue: Languages of the World, Seventeenth edition.* Dallas, Texas: SIL International. Online version: http:// www.ethnologue.com.

MINEDUC. 2000. Xk'ub'lal Li Qaatinob'aal Q'eqchi: Gramática Q'eqchi'. Guatemala City, Guatemala: Ministerio de Educación. Dirección General de Educación Bilingüe Intercultural.

Oxom, Carlos. 2014. Li Tz'iib'ak ut Aatinak Chi Chaab'il Sa' Li Aatinob'aal Q'eqchi'. Coban, A.V. Guatemala. (Available online at http://ajoxom.es.tl/Gram%E1tica-Q-h-eqchi-h-.htm, Accessed on 2015-12-08.)

P.L.F.M. 1997. Gramática del Idioma Q'eqchi. Proyecto Lingüístico Francisco Marroquín. Antigua, Guatemala.

P.L.F.M. 2003. Diccionario Q'eqchi. Proyecto Lingüístico Francisco Marroquín. Antigua, Guatemala.

Redish, Laura. 2014. Q'eqchi' pronunciation guide. On: Native Languages of the Americas website. (Available online at http://www.native-languages.org/kekchi_guide.htm, Accessed on 2014-04-28.)

Romero, Sergio. 2012. "They Don't Get Speak Our Language Right": Language Standardization, Power And Migration among the Q'eqchi' Maya. *Journal of Linguistic Anthropology*, Vol. 22, Issue 2, pp. E21–E41,

Sam Juárez, Miguel, Ernesto Chen Cao, Crisanto Xal Tec, Domingo Cuc Chen, and Pedro Tiul Pop. 1997. Diccionario del idioma q'eqchi'. La Antigua, Guatemala: Proyecto Lingüístico Francisco Marroquín.

Sedat, William. 1955. Nuevo diccionario de las lenguas k'ekchi' y española. Chamelco, Alta Verapaz, Guatemala: Instituto Lingüístico de Verano.

Wichmann, Søren and Hull, Kerry. 2009. Q'eqchi' vocabulary. In: Haspelmath, Martin & Tadmor, Uri (eds.) World Loanword Database. Leipzig: Max Planck Institute for Evolutionary Anthropology, 1995 entries. (Available online at http:// wold.livingsources.org/vocabulary/34, Accessed on 2014-04-28.)

Verdugo de Lima, Lucía (ed). 2004. Palabras: Diccionario Ilustrado Castellano / Q'eqchi' – Eb' li Aatin: K'uub'an-b'il Sik'leb'aal Aatin sa' Kaxlan Aatin / Q'eqchi'. Instituto de Lingüística y Educación, Universidad Rafael Landívar, Guatemala. 3a edición, revisada y aumentada

Xb'epo xb'een xpuktasinkil li k'anjel a'in jo'
li ch'olkutan maayab' (kelkookil ajlank):

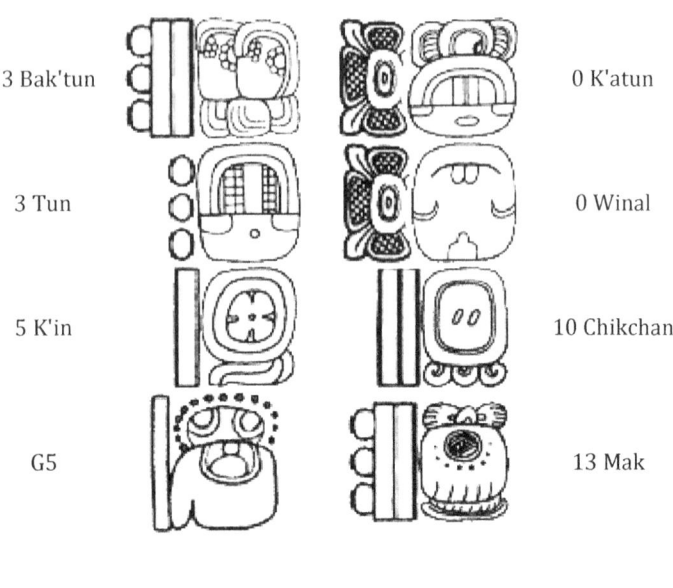

13 Bak'tun	0 K'atun
3 Tun	0 Winal
5 K'in	10 Chikchan
G5	13 Mak

Al Po

Direction: Xaman - North
Color: Sak - White
819 day count: 0.0.0.1.15 (35) 1 Ok 18 Sak
Julian Day #: 2,457,368
Maya Day #: 1,873,085
Lunar Age: 0.37 day(s)
Aztec Calendar Round: 10 Coatl 13 Tozoztontli
Mixtec Calendar Round: 10 Coo (Snake) 13 Reed

Made in the USA
Monee, IL
25 August 2020